Engendering Song

Singing and Subjectivity at Prespa Albanian Weddings

Jane C. Sugarman

The University of Chicago Press
Chicago and London

JANE C. SUGARMAN is assistant professor of music at the State University of
New York, Stony Brook.

The University of Chicago Press, Chicago 60637
The University of Chicago Press, Ltd., London
© 1997 by The University of Chicago
All rights reserved. Published 1997
Printed in the United States of America
06 05 04 03 02 01 00 99 98 97   5 4 3 2 1

ISBN (cloth): 0-226-77972-6
ISBN (paper): 0-226-77973-4

Library of Congress Cataloging-in-Publication Data

Sugarman, Jane C.
    Engendering song : singing and subjectivity at Prespa Albanian
weddings / Jane C. Sugarman.
        p.   cm. — (Chicago studies in ethnomusicology)
    ISBN 0-226-77972-6 — ISBN 0-226-77973-4 (pbk.)
        1. Albanians—Prespa, Lake, Region—Music—History and criticism.   2. Alba-
nians—North America—Music—History and criticism.   3. Folk music—Prespa,
Lake, Region—History and criticism.   4. Folk music—North America—History
and criticism.   5. Folk songs, Albanian—Prespa, Lake, Region—History and criticism.   6. Folk songs, Albanian—North America—History and criticism.   7. Wedding
music—History and criticism.   8. Albanians—Social life and customs.   9. Sex
role.   I. Title.   II. Series.
    ML3613.S93   1997
    306'.094965—dc20   96-17978
                                                                            CIP
                                                                            MN

In honor of my parents
and
of the people of Prespa:

Mali me malin nuk bashkoet;
Njeriu me njerinë bashkoet.
(Albanian saying)

Čovek so čovek se gleda;
planina so planina ne se gleda.
(Macedonian saying)

Two mountains cannot look each other in the eye;
but two people can.
(English translation)

CONTENTS

Contents

ILLUSTRATIONS

GALLERIES OF PHOTOGRAPHS FOLLOW PAGES 78 AND 204

MUSICAL EXCERPTS ON
THE COMPACT DISC

1 *Këtë fshatin tonë do ta bëjmë qytet* (We are turning our village into a town), a song of *gurbet;* Arvati, 1981. Recorded by Eran Fraenkel. Used by permission

2 *Më le xhadenë* (You have left the highway), a men's *shtruar* love song; Grnčari, 1983. From a community recording. Used by permission

3 *Malorea në shtatë male* (Malorea in the seven mountains), a women's *lartër* wedding song; Grnčari, 1983. From a community recording. Used by permission

4 *Ngreu moj Mamudi* (Get up, Mamudi), a women's *shtruar* wedding song, Grnčari, 1983. From a community recording. Used by permission

5 *Ra vesa, vesojti dhenë* (The dew fell and moistened the earth), a women's *lartër* wedding song; Krani, 1972. Selo LP-2. Used by permission

6 *Sh'të duet, moj lule, ta qëronje mollën* (Why did you have to go and peel that apple, my flower?), a women's *shtruar* wedding song; Krani, 1972. From a community recording. Used by permission

7 *Bien tri daire* (They are playing three frame drums), a north Albanian women's wedding song; Krani, 1972. From a community recording. Used by permission

8 *Duallë dy spai në lëmë* (Two *sipahi*s came out onto the threshing floor), a women's wedding song for dancing; Krani, 1980. Recorded by Jane Sugarman

9 *Moj e vogla në lëmë* (O small one on the threshing floor), a women's *shtruar* wedding song; Toronto, 1985. From a community recording. Used by permission

10 *Në divan të lartër* (On the high balcony), a women's *lartër* wedding song; Nakolec, 1980. Recorded by Jane Sugarman

11   *Atje lartër ne portë e madhe* (Up there at the great gate), a men's *shtruar* love song; Krani, 1972. Selo LP-2. Used by permission

12   *Vjeshtë e tretë më të dalë* (The third month of autumn was just ending), a men's *lartër* historical song; Krani, 1972. Selo LP-2. Used by permission

13   *Rëzonet bilbili* (The nightingale descended), a men's *lartër* song; Arvati, 1980. Recorded by Jane Sugarman.

14   *Moj syzezë e vogël* (O small, black-eyed one), a men's *shtruar* love song; Krani, 1972. Recorded by Robert Henry Leibman. Used by permission

15   *Kjo shtëpi e plakës* (This old woman's house), a men's humorous song; Krani, 1980. Recorded by Eran Fraenkel. Used by permission

16   *Po kjo anë e lumit* (On this side of the river), a women's *shtruar* song; Dolna Bela Crkva, 1981. Recorded by Jane Sugarman

17   *Muabet i shtruar* (A long, elaborate *muabet*), a men's rhymed couplet; Chicago area, 1986. Recorded by Eran Fraenkel. Used by permission

18   *Pashë një ëndërr shumë me ratali* (I had a terrible nightmare), a men's historical song sung in *lartër* style; Toronto, 1986. Recorded by Jane Sugarman

19   *Kjo Libova shumë e mirë* (O excellent Libohovë), a men's *shtruar* historical song; Toronto, 1986. Recorded by Eran Fraenkel. Used by permission

20   *Vetëtin në fund të odës* (There is something shining at the end of the room), a women's *shtruar* wedding song sung by a married couple; Toronto, 1986. Recorded by Eran Fraenkel. Used by permission

21   *Kur shkojnë pas nuses dhe kur vijnë miqtë* (When they go to take the bride and when friends arrive), performed by Prespa *daulle*; Krani, 1980. Recorded by Eran Fraenkel. Used by permission

22 *Të djelën që më saba* (On Sunday in the morning) and *Kaba;* polyphonic wedding song sung by the *daulle,* followed by a clarinet improvisation; Dolna Bela Crkva, 1981. Recorded by Eran Fraenkel. Used by permission

23 Sequence of *bejte* performed by two pairs of male singers; Chicago area, 1988. Recorded by Eran Fraenkel. Used by permission

24 Excerpt from a medley of songs from the Albanian media: *N'atë mal kur fryn veriu* (On that mountain when the north wind blows), from the Korçë region of southern Albania; and *Prej dashnisë* (Because of love), a north Albanian song from Kosova. Performed in Milwaukee, 1996, by the group Mëmëdheu, of Chicago. Selvije Mehmeti, lead vocal; Ismail Mehmeti, clarinet and backup vocal; Mikail Koço, accordion; Shpend Jonuzi, keyboard/bass; and Abdyl Mehmeti, drum set. Recorded by Ismail Mehmeti. Used by permission

NOTE ON TEXTUAL AND MUSICAL
TRANSCRIPTIONS

Prespa Albanians speak a south Albanian, or Tosk, dialect that is related to the speech of the Korçë region in southeastern Albania. It is close to the present-day literary language of Albania, with some important differences in pronunciation, vocabulary, and usage. As will be clear from etymologies given throughout the book, Prespa speech has been greatly influenced by Ottoman phraseology, as well as by the Slavic speech of Macedonian neighbors. All quotations of Prespa community members, and all song texts, have been rendered in the Prespa dialect, using standard Albanian orthography.

A number of conventions have been used in transcribing the texts of songs. For those songs cited outside the description of a specific event, the location and year of the recording from which they were transcribed are indicated after the text (e.g., Toronto, 1986). Those appearing on a commercial recording have been so noted. Except in the musical examples, all texts have been rendered as individuals would recite them, and so do not include the many verbal interpolations that would be added when sung (see chapter 2). Names inserted by the singer have been printed in capital letters; in all cases, pseudonyms have been used. Repetitions of lines have not been indicated. Refrains have been printed in italics; they are sung after any line ending with ellipsis points.

In the musical transcriptions, refrains, as well as interpolated syllables and words, have likewise been printed in italics. Before each example one note, marked "orig. pitch," indicates the actual pitch of the tonic: the drone note in polyphonic songs, and the finalis in monophonic ones. Rapid lapses into falsetto have been indicated as $_x$♭, sustained falsetto pitches as $_o$♩. Because all songs are sung with some degree of rhythmic freedom, tempo markings are approximate and may change during the course of the song. Renditions that were performed in a strict meter have been notated with solid bar lines running through the staves; those in which the meter was not always observed strictly, with dotted bar lines through the staves; those in an elastic meter, with dotted bar lines between staves. In nonmetric songs, a single bar line has been placed at the end of each line of text. In all transcriptions, a double bar line indicates the end of a verse.

PRONUNCIATION GUIDE FOR THE ALBANIAN LANGUAGE

A	a	as in st*a*r	N	n	as in *n*ice
B	b	as in *b*at	Nj	nj	as in o*ni*on
C	c	as in ba*ts*	O	o	as in m*o*re
Ç	ç	as in *ch*ur*ch*	P	p	as in *p*ut
D	d	as in *d*og	Q	q	as in *c*ute
Dh	dh	as in ei*the*r	R	r	flapped *r*
E	e	as in p*e*t	Rr	rr	trilled *r*
Ë	ë	as in (American) d*i*rt,	S	s	as in *s*top
		(English) d*i*rt	Sh	sh	as in *sh*op
F	f	as in *f*ather	T	t	as in *t*op
G	g	as in *g*ood	Th	th	as in e*th*er
Gj	gj	as in lea*gue y*ear	U	u	as in p*oo*r
H	h	as in *h*at	V	v	as in *v*oice
I	i	as in pol*i*ce	X	x	as in a*dz*e
J	j	as in *y*ard	Xh	xh	as in ju*dg*e
K	k	as in *k*ite	Y	y	as in French *u* or
L	l	as in be*l*ief			German *ü*
Ll	ll	as in hi*ll*	Z	z	as in *z*oo
M	m	as in *m*ap	Zh	zh	as in plea*s*ure

(based on Kiçi 1978 and Newmark, Hubbard, and Prifti 1982)

ACKNOWLEDGMENTS

Any ethnographic study is a highly collaborative work that involves not only researcher and subjects, but also a host of friends, acquaintances, colleagues, funding agencies, and other professionals. Of the many individuals and organizations that supported my efforts in this study, my first thanks go to two dance specialists: Steve Kotansky, who suggested, somewhere around 1969, that I listen to a recording called *Folk music of Albania,* compiled by A. L. Lloyd (1966); and Bob Leibman, whose recording, *Traditional Tosk (South Albanian) songs and dances from the Lake Prespa area* (1974), first brought the Prespa Albanian community to my attention. Although I did not travel to Macedonia with the intention of studying Prespa singing, those recordings inspired me to contact community members and thus to embark on this study.

My stay in Macedonia between 1979 and 1982 was funded by a Fulbright fellowship from the Institute of International Education. I am grateful to the members of the Institutes of Folklore and History in Skopje, as well as the Matica na Iselenicite od Makedonija, for their assistance during my stay there. A fellowship from the American Association of University Women funded fieldwork among Prespa families in North America during the year 1986–87. An initial version of this study (Sugarman 1993) was drafted during 1989–90 with the support of a Mellon fellowship from the Center for European Studies at Stanford University, where I was also fortunate to be an affiliate of the Institute for the Study of Women and Gender. Follow-up research during the summer of 1993 was made possible by an NYS/UUP PDQWL Term Faculty Development Award from the State University of New York.

Many individuals provided friendship and a home away from home during my various fieldwork stints. I wish particularly to thank the Kolarov, Donev, Siljanoski, Hoxha, and Rexhepi families in Macedonia; George Medakovich and Margy McClain in Chicago; Vlado and Vesna Ognenovski in Detroit; George and Suzanne Sawa, Christina Kramer and Richard Franz, and Louise Wrazen and Alistair Macrae in Toronto; and Tim and Ann Rice, now in Los Angeles. Special thanks are due to Ellen Koskoff, who served as midwife for my earliest ideas about music and gender; Bob Leibman (again) for use of materials from the Leibman

Library; Bob and John Filcich both for use of excerpts from Bob's fine recording; Victor Friedman, who answered many unlikely questions about "Balkan" languages; and Neil Siegel, for his computer expertise.

Portions of this volume have been substantially revised from two articles in which I presented initial interpretations of Prespa singing: "Making *muabet:* The social basis of singing among Prespa Albanian men" (*Selected Reports in Ethnomusicology* 7 [1988]: 1–42); and "The nightingale and the partridge: Singing and gender among Prespa Albanians" (*Ethnomusicology* 33 [1989]: 191–215). They are reproduced here with permission of the publishers. I also extend my sincere gratitude to the initial readers of this work at the University of California, Los Angeles, including Elsie Dunin, Robert Winter, Alessandro Duranti, James Porter, and Jihad Racy; as well as to Nazif Shahrani, who provided provocative reactions to my earliest analyses. Stephen Blum and the series editors of Chicago Studies in Ethnomusicology offered probing comments on a later version, as did Donna Buchanan and Dane Kusić on my introductory remarks. At SUNY Stony Brook, John Prokop and Susan McDonald prepared the musical examples, Lizzie Zucker Saltz drafted the maps and other figures, and Andrew Nittoli produced the master for the CD. Special thanks are due to David Brent, Matthew Howard, and Peter T. Daniels at the University of Chicago Press for shepherding the manuscript through the many stages of the publishing process.

Eran Fraenkel, my former husband, is present in many of the pages of this study. He traveled with me both to Macedonia and to Toronto, where he served as co–participant-observer, co–technician, and intellectual sounding board while he pursued his own research on Ottoman history. Several of his photographs are included here, as are selections that he recorded; and his attentive ears lie behind several of the events described. I extend my most sincere thanks for his many contributions.

My parents, Howard and Betty Sugarman, instilled in me a love of music and an abiding interest in "world cultures," and their presence too is evident throughout this work. Among other things, this book serves as a tribute to their unflagging support and enthusiasm for my various scholarly and musical pursuits.

My most heartfelt thanks go to those members of the Prespa community, both in Macedonia and in North America, who opened their hearts and homes and shared their knowledge, experience, and intellects with me. Of the dozens of Presparë who contributed to this study I wish particularly to mention the families of Selim and Refie Abdullai,

Samir and Lulieta Abdullai, Lutfi and Xhemile Abdullai, Ymet and Elizabeta Abdullai, Nuredin and Fatime Abdullau, Sulejman Abdullau, Ylldeze Abdullau, Sherif and Vezire Amidovski, Nexhmi and Myrse Asimovski, Avni and Dite Asimovski, Nuredin and Habibe Azizi, Seladin and Lude Azizi, Nazim and Anife Bako, Bedri and Elma Banushefski, Nizami and Melika Demiri, Amza and Bakie Dervishi, Zarif and Xhemile Elmazi, Beazi and Sadet Elmazi, Alber and Enisa Elmazi, Neat and Lirkë Elmazi, Sami and Dite Elmazi, Shenazi and Naxhie Halimi, Vasfi and Ismet Halimi, Kujtim and Salo Halimi, Ajredin and Tefide Isai, Murat and Dushe Isai, Ramiz and Memedie Lumani, Besnik and Xheko Lumani, Gani and Xheke Mehmeti, Astrit and Vergjenush Mehmeti, Neim and Bitie Mehmeti, Ismail and Selvi Mehmeti, Muarem Mamushllari, Bujar Mamushllari, Muarem and Ilmie Muaremi, Avzi and Beije Muaremi, Xhemall Muaremi, Fatime Nazifovski, Fatmir and Mezinet Nazifovski, Memet and Myze Nebiu, Alit and Zushe Oxha, Osman and Skenderie Osmani, Agim and Suzana Poloska, Xhafer and Alime Rexhepi, Petrit and Perije Rexhepi, Odo and Maide Sadiku, Jashar Seiti, Seit Seiti, Sami and Sadet Shabani, Neat and Mazes Shemovski, Nexhmi and Erminë Shemovski, Gani Tarevski, Zeke and Xhenet Tarevski, Nevruz and Sadber Useni, Fuat Useni, Fatmir Useni, Zarif and Kimet Veliu, Oran and Bule Veliu, Nevrus and Vergjenush Veliu, and Qani and Semie Zekirovski. Many thanks also to Ajredin Jashari, Zarif and Fatime Jashari, and Xhabil and Rinkë Jakupi, all from the village of Kišava (Kishavë) in the Bitola district; Sulejman and Agime Shabani of Bitola; and Pajazit Murtishi; from the Struga district. Lastly I wish to thank Prespa *daulle* and their families: Abdulla Islami, Sherif Islami, Ysein Islami, Ekrem Islami, Irfan Malik, and Riza Malik, all of Ohrid; Nazmi Rrushit of Ljubojno, Prespa; Ekrem Sherifi and Jashar Sadik, of Resen; Ramiz Islami, now in Brooklyn, New York; and Asllan and his band in Toronto. *Ju falemnderoj me gjith zëmbër!*

ONE

Approaching Prespa Singing

After all, why do we live, Janie? *Të durosh edhe të trashëgosh:* to get through life and see your family into the next generation. (Interview with a young woman in Toronto, 1986)

In the fall of 1985, a Prespa Albanian family in Toronto invited me to attend a circumcision celebration for a newborn boy, to be held in a large banquet hall. As I arrived and took my place in a line waiting to greet family members, the baby's grandparents greeted me warmly and immediately assured me that I would be invited to his wedding as well. Throughout the evening, as guests ate dinner and then danced to Albanian tunes played by a local band, the bandleader exclaimed between selections, *Të mblidhemi më dasmë!* "May we gather at the wedding!"

Prespa families begin looking ahead to the wedding of a son from the moment of his birth. It is not at all uncommon for relatives or family friends to bounce a baby boy on their knee and exclaim, "We're going to find a nice *nuse* ("bride") for you, a nice *çupkë* ("young girl") from Prespa!"; or for parents to promise a young son that they will hire *dy palë daulle* (two bands of Rom, or Gypsy, musicians) for his wedding. Little girls may also be bounced on a relative's knee, but no such mention is made of their eventual marriage. For Presparë, as Albanians from Prespa call themselves, having children, seeing them to adulthood, and assuring the continuity of the family line through their marriage are life's central concerns. It is the sons of a family on whom such expectations center, however, for it is they who will stay within the home and carry on the family line, while their daughters will marry out and become members of other family groups.

Weddings in the Prespa community both consecrate and reinscribe this basic set of relationships. The dramatic focus of any wedding is the point at which the groom and members of his family "take" the bride

1

and return with her to his home. A full celebration, however, fills the weeks and sometimes the months surrounding that event. During the week prior to the taking of the bride, the families of both bride and groom engage in an intensive round of activities: collecting and delivering gifts to be exchanged, preparing large amounts of food, entertaining relatives and family friends, and carrying out a sequence of ritual actions to prepare their children for marriage. Even prior to this time, the groom's family especially may begin entertaining well-wishers one to two months in advance. Once the wedding proper is over, the young couple attend a series of formal dinners at the homes of relatives and friends. Although the core of a wedding lasts for roughly a week, the period of celebration can thus continue for several months.

For the two families whose children are joined in marriage, a wedding is the culmination of a series of family celebrations that has led those children toward adulthood. Their passage into adulthood through marriage, with its implications for the continuity of the groom's household, is an event that families choose to affirm in the presence of all with whom they recognize social ties. Weddings are therefore the largest of community social events. On a symbolic level, they are also paradigmatic events for those attending: evoking, counterposing, or integrating sets of understandings regarding the organization and functioning of their social world.

With regard to their explicit purpose, weddings publicly mark the progression of individuals through the community's social hierarchy. More generally, the activities that make up a wedding celebration are structured in such a way as to articulate on many levels the internal ordering of the Prespa community. Principal among the social divisions that are articulated is that between males and females: as social groups with fundamentally different "natures" and divergent roles to play within family and community life. Weddings are thus a major site for the construction of notions of gender. At the same time, weddings address many other sorts of understandings that community members hold: of kinship ties, of interfamilial and interethnic relationships, and of the distinct stages of the life-cycle that women and men pass through. Weddings thus embed notions of gender within a far broader construction of social order.

For those in attendance, Prespa weddings accomplish more than a mere depiction of society. As active participants in the event, members of the host families and their guests negotiate their way through a

complex network of community expectations and individual assessments as to what constitutes proper social demeanor, defining through
their actions—both physically and symbolically—the terms of the social
order that the celebration constructs. Any Prespa wedding may thus be
seen as one point in an ongoing process through which community
members actively constitute, reinscribe, challenge, or incrementally renegotiate the terms through which they are connected as a community.

As Prespa families have dispersed from their home villages in the
former Yugoslavia to towns in western Europe, North America, and
Australia, their wedding celebrations have taken on a range of added
resonances. Not only do overseas weddings momentarily unite widely
dispersed family members and friends, but they also provide participants with lived representations of their community's place within new
and challenging social environments. As families introduce wedding
practices from new locales alongside those brought from Prespa, possible new subjectivities are emerging within the context of contemporary weddings.

Polyphonic singing, by segregated groups of men and women, is a
ubiquitous element at Prespa weddings. All ritual actions are carried
out through the singing of songs whose texts often address that moment in the wedding. In addition, guests who gather each evening at the
bride's and groom's homes are expected to socialize through singing, to
such an extent that extended conversation may be precluded. In the final
days before the taking of the bride, professional instrumentalists may
also be hired to sing and provide dance music for the guests. The last
two days are characterized by a continuous burst of singing and dancing, actively involving up to several hundred people.

Because singing is the principal means through which individuals
participate in a wedding, it is crucial to the processes of social reproduction and renegotiation that weddings accomplish. As a polysemic social
practice, singing allows individuals to convey a range of messages that
they might wish to make about themselves as social beings. Each rendition of each song thus serves as an embodied performance of multiple
aspects of that performer's sense of self and of community. At the same
time, each performance provides one of the myriad images which individuals within the community may subsequently draw on as they formulate their view of themselves and their social world, and thus contributes fundamentally to the ongoing consolidation of the practices
that together define the Prespa community. It is this dialectic between

singing and subjectivity, as it unfolds in the course of wedding celebrations, that is the focus of this study.

Encountering Prespa Singing

It was the people of Macedonia who, during my stay of two and one-half years in what was then a republic of Yugoslavia, first pointed me toward performance-based and symbolic approaches to the study of their cultural forms.[1] On the one hand, they were extremely articulate regarding both the inner workings of their music and dance and the ways in which those forms should be interpreted. On the other, they insisted that I get to know them not simply as musicians or dancers, but as multi-faceted, complex individuals. Whatever theoretical orientation I have developed subsequently in my inquiries into their musical activities has been pursued largely in response to their initial guidance.

I arrived in Skopje, the capital of Macedonia, in the fall of 1979, together with my then husband, Eran Fraenkel. Each of us had long-term interests in the music and dance of southeastern Europe, primarily those of Slavic villagers. I had, in fact, come to Skopje to research the singing of a very different community: Macedonian refugee families who had moved there from northern Greece after the Greek Civil War. The Skopje district is remarkable for its ethnic and religious diversity, and in our first year there we became acquainted with individuals from a variety of communities: Macedonians living in the city; Macedonian ex-villagers from various regions in the suburb where we lived; Macedonian residents of the village of Dračevo next to our suburb; settled Roma and north Albanians in other nearby villages; and north Albanians living in the old, Muslim neighborhoods of Skopje. These last families, who were among the most gracious and hospitable of our new acquaintances, gave us a glimpse of what Skopje must have been like in its days as a provincial Ottoman capital. As we sat with them on the low couches in the guest rooms of their homes, sipping black Turkish tea and listening to Turkish or Albanian music on the radio, we became ever more cognizant that our new Albanian acquaintances articulated an approach to life and a perspective on their life situations that we had not encountered among Christian Slavic communities.

Albanians are generally believed to be the cultural descendants of an Indo-European group that lived in southeast Europe in antiquity.[2] They thus predate by many centuries the Slavic groups who first entered the region in the sixth century A.D. In the past three centuries, Albanians have distinguished two sub-groups among themselves: north Albanians, or Gegs, living north of the Shkumbin river in Albania; and south Albanians, or Tosks, living south of the Shkumbin. These designations extend beyond the borders of Albania to include the more than two million Albanians living in adjacent areas of the former Yugoslavia. Over ninety percent of the Albanians living in Montenegro, in the province of Kosova (Serb. Kosovo) within Serbia, and in most of Macedonia, including Skopje, are northerners. Until recently southerners lived in only three districts, all within southern Macedonia: west of the town of Struga; south and west of the town of Bitola; and along the northern and eastern shores of Lake Prespa (fig. 1). With the exception of some communities of northern Catholics in Montenegro, Kosova, and the city of Skopje, Albanians in the Yugoslav successor states are Muslim.

In the summer of 1980 my husband and I were invited to attend the weekend portions of three south Albanian weddings in the Prespa district, near the border with Greece and Albania. I had first become attracted to Prespa singing through a commercial recording (Leibman 1974), and looked forward to hearing similar songs performed at a community occasion. The first wedding, held during Ramazan (Arab. *Ramaḍān*), the Muslim month of fasting, was somewhat subdued. At the others, held several weeks later, we found ourselves engulfed in two days and nights of virtually uninterrupted music and dance.

Among my first impressions of the community at these weddings, the strongest was that these were among the most cosmopolitan villagers I had encountered anywhere in Macedonia. Village homes were large and spacious, with such West European features as indoor staircases and flush outhouses. A few even seemed to be modeled after homes in North America or Scandinavia. Processions to fetch the bride were filled with cars with West European license plates, and we noticed that the guests often tipped the musicians conspicuously with Belgian francs or U.S. dollars. At one wedding we were caught off guard when an old man wearing a black fez scrutinized our cumbersome tape recorder and then asked, in slangy English, "How much that thing weigh?"

As we chatted with wedding guests during more informal moments, we learned that most community members were no longer subsistence farmers. A number of Prespa families were living in larger cities in Macedonia and Kosova. An even larger number, over half the total

FIGURE 1. Albanian-populated Areas in the Central Balkan Peninsula

number of families, lived abroad: in Western Europe, North America, and Australia. Most of the families then living in Prespa raised tobacco and/or apples as cash crops. Because of their long tradition of seeking work abroad, even those families were prospering by local standards and had taken on many of the appurtenances of Western life. The Presparë whom we met that first summer prided themselves on belonging to what they considered to be the most "progressive" (*përparuar*) of Albanian communities in Yugoslavia, a term that they used to allude to their adoption of the greatest range of Western social practices.

When I eventually decided to pursue a formal study of Prespa weddings and singing, I formulated my research around a set of observations and realizations made at these initial weddings. The first concerned the extent and nature of music-making. There was far more singing at these events than I had heard at other rural weddings in Macedonia, with virtually every guest and family member participating. The vitality of the singing and the degree of participation in it, even by well-educated young Presparë, seemed particularly remarkable for so worldly a community. And so I posed to myself the most obvious questions: How is it that these families have developed such a strong sense of place? What is it about weddings that makes them so central to the life of the community? And why is it so important that everyone sing at such a celebration?

The singing at these weddings was also of a markedly different character from what I had heard at other rural events. Although performed in an intricate polyphonic style that demanded close coordination among participants, the songs were far more malleable than those of neighboring Macedonian villagers, in terms of melodic contour, metric organization, tempo, ornamentation, personnel configurations, and even the content of texts. They seemed in large part to emerge in the act of performance, through an emotionally charged convergence of singers, song, and ritual moment in the crush of surrounding relatives and friends. It became clear that a sense of this repertoire could only be gained by experiencing it as performed at such events, and only through an understanding of how individual singers came to choose between various stylistic options in actual performance situations.

Perhaps the most striking aspect of these weddings for me was the marked segregation of men and women that was observed, and the strong contrast in their modes of behavior. Within each group, members of different generations dressed in contrasting ways, sat in particular places, and greeted each other with distinctive gestures. Speech was also very formal. Long formulaic interchanges accompanied each exchange of greetings and followed most performances of songs. I found myself becoming extremely attentive to where and how I stood or sat, how I greeted different sorts of people, and what I said to whom. In the midst of such orderly speech and movement, I began to view the contrasting singing styles of women and men as particularly formalized types of behavior, governed by elaborate organizational schemas to which each performer needed to be attentive. Gradually I began to theorize that a singer's choice of performance options went beyond purely musical criteria to include the same types of social considerations that lay behind other aspects of public behavior: considerations that related ultimately to the values that maintained singing as such a central celebratory activity.

At the last of the three weddings, my husband and I sat with a group of university students from the community as they debated whether or not Presparë should keep up their elaborate etiquette. The students seemed to feel that much of it was empty, insincere, pro forma. Nevertheless, in our interactions with Prespa families in those first few weeks, I began to suspect that this etiquette gave them much of their sense of identity as Albanians and as Presparë, and that even many of the young people might be loath to abandon it. At the same time as I was beginning to feel that the singing of women and men was shaped by community understandings of social order, I was thus also coming to postulate that singing, as a major component of family life, might play a crucial role in constituting and maintaining those understandings. It was this intuitive sensing of a dialectic between the singing of Presparë and their sense of subjectivity that compelled me to pursue a study of their singing.

The following summer, after seven months of Albanian language study at the University of Skopje, we were permitted to live in a Prespa village. We spent most of our time participating in farming activities with our host family: stringing tobacco, chopping wood, threshing wheat, irrigating fields, picking vegetables, herding oxen, baking bread. Fifteen weddings were held that summer in Prespa, and we attended portions of several of them, including some of the smaller gatherings that take place in the week before the taking of the bride. We spent many evenings conversing about singing and dancing with our host, one of the best-known exponents of both. Armed with some knowledge of their language, we began to learn the standard phraseology that Presparë use to speak about both their singing and their etiquette. And, in return for entertaining our family with Macedonian and north Albanian songs from Skopje, I received my first instruction in Prespa singing from our hostess, together with the family's eight-year-old daughter. The song that we learned provides a fitting introduction to the dilemmas that Presparë face as a diaspora community (CD #1):

Këtë fshatin tonë *nëne* do ta bëjmë qytet . . .	We are turning our village into a town . . .
ajde dhe moj.	(Oh, me!)
Shtëpite me tulle sa paskanë lezet . . .	The houses with tile roofs, how lovely they are! . . .
Alitrikat dritin, radioa buqet . . .	The electric lights glow, the radio blasts . . .
Telegramët vijnë, vijnë me seklet . . .	The telegrams arrive, bringing sorrowful news . . .
Ikin djemtë, nuset, shkojnë në kurbet . . .	The young men and women are leaving to work abroad . . .
po të mjera pleq mbetnë pa yzmet . . .	and the elders remain behind with no one to care for them . . .

By the time we returned to Skopje in the fall, I had begun to piece together information about the ethnic composition of the Prespa district (fig. 2).[3] In Prespa, as in many other parts of Macedonia, not only is the population diverse in terms of religious and linguistic affiliation, but it is and has been in a state of ethnic flux, primarily along religious lines. Of the Christians, the largest group are the Macedonians, who are Eastern Orthodox. They make up at least some of the population of virtually every settlement in the Prespa district. In and around the town of Resen there are also a small number of Orthodox Vlachs or Aromânii, members of an ethnic group who speak a language descending from the Latin formerly spoken in southeast Europe. Of the Muslims, most of those living in Resen and in the nearby villages of Drmeni, Lavci, Carev Dvor, and Kozjak, as well as some families in Gorna Bela Crkva and Grnčari, speak Turkish. It is possible that some of these families are descendants of Turks settled strategically during the Ottoman period in villages along what was then the main route between the towns of Bitola and Korçë. Most, however, are believed by scholars to be of Slavic origin, with ancestors who took on an ascription of Turkish ethnicity in recent centuries. Albanian-speaking Muslims live in small numbers in Resen and the villages of Sopotsko, Kozjak, and Gorna Bela Crkva. They also make up a significant portion of the population of the villages of Dolna Bela Crkva, Grnčari, Asamati, Krani, Arvati, and Nakolec. In the past there were also a number of Albanian-speaking Muslim Roma

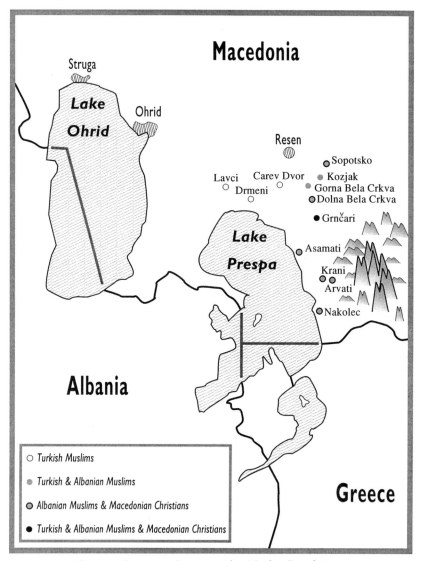

FIGURE 2. Villages in the Prespa District with a Muslim Population

living in villages such as Krani and Nakolec, including musicians who played for the weddings of all the local ethnic groups. Today most of these families live in the towns of Resen and Ohrid.

Among the Albanians in the Prespa district, I eventually came to identify three distinct groups. First are the descendants of the former

Ottoman overlords, or *beys*. Although they are sometimes referred to by themselves and by other Albanians as the *bejlerë* (from the Turkish for *beys*), they are more commonly known as *kolonjarë* ("people of Kolonjë"), since they believe that their ancestors came to Prespa in the late eighteenth or early nineteenth century from the district of Kolonjë in southern Albania. In the late Ottoman period Kolonjarë lived primarily in the villages of Ljubojno, Nakolec, and Krani. The fall of the empire, however, precipitated various population movements within the district, so that today most Kolonjarë still in Prespa live in Gorna and Dolna Bela Crkva and Asamati. Kolonjarë families belong to the Bektashi (Turk. Bektaşi) dervish order, whose doctrines have connections to the Shi'ite branch of Islam, and are thus differentiated from other Prespa Muslims, who are Sunni. Because of religious differences, and also because they consider themselves to be on a higher social level than other Prespa villagers, Kolonjarë families socialize and marry primarily among themselves. In many ways they serve as the intelligentsia among Prespa Albanians. Their speech is closest to literary Albanian, they generally know more about Albanian history and culture, and they are the most likely to provide their children with a higher education. For this reason most of the Prespa students whom I eventually met in Skopje, including my language teacher, were from Kolonjarë families.

The highest concentration of Sunni Albanians in Prespa lives in the villages of Krani, Arvati, Nakolec, and Asamati, along the eastern shore of the lake in an area referred to in older geographies as "lower Prespa" (Dolna Prespa).[4] Some of these families retain stories of ancestors who came to Prespa from various parts of southern Albania, while others consider themselves to be indigenous to the district. Kolonjarë refer to these families as *arbutë,* meaning "peons" or "commoners"; or as *të vêndë,* "local," meaning that they were already living in the area when the Kolonjarë arrived. Without an examination of Ottoman documents, it is impossible to assess how long there has been an Albanian population in this part of Prespa. In the past these Albanian villagers were able to maintain cultural ties to other south Albanians living to the west of them in what is now Albania, and their speech and folklore are close to those of Albanians in the Devoll and Korçë districts.

A third group of Albanians, also Sunni, lives in the villages of Sopotsko, Dolna Bela Crkva, and Grnčari, in the area formerly called "upper Prespa" (Gorna Prespa). Except for a few families who moved north from the lower villages, the social and economic ties of these families have been primarily to Turkish- and Slavic-speaking Muslims within that area rather than to other Albanians. In emphasizing their religious affiliation somewhat over a linguistic one, they have remained more aloof from their Christian Macedonian fellow villagers, and their cultural forms have been less exclusively Albanian. With increased intermarriage between the two Sunni Albanian groups in the last few decades, however, the distinction between them has been significantly blurred, and Albanian social practices have been strengthened among families in the upper villages.

Despite the distinctiveness of these three groups, Prespa Albanian weddings and the singing at them are remarkably uniform. With regard to the wedding ritual itself, there is almost no significant variation.[5] Eventually, however, I was able to identify some differences in singing style and repertoire between Kolonjarë and other families, and between families from the upper and lower villages. I also came to regard lower Prespa as the area in which polyphonic singing is most firmly established. For this reason, and because of my more extensive connections with families from the lower villages, my subsequent fieldwork and writings have concentrated on families with ties to the villages of Krani, Arvati, and Nakolec. Thus, when I speak of "Presparë," unless the context indicates otherwise, I am referring primarily to families with origins in these villages.

In the months that followed our second summer in Prespa, I seriously reconsidered my research in Macedonia. My work with the community from Greece had been difficult in many respects, and so I discussed with some of my colleagues the possibility of conducting a study of singing at Prespa weddings. This type of project, however, would have required me to observe and document a number of actual events, thus remaining in Prespa for an extended period, and I came to realize that such a study was not feasible. In this period, at least, no foreigner in Macedonia could expect to reside long-term in a rural area, within sight of the Greek and Albanian borders, in daily, informal contact with villagers of any sort, let alone members of an ethnic and religious minority.

I decided instead to seek out Prespa families in North America and to study their singing within that context. Initially I planned a different kind of study, one focusing on Presparë as an immigrant community and comparing them to their counterparts in Macedonia. In 1985, I visited Prespa families in Toronto, Detroit, and Chicago, some of whom I had known from Macedonia, and then returned to Toronto to live for three months with two different Prespa families. In the following year my husband and I traveled together to Toronto. Using that city as a home base, I carried out eight months of intensive research in the Great Lakes area, followed by a few short return visits to various cities. It was to be expected that my experiences with Prespa families in Macedonia, including knowledge of their dialect and singing, would prove invaluable once I began my research in North America. But I also found that what I learned subsequently about Prespa families in the United States and Canada greatly influenced my perspective on families who have remained in Macedonia.

Until the dismantling of the Ottoman provinces of Europe in 1913, the peoples of Macedonia lived under a feudal system that enforced large economic distinctions between overlords and commoners. As Muslims, all Prespa Albanians were members of the favored religious group within the Empire, and the Kolonjarë in particular were at the top of the local social ladder. But all this was to change drastically. Around the turn of the century the Prespa district became a hotbed of anti-Ottoman activity. When a Macedonian-led uprising against Ottoman rule failed in 1903, several villages were burned and villagers suffered extreme deprivation (see Durham 1904, Perry 1988). After this period, Macedonian men from the lower Prespa villages initiated a pattern, referred to as *gurbet*, of traveling overseas to earn money to support their families. The destination of most was the United States. During World War I, the lower villages again came under siege. Many villagers temporarily fled to other settlements, and substantial numbers of homes were destroyed. Once the war was over, around 1920, Albanian men from Krani and Nakolec also began to go on *gurbet* to America. They went primarily to industrial centers such as Dearborn, Michigan, and Bridgeport, Connecticut, where they became factory workers or found jobs in the restaurant business. After a stay abroad of several years, most returned to their villages and invested their foreign earnings in their farms.

With the fall of the Ottoman Empire and the subsequent inclusion of the Prespa district within the new Yugoslavia (1918–1944), Albanians there found themselves cut off from their compatriots to the west, and learning to function within a new capitalist economic system. Under the pressure of heavy taxes, many Kolonjarë sold off their surplus land and became subsistence farmers like their former subjects, often moving to a different village in the process. To counteract what might have been an equalizing trend, certain former commoners' families became so prosperous through foreign earnings that they began to hire their fellow villagers to work their land, and thus discrepancies arose among the Sunni families where few had existed before. As neither Slavs nor Christians, all Albanians in Prespa found themselves in the position of being simultaneously a linguistic and a religious minority. Once schools were opened, classes were conducted in Serbian, with one day a week of religious instruction in Turkish and Arabic for all Muslims.

A new set of changes occurred with the coming of socialism in 1944. In the years following World War II, an attempt was made to collectivize the land in Yugoslavia. Many families with large holdings, mostly Kolonjarë, felt extremely disaffected by the system, and numbers of them emigrated permanently. A large number of Kolonjarë moved at this point to Detroit, where Bektashi families from Albania had begun to congregate. Some Muslim families from the upper villages went to Turkey. The majority of Prespa Albanians, however, remained in Yugoslavia, encouraged both by an opportunity to acquire farmland of their own and by the policy of cultural pluralism that became a hallmark of postwar Yugoslavia. For the first time, Albanian-language primary schools, which both boys and girls were expected to attend, were opened in several villages. The families who remained in Yugoslavia set about to fare as best they could within the new system, and many succeeded. A disproportionate number of the Albanian professionals within the former Yugoslavia—government officials, teachers, doctors, lawyers, and political leaders—came from Prespa.

In the mid-1960s, however, Yugoslavia went into an economic decline, and the idea of *gurbet* and its promise of economic advancement once again began to lure Prespa men overseas. At first younger men, not yet married and full of curiosity and a desire to travel, set off by themselves to work in the United States, Canada, Australia, and western Europe. Some returned to their villages, married, and resumed their farming life. Others sent for brides and set up house abroad. Gradually, many who had returned to marry then chose to go abroad once more, taking their families with them. By the mid-1970s Prespa families, including those of older men with established means of livelihood, were setting out from Yugoslavia in all directions.

Today there are large colonies of Prespa Sunni Albanians living in and around Sydney and Melbourne in Australia, and there are smaller communities in Sweden, Denmark, and Belgium. In North America there are a few hundred families living in Toronto and London, Ontario, and in greater Chicago and Detroit, with small clusters of families in Connecticut, Florida, and Nevada. Virtually all families retain their land in their villages, and many have built impressive new homes there. With the exception of vacation periods, however, the lower villages especially are severely depopulated. The situation was poignantly illustrated to me in 1985 when a woman in Toronto showed me a photograph from around 1960 of her grammar-school class in Krani. Out of 29 Albanian children, all but three were then living outside Yugoslavia, and the teacher was in Detroit.

Some families living in western Europe have returned to Prespa for a month virtually every year. The situation has been different, however, for families in North America and Australia. Some have embraced overseas life and its material advantages to such an extent that they have shown no interest in returning, and have rarely gone even to visit. Others have returned during the summers as often as they can. During the period that I was conducting research in North America, a substantial number of families found the clash between their traditional values and those of mainstream North America to be so threatening to them and their children that they viewed their stay abroad as a temporary one and devoted considerable thought to making plans for returning to Prespa to live. Of the families living in Toronto in the mid-1980s, for example, around ten had come to Canada about a decade earlier, had returned to Prespa in the late 1970s and early 1980s for stays of up to eight years, and had then decided to return to Canada for economic reasons. Some of them still planned to return permanently to Prespa, although most eventually did not. What is important to note in all this shuffling from locale to locale is the primary allegiance that families have shown to the Prespa district and to the set of values to which adult generations were socialized. To whatever extent possible, they have tried to live overseas as if they were still in their villages, raising their children according to the values they grew up with and socializing almost exclusively with other Prespa families. To outsiders they are an "invisible" community, in that they have not associated with Albanian-American organizations, nor drawn attention to themselves by opening Albanian businesses or sponsoring Albanian folklore groups.

Large occasions such as weddings have been an important means for families to keep in touch. When I was in Prespa in the early 1980s, the wedding season extended from late May to late September. There was at least one wedding every weekend, and sometimes two or three were held simultaneously in the same village. Families living elsewhere in Yugoslavia, as well as those living overseas, returned to Prespa in large numbers to attend. In addition, many families living overseas returned to their village homes for their sons' weddings, bringing a large entourage of relatives. It was not unusual, therefore, for a wedding held in Prespa to be peopled largely by families who no longer lived there. In North America, most weddings are also held during the summer, although they may occur at any time of year. Families travel from all over the United States and Canada to attend these events, and there are often guests from Australia and western Europe as well. Families in Prespa who still live by farming find it difficult to leave during the summer work season, but those who can afford to do so may visit relatives abroad during the winter. There is thus a constant flow of Prespare from one continent to another.

When families in North America hold a wedding, it attracts several hundred guests and culminates in an elaborate dinner in a banquet hall, with dancing to an amplified band. Leading up to the taking of the bride, however, many families choose to hold gatherings at their homes for days or weeks beforehand, to carry out the various ritual preparations, and to do all this through singing. Of necessity, the sequence of ritual activities and the extent of singing must be accommodated to urban work schedules, apartment living, and other exigencies. Nevertheless, most adults formulate their song performances around the same considerations that I first noted at weddings in Prespa, and the capacity of weddings to evoke and transform an individual's sense of self and community is no less potent than in Prespa. I have chosen, therefore, not to frame this study of Prespa singing in terms of contrast and change between two separate, historically related communities; but rather to explore both continuities and disjunctures in the musical practices of families living in two distinct locales who nevertheless regard themselves as part of a single diasporic community.

Researching Prespa Singing

For my North American fieldwork (1985–87), in contrast to my two summers in Prespa, I worked with a definite research agenda in mind. The prospect of being included in the daily activities of community members was made easier during my first stay by my consecutive residence in Toronto with two different families. When I returned the next year with my husband, we maintained our own apartment there, but by that time there were at least three families who regarded us as close friends and who treated us in certain respects as if we were members of their households.

Life for families in North America is hectic. During the week younger adults are at work, the children are in school, and only the grandparent generation is home. Weekends, and especially Sundays, are devoted to socializing with other Prespa families. The constant visiting back-and-forth between households is not merely for amusement: it involves the living out and constant renewal of extensive social obligations. For most families the weekend calendar is so packed with social occasions that there is little time for housework, shopping, or a leisurely outing with the children. Because of this schedule, my initial contacts were concentrated in the weekend rounds of visiting. Most common were small gatherings involving a few households of close relatives or friends. At first I was a bit of a curiosity, but eventually the novelty of my presence wore off and people conversed about whatever was on their minds, while I followed the conversation as best I could. Gradually I began to visit single families by myself, and later with my husband; subsequently I took a more active part in structuring conversations.

Whereas in Prespa we had mostly attended weddings, in North America we were included in a variety of other large social occasions: ceremonies called *mevlyd*s, held upon the birth of a child; dinners held in honor of visiting relatives; and celebrations of circumcisions. It was at such larger events, and at weddings, that we encountered the greatest number of community members, but there was little time to converse. At a *mevlyd* a Muslim religious leader (*oxha*) or other man knowledgeable in Qur'ānic recitation leads a prayer service. At all other events, when not eating, individuals interact primarily by singing and dancing. We had already learned in Prespa that our participation in the dancing was a way to express our interest in the community and to break the ice in meeting new families. In North America, depending on the formality of the occasion and our closeness to the hosts, I might also be asked to participate as a singer.

In a very real way, the structure of Prespa social life dictated the types of contacts that I made, and hence the list of those who became my major consultants. Virtually all large social occasions are family-based, hosted by a single household that composes the guest list. For reasons that will be explored later, there were virtually no events sponsored by the mosque or by some sort of community organization that would include all families living in a particular city. And so, from the moment that I arrived in Toronto and took up residence with my first host family,

I became associated with them, their relatives, and their circle of neighbors and other acquaintances. All the individuals whom I eventually interviewed and with whom I exchanged ideas were contacted through an elaborate network of families that emanated ultimately from a very few initial contacts in Toronto, Detroit, and Chicago.

Generally only Prespa Albanians are included in large family celebrations. Because some of the Toronto families have intermarried with south Albanian families from the Bitola district east of Prespa, the two frequently socialize together. But even these families from Bitola are excluded from some Prespa events. As *anglezë* ("English people"), our presence at any such event was thus highly unusual, and we were only permitted to attend events hosted by families who felt they could trust us. Ultimately, this trust required months of cultivation on our part. Some families in Toronto and the greater Chicago area were willing to include us in activities solely because we were vouched for by acquaintances from our time in Macedonia. Others needed to observe us, converse with us, and then discuss us with other families before they were willing to extend an invitation. Many were impressed with our knowledge of their singing and my ability to participate in it. But they were even more pleased that we attempted to master their complicated etiquette, which they took as a sign of our respect for them. Some others became suspicious of our knowledge of their dialect and music, and feared that we were somehow spying on the community, or worried that I would depict them in my writings as "conservative" or "backward." While most individuals eventually overcame such suspicions, a few held to them for the duration of my fieldwork. We thus found ourselves excluded from some events where our presence might have offended certain guests.

For these reasons, I came to know the North American Prespa community from the particular vantage point of my network of contacts. I also concentrated my most intensive interviewing and documenting within a few clusters of families in Toronto and Chicago. Within these clusters were a large number of the most highly regarded singers in North America, including a number of those on the Leibman album or a more recent one recorded by Herman Vuylsteke (Vuylsteke 1981). But I also worked with a number of average singers, as well as a few individuals who, while admiring the singing of community members, do not themselves sing. What I lost in the way of breadth of coverage within the community, I gained in the depth of subject matter that I was able to explore with them and in the range of activities in which I was encouraged to participate.

In our first weeks among North American families, we visited a man outside Chicago who was known as a clarinet player and singer. He and a fellow musician serenaded us with songs and dance pieces from their repertoire, and I sang a song or two with his wife. At the end of the evening he took us into the family room, brought out an impressive video camera and recorder, and filmed a sort of talk-show interview with us, which he then played back for us on his television set. On a return visit, he showed us some videos he had made during the previous year: a wedding in Ontario, a New Year's party at his home. This was my first encounter with the voracious appetite of Prespa families for the electronic media. In the months to follow I found that most families had long ago begun to make audio recordings of singing events, both in Macedonia and abroad, and that many had now switched to video. Individual families also owned commercial videos of music and dance from Yugoslavia and Albania, as well as cassettes that they had recorded from Yugoslav or Albanian radio of commercial song performances.

Following the lead of community members, I returned to Toronto in 1986 with a video camcorder and a VCR to duplicate community recordings, in addition to the still camera and tape recorder that I had used in earlier fieldwork. Ultimately, the interest of Prespare in electronics proved advantageous to my work in two ways. On the one hand, my husband and I were rarely the only people recording an event, and our equipment was generally more modest than that of community members. We were even able, toward the end of our stay, to be the official video team for some events, thus allowing relatives of the host family to join actively in the celebration. On the other hand, I was eventually able to draw on community recordings dating back to the late 1960s in preparing my account of Prespa singing, some of which are featured on the accompanying CD. These included recordings of men's social gatherings of a type that I, as a woman, had sometimes been excluded from attending.

Gradually I became aware of the cycles of Prespa social life. Major celebrations such as circumcisions, betrothals, and weddings were clearly the highlights. Families spoke about them for weeks in advance, fussing over what they would wear and trying to predict what sorts of affairs they would be. Once an event had passed it became a major topic of conversation at all smaller gatherings for weeks thereafter. Everything was discussed and critiqued: the menu, the clothing of hosts and guests, the host family's attention to all the fine points of ritual, the atmosphere that the event generated, the band, the dancing, and—quite prominently—the singing. Often we were included in viewing sessions of videos made of the event, or even provided the video ourselves, and were therefore privy to many rounds of commentary about everything that had been recorded. When I felt that it was time to begin formal interviews with individuals, I already had some sense of what was important to community members about these events, what sorts of questions to ask, and what sort of vocabulary to use in my questions, in addition to drawing upon my own observations made at events.

In my initial rounds of interviews I focused on how individuals speak about singing. I was particularly curious as to how today's adults had learned to sing, for I surmised that their perceptions of singing must have been shaped to a great extent by the ways in which they were initially exposed to it. Were they taught set versions of songs, or were they expected to come up with their own versions? Had they been coached or corrected by older singers? About which aspects of singing had they received instruction? Had there been contexts in which young people practiced singing prior to performing songs "in public" at social events? I also had many logistical questions regarding singing at weddings: How is the particular order of singers determined? Who sings with whom? How does a person choose which song to sing? Which songs are associated with which points in the wedding ritual? Precisely what are singers and listeners saying to each other in the flowery spoken exchanges that follow most song performances? I wanted to clarify the meaning of the various technical terms that singers use to coordinate their singing and to evaluate their own and others' performances. Lastly, I wanted to identify performers and to transcribe and translate the texts as sung on my growing collection of recordings, a task made infinitely easier by the excellent English spoken by some of the most knowledgeable singers.

One point that came through in early interviews was the complex relationship within their commentary between musical and social, or even moral, considerations. First of all, individuals rarely spoke in terms of a "singing tradition" that possessed certain codified rules. When presented with abstract questions about techniques or terminology, they looked blank. The questions that made more sense to them were ones that addressed their experiences as singers or their evaluations of others, preferably with reference to specific events. I therefore turned increasingly to playback interviews structured around audio or video recordings (see Stone and Stone 1981). Here the advantages of video were immediately apparent. Not only was it easier to identify all the participants in a singing occasion, but the songs could be correlated more precisely to other activities taking place.

Individuals also evaluated one another's performances from two vantage points. On the one hand they appraised technical aspects such as the singer's intonation, execution of ornamental techniques, and tempo. These sorts of "musical" evaluations were generally expressed in a tolerant manner. Good singers were spoken of as those who understand how the "system" of Prespa singing works and who exploit its expressive possibilities successfully: in short, those who "know how to sing." Poor singers were regarded as well-meaning individuals who had never fully caught on to the style.

Other comments, however, were expressed in a far more critical, even self-righteous tone, and I sensed that my questions had penetrated to the bedrock of the community's social ideology. These "moral" evaluations covered aspects of singing as diverse as the point in the ritual when a person sang, the singer's choice of song and rendering of the text, vocal timbre, and type of ornamentation. Here again video recordings proved their worth, in that some comments had to do with a singer's physical stance and overall demeanor. It was these aspects of singing that individuals seemed to most enjoy discussing, and for which they seemed to have the most extensive vocabulary.

At an intermediate stage, therefore, I moved in my interviews from more technical, musicological concerns toward an exploration of the connection between singing and community notions of social and moral order. Eventually, as I came to recognize just how fundamental that relationship was, I expanded my observations and interviewing to include a broad range of issues that are central to the community's social practices: gender, kinship, means of production and division of labor, relations between families, and relations with mainstream North American society.

Early discussions of the moral aspects of singing tended to elicit what I came to refer to jokingly as The Party Line: standard explanations of singing worded in stereotypic ways. So uniform was this phraseology that I came to identify it as an explicit discourse linking performance forms to community notions of morality. As I spoke more intensively with individual singers, however, their comments and observations became increasingly idiosyncratic. Often we found ourselves negotiating a new vocabulary in order to discuss ways of thinking about singing that they had never before verbalized, perhaps, or even explicitly thought about.

I also sensed in the more personal commentary of singers a relationship of creative tension that exists in any performance between what I think of as the aesthetic and social aspects of singing (cf. Turino 1993: 63). Individuals frequently complained that their singing at an event was to some extent undermined by social exigencies: that considerations as to when to sing or with whom or which type of song was appropriate had prevented them from achieving the most aesthetically satisfying performance. Less frequently, singers spoke of encountering an almost ideal atmosphere and set of circumstances that enabled them to sing better than they had ever been known to before. These were the moments that singers and listeners at an event came to await with eager anticipation. Not only were they remembered long after the occasion was past, but they also set the standards for future performances.

Ultimately, I found, Prespare give precedence to social considerations: they speak of singing less as an end in itself than as a means to social ends. It thus became very clear that it would be misleading for me to present the aesthetic aspects of Prespa singing as a closed musical system. Rather, in my analysis, I focus upon the two-way interaction between aesthetic and social considerations that occurs at any event: on the one hand, how social constraints affect individual performances; on the other, how aesthetic techniques contribute to the community's ongoing formulation of its notions of society and morality.

Theorizing Prespa Singing

While still in Macedonia I began to lay the scholarly groundwork for my study by searching for ethnographic writings on Albanians. What I found was a body of travel accounts and ethnographic reports written by west Europeans and North Americans in the early decades of the twentieth century. Prompted by reports of fearless mountain men living according to an ancient code of honor enforced by tribal law, adventurists and journalists had flocked to the highlands of northern Albania in search of what they imagined to be a sort of primitive European clansman. One of the most thorough of these writers was Mary Edith

Durham, a plucky Englishwoman who traveled with mule and guide into the most remote parts of the northern highlands. Her sympathetic analyses of rural Albanian life (see, for example, Durham 1909, 1928) have been consulted repeatedly over the years by most subsequent writers on Albanians, including Albanian scholars. In their quest for the exotic, however, Durham and others all but overlooked south Albanian communities, whose way of life has been much closer to that of neighboring Greek and Slavic villagers. Until very recently, Albania was so inaccessible to anyone in the West that these early accounts still provide many of the common stereotypes about Albanians. Their emphasis on northern communities, however, renders them of limited usefulness to any appraisal of southerners such as Presparë.[6]

To overcome this lacuna regarding southerners, I turned to a broad selection of ethnographic studies of communities in various parts of the eastern Mediterranean.[7] Since the mid-1960s much of this literature has been concerned with the structure of Mediterranean societies, as well as with certain core concepts, such as "honor" and "shame," that propel and shape activities in such communities. Many of these concepts have strongly gender-specific associations, with the result that a number of these studies have also examined the ways that community notions of gender have been constructed through time. Since Presparë recognize a fundamental distinction between men's and women's singing styles and song repertoires, I gradually focused on gender as the central component in my analysis of Prespa singing.

Through my acquaintance with a range of south Slavic and Albanian communities, it had already become clear to me that substantial variation in the interpretation of such terms exists within the Mediterranean area, even within and between communities of the same ethnicity (cf. Herzfeld 1980). I therefore realized that I could not directly use the analyses presented in these various regional studies in my account of Prespa social practices. I could and did, however, use this literature to suggest which avenues of observation and interviewing to pursue, and which directions to take in my eventual interpretation of Prespa social life. That the most relevant writings proved to be those concerning Greek, Turkish, and Arab communities only reinforced my impressions from Macedonia of the marked differences between Albanians and the Slavic groups among whom they live.

What had struck me most forcefully during my stay in Macedonia was a sense of Prespa weddings as arenas within which aspects of social identity were continually produced and negotiated, and of singing as a major means through which any individual would engage in that process. That sense of singing as a site for the renegotiation of identities came into sharper focus as I continued my research among families in the Prespa diaspora, for whom various performance forms offer a means of addressing the challenges that North American society presents to their views of social life.

The Interpretive Paradigm

At the time that I began to formulate my approach to such processes, the dominant paradigm influencing ethnomusicological studies of individual communities was that of interpretive anthropology, so named for the writings of Clifford Geertz (1973a; see also Marcus and Fischer 1986). Strongly influenced by hermeneutic theory, particularly as set forth by Ricoeur (see especially Ricoeur 1971), Geertz and his followers promoted a notion of culture as a web of socially shared meanings, and a view of social action as a "text" that could be read interpretively by the ethnographer, who put forth his or her account as a form of "cultural translation." Following Geertz's lead, ethnomusicologists working within this paradigm have analyzed musical performance as an expressive activity that communicates social meanings, and as a realm within which a community's fundamental values are evoked and confirmed. They have thus defined their task as conveying the "lived experience" of individuals participating in a musical tradition by elucidating the meanings that community music-making holds for its members.

In early studies within this paradigm two distinct types of analysis were widely employed. First was the postulation of structural homologies between musical forms and aspects of either social ideology (Kaeppler 1978) or cosmological belief (Becker and Becker 1981) or both (Hill 1979, Seeger 1980). The premise behind this manner of analysis, which Kaeppler termed "ethnoscientific structuralism" (1978:261), was that a community makes the music it does because something in that music's structure or style is logically consistent with central patterns of thinking and of behaving within the culture. Such homologies were often postulated without reference to community verbalization about either musical practice or the larger realm of shared meanings, the assumption being that community members were not consciously aware of inherent consistencies between conceptual domains. The Beckers' refinement of this approach (1981) was important in emphasizing the extent to which members of a society come to regard "iconic" constructs in music, not as metaphors for other domains of experience, but rather as expressions of the natural order. A second approach, often referred to as "ethnoaesthetics," focused upon verbalized accounts of music-making among communities whose members explicitly recognize links between musical and non-musical domains, and for whom music serves as a conscious metaphor of specific clusters of beliefs (Robertson 1979; Feld 1982, 1984; Roseman 1984, 1991). In practice, these two types of analysis have been complementary rather than mutually exclusive. More recent studies have often combined the two (Seeger 1987, Waterman 1990, Rice 1994), and scholars have in many cases been able to situate instances of homology or iconicity within community discourses (Feld 1989, Turino 1993).

The interpretive paradigm has transformed the work of Western ethnomusicologists in several crucial ways. We have learned to give serious attention to the ideas and interpretations of musicians and their constituencies, to carefully render the terminology that they use to convey their ideas and the collective meanings that music is said to generate, and to recognize the importance of individual agency in the formulation of musical practices. Together with a number of scholars, however, I have come to view this paradigm as "necessary but not sufficient": as in need of refinement and expansion, in part because of shortcomings that became evident to me in the course of my fieldwork.

First, ethnoaesthetics in particular is a logocentric methodology, in that it gives precedence to those aspects of music-making for which there exists some sort of standard parlance. In the case of the Prespa community, as already noted, singers do indeed share a well-developed discourse that outlines the moral aspects of singing, one formulated around the concept of "honor." But there are also many aspects of singing that community members do not speak about, and these are often the aspects that relate most directly to issues of gender. It is implicit understandings of music, acquired through nonverbal means, that have been addressed to some degree by ethnoscientific structuralism. But ethnomusicologists have rarely tackled the question as to why certain aspects of music are verbalized about while others are not, nor what effect a lack of verbalization might have either on musical practice or on the understandings that individuals maintain of themselves and their community.[8]

Second is the more complex issue of postulating a culture, belief system, or meaning system as something holistic and internally consistent that a musical performance "mirrors" or "articulates." If we view culture as a monolith, we ignore the contestation and renegotiation of meaning that continually take place among community members. As I have interviewed individual Prespare, I have found that behind the community's musical discourses and highly formalized practices lie all sorts of idiosyncratic viewpoints that represent quite individualistic versions of a Prespa "culture."[9] It has thus become a major concern for me to provide an account of their singing that addresses the tension that often exists between shared understandings and the idiosyncratic and at times conflicting interpretations of individuals.

It is also clear that periods of major discontinuity, such as population movements or changes in the political, economic, or religious order, have often prompted fundamental refigurings of the meaning of musical activities. Such transformations, however, are never so thorough as to reconcile the many disjunctures and contradictions that result from social change, and that create points of continual tension within social life.[10] Working with immigrant families who have found their views of social order radically challenged by those of mainstream North America, I have had to give particular attention to the renegotiations of meaning that are currently taking place among diaspora families within and through musical performance, and to the ways that musical practices may address, or mask, societal tensions.

The notion of a unitary culture has thrived within the anthropological tradition of cultural relativism, through which ethnographers have defended a community's right to formulate a view of the world that is distinct from that advanced by Western powers. However oppositional our intentions might be in taking on such a role, in doing so we may unwittingly valorize whatever hierarchical relations pertain within a community. This, of course, is a problematic stance to adopt when appraising any type of asymmetrical social arrangement based on aspects of identity such as gender, age, ethnicity, or class. Indeed, the distinct subject positions that individuals occupy within a social formation often generate particularly contrasting accounts of "culture." Often we have seemed most willing to examine questions of power when they concern the relationship between the individual communities that we study and larger national or international processes. Indeed, some of the most compelling ethnomusicological accounts in recent years detail unfolding encounters between local communities and the hegemony of a ruling elite or of an expanding global economic system.[11] But we also need to be cognizant of the dynamics of power relations as they unfold within localized communities, particularly as they are affected by national and global concerns.

Theories of Subjectivity and Power

If we posit a dialectical relationship between performance forms and the social configurations of the communities that perform them, then the interpretive approach may be viewed as privileging one phase of that dialectic: the evocations of self and of community that musicians accomplish through their performances. In order to address its other phase, I have turned to the work of social theorists who have had as their concern the ways that subjectivity is constructed and negotiated through cultural forms. These writers invite us to broaden our analysis beyond a consideration of lived experience to encompass what might be termed the "social effects" of musical practices: the ways that music-making participates in the very construction of agency and experience; and the ways that the actions of individuals implicate them in continual renegotiations, not only of their musical practices, but also of the relations of power that organize their society. Such a perspective suggests a break with certain of the conventions of interpretive scholarship, including some of its core vocabulary. It suggests that musical performance is not so much an "expressive form" that evokes a world of meanings located in other realms of experience, as it is a form of representation that participates fundamentally in constituting those worlds (cf. Seeger 1987). It suggests that performance forms be seen both as structured by a range of shared meanings, and as structuring, in their capacity to shape ongoing social formations.

Among recent theorists, Bourdieu situates this dialectic within the realm of social practices, which he sees as emerging through an oscillation of "objectification and embodiment" (1977:87–95). The underlying structures that characterize a social formation are "objectified" through symbolic forms of behavior such as ritual or musical performance, or the tangible products of behavior such as architectural plan or clothing style. As an individual interacts with a world filled with such objectifications, those structures are internalized in bodily form within the individual as his or her "habitus." Any instance of social action, shaped in line with the actor's habitus, both provides a new objectification of societal structures and serves as a vehicle for their ongoing internalization by other community members.

Since an adult acts on the basis of structures, themselves historical products, which were inculcated in him or her beginning in early childhood, Bourdieu sees habitus as predisposing individuals to reproduce those structures through their actions in the great majority of instances, rather than to act in ways that might challenge and transform them. He

27

thus views symbolic practices as crucial vehicles for the reproduction of social relations, preserving the positions of those within a society who are able to exercise the greatest power and authority. Through his postulation of the collective habitus of a community as the repository of its deep structures, he also addresses the iconicities that may often be identified between domains of human activity, and that are particularly apparent in ritual and performance forms. Here he speaks of

> the magic of a world of objects which is the product of the application of the same schemes to the most diverse domains, a world in which each thing speaks metaphorically of all the others. . . . The mind born of the world of objects does not rise as a subjectivity confronting an objectivity: the objective universe is made up of objects which are the product of objectifying operations structured according to the very structures which the mind applies to it. The mind is a metaphor of the world of objects which is itself but an endless circle of mutually reflecting metaphors. (1977:91)

In line with the Beckers' notion of "iconicity," Bourdieu emphasizes that the effect on members of a society of extensive homology across domains of experience is one of a "world of tradition experienced as a 'natural world' and taken for granted" (164).

Foucault's writings carry us still further from the conventions of interpretive scholarship. Whereas Bourdieu assumes history, Foucault traces it by providing "genealogies" of what he terms "discourses." His best known definition of discourses, as "practices that systematically form the objects of which they speak" (1972:49), would seem to suggest entities akin to Bourdieu's notion of "practice." But Foucault more commonly documents the deployment of authoritative texted arguments that he views as productive of relations of power. As with Bourdieu, power relations for Foucault permeate social life and are exercised in every instance of human interchange, but his vision of power is more fluid. While he recognizes that relations of power within different domains may come together to reinforce each other, forming in the process "a chain or a system" (1980:92) that is enforced by state institutions or hegemonic societal constructs, they may also be constituted within a society in contradictory, disjunct ways. A discourse that is deployed in the name of dominant interests in one historical moment may be taken up as a site of resistance in the next, only to plunge those who have adopted it into new and unforeseen strategies of power at some point in the future. Social relations thus unfold through processes of continual contestation along axes of power.[12]

Foucault's notion of "discourse" provides a means of organizing much of the "native terminology" that has formed the basis of ethnoaesthetic inquiries. By viewing such terminology not as the creation of a single localized community but as arising from discourses that are widely disseminated and of considerable history, and that have often reached communities through the authority of the state or of religious institutions, we are better able to understand the ongoing capacity of a community's speech patterns to construct social reality for its members. The official character of many such discourses may also account for the similarities in musical parlance as well as practice that may be traced throughout large geographic areas that share a common history. Much of the richness of Prespa phraseology, for example, stems from a legacy of Ottoman and Islamic discourses that Albanians share with many other communities in former Ottoman territories.[13] By positing the existence of multiple, competing discourses, Foucault's approach also challenges the predilection of both Bourdieu and interpretivist scholars to characterize communities in terms of a single, monolithic culture, belief system, or set of coherent structures. For any community it should be possible to identify a range of discourses that have arisen in different periods and historical circumstances and that, through a dense web of interaction, construct an individual's subjectivity in multiple and contradictory ways. Although many discourses circulate within a community, each individual chooses which of them to invoke and how he or she will be situated within them, and the precise interpretation of any discourse is open to continual debate. Such an expansion and complication of the concept of culture holds much promise for understanding the complex ways that performance forms with traditions of long standing have served over time as sites of identity construction.

But is a focus on verbal discourses sufficient for an account of the processes of social reproduction and renegotiation that musical performance brings about? And are forms of music-making, which involve such a rich array of communicative channels, to be considered merely as "discourses"? Here Bourdieu's attention to nondiscursive, experiential domains provides a necessary counterbalance. In his view, individuals acquire assumptions regarding their social world in the course of living out their daily patterns of activities, often without any type of verbal explanation as to why those activities are ordered as they are. What they acquire in the course of their lives is a "sense" (1977:15) or "practical mastery" (88) of those assumptions that enables them to act in a socially appropriate manner, rather than the "symbolic" mastery that one might acquire through a conscious application of explicit rules as laid out in a formal discourse. An individual's knowledge of certain domains of activity may thus be largely "implicit" (27). When individuals formulate their actions within such a domain, they do so without conscious reference to its underlying assumptions, much as a person speaks spontaneously without reference to grammatical rules. Certainly many musical traditions, including that of Prespare, have been maintained largely in this manner.

The implicit status of many community understandings most certainly accounts for the inability of individuals to verbalize about certain aspects of musical practice. More importantly, a recognition of the epistemological transformation that is brought about when such implicit understandings are brought to the level of discourse should prompt researchers to present their analyses in such a way as to convey the means through which they, as well as members of the society that they study, have come to "know" what they "know." This requires an attention to practice: that is, to the ways that individuals learn of aspects of social life and then draw upon their understandings to formulate their actions. Here we are very close to the performance perspective as it has developed in the field of folklore, as well as in anthropological accounts of ritual events, for attention to these matters requires attention to specific moments of musical performance and to the assumptions that emerge in their course.[14] An exclusive focus on practice, however, may overlook the extent to which communities, including nonliterate ones, maintain formal discourses that consistently mediate certain domains of action. Analysis of performance forms thus also requires an attention to discourse: to the ways that distinct historical discourses shape activities within the performance arena; to those sites where discourses are produced as individuals anticipate, evaluate, or reflect on moments of performance; and to those realms of musical practice where discourse is striking in its absence. It is this vision of an intricate interplay between discourse and practice within the sphere of performance that most deeply informs my assessment of the "engendering" capacities of Prespa song.

Toward a Critical Ethnomusicology of Gender

Considerations of subjectivity and power should be central to any analysis of music as a gendered activity. How do individuals within a community come to regard themselves as gendered beings, and to appraise certain qualities and activities in gendered terms? How is power exerted and experienced in gender relations? How are asymmetrical power relations, as gender relations often are, reproduced from one generation to the next, even with the willing complicity of those who are subordinate? How is it possible for individuals to challenge or renegotiate the terms of such relations? What roles does musical performance play in each of these processes?

Until recently, much of the gender-based research in ethnomusicology was descriptive and compensatory in character, with a focus on the many and varied musical contributions of women.[15] Such studies have been of undeniable importance in redressing an earlier emphasis on male performance genres, as well as male-centered views of individual societies, but an explicit examination of how women's music-making relates to gender relations as a whole has often been lacking. Those ethnomusicological studies that have been concerned with broader issues of gender have generally derived their approach from interpretive writings in anthropology. Such analyses were among the first in any discipline to emphasize gender as something that is culturally constructed. Often, however, they have been presented in terms of a "gender ideology" (Ortner and Whitehead 1981) or "sex/gender system" (Rubin 1975) that has been abstracted, somewhat artificially, from the greater complexities of social life. Taking the Prespa community as an example, I see their notions regarding gender identity as both enmeshed within and central to a far broader view of society that emphasizes the precedence of patrilineal descent. It is thus a whole social order, and perhaps a cosmology as well, that must be appraised in any consideration of the relation of music to gender.[16]

There has also been a tendency in this literature to present too consistent a view of any social formation. Here the analysis of musical forms presents a particular challenge. Musical practices, like other types of formalized behavior, often construct an idealized and overly cohesive image of social relations. Researchers have at times unwittingly taken that image at face value, with the result that discourses and practices that prevail in other domains of action have not been adequately considered or counterposed.[17] As George (1993) has recently illustrated in his study of an Indonesian community, even small and relatively isolated communities maintain multiple discourses and practices regarding gender that construct the local social order in contradictory ways. It is thus crucial to examine the role that music-making plays in mediating, or exacerbating, the societal tensions that result.

Finally, most studies of music and gender to date, like many of the musical traditions that they document, have participated in a reinscription of binary notions of gender, assuming that any social formation is composed of two gender categories of heterosexual "men" and "women." (This is true also for my own earlier formulations; see Sugarman 1989.) As is becoming clear, musical activities have long been associated with individuals who have identified themselves through alternative gender designations, or whose sexual orientation has not been heterosexual. This is perhaps the most under-acknowledged area within studies of music and gender.[18]

It would seem that ethnomusicologists now need to embark on what might be termed a critical approach to the question of music and gender. On the one hand, we need to focus on the capacity of musical traditions not merely to reinforce gender relations within other domains but to actively *engender* those individuals who participate in them. Here the notion of habitus can be particularly helpful. Each of us as individuals, whether we be cosmopolitan academics or perhaps no-less-cosmopolitan members of the communities that we study, invariably carry with us through life what are often "residual" notions of gender (Williams 1977: 122–23): notions that vie with the more explicit, verbal formulations that we have developed for ourselves on an intellectual basis. Often it is highly symbolic practices such as music-making that have helped to inscribe and maintain those notions deep within our beings, and their very beauty and power have often distracted us from noticing the assumptions that they embody. From this perspective, so long as we operate within gendered social worlds, gender is intrinsic to our musical performances, and any musical performance is thus also a performance of gender. On the other hand, we are all currently encountering and contributing to a global proliferation of gendered and engendering discourses and practices. We need a notion of culture as something that is multiple and disjunct in order to chart the ways that individuals and communities are incorporating, resisting, or reformulating these discourses and practices through musical means, at times interrogating the concept of gender itself.

Such an approach has been taken in recent years by a number of anthropologists researching performance forms. A similar orientation may also be discerned in some of the recent work in both Western musicology and popular music studies.[19] A critical approach to studies of music and gender should not simply resort to an analysis of "music as text," however, as some studies of Western music have done. In drawing on social theory we should not by any means set aside questions of the meaning of musical activities or of the lived experience of participants in musical practices, nor should we ignore the agency of individual performers. All these are crucial factors that must be considered in their historical and cultural specificity, and the actions and observations of the individuals whose lives we study deserve particular prominence in our accounts. But we then need to extend those accounts by examining the constitutive processes through which actors come to experience themselves in gendered terms and then formulate their individual actions on that basis. Only through a detailed appraisal of the lived experience of gender can we understand the power of musical performance to shape that experience, often encouraging members of any gendered group to regard their position within society as unquestionable.

Representing Prespa Singing

The representation of one group of people by or for another is today the most vexing issue for ethnographers, and it is one with which I am not yet at peace. Like questions concerning the construction of gender, it has been illuminated in recent years by writers who have pointed out the ways that ethnographies, often unwittingly, have had the effect of asserting the precedence of Western discourses, and thus consolidating the power of the West over its non-Western ethnographic subjects. The issue has been particularly acute in studies of women and/or gender, where it has been noted that European and Euro-American women scholars have often imposed their own social aspirations upon their women subjects, producing through their writings a generalized "third world woman" who, in her passivity and subjugation within various societal institutions, comes to represent everything that they as "first world women" are not.[20] In light of such critiques, ethnographers such as myself need to consider with great care what sorts of power relationships we put into play through the various strategies that we employ in our work.

At the same time, our representations of musical communities are not produced in a vacuum. They now enter a discursive space filled with verbal, visual, and aural depictions of "world musics," prompted by every sort of motivation from the unselfconscious interest of cosmopolitan aficionados to the ideological formulations of national governments to the commercial bottom line of transnational media conglomerates. Our writings do not establish a relationship simply with the individuals and communities whom we represent, but enter a complex field of competing, and often far more powerful, representations of them, many of which employ the tropes now so familiar to us through critiques of ethnography. Given this situation, I approach the ethnographer's dilemma by asking myself: How can I incorporate lessons from the many critiques of my enterprise into my research methods and writing strategies? Have I chosen approaches to analysis that I would comfortably use to speak of my own life? How can I exert the "power" that is inherent in my position as an ethnographer to constructively reconfigure the "knowledge" that has been produced thus far about the sorts of communities of whom I write?[21]

Like several other North American scholars of southeast European cultural forms, I was first introduced to the music of that area as a teenager, when a craze for international folk dancing swept through my mostly white, middle-class, suburban community in the late 1960s. Already having a penchant for various types of American vernacular musics, I quickly extended my interest from the dances to the songs and instrumental music that accompanied them, and began collecting recordings of village music and attending concerts by touring ensembles. This was a period of increasing U.S. political and economic expansion, and the proliferation of recordings of various types of "ethnic music" encouraged me to view the world of music as being at my fingertips and there for eager consumption.

My first impressions of the singing that I heard on these recordings, mostly of south Slavic communities in Bulgaria and Macedonia, were mediated by the often romanticized depictions of village life that were propagated on record jackets and concert programs at that time: visions of communities in which singing was central to all of life's activities, and in which women joined their strong, resonant voices together to develop a vibrant women's "art form." Although the texts of songs were often translated in the jacket notes of recordings, they were rarely contextualized in terms of village life. It was only during my extended stay in Macedonia, when I was in my early thirties, that I was able to place in context the words to Slavic women's songs: accounts of backbreaking work in the fields all day, of being carried off by a Turkish overlord, of being beaten by a drunken husband or chastised by a cruel mother-in-law. For many south Slavic village women, singing, which had indeed served them as a major form of socializing and of aesthetic expression, had also been a means of commenting on, and at times resisting, their hard lot in life (cf. Rice 1994:115–26). Whatever their songs had come to mean to me, I was learning that they meant something quite different to those who had created and maintained them. Although I became an avid singer of Bulgarian and Macedonian songs, I ultimately made a decision to represent singing from these communities primarily as a scholar and teacher rather than as a performer, and to place a priority on the ways that singers themselves have spoken with me, and with each other, about their musical involvement.

My stay in Prespa provided me with my only extended, first-hand experience of the life that village songs depict, as well as an introduction to a very different sort of rural singing. I lived with a family in which relations between men and women seemed at times more complementary than hierarchical, and in which age was arguably a more salient axis of power than gender. Particularly among my host and hostess I found that a woman's—and a man's—response to a harsh life was often a zany sense of humor. I encountered the exquisite poetry and tender sentiments of the women's wedding songs, and a men's singing tradition that is as vibrant and as carefully cultivated as is the women's, to an extent probably unparalleled in all of southeastern Europe. Whatever Prespa singing meant to its practitioners, and however closely it was implicated in gender relations within the community, I was learning that I could not adequately explore that relationship in terms of standard, monolithic formulations about "patriarchal" societies.

As I have continued my research on Prespa singing among overseas families, I have found that individuals in the community maintain highly disparate and often inconsistent attitudes toward their singing, depending on their age, their gender, and a whole range of life experiences. For some individuals, singing is an absolute fixation: life's raison d'être. For others it is just another social obligation that they perform in a perfunctory manner. For some younger community members, skill as a singer is an aspect of their heritage that they wish they had acquired in their youth; for others, it is a symbol of a patriarchal past that they would gladly trade for a sensuous Turkish dance melody or a song by Janet Jackson. This ambivalence on the part of many Presparë has its source in the tensions that individuals are feeling as they find themselves negotiating between two quite different social environments: that of their own community, and the wider, predominantly Euro-American environment of North America. If singers are reexamining their relationship to their received repertoire of songs, and at times experimenting with new ways of rendering it, their efforts are part of a far more pervasive reexamination of social relations. Any connections that I draw between Prespa singing and gender relations must allow for a consideration of the sorts of tensions and contradictions within which individuals in the community are currently operating (cf. Ong 1988, Mohanty 1991).

In fashioning this study I have had as my first goal to provide a vivid and nuanced evocation of Prespa weddings and singing, of Prespa social life, and of the individuals who currently regard both with passion as well as ambivalence. At the same time, I have sought to foreground what I believe are the inevitable links between any musical practice and issues of subjectivity and power, and thus to contribute to scholarly understandings of the relationship between music and society. In the former goal I have been helped by the example of recent anthropological writings that have abandoned normative descriptions in favor of ones that place the ethnographer squarely within the written account, that emphasize the individuality of those whose lives they write, and that highlight the varied options that individuals exercise as they live (see for example Cowan 1990 and Abu-Lughod 1993). Such writing strategies do much to de-exoticize the communities that we represent, and to bridge the ontological gap between researcher and ethnographic "other." But accounts constructed solely around the activities of known individuals may be overly intrusive in instances such as mine, when one's subjects will also be one's readers (cf. Stacey 1988); and they do not permit the sort of extended consideration of theoretical questions that I believe need to be addressed within music studies. I have thus chosen to organize my account in a way that moves between two contrasting types of writing: one that highlights specific events and individuals, and another that deals in more normative terms with theoretical concerns.

By organizing my text in this way, I hope to model two sorts of processes. First is the dialectic between singing and subjectivity that forms the heart of my analytic argument. Second is the process through which I as a fieldworker gradually constructed my interpretation of Prespa singing. During my stay in Macedonia and the period of my research in North America, I attended portions of approximately fifteen Prespa weddings. For the first three that I attended, I knew no more than ten words of Albanian, and so was unable to follow many of the details of the event. Although various guests provided some explanation in Macedonian or English, my first "understandings" of these weddings, and of the singing that dominated them, were multisensory but largely nonverbal. As I attended more weddings, I began to note consistencies both in the way that songs were performed and in the way that wedding celebrations were organized. Once I began to learn the Prespa dialect and was able to speak with participants during and after these events, I began to link the practices that I had observed with the discourses through which community members interpret and evaluate them. In the years to follow, as I participated in daily activities in the village and then lived with Prespa families in Toronto, I began to draw parallels between the practices of Prespa weddings and those that characterize many other domains of community life. As I was gradually drawn into conversations on a wider range of family and community concerns, as I broadened the scope of my interviews with community members, and as I began to delve into the history of the community, I was able to postulate connections between singing, weddings, and the broader range of discourses and practices that have shaped community constructions of self and society.

Each of the chapters that follow begins with a description of a segment of a wedding celebration held either in Prespa or in North America between the years 1972 and 1988 (see table 1). These descriptions invite the reader to "attend" a number of weddings before beginning, with my prompting, to mediate them with various community-based or theoretical discourses. The descriptions encompass such facets of the event as the individuals that were present and their relationships to each other, the texts of the songs that were sung, the styles of singing used, the etiquette surrounding the performances, the refreshments served, the spatial arrangement of participants, their dress and demeanor, the interactions that developed, and the emotions that were generated. Through these seven segments, the central portion of a Prespa wedding celebration is traced from its first day to its culmination a week later. I have excerpted segments from a number of different weddings taking place in different locales and time periods so as to highlight the variety of strategies that individuals and families have employed in structuring both their wedding celebrations and their song performances. At the

TABLE 1 Segments of Weddings

Chapter	Segment of Wedding	Place and Year of Wedding
2	Singing at the groom's	Grnčari, 1983
3	Women's singing at the bride's	Krani, 1972
4	The bride is adorned	Toronto, 1986
5	Men's singing at the groom's	Chicago, 1986
6	A men's *konak* at the groom's	Chicago, 1988
7	The groom bathes and is shaved	Connecticut, 1985
8	The bride is taken	Chicago, 1986

same time, I mean to illustrate precisely how events exhibiting such diversity and variation also betray much underlying consistency, thus reinscribing fundamental aspects of social order.

The description that initiates each chapter is followed by an exposition of some specific aspect of Prespa social life. I begin with the particulars of Prespa singing (chapters 2 and 3) and of the wedding ritual (chapter 4), and then expand the analysis to encompass community views of self, family, and community (chapter 5). As I do so, I move from a more interpretive focus on community parlance and the lived experience of community members to a more critical examination of the ways that singing structures that experience and engenders those who sing (chapters 6 and 7). Finally, I consider the ways that Prespari are restructuring weddings and singing in North America so as to explore a range of new forms of subjectivity (chapter 8). These more theoretical sections are intended not so much to comment on the event whose description they immediately follow as to expand the reader's interpretation of the events presented in subsequent chapters. In order for the analysis to have its full effect, I would suggest that the reader conclude this study by rereading in succession the initial section of each chapter.

Each phase of this analysis is illustrated by selections on an accompanying CD, which showcases the range of musical styles that community members currently perform. A number of the examples are taken from recordings made by my former husband or myself, whether audio recordings or the soundtracks of video recordings made in North America. Several have been taken from recordings or videos made by community members for their own enjoyment, and a few are drawn from a commercial release of Prespa music (Leibman 1974). While audio quality is not always of the highest order, these performances are often characterized by an intensity of involvement and emotion on the part of the performers that is rarely captured in an artificial recording situation. They thus represent particularly fine examples of Prespa music-making.

A second concern in the organization of this study has been how to give voice to the individuals who have contributed so fundamentally to it. I have opted to sprinkle my text liberally with the comments of community members: some in the form of traditional sayings, some casual comments made in the midst of lively conversations, and some excerpted from formal interviews. My hope is that an image will emerge of a community composed of particularly articulate, thoughtful, and witty individuals, whose struggles with issues of modernity will surely resonate strongly with those who read about them.

Having shared with individuals their often candid and intimate reactions to the events in their lives, it has also become especially important to me to preserve the trust that they have placed in me. I have thus
made a conscious attempt to preserve the anonymity of the individuals
whose remarks and song performances are presented here. In the case
of quotations, I have indicated the place and year of those making the
remarks, but have not cited their names. For all accounts of wedding
singing, I have given the names of the bride and groom as pseudonyms, and have identified other participants only through kinship
terms. These practices are in no way meant to deny either the artistry
of many Prespa singers or the contributions of many individuals to
my account of Prespa singing. Those community members who have
shared in the creation of this work are credited, by name, in the opening
acknowledgments.

TWO

Singing as a Social Activity

Këngë është muabeti i dasmës. Singing is the *muabet* of the wedding.
(Prespa saying)

SINGING AT THE GROOM'S

In the summer of 1983, a Prespa family living in Chicago returned to the village of Grnčari (Gërnçar) in Prespa for the wedding of Asan, their third and youngest son. Breaking with Prespa custom, Asan was to marry a young north Albanian woman from Kosova named Sevdie, chosen for him by an older sister who lives there with her husband. Beginning on a Sunday evening, gatherings took place at Asan's home or at neighboring homes of the *xhaxhallarë*, his father's male kin, for a week in succession. Singing was a major activity during each gathering.

On Tuesday evening the women sang as they packed the *rroba*, the clothes and other personal items that are given to the bride by the groom. These were then taken to Sevdie's home in Kosova on Wednesday by Asan's oldest brother. He returned on Thursday afternoon in time for the crushing of the *qeshqek*, wheat berries that are later made into a special wedding meal. This was a particularly festive occasion, with hearty singing by older men of the family and instrumental music provided by some of the best Rom musicians in the region. The noise of the long, T-shaped poles striking against the trough filled with wheat, and the sight of them rising and falling above the walls surrounding the family compound, served as an announcement to the whole village that a wedding had begun (cf. plate 2).

On Saturday the groom's party traveled to Kosova by bus, stopping at a restaurant along the way for a celebratory luncheon. After their arrival in the town where Sevdie's family was living, they caused quite a stir as both women and men processed through the streets, singing polyphonic wedding songs (among north Albanians, women do not sing in public during a wedding, nor does the groom go to fetch the bride). In the evening they were hosted by Sevdie's family before setting out with her for Prespa on Sunday morning. Once the groom's party had returned to his village, Asan was taken out into the family's courtyard for a ritual shaving by his older brother, and the "bride's dance" was danced (cf. plate 10). Then, at night, Asan and Sevdie were "closed in" at Asan's home for the consummation of their marriage.

In many ways, Asan's was a typical Prespa village wedding, but it was also unusual in two respects. First, Sevdie was not a Presparkë, and the usual wedding schedule had to be significantly rearranged because she lived so far away. Second, Asan's family brought a video camera with them and filmed much of the wedding. To their knowledge, this was the first Prespa wedding to be filmed. What follows is an account of the singing that took place on Sunday evening, one week before the bride was taken, based on that video as well as conversations with family members.

The Sunday evening gathering was a particularly intimate and informal event. Coming so early in the wedding period, it involved only members of Asan's immediate family and those of his father's extended family who lived nearby in the same village. Because nearly every male present was of the same lineage, the gathering symbolically reconstituted the large, extended-family household in which Asan's father and his brothers and cousins had grown up. It was only later in the week that other types of relatives living in other villages or in towns outside Prespa arrived for the celebration.

Because only a small number of people attended, men and women gathered together at Asan's uncle's home in the *odë*, a room at the front of the house that is reserved for receiving guests. The seats in the *odë* were arranged in a horseshoe along three of the four walls, opening toward the doorway into the kitchen (fig. 3). The men took seats on the couches and armchairs farthest from the doorway, with the oldest men seating themselves in the left-hand corner. Older women sat on the left-hand couch nearer the door, while younger women sat on the right-hand couch or on the floor. Despite their age, a few older women also chose to sit on the floor. Asan's two young sisters-in-law, the wives of his two older brothers, sat in the doorway. Opposite the older men a small coffee table was set out, and beer and appetizers were placed on it for the male guests. As the evening progressed, one of the daughters-in-law cared for her young baby, while the other moved back and forth between the kitchen and the *odë*, serving refreshments to the men.

Among the older men sat the host, dressed in a dark suit with vest

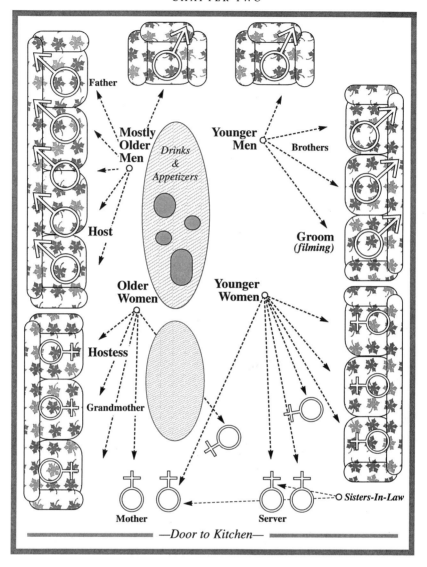

FIGURE 3. Singing at the Groom's, Grnčari, 1983

and a wool fedora hat. He began the evening's activities by initiating a slow, drawn-out love song, accompanied on a second melodic line by Asan's father, his first cousin. All the other men sang a textless drone in unison beneath the melodies of the two soloists. The song recounts a conversation between a man's wife and his mistress. As the song begins, the wife describes how the mistress's life is slowly moving from bad to worse. Eventually, however, the wife admits ruefully that the mistress is indeed an especially attractive woman (ex. 2.1; CD #2):

Më le xhadenë, më mori rrugën . . .	You have left the highway and taken the country road . . .
m'u bëfsh kurban sa ma dashke burrën!	(May you become my sacrifice, so much do you desire my husband!
m'u marrç të keqën sa ma dashke burrën!	May you take all my sorrows, so much do you desire my husband!)
Ne baltë e madhe më umbe gjurmën . . .	In the deep mud you have lost your way . . .
Me perje të bardhë ma qendis gunën . . .	With a white thread you embroider your cloak . . .
Më zbrite kalën, ma ipe mushkën . . .	You have gotten down from the horse and mounted the mule . . .
Qelibar stambolli ma paske undën . . .	My, but your nose is [as finely chiseled as] amber from Istanbul . . .

As the person initiating the performance, the host was considered to be the "singer" of the song. At its conclusion, he exclaimed: *Ajde gëzuar!* ("Happiness!"). The other men then called out their compliments on his performance: *Si goja e zëmbra!* ("May your heart be as happy as the sentiments that you have uttered!") and *Të trashëgoet!* ("Congratulations! May the groom lead a long and happy married life!"). This was the extent of the men's singing. Because the gathering involved only close relatives, the men did not feel obligated to sustain a formal evening of singing, as is the custom at such a gathering. Instead they spent the remainder of the time chatting and telling stories, leaving the singing to the women.

The first of the women to sing was the hostess, a dignified older woman wearing a dark dress and sweater. Like most women of her generation, she had covered her hair with a Turkish scarf of cotton gauze printed with a floral pattern and tied neatly at the side of her head. A woman in her fifties moved across the floor toward her to accompany her song. The hostess chose a song that can be sung by either men or

EXAMPLE 2.1. *Më le xhadenë, më mori rrugën*

44

women, and inserted the groom's name at an appropriate spot. All the other women droned:

Vjen një lumë plot mi plot . . . *zerdelia plot.*	A river fills to overflowing . . . (O ripe apricot)
Janë tri vajza, e s'kalonin dot . . .	There were three girls and they couldn't cross it at all . . .
ASAN beu ç'i ra me not . . .	ASAN *bey*[1] crossed it swimming . . .
Më të madhe që kërkonte shok . . .	The oldest one looked for a friend [to help her] . . .
Ato më së vogla qanin me lot . . .	The younger ones were crying with tears . . .
ASAN beu ç'i ra me not . . .	ASAN *bey* crossed it swimming . . .
Më e mesmja e kërkonte shok . . .	The middle one sought him as a friend . . .
Ato më të vogla qanin me lot . . .	The younger ones were crying with tears . . .

Throughout her song, the men's conversation continued quietly at the other end of the room.

At the song's close the singer exclaimed *Gëzuar e mirë! Të trashëgoet!* ("Happiness and well-being! Congratulations!"). Both men and women called out salutary phrases in response: *Si goja e zëmbra, nëno!* ("May your heart be as happy as the sentiments you have uttered, mother!") and *Arrifshi më nipçinat!* ("We look forward to the weddings of your grandchildren!"). Several women reached forward to shake her hand. When these exchanges were completed, the groups of men and women each broke into animated conversation.

After a minute or two the oldest woman present, Asan's grandmother, was encouraged to sing and was accompanied by the same middle-aged woman. The grandmother too was wearing a gauze headscarf, together with a dark dress with small polka dots and a dark sweater. The song that she chose is an extremely popular one, especially for relatives on the groom's side. It is generally sung in a lively style: rapidly and with moderate ornamentation. Midway through the song she inserted Asan's name into the text. She then repeated the final two lines twice more, mentioning two of his male cousins (ex. 2.2; CD #3):

EXAMPLE 2.2. *Malorea në shtatë male*

Malorea në shtatë male . . .	Malorea in the seven mountains . . .
moj Malorea.	(O Malorea)
shtatë male dhe një fushë . . .	seven mountains and a field . . .
N'atë fushë paska një kullë . . .	In the field there's a tower . . .
n'atë kullë paska një vajzë . . .	in the tower there's a young girl . . .

do ta marrim për ASAN benë . . .	we'll take her for ASAN *bey* . . .
N'atë fushë paska një vajzë . . .	In the field there's a young girl . . .
a ta marrim për AVDYL benë . . .	let's take her for AVDYL *bey* . . .
N'atë fushë paska një vajzë . . .	in the field there's a young girl . . .
a ta marrim për YSEN benë . . .	let's take her for YSEN *bey* . . .

While she sang, the men continued to converse quite loudly, as they did through most of the remaining songs, stopping only to praise the singers once their performances had ended. When she had finished her song, she too exclaimed "Happiness and well-being!" and was heartily congratulated by all present. Each woman, even the older ones, rose to embrace her and kiss her hand.

After a short pause, the woman who had been accompanying the other singers began a song. She was dressed particularly austerely, in a plain, dark brown dress and dark, flowered polyester headscarf. A younger woman moved near her to accompany her. The two are regarded by Asan's relatives as the finest women singers in their family, and so their singing was especially moving for those listening and droning. The "singer" chose an unusual song for this point in a wedding, one that depicts a conversation between an unhappy bride-to-be and her mother as they await the groom's party (ex. 2.3; CD #4):

Ngreu moj Mamudi, ngreu, për perëndi.	Get up, Mamudi, get up, for God's sake!
S'mund moj nëne, s'mund moj të keqën,	I can't, mother, I can't, I beg of you,
se jam e sëmurë, po dergjem . . .	for I am sick, I am languishing . . .
Ngreu moj Mamudi, ngreu, për perëndi.	(Get up, Mamudi, get up, for God's sake!)
S'mund, moj nëne, s'mund, moj kurban nëne.	I can't, mother, I can't, mother, I beg of you.
Ngreu që të vërë nënja kënaun . . .	Get up so that your mother can put on the henna . . .
Se na erdhë krushqit brënda në shtëpi . . .	for the wedding party has come into the house . . .

EXAMPLE 2.3. *Ngreu moj Mamudi*

As she sang, she injected into the text a great many exclamations, ones that express a particular intensity of emotion:

> *o-i* Ngreu moj Mamudi, *aman aman* ngreu për perëndi . . .

She also ornamented the melodic line so intricately that any sense of a steady pulse was undermined.

Why did this woman choose to sing such a sad song? And why did she perform it in such an elaborate, evocative manner? Asan reasoned to me several years later that she had lost her first husband when still quite young, and had then been married to his younger first cousin so that she would remain within the lineage. Perhaps the wedding taking place brought to mind ambivalent feelings about marriage, prompting her to choose a song about a bride's sorry plight and to ornament it in an overtly emotional way. It is just as likely, however, that she chose the song for aesthetic reasons, because of the appeal of the melody or the phrasing of the text. As she finished her song, she too exclaimed "Happiness and well-being!" Her performance was praised enthusiastically by all present. In response she was wished, "We look forward to the weddings of your grandchildren!"

From this point, one performance followed closely on another. As each song ended, the older women conferred among themselves as to who should sing next and gently encouraged each woman in turn. Slowly the order of singers progressed, roughly from oldest to youngest, so that it followed the seating order fairly closely. The host's daughter, dressed in a dark, flowered dress and gauze headscarf, was next to sing, accompanied by one of the younger women. She chose one of the most widely sung Prespa songs. In the proper points in the text she mentioned not only Asan but also several of his male cousins. These she named in a particular order: first the grandson of the host and hostess, then three others in order of the age of their parents, from oldest to youngest:

Të këndon bilbili kryeqytetit	The nightingale sings to you in the capital city,
tri saatë matanë detit.	three hours across the sea.
Jep të fala mbretit	Give our greetings to the king,
të na japë të tri të bijat:	that he might give us his three daughters [in marriage]:
të madhen për ASAN benë . . .	the oldest for ASAN *bey* . . .
moj sytë na mbenë.	(we can't take our eyes off of him).
të mesmen për YSEN benë . . .	the middle one for YSEN *bey* . . .
të voglën për AVDYL benë . . .	the youngest one for AVDYL *bey* . . .
më pastajzë për NEIM benë . . .	the one after that for NEIM *bey* . . .
më së fundit për ZENEL benë . . .	the last one for ZENEL *bey* . . .

When she had finished she kissed the hands of the older women as they complimented her performance. Then, as the daughter of the host, she rose and shook hands with each male guest before resuming her seat.

Following her was the middle-aged woman who had accompanied the evocative performance of a few minutes before. In contrast to the older women, she was wearing a colorful, floral print dress, and her neatly coiffed hair was not covered with a scarf. The woman whom she had accompanied earlier now accompanied her. She chose to sing a more unusual song, one that is particularly appropriate for the groom's relatives to sing on such an occasion. Like the previous singer, she too mentioned several of Asan's male cousins at the song's close:

Të shkon rruga pranë shtëpisë . . .	The road goes by your house . . .
buzëkuqe, ajde moj sylarushe.	(Red-lipped one, O hazel-eyed one)
Të qan djali, jep i për të pirë . . .	Your baby boy is crying, give him something to drink . . .
Ap sepetnë të nusërisë . . .	Open up the marriage chest . . .
zir ca qelqe të rakisë . . .	take out some glasses for brandy . . .
të pinë këta bejlerë . . .	for the *bey*s to drink . . .
do martojmë ASAN benë . . .	because we're marrying off ASAN *bey* . . .
arrifshi më YSEN benë . . .	and we look forward to [the marriage of] YSEN *bey* . . .
më pastaj më AVDYL benë . . .	after that [the marriage of] AVDYL *bey* . . .
arrifshi më ZENEL benë . . .	and we look forward to [the marriage of] ZENEL *bey* . . .

The two women sang in a florid manner, injecting emotional exclamations such as *o-i* and *ajde moj* into the text and ornamenting the melody to such an extent that the song's meter was loosened somewhat. They seemed so relaxed and so involved in their performance that they scarcely moved as they sang. Clearly their singing also affected the other women, who listened intently as they droned. Even the men's conversation slacked off. When the song had finished, the singer was warmly kissed and embraced by those around her.

Another younger woman in a sleeveless print dress sang next, choosing a song that may be sung on either the groom's or the bride's side of a wedding. On the one hand it speaks of the beauty of the bride, while on the other there is a point in the text where the groom's name may be inserted:

Që naj mali rëzonesh në fushë . . .	From the mountain you descend to the field . . .
moj sylarusheja.	(O hazel-eyed one)
Ç'deshe ti në fushën tonë? . . .	What is it that you wanted in our field? . . .
Fusha tonë paska trendëlinë . . .	Our field has clover . . .
trendëlinë për anëm nënenë . . .	clover for the lady of the house . . .
guguçja për ASAN benë . . .	and a turtledove [the bride] for ASAN *bey* . . .

As a less experienced performer, the singer sat rather self-consciously as she sang, staring at a spot on the floor in front of her and clasping her hands before her. The woman who had sung just before accompanied her and continued to accompany the next few singers, all of whom were sitting near her.

She was followed by an especially outgoing and jovial young woman with thick, curly blond hair, dressed in a flowered apron worn over a simple dress. Rather than choosing a song about the groom, she selected one intended to "honor" his father:

N'atë mal ngreur një qoshk	On that mountain rose a kiosk,
por sa mirë, sa bukur shtruar.	how well, how beautifully laid out.
Nusja e ASAN beut që u ndodh atije	The bride of ASAN *bey* who was to be found there
me veilo mbuluar,	[was standing] covered with a veil,
me florinj ngarkuar.	laden with gold coins.
ASAN beu që do ta marr	ASAN *bey*, who is to marry her,
një pëllumb, syret i shkruar.	is a beautiful speckled dove.
Beu i madh që i rrinte pranë	His father standing beside her
fortë një zot i zotëruar.	is a very gracious host.

Now came the turn of a young woman from a Turkish-speaking family, recently married to the son of the host and hostess. As their family's new "bride" she was especially dressed up, in a crisp pastel dress with eyelit collar and cuffs. At her neck she wore two simple gold chains. She had spoken no Albanian when she married into the family, but was now conversant and had learned one easy Prespa song. After some encouragement she began her song and performed simply but with ease:

Ato ftojnë që solli lumi . . .	Those quinces that the river brought . . .
me aman, me o-i.	
ASAN benë nai zënka gjumi . . .	Sleep has overtaken ASAN *bey* . . .
Me gadale, mos e zgjoni . . .	Go softly, don't awaken him . . .
është i vogël ta martoni . . .	he's still young for you to marry off . . .
me një nuse ta gëzoni . . .	for you to make him happy with a bride . . .

At this point the groom's mother suggested to the outgoing blond woman that she sing a song for her sister-in-law, who had not yet arrived for the celebration. Because all kin are expected to sing at such an occasion, it is common for a close relative to stand in for them in the event of their absence. She began a lively song that her sister-in-law is known for singing (ex. 2.4):

As ja merr, ja thuaj një erë . . .	Won't you sing for me just once? . . .
tinë o bilbil aman e, *o bilbil aman aman o-e.*	(O nightingale)
Çak e çak ja bën bilbili . . .	Chak-chak goes the nightingale . . .
o more bilbil aman e, *o bilbil aman aman o-e.*	(O nightingale)
Bilbil, seç m'u nqase pranë? . . .	Nightingale, why did you come near me? . . .
Çak e çak ja bën bilbili . . .	Chak-chak goes the nightingale . . .

As she reached this point in the song she suddenly began to giggle, in part because the song is lighthearted, in part because she could not

EXAMPLE 2.4. *As ja merr, ja thuaj një erë*

remember the words. It would have been unbecoming for her to stop her performance midway, especially out of laughter, and so she tried her best to regain her composure. In the moment that she had to take a breath between lines, she explained her predicament to a woman near her, who mumbled the words of the next verse to her under her breath. In all the commotion, one crucial line was omitted:

[seç m'u mallengjive xhan-   Why did you upset my
    e . . .   soul . . .]

but she eventually completed the song:

porsi vajzë tamburanë? . . .   as a *tambura* [long-necked
                                                   stringed instrument] stirs a
                                                   young girl? . . .

Çak e çak ja bën bilbili . . .   Chak-chak goes the
                                                   nightingale . . .

A few minutes of laughter and joking followed her performance. Asan's father then turned to the young wife of his oldest son, sitting quietly in the doorway in a cream-colored T-shirt and slacks, and asked her to sing. Not having a large repertoire of songs to draw on, she sang a song that had already been performed earlier in the evening (*Të këndon bilbili*), and carefully inserted the names of Asan's cousins in the proper places. Her sister-in-law, married to Asan's other brother, took a seat next to her and accompanied her.

Both women were somewhat new to this large family, and the youngest married women there. As recent brides they knew that their behavior was being scrutinized particularly carefully by other family members. As they sang, they sat extremely demurely: legs tucked under them, hands folded in their laps, their eyes cast downward. Meanwhile, the woman who had sung before them had not succeeded in suppressing her giggles, and she occasionally burst out in muffled laughter. As her laughter continued, the young bride singing the accompanying line struggled to contain her own mirth. Finally, with a great deal of effort and poise, the two concluded the song without interruption. At its close the singer rose and kissed the hands of each male guest.

During the women's rounds of singing, the men had become restless. Toward the end of this song, one of the older men began a long historical anecdote that the other men found particularly intriguing. Asan, who had been filming up to this point, panned his camera over to film the speaker. At this the women, seeing that the men's attention had been drawn elsewhere, likewise broke into conversation. After a few minutes, however, the second bride of the groom's household was asked to sing, and Asan redirected the camera toward the women. This bride too was wearing a light T-shirt and had a flowered apron over her skirt. She chose one of several Prespa songs about three young men, an appropriate song for a groom who is the youngest of three sons, and was accompanied by Asan's mother, who otherwise did not sing that evening:

De gjol'i Orisë ma shkove bejar . . .	You passed the summer at Lake Ohrid . . .
ruaj u, moj Gjermankë, se do gjesh belanë.	(Watch out, German girl, or you'll find yourself in trouble!)
Nja dy-tre djem nga Korça sh'tashti në sevdanë . . .	Now two or three young men from Korçë are in love [with you] . . .
Ay më i madhi qënka i martuar . . .	The oldest one turns out to be married . . .
Ay më i mesmi qënka i fejuar . . .	The middle one turns out to be engaged . . .
Ay më i vogli sh'tashti rri sevdanë . . .	The youngest one is now in love [with you] . . .

She then "honored" Asan's parents by adding to her song a rhymed verse sung in triple meter (ex. 2.5):

Do të loz, do të këndoj,	I will dance and sing,
ASAN benë ta martoj,	to marry off ASAN *bey*,
prindërit do t'i gëzoj.	to make his parents happy.

Now came the turn of the one unmarried woman present, a teen-aged cousin of Asan's. At such informal occasions, unmarried men and women are often encouraged to practice singing "in public," usually accompanied by a close relative. In this case she chose a song originally learned by Prespare from Albanian radio that became one of the most popular wedding songs of the 1980s. She was accompanied by her grandmother, the older woman who had sung so poignantly earlier in the evening:

EXAMPLE 2.5. *Do të loz, do të këndoj*

Ap i sytë e zezë të nai sjellç
  bejar.
Sa të desha tynë si nënja
  evlanë.
Me doçkat përveshur më
  mbledh manushaqe,
t'i kam për t'i ngrënë me
  gushë e me faqe.

Open your black eyes and
  bring us summer.
I loved you as much as a
  mother loves her child.
With your sleeves rolled up
  you gather violets for me,
for me to have to eat with my
  throat and my face.

Në një thellësirë ta dëgjova zënë.	In the darkness I heard your voice.
Të dinja bilbil, më dolle fëllënxë.	I thought you to be a nightingale, but you turned out to be a partridge.

As with the two young daughters-in-law, the singer, dressed in a sleeveless sundress, sat extremely demurely and self-consciously, and she fidgeted with her hands as she sang. Despite her inexperience, she performed in an accomplished manner, decorating her melody line with delicate ornaments. Hers was the final song of the evening.

Weddings and Singing

Throughout the course of a Prespa wedding, relatives and friends are invited to the homes of both the groom's and the bride's families for evening social gatherings such as this. Guests may begin to assemble at the groom's home during weekend evenings weeks or even months before the culmination of the wedding. During the final week before the wedding day, it is customary for gatherings to take place at the groom's home during each evening. At the bride's, similar gatherings are held on the final three evenings before she departs for her new home.

Families say that they attend such gatherings in order to *nderojnë* ("honor") or *respektojnë* ("show respect for") the host household. Secondarily, wedding gatherings provide families who attend with an opportunity to renew ties with many family and community members whom they might not otherwise see regularly. During the ritual portions of a wedding that take place during the day, participants are expected to focus their attention on the activities taking place and on the personages of the bride and groom. At evening gatherings, however, the emphasis is on interchanges between members of the host household and its guests.

Although conversation does indeed take place throughout wedding celebrations, hosts and guests interact much of the time through singing. To do so they draw on a repertoire of several hundred preexisting songs, which they occasionally augment with extemporized verses based on well-known formulas. There are a number of specific songs that are associated with each of the major ritual activities that constitute the wedding, as well as songs customarily sung at evening social gatherings. Singing is not an activity that is exclusive to weddings, but it is more closely associated with them than with any other setting, and virtually any song known to Prespari may be appropriately sung at a wedding.

The primacy that Prespari grant to singing at weddings is best understood in the context of their more general attitudes toward singing as an activity. First, they view it as an activity reserved for social settings. Unlike many other southeast European communities, Prespari do not have a special repertoire of songs that they sing while doing field or household work, nor do they celebrate a yearly cycle of agricultural rituals with its own repertoire of songs. This absence of singing in work contexts seems to be deliberate. For Prespari, singing is one of the features that marks social occasions as set apart from the mundane and particularistic concerns of a household's working life.[2]

Singing also has a specific role at a social occasion. Individuals often explain that *kënga është muabet:* "song is *muabet.*" At any gathering, it is important that the psychological barriers dividing those in attendance be broken down so that a state of *muabet*—of openness and affection—may be nurtured among those present. *Muabet* can be "made" or induced at a gathering through any of a variety of activities. It is possible to "make *muabet*" through conversation, storytelling, singing, dancing, and/or playing musical instruments. One man, for example, speaking of informal gatherings held by families in Toronto when they first immigrated there, recounted to me enthusiastically that his cousin could "really make good *muabet* with his accordion." Families from the lower villages of Prespa, however, regard singing as by far the most efficacious means of "making *muabet.*" As will become clear in subsequent chapters, Prespa singing is structured in such a way as to channel participants into a particularly attentive, engaged form of interaction. As such, the sound of their communal voices raised in song has come to be apprehended by Prespari as a sonic embodiment of *muabet.*

Among all social occasions, singing is particularly associated with life-cycle celebrations, but only certain types. When a child is born, a family invites the *oxha* (Tk. *hoca*), the community's religious leader, to recite the Mevlyd (Tk. Mevlûd) at their home. This is a poem composed during the Ottoman period that recounts the birth of Muḥammad (see Süleyman Çelebi 1943). At such gatherings various prayers are recited by those attending, but the singing of Albanian songs is not considered appropriate. Likewise, when a family member dies, the *oxha* is invited to the home to recite from the Qur'ān. The women of the household often lament the deceased in the period immediately after the death. Once the *oxha* has arrived, however, Qur'ānic recitation is considered to be the only appropriate form of vocalization. At any other type of life-cycle occasion, whether a son's circumcision (*synet*, Tk. *sünnet*), a child's betrothal (*ndërtim* or *fejesë*), or a wedding (*dasmë*), singing in Albanian is the expected form of vocalizing.

It seems to me that this division of community occasions by type of vocal genre is based on an implicit distinction made between those moments in life over which only God has control—birth and death—and those which represent a point in an individual's passage through life that is ordained and sanctioned by the community. For birth and death, it is the word of God that should prevail. On other occasions, it is the voice of the community and of the Albanian people that is heard through its legacy of songs.

Although individuals "honor" the host family by their presence at a social occasion, their attendance is not in itself a sufficient gesture of respect. Guests are expected to express their happiness in the occasion being celebrated by actively contributing to the "making" of *muabet* through their singing and perhaps also dancing. And so a second crucial aspect of singing for Presparë is that it is a social obligation. As an important means of asserting one family's respect for another, singing is regarded as a moral act. What this means, practically speaking, is that each guest at a wedding who attends an evening gathering, or who participates in any ritual activity, is expected to lead, or "sing," at least one song on each occasion.

It is the adults who represent their household at any community event, and thus Presparë regard singing primarily as an adult activity. As with other aspects of social responsibility, children are considered to be in an apprenticeship position as singers until they marry. Often they begin to learn to sing as early as age six or eight, but there is no formal mechanism for their inclusion in singing at social gatherings until they are married. The very structure of the Prespa song repertoire is difficult for children to learn. Often their acquiring competence in it is taken as a sign of coming adulthood. An older relative might comment that a young boy sings "like a man," or a girl who sings well will be pointed out as being particularly *e mënçme* ("mindful"), in the sense of having been socialized to adult behavior. Formerly at weddings, the bride and groom each signaled their coming of age by leading a short song on their first day as a married couple. Today this practice is rare, but they are still often expected to participate in the singing that takes place at the various

59

dinners held in their honor in the weeks after their wedding, and in so doing to take their place in adult society.

The Prespa community's view of singing as a necessary adult social skill has provided much of the impetus for the preservation of their singing as a participatory activity. This situation contrasts strongly with that among neighboring north Albanians in Macedonia and Kosova. In many northern communities, professional male wedding singers are hired to perform for male wedding guests, who simply recline and enjoy the performance of music specialists. Female Rom singers might also be hired to sing songs to accompany the women's dancing (for both instances see Traerup 1974). At a Prespa wedding, however, every adult who is able to project his or her voice and sing reasonably in tune, and who is not overcome with embarrassment at singing in front of others, is actively encouraged to "sing" at least one song, and the badgering of recalcitrant singers is a prominent aspect of wedding gatherings.

Of the current adult generation of Presparë, many were already accomplished singers by the time they married. Others assembled a minimal repertoire of three or four songs shortly before their marriage so as to be able to participate fully in adult society. While the obligatory nature of singing puts pressure on individuals to learn to sing, they also realize that singing can be a means of gaining attention and admiration from others, and of feeling that their presence is felt at a social occasion.

A third aspect of singing for Presparë is that it is an expressly emotional form of communication. Presparë regard singing as emblematic of *gëzim*: "joy" or "happiness." Indeed, in expressions such as *I këndon zëmra*, the verb *këndoj* may be translated as both "to sing" ("His heart is singing") and "to be happy" ("He is very happy"). In women's songs, birds like the nightingale sing in anticipation of a happy occasion such as a wedding:

Tak-tak-tak ja bën bilbili.	Tak-tak-tak goes the nightingale.
Të këndoj më trëndafili,	I sing in the rosebush,
të këndoj e mos pushoj,	I sing without letting up,
[groom's name] benë e martoj,	to marry off [the groom],
edhe nënën e gëzoj.	to make his mother happy.

(Portion of a women's wedding song, Krani, 1972)[3]

Individuals often explain that people sing at a family celebration *nga gëzimi* ("out of joy"), as if the act of singing is a person's spontaneous and unavoidable response to a happy event. More pragmatic individuals view singing more as an obligatory activity that lends an auspicious air to the occasion.

Singing may also express a more generalized state of heightened emotion or elation, generally referred to as *qejf* (Tk. *keyif,* from Arab. *kayf*). At a social occasion a person can become elated or *qejfli* not only because of the event being celebrated but also because of a variety of feelings that are triggered through interaction with others. Individuals generally choose to sing songs that they are particularly drawn to, often ones whose texts have personal meaning for them. Singers frequently say that the connection they feel to the song enables it to serve as a vehicle for the expression of the *qejf* the occasion has induced in them. Through its embodiment of a sense of elation, their performance is then capable of inducing *qejf* in those listening. In short, singing is seen as an expressive medium that both conveys the emotional state of the singer and evokes an emotional response in others.

If singing indicates "joy," then abstention from singing signals personal sorrow. As with other southeast European communities, Preparë have traditionally commemorated death through women's lamenting, a type of vocalizing whose sound contrasts strongly with singing. Today lamenting is very much circumscribed among Preparë because it is regarded as challenging God's will that an individual should die. Nevertheless, it is performed in many households for a short period of time immediately following a death. Many individuals also refrain from singing for a certain length of time, generally six months, following the death of a close relative. After this comparatively short interval, they are expected to return to regular activities, including singing at community events.[4]

Preparë regard weddings as the most joyful of all celebrations, and they consider it natural that relatives and friends of the families involved would wish to share that joy with their hosts. Singing is a tangible way for participants in a wedding to express that joy and to recognize the auspiciousness of the occasion. It also provides a particularly constructive and orderly format for social interaction at an occasion that brings large numbers of people together. There is a third important reason for the appropriateness of singing to weddings. Just as weddings are structured around many of the central concerns of Prespa families, so singing compels participants to behave in ways that both articulate and affirm fundamental beliefs that community members hold about their social world. It is for all these reasons that Preparë often speak of singing as *muabeti i dasmës:* "the *muabet* of the wedding."

The Structure of Prespa Songs

The social nature of Prespa singing is evident in the very structure of the community's song repertoire. Any Prespa song requires three individuals to perform it at all, and several more than that to achieve an optimally balanced sound. Like the songs of virtually all south Albanians, those that comprise the local Prespa repertoire have a polyphonic texture, in contrast to the monophonic or heterophonic texture of most north Albanian styles. Prespa songs are similar to those of southerners living in the regions within Albania known as Myzeqe (on the western coast, south of the Shkumbin river), Toskëri (also south of the Shkumbin, but lying along the eastern border adjacent to Macedonia), and Çamëri (straddling the Greek and Albanian border at the far south of the country); as well as south Albanians living in the Struga and especially the Bitola districts of Macedonia (see fig. 1). In these areas virtually all men's, and most women's, songs have a structure in which two soloists sing melody lines that interweave over a choral drone. Albanian ethnomusicologist Beniamin Kruta has termed this particular style of singing "Tosk" polyphony, in contrast to the "Lab" style found in the south central Albanian region of Labëri.[5]

For Preparë, any such "song" (*këngë*) consists of a particular pairing of textual and musical elements, each of which is referred to with specific terminology. For its musical portion, they speak interchangeably of a song's *melodi* ("melody") or *zë* (literally, "voice").[6] Here they are not referring to the note-to-note melody line that a singer might perform on any single occasion. To understand their notion of "melody," it is important to realize that their repertoire is made up of a limited number of distinctive melody types. These melody types are so flexible that they may incorporate refrains or patterns of repetition, and most of them may be performed in several different meters such as 2/4, 3/4, and 7/8. It is the basic skeletal tonal structure of a song that individuals often allude to, such as when men point out somewhat condescendingly that women "always sing with the same *melodi.*"

Preparë also speak of the *fjalë* ("words") or *llafë* (from Tk. *laf,* "word") of a song. Those who received more education in Yugoslavia in the Albanian language might use the term *vjershë* ("verse"), which otherwise refers to a cultivated "poem." This is not an inappropriate term, since some of the men's songs now sung widely in rural Albanian areas originated as nationalist or religious poems written by members of the intelligentsia during the last century. For each type of melody, there are anywhere from two to ten textual formats that are commonly employed. Each format is distinguished by the length of its individual lines, patterns of repetition of lines, or the absence or presence of a refrain. The greatest task for a singer in learning to perform a new "song" is not to learn the melody line or the way that the verses scan, since he or she is already conversant with such matters from countless other songs, but simply to learn the song's particular "words." Once that is accomplished, an experienced singer can draw on his or her knowledge of common textual formats and melody types to perform a new song with assurance.

The poetic conventions of Prespa song texts are most evident in instances when individuals recite the words of a song rather than sing them. When an older relative or family friend teaches a child a song, for example, he or she recites the words to the child line by line as if it were a spoken poem. Similarly, adult singers often confer on the details of a text before beginning to sing by going over individual lines. Even in the midst of a performance, as we saw at the gathering of Asan's relatives, one of the soloists might have to be prompted if she or he is less familiar with the song.

As they might be recited, the words to one popular women's song, sung by members of the groom's family as they set out to take the bride, are as follows:

Ra vesa, vesojti dhenë.	The dew fell and moistened the earth.
Ku jemi nisur ne te vemë?	For which place have we set out?
Jemi nisur për dë Kranjë	We have set out for [the village of] Krani
ta bastisim NN benë,	to fall upon NN *bey*'s house,
t'ja marrim të bijënë,	to take his daughter,
atë më të mirënë,	the best of all,
atë ballëkartënë,	with a forehead [as white as] paper,
atë gojëmjaltënë.	with a mouth [as sweet as] honey.

At the heart of this or any song lies a text organized by poetic meter and ending rhymes. Either of these might change in the course of the text, as does this song beginning with line 5. As with many wedding songs, the one given above includes a space, marked NN in the transcription, where the appropriate person's name should be inserted: in this case, that of the bride's father.

When a person sings a song, he or she generally obscures this neat poetic form by adding a variety of elements to the song's core text. Often the singer begins each line of text with a single vowel sound such as *e* or *a*, a practice that seems to serve merely to get the person's voice started. He or she might also insert words or sounds such as *mori, aman, ajdo,* and *o-i* throughout the text. All these are sounds that are also common in the speech of Presparë. Many are what Irvine (1982:40) has referred to as "intensifiers": words that do not of themselves imply any particular affect, but which intensify whatever affect is associated with an utterance. Usually there are specific points in each line where these insertions are customarily made, but a singer is also free to add other ones spontaneously. The same text, as sung in one performance by the first soloist, is given below. Non-lexical additions have been rendered in italics:

e	Ra vesa	*moj*	vesojti dhenë
a	ku jemi nisur	*moj*	ne të vemë?
a	Jemi nisur	*moj*	për dë Kranjë
a	ta bastisim	*moj*	NN benë,
a	t'ja marrim	*moj*	të bijënë,
e	atë më	*moj*	të mirënë,
e	atë ballë-	*moj*	kartënë
e	atë gojë-	*moj*	mjaltënë.

(Leibman 1974, B1; recorded in Krani, 1972)

In the course of a performance, the first soloist (I) also inserts certain mandatory elements that serve as a form of punctuation. Before beginning the song proper, he or she intones the syllables *e-o*. This intonation serves in part as a signal that someone is about to sing and that others in the room should curtail their conversations and prepare to join in on the drone. After the intonation the first soloist generally sings the complete first line of the song's text. On the repetition of that line, he or she drops out to take a breath before its completion, omitting the last one or two syllables (indicated by the symbol =):

I	*E-o*	*e*	Ra vesa	*moj*	vesojti dhenë,
I		*e*	ra vesa	*moj*	vesojti=

The second soloist (II) generally begins as the line is repeated, entering a few syllables into the line and completing the text:

I	*E-o*	*e*	Ra vesa	*moj*	vesojti dhenë,
I		*e*	ra vesa	*moj*	vesojti=
II			=sa	*moj*	vesojti dhenë . . .

Subsequently, neither the first nor the second soloist sings the full text of this or any other line of the song.

Those singing the drone (III) have some degree of leeway as to when they will enter. The most usual point is the moment when the second soloist begins his or her descent to the pitch on which the drone is sung. This drone is sung to the vowel sound *e:*

I	*E-o*	*e*	Ra vesa	*moj*	vesojti dhenë,
I		*e*	ra vesa	*moj*	vesojti=
II			=sa	*moj*	vesojti dhenë . . .
III					E——

Once all three parts have entered, the two soloists proceed in overlapping alternation. The first soloist omits the end of each line and breathes before beginning the next line. The second soloist sustains the last syllable of each line and eventually takes a breath before reentering part way through the next line:

Verse One:

I	*E-o*	*e*	Ra vesa	*moj*	vesojti dhenë,
I		*e*	ra vesa	*moj*	vesojti (BREATH)
II			(BREATH) sa	*moj*	vesojti dhenë
III					E——

Verse Two:

I	*a* ku jemi	nisur	*moj*	ne të (BREATH)
II	(BREATH)	nisur	*moj*	ne të vemë
III	*e* --			
I	*a* ku jemi	nisur	*moj*	ne të (BREATH)
II	(BREATH)	nisur	*moj*	ne të vemë . . .
III	*e* -- etc.			

This type of alternation serves much the same purpose as does antiphonal singing among many other European communities: it enables the

EXAMPLE 2.6. Pentatonic Scales on which Prespa Songs Are Based

singers to maintain the rhythmic momentum of a song when there is no instrumental accompaniment.

As sung by Presparë, the two solo lines of any song are drawn from the pitches of a pentatonic scale (ex. 2.6). By far the most common is scale (a); scale (b) is found in a few songs, while (c) is rare. Singers may, however, "decorate" (zbukurojnë) the melody with rapid, melismatic ornaments that employ pitches outside the basic scale. One pitch, indicated by a whole note, serves as the tonal center, in that it is heard through most of the performance as a drone. Texted portions of the solo lines are sung to phrases that move above the drone. Phrases characteristically descend from a higher pitch to the drone note, or they begin and end on the drone note, forming an arched contour. Singers reserve the pitch a minor third below the drone note, together with ornamental pitches lying above and below it, for the various punctuating intonations sung to the syllables e-o. This is true regardless of the scale of the song being performed.

The song Ra vesa, vesojti dhenë is sung to one of the most common melody types for women's dance and ritual songs, probably the one that men think of as the "women's melodi" (ex. 2.7; CD #5). Once the song is under way, singers of the drone stagger their breathing in order to provide a more or less continuous drone, sometimes sliding up to the drone note from a lower pitch as they reenter.

In any song, if the first soloist wishes to pause between lines or verses, he or she reenters on the syllable e at the end of the repeated line. This signals to the others that there is to be a break at that point. Those singing the other parts sustain the drone pitch and then, initiated by the first soloist, all complete an intonation on e-o. The first soloist then begins the next line of text alone, the second soloist reenters, those singing the drone reenter, and the song proceeds as before (ex. 2.8; CD #5). In some songs it is customary to pause after every line or pair of lines. For others, the first soloist is more free to initiate pauses at will. Singers also perform this type of communal intonation at the very end of a song.

Ra vesa is typical of most Prespa songs in the way the two solo parts

EXAMPLE 2.7. *Ra vesa, vesojti dhenë*

cross each other. For each line of the text, the first soloist begins several
pitches above that of the drone. As she descends to the drone pitch toward the end of the line, the second soloist enters above her, moving
through the range of higher pitches that the first soloist had initially
defined. While the voices cross just once per line in most *melodi*, there
are *melodi* in which the voices cross three or more times. It is this continuous weaving back and forth of the two solo vocal lines that gives
the Tosk style of polyphony its distinctive sound, and that presents the
greatest challenge to both performers and listeners. If the voices of the

EXAMPLE 2.8. *Ra vesa, vesojti dhenë*: First Soloist Initiating Pause between Verses

two soloists are particularly well matched, it can be difficult for a listener to decipher which soloist is singing which pitches. For a beginning singer, it is particularly difficult to learn to hold one's part securely against that of the other soloist.

Singing Terminology

Whenever singers wish to describe a past performance, decide on personnel for an upcoming performance, or urge someone to join in during the course of a performance, they draw on specific terms that refer to each of the three lines of their polyphony. Commonly they say that the first soloist *këndon* ("sings") the song. In its primary meaning the verb *këndoj* refers to any form of singing, not only by humans but also by birds. Presparë use it not only for their polyphony, but also in reference to any type of unison singing, such as for a Macedonian or north Albanian song. As already noted, it may also be used figuratively to mean "to be happy." South Albanians in particular use *këndoj* to mean "to read," as in, "He knows how to *këndojë* and to write Albanian language." And they use it in the sense of "reciting" a text aloud, specifically when they speak of "reading" the Qur'ān (see Kostallari 1980:816–17).

Within the context of polyphonic singing, the first soloist is thought of as "singing" a song as his or her gesture of "honor" toward the family hosting the social event. It is the first soloist who chooses the specific song to be sung, and who is the only person who needs to remember the text in full. Because the second line enters after the first, the second soloist need not remember how each line begins, but can be cued by the first. Thus it is that only the first soloist is said to *këndon* the song. In place of *këndon,* one woman that I interviewed used the verb *thotë,* which means "to say," as if to emphasize the first soloist's role as the declaimer of the song's text.

More rarely, the first soloist may be said to *merr* ("take") the song. Presparë use this verb most often in the sense of "taking up" or "beginning" a song. When others wish an individual to begin singing, for example, they will call out for him or her to *merr ja këngës!* ("Take up the song!"). Or one singer will indicate to another that "I will *marr* the song, you [most often] *mban* it."

The second soloist *pret* or *mban* the song. Presparë use both these verbs as specific musical terms to such an extent that they do not relate their musical usage to their meanings in other contexts. Nevertheless, if one explores related meanings of each word, some insight may be gained into the way that their polyphony has historically been conceptualized. There are, in fact, two verbs *pres,* each conjugated differently. The first means "to wait" (past participle *pritur*), the second "to cut" (p.p. *prerë*). Most Presparë use the form *prerë* when speaking in the past tense, but even here I did not find complete agreement on usage. It might seem logical to assume that the second soloist "waits" for the first to begin. Albanian sources, however, derive the usage from "to cut," presumably in the sense of "interrupt," since the first soloist is "cut off" from completing the line of text once the second has entered (see Kostallari 1980:1541–42). Aromân singers from southern Albania, who sing in the same style, also say that the second soloist in their polyphony "cuts" (see Lortat-Jacob and Bouët 1983).

The principal meaning of *mbaj* is "to hold" or "to support." It is possible that the word as a musical term developed out of the close relationship between polyphonic singing and dancing. When men or women perform dance songs, several individuals join hands and form a line which moves counterclockwise in a semicircle as all perform the same sequence of steps. The person at the head of the line "sings the song" (*e këndon këngën*) and also "dances the dance" (*e lot vallen*). The person second in line *e pret* or *e mban* the song. At the same time, he or she "holds" or "supports" the first dancer (*e mban*) by raising the right hand to shoulder level and keeping a firm grip on the hand of the leader. In some men's dances, the first dancer performs various acrobatic movements and is very much in need of a strong second dancer who will physically hold onto him with his arm. It seems to me that, at present, more women than men use the term *mban*, perhaps because they are the ones who still actively perform dance songs.

With the exception of the use of the verb *këndon* for the first solo line, the terms discussed thus far (see table 2) are used widely wherever the Tosk style of polyphony is sung (see Dheri, Daiu, and Haxhihasani 1964; Dheri, Daiu, and Mustaqi 1966).[7] Some other terms commonly used in Prespa, however, have not been noted for other southern song styles. Many individuals regularly said that the second soloist "goes behind" (*vete pas* or *shkon pas*) or "comes [from] behind" (*vjen pas*). More rarely, the first soloist was said to "drive" (*nget*) the song, or to "set out" or "initiate" (*nis*) it. One couple used similar spatial imagery when they said that the first soloist "sings in front" (*këndon perpara*), while the second "goes behind" (*vete prapa*). Similar terms are used by south Slavic singers in some regions, although they are not necessarily the most prevalent in any area.[8]

For the drone part, virtually all Presparë other than Kolonjarë say that the performers *rënkojnë*, from the verb *rënkoj*, which means to "moan" or "groan"; hence the designation of *këngë me të rënkuar* (lit. "songs with moaning") for their polyphonic repertoire. This same verb

TABLE 2 Terms Used for Tosk Polyphony

	Prespa	Korçë	Pogradec	Përmet	Lushnjë	Berat
I singer	këndon (merr) (thotë)	këndon/thotë	merr	merr/thotë	merr	merr
II accompanist	pret/mban	pret	pret/mban	mban	mban	pret
III drone	rënkojnë	mbajnë zë/zjejnë	bëjnë iso	bëjnë iso	mbajnë zë	kaba

rënkoj is also used to describe the intonations performed at the beginning of a song, before pauses between verses, and at the end of a performance, all sung to the syllables *e-o*. Occasionally I heard someone refer to those droning as *e mbajnë zë* ("they hold the voice"). Kolonjarë in Prespa use instead the phrase *bëjnë iso* ("do a drone"), and refer to their songs as *këngë me iso* ("songs with a drone"), a designation that is more common in Albania.[9] All Albanians in Prespa use the term *iso* when urging others to join in on the drone. My field recordings are peppered with individuals calling out loudly, *Bëni iso!* or *Bëni isa!* ("Do a drone!"). Or they might exclaim, *Ajde, mbusheni!* ("Come on, fill it!").

While the word *iso* and the phrase *e mbajnë zë* are used in many parts of southern Albania (table 2), the Prespa community is the only one to my knowledge that uses the verb *rënkoj* for the drone. In the Berat district, singers evidently use the Turkish word *kaba*, which often indicates a melody performed in a low register; while some singers in the Korçë district use the verb *zjejnë* ("to boil"). Slavic families who formerly lived in the Kastoria district of Greece along the Albanian border, however, and who sing a similar type of three-voiced polyphony, say that those who perform the drone line *grčat* or *grtat* ("groan"; cf. *rënkojnë*). They thus call their three-voiced songs *grteni pesni*, an equivalent of *këngë me të rënkuar*.[10]

Interpreting Prespa Terminology

When Presparë speak of their experiences as singers, or when they evaluate the performances of others, they draw upon a practical discourse that includes such terms as well as a shared phraseology concerning various aspects of performance. When I asked individuals to, as it were, peer behind this discourse to translate it for me or to explain to me how they relate it to their own experiences, they offered an array of idiosyncratic, metaphoric images concerning song performance.

In order to understand their explanations and images, it is helpful to recall how songs unfold in the course of an event such as the evening gathering described earlier. Everyone at an event takes a turn "singing" one song, in the sense of performing the first solo line. The singer of this line has generally learned it in a fairly set form, perhaps even with specific verbal interpolations and melodic ornaments. Not everyone, however, is expected to be able to perform the second line of a song well. Often the second soloist is one of a few more experienced singers who take turns performing this line for the various "singers" throughout the course of the event. In the event just described, for example, the two most accomplished women singers took turns "accompanying" almost all the songs that were sung.

What the second soloist performs is not a set melody line, but rather a flexible, semi-extemporized line that complements and holds together the performance of the first. Individuals often say that it is the role of the second soloist to *rregullon* ("regulate" or "put in order") the song, meaning that he or she should pull the performance together and make it sound acceptable. Because everyone present takes turns "singing," regardless of their skill as singers, it is to be expected that some individuals will hardly be able to get through their line of the song. It is not uncommon, for example, for the first soloist to begin to sing out of tune, or to not observe the song's meter consistently. In such instances the second soloist, who should be a strong singer, is expected to keep the first soloist's performance on track. Although rarer, the reverse is also a possibility. If a less accomplished singer volunteers to sing the second solo line, he or she may spoil even the best performance on the part of the person "singing."

Because of this relationship between the two soloists, many Prespparë associate the term *mban* with "hold" in the sense of "support." Thus, *ajo e mban këngën* means for them: She supports the "song" as sung by the first soloist. Similarly, they use the word *pret* in the sense that it is used when speaking of social etiquette. At any occasion, a host or hostess is expected to both *pret* ("wait upon") and *përcjell* ("accompany" to the door) the family's guests.[11] Thus, a younger man explained to me that *"Këngën e rregullon ay që e pret, ay që e përcjell"* ("The song is regulated by the one who *pret*s, the one who *përcjell*s"). A younger woman, speaking in English, explained the term *pret* in this way: "*E pret* is 'follow.' 'It catches'—she comes right after you, she's singing it, she's helping you sing the song. . . . [*E pret këngën*] is 'singing after her.' . . . It helps her to make a better melody." She was pleased to have arrived at the word "help" as a translation for *pret,* and henceforth continued to use it throughout the interview. Because of such explanations on the part of community members, I have chosen to refer to the second soloist as "accompanying" the first.

In most situations the second soloist is expected to adjust his or her performance to that of the first. Such adjustment is particularly crucial at large occasions such as weddings, when two singers who have never met before might come together, as it were, through song. In such cases they might not even know the same version of the words, and so the second soloist should adjust his or her text as well:

. . . You have to see how she goes, whether fast or slow. So that's why you have to wait. Once she says one sentence while she's singing, you have to listen to how fast or slow she's going, and then you follow her. [JS: What if you don't know the same words?] Oh, you make a mistake. If you don't know, it's a mistake. . . . You'll just have to follow her. (Interview with a younger woman in Chicago, 1987)

Ideally the two solo parts in any song should interweave in a smooth, unbroken flow. *Si zinxhir* is the way one man described a particularly good performance: "like [links in] a chain."

At any social occasion, every person in the room of the same gender as the soloists is expected to join in on the drone. From my perspective the drone provides the soloists with a clear reference pitch. When they cannot hear it well, they are apt to lose their sense of tonality and sing out of tune. Prespare, however, speak of the drone in aesthetic, rather than technical, terms:

We often say, *Bëni ca isa! Bëni isa!* ("Do some droning! Do the drone!") . . . so that the song will "go." The song only "goes" with a drone, with droning. Why do we call them "songs with droning"? You have to drone! It's not that it's harder to sing when they don't drone, but that the song doesn't "go." It doesn't sound good. It *s'ka lezet* [has no taste]. (Interview with a younger man in Toronto, 1986)

Often they speak of the drone as "filling" (*mbush*) the song, in the sense of giving the performance a full, resonant sound. Indeed, the vocal timbre of Prespa singers, which is rich in upper partials, combines with the beats caused by slight differences in intonation to produce a particularly vibrant acoustic backdrop.

In the years that I was actively researching Prespa singing, I found that I had arrived at my own metaphoric image of its polyphonic structure. In the course of a song performance, I thought, the soloists' lines rise and fall above the drone, resonating in turn with the various overtones that it sets forth, much like individual waves cresting above the surface of a sea. Several years after I first formulated this metaphor for myself, I found that I was not alone in thinking of the singing in this way. During a visit with a younger man in the community, he described to me his ideal for Prespa instrumental music: tunes for listening and dancing that are patterned on the vocal repertoire. "When the clarinet plays," he explained in English, "the accordion should 'come behind' [his translation of *vjen pas*] and [move] below the clarinet. Then, when the clarinet goes down, the accordion comes up." As he spoke, he made wavy rising and falling gestures with his hands. "Like *këngë me të rënkuar?*" I asked, and he agreed. "Our Tosk music goes . . ." and here he gestured again up and down with his hands. "You know . . . like the water."

Acquiring a Repertoire

One of the things that most intrigued me when I interviewed adults in the Prespa community was how they had learned to sing their complicated style of polyphony. Most started at age six or eight, largely without formal instruction. In the course of attending frequent gatherings that involved singing, they watched and listened, and eventually began trying to learn a song themselves:

> I learned to sing when I used to go to wedding gatherings and I listened to the older men when they sang. As they sang I practiced along with them. I would plop myself in a corner on one side of the room and they would sing, and I would sing softly so that I wouldn't spoil their song. I would sing softly along with them and . . . you sing a little today, and a little tomorrow and then . . . you've learned. (Interview with a younger man in Chicago, 1985)

Once a child showed some interest, a parent or other relative would intervene and offer pointers and corrections. Most of my interviewees spent a couple of years learning to "sing" various songs before they began to learn to perform the second, accompanying line.

Once children who were interested in singing were conversant with the style, they practiced constantly, with both relatives and friends. Boys would sing together while they herded livestock, girls while they strung tobacco. I was able to witness such a practice session in 1981 when I attended the bride's side of a wedding in a Prespa village. As we waited for the groom's party to arrive to take the bride, a group of girls aged fifteen or sixteen sang a few simple songs over and over. Sometimes two girls sang the top two voices with no one droning; at other times one girl sang the first line while two or more sang the second line together, again without droning. As they sang verse after verse, they gradually performed their parts with greater assurance.

Individuals also spoke of their eagerness to perform *dë mexhelis* ("in public") when there was a wedding or other large occasion. This is again something that I saw at several weddings in both Prespa and North

America, where a child with a particular *merak* ("passion") for singing was showcased at a more informal singing gathering, generally accompanied by an older relative. One particularly esteemed singer in Prespa recounted to me how, as a boy, he had frequently been asked to sing at men's evening gatherings. He would be placed on the polished earthen floor in front of the fireplace, near where the oldest men were seated. When he had finished, he would be passed hand to hand around the room until he reached the area near the doorway, where the youngest guests customarily sit. Not all children showed such an early willingness to learn. If a child was approaching marriageable age and still had not begun to sing, a parent generally took the child aside and taught him or her a few songs. For the generation of Presparë who are now adults, it was simply imperative that they be able to sing by the time that they were married.

Individuals of this generation have gradually pieced together a personal repertoire of songs from quite diverse sources. This process has been facilitated by the similarity of songs sung throughout the region where Tosk polyphony is found. Whenever I have read about Tosk singing or looked through collections of Tosk songs, I have always found many textual variants of songs sung by Prespa singers. Even when not variants, songs from other regions are often indistinguishable from those sung in Prespa in terms of their basic textual and melodic structure. It seems that this entire area may be regarded as a single musical zone within which extensive interchange, particularly of song texts but also of melody types, has taken place.

When Presparë speak about songs in their repertoire that are "old," or even just "ours," they mean songs that were made up locally or that families are thought to have brought with them when they settled in Prespa centuries ago. Songs "from Albania," on the other hand, are ones clearly originating in Albania itself that Prespa singers have learned at some point during the past century. Until World War II, when passage across the border into what is now Albania was forbidden, Albanians in lower Prespa were in constant interaction with families living in the Devoll district and beyond. Brides were often taken from villages in that area and came to Prespa knowing a full repertoire of songs that other women then learned from them. Prespa men traveled to market in Korçë, as well as to more distant towns such as Tiranë, to sell produce and buy supplies. There they often congregated with other men to socialize and swap songs. Beginning with the Balkan Wars of 1912–13, men who fought in one or another of the armed forces involved in regional disputes learned songs from fellow soldiers. As one example, a man in Krani learned a number of unusual songs during World War II that he eventually performed at folk festivals and on Yugoslav radio with other Prespa men. Since the 1960s Presparë living overseas in places such as North America and Australia have continued to learn songs from singers from Albania.

Since World War II, families in Prespa have learned new songs primarily through the electronic media. After the war, both Albania and Yugoslavia initiated regular radio broadcasts of folk music. For Presparë, Radio Tiranë at once became the major source of new songs for both men and women. The radio served as a substitute for live contact with singers in other districts and contributed as well to a sense of pride in their distinctively Tosk culture. When I was in Prespa in the early 1980s, Radio Tiranë broadcast several hours of folk songs each day. One young woman described for me how she used to keep a sheet of paper and a pencil by the radio so that each time a song that she was interested in was played, she could jot down a few more of the words. Once cassette players became available, families recorded broadcasts and then played songs over and over until they had learned them, much as I have done in learning songs from recordings of Prespa singers.

The sampling of songs played on the radio in that era was broad. Polyphonic songs from southern districts were clearly favored, in line with a general preference shown toward southern speech and cultural forms within socialist Albania. But northern heroic songs, as well as songs in Turkish or European style from towns such as Shkodër and Elbasan, were also included. Most songs were sung with their village texts, although more and more frequently songs were broadcast with new texts that spoke glowingly of Enver Hoxha, then the leader of Albania, and of the *Parti* (Communist Party). Presparë showed little interest in any but the older polyphonic songs, whose themes and melodies were similar to those of their local repertoire. Most of the songs that they chose to learn from Albanian radio were in a style similar to their own, the majority coming from districts such as Korçë, Kolonjë, and Përmet. Often they were textual and/or melodic variants of songs already known in Prespa.

Until the mid-1980s, Yugoslav radio broadcast very little south Albanian music other than a few songs recorded years ago by the men's performing group from Prespa. Presparë have, however, learned many monophonic north Albanian and Macedonian songs from the radio. The

Rom musicians who play for weddings in Prespa also perform many north Albanian songs disseminated through the media, and Presparë have learned some such songs from them. Additional northern songs and urban Albanian songs were taught to Presparë in grammar school, or were learned by men while serving in the Yugoslav army.

The media have continued to serve as the principal source of new songs for overseas Presparë. Cassettes recorded from the radio are sent to them by relatives in Prespa, or are recorded during return visits to their villages. In addition, Presparë have had available to them a variety of commercial audio and, more recently, video recordings. In the 1960s and 1970s, older recordings of southern singers, issued in the United States on labels such as "Liria" and "Strictly Albanian," were circulated among Albanian communities, and these performances are now re-garded as classics. Small 45 rpm discs of Yugoslav singers, including Albanian ones, were available in Yugoslav record stores. Since the 1980s, Presparë have been able to purchase videos from Albania of folk festi-vals, as well as of feature films that take place in southern Albania and that feature speech and folklore similar to their own. Until the dissolu-tion of Yugoslavia, there were pan-Yugoslav radio programs in North American cities that played the latest folk-pop hits, and stores that sold a wide variety of Yugoslav recordings and videos. In an interesting twist, one of the most popular videos of the 1980s featured "Ibe Pali-kuqa," a student group of north Albanians from Macedonia, performing southern songs that were popular on Albanian radio perhaps thirty years ago, together with a Prespa song ("*Dardhë rrumbullake*"). For the first time, Presparë heard south Albanian music enter the mainstream of the Yugoslav Albanian media.

As already noted, Presparë other than Kolonjarë refer to songs in the Tosk polyphonic style as *këngë me të rënkuar*, "songs with droning." In part because of the Albanian media's preference for southern styles, Presparë tend to think of their songs as being particularly "Albanian." When comparing them to other types of songs that they sing, they may simply refer to them as *këngë shqipe*, "Albanian songs." One older woman, for example, told her family that I could sing *maqedonçe, shqip, dhe gegnisht:* "Macedonian, Albanian, and Geg [songs]." Monophonic Albanian songs, whether from the north or part of the urban repertoire, are more often dubbed *këngë popullore*, a designation common in the me-dia in Albania and the former Yugoslavia that corresponds to Serbo-Croatian or Macedonian *narodna muzika:* "national" or "popular" or "folk" music. Presparë also frequently speak of them as *këngë pe shkolla* ("school songs"), since these are the types of songs that they were taught in school.

Virtually any song known to Presparë, whether new or old, whether polyphonic or monophonic, whether Albanian or south Slavic, may be sung at some point during a wedding. The only major criterion is whether the singer deems its text, or the overall sentiment that is associated with it, to be appropriate to the point in the wedding celebration at which it is sung. I was quite surprised, for example, to hear an excellent singer in Prespa declare that one of his favorite songs for late-night men's gatherings was *"U Novom Sadu"* ("In Novi Sad"), a radio-disseminated song from Vojvodina in northern Serbia. In this respect, Prespa weddings have often been, as one younger man quipped, "a multicultural experience." Weddings and other large celebrations are in fact the primary context within which new songs are picked up by others and eventually spread throughout the Prespa community. "I first heard Selim sing that at Ali's wedding," people will say about an addition to the repertoire. Or, "I learned that song from a cassette of Sherifa's aunts singing at her wedding." In these ways, songs from the outside have quickly entered the community's oral tradition, and the Prespa song repertoire has continually been replenished.

WEDDINGS IN PRESPA
1980–1995

1. A mother and daughter departing for a wedding. The mother holds a *bakllava* decorated with fresh flowers; her daughter carries a white *boçe* wrapped around gifts of clothing for the groom. (Arvati, 1981; photograph by Eran Fraenkel)

2. Crushing the *qeshqek*. While two men crush wheat berries for the wedding banquet, the groom's closest male relatives sing ritual songs. (Krani, 1995; photograph by Eran Fraenkel)

3. Dancing in the groom's courtyard. On the day before the taking of the bride, guests of the groom's family dance to music provided by the *daulle*. (Grnčari, 1980; photograph by Jane Sugarman)

4. Entertaining the guests. On the day of the taking of the bride, the *daulle* play an instrumental improvisation (*kaba*) for male guests of the groom's family. (Sopotsko, 1981; photograph by Eran Fraenkel)

5. Fetching the dowry. Early on the wedding day, children parade small items in the bride's dowry from her house to that of the groom. (Grnčari, 1980; photograph by Jane Sugarman)

6. Shaving the groom. The groom is shaved and has his hair combed by a male relative as men of his wedding party sing ritual wedding songs. (Grnčari, 1980; photograph by Eran Fraenkel)

7. Combing the groom's hair. Just before the groom's party sets out to take the bride, his female relatives sing to him as they comb perfume through his hair. (Nakolec, 1980; photograph by Jane Sugarman)

8. Taking the bride. The groom poses beside his bride in the doorway of her home just before she is taken by his wedding party. A recent bride, also in a white wedding dress, attends her. (Grnčari, 1980; photograph by Eran Fraenkel)

9. Departing from the bride's home. Female relatives of the groom (standing in a semicircle in the foreground) sing as the bride and groom approach the car that will carry them back to his family's home. (Dolna Bela Crkva, 1981; photograph by Eran Fraenkel)

10. Dancing the bride. A relative of the groom leads the bride and groom in the "bride's dance" (*valle e nuses*), accompanied by the *daulle*. (Dolna Bela Crkva, 1981; photograph by Eran Fraenkel)

THREE

Singing as a Gendered Activity

Gratë kanë tjetër muabet. Women have their own *muabet.*
(interview with an older couple, Detroit 1987)

WOMEN'S SINGING AT THE BRIDE'S

During the 1970s a great many marriages took place between young Prespa men who had been working overseas and young women still living in Prespa villages. If the young man returned to Prespa to marry, then a large celebration was held at his home. If, however, he remained overseas, then his bride was sent to join him and the wedding was celebrated there. Such was the case with a marriage that took place in 1972 between Ruzhdi, a young man who had then been in Canada for several years, and Aiten, a young woman from the lower village of Krani (Kranjë). Even though the ceremony itself was not to be celebrated in Prespa, evening gatherings were held at the homes of both Ruzhdi's and Aiten's parents during the week before her departure for Canada.

On the final evening before she left, men and women assembled in separate rooms at Aiten's home for a night of singing. A neighbor who had lived in Australia lent her family a portable tape recorder that he had purchased there so that they could record the event. In somewhat of a break with tradition, they chose to record the women's gathering rather than the men's. The recording, together with one of a gathering held earlier at Ruzhdi's home, were then sent to Canada with Aiten for relatives of both families to hear. It is upon this recording, together with many discussions with the couple and other relatives, that the following account is based.

One of the unusual features of this gathering was that the groom's mother and a female cousin of his father's were both present at a gathering held at the bride's home. Usually only her own relatives would have attended. A second unusual feature was that Aiten's north Albanian pen pal from western Macedonia, together with her young cousin, had traveled to Prespa for the occasion and participated by singing northern songs. Once the guests had departed, the singing continued as a series of Aiten's young relatives came forward to have their singing immortalized on tape.

The recording provides a valuable record of women's singing in Prespa at a time when most families were still living there, and when polyphonic singing flourished among even the youngest generation. It also illustrates the way women singers in particular may adjust their repertoire to suit a given event. During the course of the evening, women addressed songs to both Aiten and Ruzhdi, frequently inserting their names into the songs' texts. Singers also chose songs that drew attention to Ruzhdi's absence from the village and Aiten's long journey to her new home, occasionally changing individual lines of songs and adding new lines to make them, as Aiten later explained to me, *tamam si ç'duet*: exactly suited to the occasion.

Prespa families began to record their singing to send to relatives overseas sometime in the late 1960s; it was thus a common practice at the time this recording was made. As had become standard, each singer introduced her song with a speech addressed to those abroad. The first to sing was Aiten's mother, the hostess for the event. She prefaced her song with long remarks to each of her relatives in Canada and to their spouses, children, children's spouses, and grandchildren. To each she exclaimed, *Të trashëgoet!* and *Me jetë të lumtur!* ("May the bride and groom have a long and happy life!") on the occasion of her daughter's marriage. She then offered specific congratulations regarding recent weddings held in Canada. When these greetings were concluded, she sang a song that expresses a mother's concern for her daughter (ex. 3.1; CD #6):

Sh'të duet, moj lule, ta qëronje mollën?	Why did you have to go and peel that apple, my flower?
Të shpëtoi çarkia e ta previ dorën:	The knife slipped and cut your hand:
jo të tërë dorën por një cikë gishtin.	not the whole hand but a bit of your finger.
Asaman, moj lule, ma këpute shpirtin!	O my flower, it unhinged my soul!
Kur m'i ngjitnje shkallet pas parmak vështetur,	As you went up the stairs leaning against the balcony,
asaman, moj lule, me këtë të qeshur.	O my flower, you were still laughing.

EXAMPLE 3.1. *Sh'të duet, moj lule*

Accompanying her was a first cousin of Aiten's father, a woman then about forty years old who is often spoken of among families from the lower villages as the finest woman singer of her generation. As Aiten told me, "She was first in the village in everything": a model cook and homemaker as well as singer. She and her sister were known for singing a few particularly elaborate men's songs on occasion, and had even sung outdoors at weddings accompanied by the Rom musicians, something that women would otherwise not do.

More than any other woman that I have heard, Aiten's cousin was capable of "regulating" song performances through her confident and highly ornamented renditions of the second solo line. In this case, Aiten's mother sang simply while the cousin performed a florid second line, always careful to remain within the meter established by the "singer." She continued to accompany virtually all performances by the adult women present. When the song was finished, Aiten's mother exclaimed "Congratulations! May they live a long life!" and then addressed Ruzhdi directly on the tape, wishing him a long life.

Had this gathering included only Aiten's relatives, the guests would now have sung in descending order of age. Instead, Ruzhdi's relatives were asked to sing next. First was his mother, who began with a long speech thanking the host family and sending best wishes to relatives in Canada. She then sang a song that begins with references to the bride's beauty:

Sh't'është nxirë vetulla tynë? . . . *edhe moj, ajde dhe moj.*	Is it that your eyebrows have been blackened? . . .
Mos ta kanë shtënë mazinë? . . .	They haven't put makeup on you, have they? . . .
Jo për jo, për perëndinë . . .	Oh no, in God's name . . .
ashtu ç'e ke bukurinë . . .	that is the nature of your beauty . . .

The song continues by speaking of a young man who has gone to a faraway place, which may be taken as a reference to his new life in Canada. Ruzhdi's mother inserted his name in the text, and changed the usual phrase *në fshat të uaj* ("in a foreign village") to *në qytet të uaj* ("in a foreign city") to suit his situation more closely:

RUZHDI beu në qytet të uaj . . .	RUZHDI *bey* in a foreign city . . .

| Mollënë në xhep ja ruaj . . . | I keep the apple in my pocket . . . |
| Ç'u kalp molla, ç'u gëris xhepi . . . | The apple rots, the pocket tears . . . |

The final two lines of the song are often taken to mean that the young man runs the risk of staying away so long that the young woman loses interest in him.

Ruzhdi's mother had attempted without success to get a visa to attend his wedding in Canada, and was distressed that she could not be present. And so, when she had completed her song, she extemporized a few rhymed couplets based upon standard formulas. These were addressed to her own mother, then living in Canada, asking her to watch over the young couple:

Amanet, moj nënkë, të kam lënë malit:	My little mother, I have left something in the mountains for you to care for:
Kur të më kujtosh mua të ma shikosh djalën.	Whenever you think of me, may you look after my son.
Amanet, moj nënkë, të kam lënë fushën:	My little mother, I have left something in the fields for you to care for:
Kur të më kujtosh mua të ma shikosh nusen.	Whenever you think of me, may you look after my daughter-in-law.

After her sang Ruzhdi's father's cousin. She chose a fast-paced song appropriate to the groom's side of a wedding, adding Ruzhdi's name in the customary place:

Dëgjoni, zonja, dëgjoni . . .	Listen, ladies, listen . . .
moj zonja dëgjoni.	(ladies, listen)
vallë që thotë telefoni . . .	to what the telephone says . . .
RUZHDI benë ta martoni . . .	that you should marry off RUZHDI *bey* . . .
Nëna jonë në mos dashtë . . .	If his mother doesn't wish it . . .
ta gënjejmë me gjëkafshë . . .	we'll bribe her with something . . .
me një boçe pe mëndafshtë . . .	with a silken cloth [wrapped around presents for her] . . .[1]

EXAMPLE 3.2. *Bien tri daire*

Now the two young north Albanian women were asked to sing. Aiten's pen pal, together with her cousin, sang a unison song that had recently been a hit on the radio among Yugoslav Albanians and is still sung by Presparë. Although it describes the very different status of a northern bride within her new family, it was nevertheless especially appropriate to this event because of its theme (ex. 3.2; CD #7):

Bien tri daire, moj nane,	They are playing three frame drums, mother,
të trijat nji soj.	all three the same.
A s'e din, moj nana ime,	Don't you know, O mother of mine,
se un' nesër shkoj?	that I go [to be married] tomorrow?
Dhe në shkofsh, moj bija ime,	If you go, my daughter,
të qoft' rruga e mbar':	may you have a safe journey:
tuj qendis gjergjefin, moj bije,	as you embroider on your hoop, my girl,
tuj m'i bo çorap'.	as you make a pair of socks.

Se kur t'shkojsh ke nana jote,	When you go back to your mother's
do t'rrish si mikesh.	you will have to behave like a guest:
Kur të haet buk', mori bije,	When you want to eat bread, my girl,
ke magja s'un veç.	you won't be allowed to go to the kneading trough.
Kur të piet uj', mori bije,	When you want to drink water, my girl,
shtambën s'un e ngresh.	you won't be allowed to lift the water jug.
Edhe unë, si gjith' shoqet,	I too, mother, like all my friends,
edhe un' do t'shkoj.	I too will go.
Der sa t'jem un' ngjall', mori nane,	But for as long as I live, mother,
fjalët s'i harroj:	I won't forget your words:
Se ajo der' e huj, moj bije,	At that foreign door, my girl,
m'i asht' shum' e rand':	life is very hard:
se t'jet' dit'n e lum-e, moj bije,	even when there is a holiday, my girl,
duet më rrish në kamb',	you must remain on your feet,
edhe f'mijve t'djepit, moj bije,	and even before the babies in the cradle, my girl,
temena me u marr.	you must perform a *temena* in respect.[2]

The cousin followed this with another north Albanian song.

At this point the singing of Aiten's relatives began in order of age with the mother of the cousin who had been accompanying each singer so consummately, and who now accompanied her mother (sung to the same melody as ex. 3.1). Her song depicts a beautiful young bride and the consideration that the groom's family is expected to show toward her. This was the first song into which Aiten's name was inserted:

Lule e bukur me bojë allit	Beautiful, bright red flower
duke dalë për rrëzë malit	blooming at the edge of the mountain
gjer e zgjodhe bashnë e djalit.	until you found the best possible young man.

AITEN lule me bojë allit	AITEN, bright red flower,
duke dalë për rrëzë fushës	blooming at the edge of the field
gjer të zgjodhë bashnë e çupës.	until you were found to be the best possible young lady.
Ruaj, O AITEN, se mos të shkelin!	Be careful, AITEN, that they don't trample you!
Jo, more baba, nuku më shkelin	Oh no, father, they won't trample me
se më kanë nuse, më përkëdhelin.	for I am their bride, and they pamper me.

Following her, and breaking with the customary order, the younger cousin sang, perhaps because her beautiful singing had the potential to enliven an otherwise sorrowful occasion. She was accompanied by Aiten's *allo* (father's sister), who is not a strong singer. As the cousin sang, realizing that the accompaniment was weak, she gradually simplified her melody line, eliminating many of the ornaments that she would normally use.

Hers was a moving performance nevertheless. The song she chose reminded all present of the poignant circumstances of the wedding, and she adjusted the words so as to make it even more suitable to this event. At the beginning of the song, which is about a daughter's departure from her mother's home, she added a line to point out that Ruzhdi was also away from his parents:

U këput ylli nga ëna . . .	A star separated from the moon . . .
bir more.	(O child).[3]
(added line:) Se ç'u nda djali ngaj nëna . . .	As a son separated from his mother . . .
u nda AITENI nga e ëma . . .	so AITEN separated from hers . . .
Bir, më ike, m'u largove . . .	Child, you ran from me, you went far away . . .
nënënë ç'e përvëlove . . .	you broke your mother['s heart] . . .

She then extemporized several lines to the same tune which were formulaic enough that the second soloist could follow them:

Për nënën mos kesh gajle . . .	Don't worry about your mother . . .
se nënkoa do të ju urojë . . .	for your mother will rejoice . . .
Rrugën të mbarë të ma kesh . . .	May you have a safe journey . . .
Edhe atje ku do veç . . .	And there where you are going . . .
kësmet edhe air të kesh . . .	may you have good fortune . . .

Now was the turn of the *allo*, a woman in her forties, to sing. She first gave a long speech to those in Canada, congratulating Ruzhdi and his family and then greeting her own relatives. As she listed the names of those who had left, her voice became choked. She seemed to recognize at that moment that Aiten was but one of many close relatives who had departed for North America over the past few years, and who were rarely able to return to visit. On the verge of tears, she curtailed her speech in order to address a song to Aiten. She began a more standard version of the song that had just been performed, adding lines referring to Aiten's imminent voyage and her parents' sorrow:

Ç'u këput një yll nga ëna . . .	A star separated from the moon . . .
moj bir more.	(O child)
ç'u nda AITENI nga e ëma . . .	AITEN separated from her mother . . .
Bir, m'u ndave, m'u largove . . .	Child, you left me, you went far away . . .
(added lines:) nëpër det më udhëtove . . .	you traveled across the ocean . . .
baba, nënë s'i mentove . . .	you didn't think of your father and mother . . .

At this point in her performance she became overcome with sadness and began weeping, unable to complete her song. A younger singer would probably have been expected to regain her composure and finish her performance. Because she was older and a particularly close relative, however, she continued to cry while the singing resumed.

Next was the turn of Aiten's *xhaxhicë* (wife of her father's brother). In her speech she addressed various relatives of Ruzhdi's and then enumerated several of the children of her relatives in Canada, mentioning the boys by name and the girls as *çupka* ("girls"). Although a relative of the bride's, she then sang a short song customarily sung on the groom's side. As is usual, she inserted Ruzhdi's name in the proper place but then, since she represented the bride's side, she continued by enumerating two of the boys that she had just mentioned, who are Aiten's cousins:

Merr gjergjefnë edhe aj të rrimë . . .	Grab your embroidery hoop, let's sit for awhile . . .
edhe more trëndafil.	(O rose)
Unë vij po s'ja kam ngenë . . .	I would come but I don't have time . . .
se martojmë djalin RUZHDI benë . . .	because we're marrying off RUZHDI *bey* . . .
arrifshi më DAUD benë . . .	and we look ahead to [the wedding of] DAUD *bey* . . .
më të fundin FERAT benë . . .	and finally FERAT *bey* . . .

She was accompanied by her daughter, who now addressed another song to Ruzhdi and his family. She prefaced her singing with an emotional speech to her relatives, in which she "kissed the eyes" of several young cousins and exclaimed that, "since you left, all I do is cry." To a certain extent, the process of sending recorded greetings to relatives abroad was becoming the emotional focus of the gathering, adding significantly to the sorrow that the women felt over Aiten's imminent departure.

Leskoviq bënet pazari . . .	They're having market day in Leskovik [a town in southern Albania] . . .
edhe ajde dhe moj.	
Aj të vemi Leskoviq . . .	Let's go to Leskovik . . .
të marrim një xhufkë ari . . .	to get a golden tassel . . .
që t'ja vëmë atij shalli . . .	to put on the shawl . . .
atij shalli t'RUZHDI beut . . .	the shawl of RUZHDI *bey* . . .
që ta ketë për dhëndëri . . .	to have for when he is a groom . . .
ta gëzojë babanë e tij . . .	to make his father happy . . .

Last of the married women to sing was another cousin of Aiten's father. She again sang a song often sung on the groom's side, one which depicts a conversation between a young woman and her beloved who is away on *gurbet*. It thus addressed a situation that Aiten and Ruzhdi had faced living so far from each other. In this instance the singer inserted the names of both into the song:

RUZHDI beu, qysh e bëmë fjalën	RUZHDI *bey*, since we gave our word
të piqemi bashkë pa mbushur javën.	that we would see each other before the week is out,
Letër të dërgova, letër s'ke këthyer.	I sent you a letter, but you didn't return one.
A më ke dër ment apo më ke arruar?	Are you thinking of me or have you forgotten me?
AITEN, dër ment të kam, s'të kam arruar.	AITEN, I am thinking of you, I haven't forgotten you.
Sheqer e llokume bashkë janë gatuar.	[Like] sugar and *lokum* [Turkish delight] [we are] bound together.[4]

Now that all married women had sung once, the first unmarried woman sang, a distant cousin of Aiten's who was also her close girlfriend. The song that she sang is appropriate to either side of the wedding, and was also sung at the gathering on the groom's side discussed earlier (*Që naj mali*). In its final line she once again inserted Ruzhdi's name.

The remaining singers were teenage girls: Aiten's sisters, cousins, and girlfriends. Both their choices of songs and their performances provide a glimpse of some of the challenges and pitfalls of learning to sing the Prespa repertoire. For the most part the girls chose fast-paced songs that are easy to sing, and ones with more lighthearted themes, helping to diffuse somewhat the melancholy atmosphere that had built up during the past several songs. The younger sister of the previous singer, for example, sang a humorous song more often sung by men:

Më martoi nëneja që në vegjeli . . .	My mother married me off when I was still young . . .
Asaman aman, asaman o-i.	(O poor me)
dhe më dha një burrë, bënet axhami . . .	and gave me a husband who acts as if he's completely naive . . .

Unë vete në magje, ay më vjen pas . . .	When I go to the kneading trough he tags along after me . . .
dhe më thotë: Nënkoa, bë më një kullaç . . .	and says to me: "Mama, make me a loaf of bread" . . .
Unë s'jam jot ëmë, moj qafë më paç . . .	"I'm not your mother, I swear to you . . .
po jam jote shoqja, me shokë mos dalç . . .	I'm your wife, and may you always be ashamed to show your face in front of your friends!" . . .

For young Presparë, one of the hardest aspects of the singing to master is the ability to sustain the first solo line once the second soloist has entered. This is particularly difficult because the second line is usually higher in pitch than the first and has more of a contour, while the first line may proceed on one or two pitches. In my experience, many young singers initially hear the "melody" of a song as a combination of the two parts, composed of the portions of each line that are higher in pitch. It is this sort of "melody" that another of the bride's cousins performed on this occasion, with the result that the two soloists concluded each verse in unison (ex. 3.3):

EXAMPLE 3.3. *O borsilok,* as Sung by Two Young Girls

O borsilok i dëndur,	O dense basil,
mos u bëj i dëndur,	don't make yourself so dense,
se vijnë dasmoret,	because the groom's party is coming,
do vijnë të marrin . . .	they are coming to take [the bride] . . .

In a proper performance, the first soloist would reiterate the pitch of the choral drone once the second voice enters. As I heard one woman comment of another such performance, *Edhe këndon edhe pret:* "She is both 'singing' and 'accompanying.'"

As young singers, girls often do not have a large enough repertoire to choose songs that are appropriate to the occasion. One of Aiten's girlfriends, for example, chose to sing a song customarily addressed to the groom at important ritual moments. In this instance, since the singer did not know Ruzhdi's family, she inserted into the text whichever kinship terms came to mind, including the word for "sisters," even though Ruzhdi has none. Such an oversight would not have been made by an adult singer:

RUZHDI beu nëpër limoj . . .	RUZHDI *bey* under a lemon tree . . .
moj nëpër limoj.	(under a lemon tree)
ç'e zu gjumi, ç'e qëlloi . . .	Sleep by chance overtook him . . .
Vai BABAI, NËNEJA ç'e zgjoi . . .	His FATHER AND MOTHER went to wake him . . .
Vanë XHAXHALLARË, E MOTRA ç'e zgjoi . . .	His UNCLES AND SISTERS went to wake him . . .
Ngreu O bir të të martoj . . .	"Wake up, child, so I can marry you off . . .
me $\left\{ \begin{array}{l} \text{një nuse} \\ \text{AITENNË} \end{array} \right\}$ të të gëzoj . . .	and make you happy with a bride!" [sung with Aiten's name on the repeat]

At age fourteen, this singer was the youngest to perform that evening. Once the guests had gone, however, several relatives who were even younger sat up recording songs onto the tape for Aiten and Ruzhdi. A male cousin sang a wedding song, a Serbian popular song, and then a men's heroic song, accompanied tentatively by an older woman who clearly did not know the words. The older two of Aiten's sisters sang two wedding songs and then a Macedonian village song that had been popularized through the radio. Youngest of all were Aiten's eight-year-old sister and five-year-old cousin, who each sang a polyphonic song quite competently, accompanied by older relatives. All in all, the recording is witness both to the extent of polyphonic singing among children during this period, and the eclectic listening and performance tastes of Prespa singers, especially when singing outside a ceremonial context.

Women's and Men's Singing

When Presparë get together to socialize, it is most often in groups that are segregated by gender. When such a gathering includes singing, then that singing generally takes place among groups of all males or all females. Indeed, Tosk polyphony would seem to be premised upon gender segregation, since songs are structured around three vocal lines that move within the same range of pitches, and hence favor singers whose voices have roughly the same tessitura.

Presparë regard women and men as having contrasting natures, and they expect the particular character of the *muabet* that they cultivate through their singing to be somewhat different. It follows that the singing styles of men and women, as embodiments of their contrasting sorts of *muabet*, are also expected to differ. Furthermore, men and women are assigned contrasting roles within family and community life. They are thus expected to play contrasting roles as singers in community events, particularly during ritual occasions, and to address different sorts of subject matter in their songs. On the basis of both subject matter and performance style, then, Presparë divide their song repertoire into "women's songs" (*këngë të grave*) and "men's songs" (*këngë të burrave*). These designations indicate not only different repertoires, but also different styles of performance, in that the same song will be rendered somewhat differently by women and men.

Women's Singing

Like most southeast European villagers, Prespa men and women virtually always sing in their chest register, although with somewhat different vocal placement. Women are generally said to sing in a "thin voice" (*zë të ollë*). Those who fit this description most often arch their palate and lower the velum while singing, producing a somewhat nasal tone.

They also pitch their songs in a relatively high tessitura, so that the drone falls between middle c and e. Not all women, however, sing in this way. Some sing much lower, so that the drone is pitched as low as F or G. Others sing at an extremely high pitch level, around f or g, and very occasionally in falsetto. Either extreme is regarded somewhat negatively by other women. Very high-pitched singing in particular is thought of as shrill, and may be described as *si pizgë:* like the piercing, high-pitched shawms that Rom musicians used to play for village weddings.

The nasal quality of much of the women's singing has the effect of muting the resonance of their voices. At present-day social occasions, their relatively subdued singing often contrasts strikingly with their more boisterous and animated conversational style. Neighboring Slavic women in rural areas have traditionally sung in a highly resonant style that has enabled their songs to carry long distances across the fields during work periods or across the village square for public dancing. But for Prespa women, singing has been largely an indoor activity associated with intimate social gatherings. Their characteristic vocal quality is thus appropriate to the setting within which their singing takes place. In rare cases where a Prespa woman does sing in a more resonant manner similar to that of Macedonian women, her vocal quality may also be regarded negatively. *Si kaurkë këndon* might be the comment: "She sings like a *kaur*," a derogatory Ottoman word for a non-Muslim. It therefore seems that the muted quality of Prespa women's singing is apprehended to some degree as an ethnic marker.[5]

Within their repertoire, women distinguish between two main categories of songs according to the manner in which they are performed. At any type of social gathering, those women present might decide to perform a sequence of *këngë pe më mbythë* (lit. "songs sung on one's behind"), songs that are sung while seated; or they might perform *këngë pe më këmbë* (lit. "songs sung on foot"), songs that are also danced. For the latter, women grasp hands at waist height and form a line that will move counterclockwise. The woman who is to "sing" the song stands at the head of the line holding a small kerchief (*shami*) in her right hand, while the woman who will accompany her stands to her left, holding her hand at shoulder height. All others in the line will drone as they dance. As the singer begins the first line of the song, she sways slowly back and forth, not always in time to the singing. Then, after a few syllables, she begins a six-measure sequence of steps which the others in the line perform with her (ex. 3.4; CD #8). Most dance songs have phrases of

EXAMPLE 3.4. Women's Song with Dancing: *Duallë dy spai në lëmë*

TABLE 3 Footwork for Dance Song

Measure of Song	Measure of Dance	Footwork
1	1	Facing diagonally to right, dancers step to right with right foot.
2	2	Dancers step to right with left foot.
3	3	Facing into center of semicircle, dancers step to right with right foot.
4	4	Dancers close left foot to right.
5	5	Still facing into center, dancers step to left with left foot.
6	6	Dancers close right foot to left.
7	1	Facing diagonally to right, dancers step to right with right foot.
8	2	Dancers step to right with left foot.
1	3	Facing into center of semicircle, dancers step to right with right foot. . . .

four or eight measures, and so their structure does not coincide with that of the accompanying dance step (see table 3). If the singer initiates a pause between verses, she also momentarily stops the dance. She then resumes both the song and the dance step, and the other women follow:

Duallë dy spai në lëmë . . .	Two *sipahi*s [Ottoman over-lords] have come out onto the threshing floor . . .
nën' moj nën', bij' moj bij'.	(O mother, O daughter)
E kërkojnë çupën tonë . . .	They are asking for our young girl . . .
Çupa jonë s'është bërë . . .	Our girl isn't ready yet . . .
duart në brumë s'i ka vënë . . .	She hasn't yet put her fingers into the bread dough . . .
pe, gjilpërë me dorë s'ka zënë . . .	she hasn't yet taken a needle and thread in hand . . .
	(wedding in Krani, 1980)

Both gatherings described thus far featured songs sung while seated. The two types of songs are not mixed. It would be inappropriate, for example, to sing a *këngë pe më këmbë* while seated, or to try to dance to a *këngë pe më mbythë*. Songs sung only at ritual moments during a wedding fall outside this form of categorization. For their performance the singers might be either seated or standing, but such songs are never danced.

Women also distinguish between two main styles of song perfor-mance that cut across the categories just discussed. A smaller number of songs are performed *lartër*, a word that means both "loud" and "high-pitched." Prespare do not consider the two qualities to be separable: as they see it, when one sings at a higher pitch level one naturally sings more loudly. For younger women, whose voices are thought of as being in their prime, performing a song *lartër* means pitching the drone some-where above middle c. *Lartër* songs are generally sung more rapidly, with moderate ornamentation. Most of the songs characterized in this way are dance or ritual songs: songs sung in contexts where there is a need for the singer to project her voice more (as in ex. 3.4; CD #8). But there are also a few "sitting" songs that are characteristically sung at a brisk tempo (as, for example, ex. 2.2; CD #3).

Most women's performances are in a style referred to as *shtruar*, or "drawn-out." *Shtruar* is an overriding aesthetic concept in Prespa singing. However else one sings, one should sing *shtruar*: taking one's time, not straining one's voice, and giving weight to each syllable of the text so that it is clearly understood. Prespare sometimes speak of *këngë tona të shtruara* ("our *shtruar* songs") when they contrast their repertoire with that of other southern Albanian areas. In its narrower meaning, *shtruar* can refer to a specific style of women's singing in which a song is performed more softly, perhaps at a lower pitch level, and at a leisurely tempo that allows the melody line to be "beautified" or "decorated" (*zbukuruar*) with ornamentation.

When accomplished singers have spoken with me about singing, they have been very detailed in their descriptions of how to sing *shtruar*. First they have emphasized that each syllable needs to be drawn out so that it is heard fully before the next syllable follows it. One woman included as part of this process "bringing out the sound from your chest" rather than your throat, by which she seemed to mean supporting the voice with the diaphragm. A singer who draws out the vocal line in this manner is said to *e vazhdon zënë* or *e zgjat zënë*: to "continue" or "extend" the "voice/melody line." It is not considered good singing, however, merely to perform the skeletal melody of a song in a drawn-out manner. As part of "extending" the melody line, each soloist is expected to *e dredh zënë*, literally "wind" or "twist" the melody by adding rapid turns or other types of melismatic ornaments. Some women singing the first solo part like to begin a performance with a particularly florid version of the melody line (ex. 3.5; CD #9):

Moj e vogla në lëmë . . .	O small one on the threshing floor . . .
moj e vogëla.	(O small one)
sh'të ndritin tynë ato llërë . . .	my, how your forearms are glistening . . .
Do t'i mbash t'i bësh gjëlpërë . . .	You must ask them to hold a needle . . .
që ta qepç pajën e tërë . . .	so that you can sew a complete dowry . . .
që ta mbash me NN benë . . .	for you to keep for NN *bey* . . .
që ta mbash, të trashëgoesh . . .	to keep, to live a long and happy life . . .

(New Year's Eve gathering in Toronto, 1985)

More often, however, it is the second soloist who *dredh* her line more extensively, as was the case with Aiten's cousin's performances above, while the first part is performed more simply (ex. 3.1; CD #6).[6]

There are two additional techniques that the singer of the second solo part may employ to "extend" her melody line. The first involves a descent to the drone pitch by means of a slight portamento. The second is the performance of a rapid glottal ornament, in which the singer

EXAMPLE 3.5. First Soloist's Ornamentation of Melody Line: *Moj e vogla në lëmë*

97

momentarily produces a note in falsetto or head register (notated as $_x^♭$) just before she sings the final syllable of a line. More rarely, such ornaments may be performed elsewhere in the melody line by either soloist (both techniques are illustrated in ex. 3.5).[7]

As in all Prespa singing, women generally embellish the basic text of a song in various ways: by interrupting words, repeating syllables, or inserting non-lexical words and syllables. For some women's songs, particularly ones performed in *lartër* style, all singers learn and perform these embellishments in a highly consistent manner. Such is the case with one of the most popular wedding songs, *Në divan të lartër,* sung by close relatives of the groom when they take the bride. The text of the first verse with refrain, as it might be recited, is as follows:

Në divan të lartër ke dalë e më rri . . .	On the high balcony you have come out to sit for me . . .
vajzë e parritur pa vënë stoli.	(O girl not yet grown up, with your wedding finery not yet put on.)

It is sung, however, in the follow manner (ex. 3.6; CD #10; all non-lexical verbal interpolations have been rendered in italics):

I Në divan të la=*moj* të lartër*ë* ke dal' e më=
II   ke dal' e më-*ja*-rri

I më rri (*e moj*) *vajzë e pa=*   *parriturë pa vënë sto=*
II   *vajzë e pa-ja-rri=*   pa vënë sto-*ja*-li.

In the verse, the first soloist interrupts the word *lartër(ë)* ("high") and then reiterates it after interpolating the word *moj.* Likewise, in the chorus, she interrupts the word *parritur* ("not yet grown") and then reiterates it. She also adds a final *ë* to both words so as to create an extra syllable. On the final word of her line, the second soloist adds the syllable *ja* as she descends to the drone note. This playful manipulation of the text, together with the rhythmic interest that the interpolation of extra syllables creates, are particularly appealing features of such songs.

In most *shtruar* songs, textual embellishment is expected but not absolutely set. Generally there are standard places in the text where an exclamatory word may be inserted, but the specific choice of a word is up to the soloists. Women most commonly use words such as *ajde* (or *ajdo*), *aman, mori,* and *moj* in their performances. All of these are words that are also commonly used in conversation, each with a somewhat

EXAMPLE 3.6. Women's Song in *lartër* Style: *Në divan të lartër*

distinctive meaning. *Ajde* may be used to mean "come on" or "come along," although its meaning is not always so specific. *Mori* and its contraction *moj* indicate direct address to a female, whereas *more* (not used in women's songs) indicates direct address to a male. *Aman* signals an experiencing of somewhat heightened emotion. All serve as intensifiers, in that they imply a mild emotional reaction and degree of engagement on the part of the speaker to what is being discussed. When two women are sharing bits of local news, for example, one might respond to the other by exclaiming: "*Aman mori* Fatime! Did she really tell you that?!"

In singing, these words may be inserted interchangeably into a text, thus losing even the minimal specificity of meaning that they have in speech. They therefore have no direct bearing on the meaning of the text. By inserting them into the song's text, a woman signals her interest in the event taking place and her emotional involvement in her performance. Some songs, both *lartër* and *shtruar*, have refrains consisting entirely of such words. The refrain *edhe moj, ajde dhe moj* ("and *moj, ajde* and *moj*") is particularly common. In such instances the words serve essentially as vocables that carry no semantic meaning.

Regardless of the style in which a song is performed, an essential feature of women's singing is that it is consistently metric. A woman may "extend" her melody line through various types of ornamentation, and may insert exclamations, interruptions, and repetitions throughout the song's text. All such "decoration" of the song, however, should be performed within the framework of a clearly articulated pulse. The metric quality of women's singing will prove to be particularly significant when women's and men's performances are compared.

Men's Singing

Prespa men are stereotypically said to sing in a "thick voice" (*zë të trashë*), in contrast to the "thin" voice of women. Men who are described as having such a voice generally sing with a greater tensing of the muscles in the throat than is the case for women, producing a tone that is particularly rich in upper partials. Unlike women singers, most men do not lower their velum as they sing, so that their vocal quality is not nasal.[8] The more resonant manner of singing that results is also described by singers as *plot:* "full." In most respects, this type of vocal production is similar to that of Christian men and women in most south Slavic communities.

Early on in my contacts with Presparë, a young man from a Kolonjarë family told me a story about helping to tear down his uncle's old stone house in the village. He and his cousin found that an empty earthenware pot (*saksi*) had been built into each of the four walls of the *odë*, or reception room, so that the mouth of each pot faced into the room. When his cousin teased his mother that they had been hiding gold in the pots, she explained that the pots were meant to make the room more resonant for the men's singing. The young man added that he had been in one old house whose *odë* had been especially resonant, and he suspected that it too had such pots built into the walls. I was never able to confirm this detail of local house construction in my subsequent conversations with non-Kolonjarë. Nevertheless, one of the aspects of men's singing that was most striking to me when I first attended weddings in Prespa was the pulsating sound that resulted when the twenty or more men who were gathered in an *odë* droned for the two soloists.

Because the men's repertoire has a greater range of themes than does the women's, Prespa men distinguish between different types of songs according to their subject matter. The two principal types they speak of are "love" songs (*këngë dashurie*) and "heroic" or "historical" songs (*këngë trimërie* or *këngë istoriake*). Men also sing a few songs about the beauty of the countryside, about the experience of working abroad (*këngë të kurbetit*), and about the foibles of relations between the sexes.

Like women, men also recognize distinct styles of songs within their repertoire. They even use some of the same terminology to describe these styles, although the terms have different connotations for men than for women. Men consistently refer to one group of songs as being *këngë të shtruara*: songs sung in a *shtruar* manner. As with the women's repertoire, *shtruar* for them refers to a softer, slower, more drawn-out way of singing. Unlike women's *shtruar* songs, however, the men's songs that are specifically designated as *shtruar* are sung with very little ornamentation. Generally they have a relatively small ambitus, extending no more than a fifth or sixth above the drone note. Although they may be considered to be metric, a singer customarily relaxes the pulse of such a song in performance (ex. 3.7; CD #11; also ex. 2.1; CD #2).

The most esteemed songs in the men's repertoire are those known as *këngë të lartëra*. Here, as with women's singing, *lartër* may be translated as "sung in a loud/high voice," but the style of execution of these songs is unlike that of any in the women's repertoire. Men's *këngë të lartëra* are among the only nonmetric songs in the Prespa repertoire. They are generally sung to the same *melodi,* characterized by an ambitus that extends an octave or more above the drone pitch, and the melody may be varied considerably from verse to verse. Singers most often pitch these songs with the drone on F# or G so that the highest notes fall at the very top of their range, and they sing them at full volume (ex. 3.8; CD #12).

Most *këngë të shtruara*, like that in ex. 3.7, are about love or events of everyday life:

EXAMPLE 3.7. Men's *shtruar* Song: *Atje lartër ne portë e madhe*

EXAMPLE 3.8. Men's *lartër* Song: *Vjeshtë e tretë më të dalë*

Ajte lartër ne port'e madhe,	Up there at the great gate,
ryn' e dalin nja dy sarkadhe.	two deer [young girls] go in and out.
Njëra më e vogël, tjetra më e madhe . . .	The one smaller, the other larger . . .
më ta marrça myzeqaren.	(May I take the one from Myzeqe.)
[Këmka të shkurtra si pe kunadhe . . .]	[With short legs like a marten's . . .]
Do ta marr ogiç manare . . .	I'll take her as my tame lamb . . .
Do ta gjezdis stane mi stane . . .	I'll lead her from dairy to dairy . . .
Do ta yshqej me mish me bukëvale . . .	I'll feed her meat and bukëvale . . .⁹

(Leibman 1974, B2; recorded in Krani, 1972)

The great majority of *këngë të lartëra*, however, recount the exploits of men who fought for Albanian independence, whether against the Ottoman regime at the turn of the century, Greek forces in the Balkan Wars, or Nazi occupation in World War II. The song in ex. 3.8, for example, describes a battle against Greek units that took place in 1916 (see Panajoti 1982:136):

Vjeshtë e tretë më të dalë	The third month of autumn was just ending
ç'u fillua Komiteti.	when the guerrilla movement began.
Komiteti mori mali	The guerrillas took to the mountains,
Panarit më luftë ranë	Panarit [a town in southern Albania] fell in battle,
u vranë dy kapetanë	and two captains were killed:
Nebi Kuçi me Rizanë.	Nebi Kuçi and Riza [Panariti].
Sali beut aber ja dhanë	The news was brought to Sali *bey*
[për Nebinë e Rizanë.]	[about Nebi and Riza.]
Sali beu tha nja dy fjalë:	Sali *bey* said a few words:
Mos, burra, qani si gratë!	Men, don't cry like women!
Mengoni nesër me natë!	By tomorrow night you must be gone!

(Leibman 1974, B6; recorded in Krani, 1972)

Several *këngë të lartëra* also originated as literary poems. A few popular heroic songs derive from poems by the patriot Sali Butka, the "Sali *bey*" mentioned in the preceding song (ibid.: 114, 127–28). Another song, filled with idealized images of the Albanian countryside, incorporates lines from a poem by Naim Frashëri, the foremost Albanian poet of the nineteenth century: [10]

Ku më zien capi me zile	Where the goat bleats with its bell,
atje fryn veri me erë	that is where the north wind blows.
për atje qan zemra ime	For there my heart weeps,
që të rri një copë erë	that I might rest for a moment's time
të më fryn veri me erë.	that the north wind might blow on me.
Malet e Shqipërisë	The mountains of Albania,
kur mbushin me tufë lule	when they are covered with bouquets of flowers,
i ka dhënë i madhi Zot	the great Lord has given them
për qejfin të njerëzisë.	for the pleasure of mankind.
Edhe qyqja kur këndonte,	And the cuckoo when she sang,
dru me dru vinte, qëndronte,	going and alighting on each tree:
lum e lum ajo botë	how lucky was this world
zënë e saj kur e dëgjonte.	when it heard her voice.
	(Wedding in Krani, 1980)

It is in the performance of *këngë të lartëra* that both the first and second soloist can most fully demonstrate their proficiency as singers. Both are expected to *dredh* their melody line by ornamenting it with turns and other rapid running ornaments. The second soloist in particular is also expected to "extend" (*zgjat*) his vocal line with an exaggerated portamento (ex. 3.8; CD #12), or with a series of turns on one of the upper notes of his melody. Each of these techniques delays his descent to the drone pitch, injecting moments of suspense into the performance. Because of extensive ornamentation, either soloist may sustain individual syllables to such an extent that any sense of a steady rhythmic basis is distorted.[11]

A few highly regarded singers of *këngë të lartëra* interject sustained falsetto pitches at points during their performance. They might also move between chest and head registers, either by yodelling or by inserting rapid glottal ornaments into their melismas. Two of these techniques may be heard in a performance by two elderly brothers from the village of Arvati (CD #13). As shown in ex. 3.9, the second soloist often yodels as his melody line descends to the drone note, while the first soloist lapses into falsetto (notated as ♩) toward the end of some verses. These various techniques are referred to as *me të qarë*, "with crying," and are said to be an imitation of women's funeral lamenting. They are considered both to "decorate" (*zbukurojnë*) a song and to make it *mallengjyer*, that is, expressive of a sense of deeply felt longing. As one man described this performance, "It's as if he is crying the song." The text of this song is particularly evocative and melancholy:

Rëzonet bilbili që ngaj mali	The nightingale descends from the mountain
o bilbil	(O nightingale)
pi ujë në stenë . . .	to drink water at the fence . . .
As ja merr një erë, nja dy erë, o bilbil, për ashik e mi.	(Why don't you sing once, twice, O nightingale, to fill me with longing.)
Ty sh'të zur' dëborë e marsit, ta mbuloi folenë . . .	The snows of March overcame you and they buried your nest . . .
Por ca vezë që pate tinë të mbetnë panxirrë . . .	Some of the eggs that you had remained unrescued . . .
Pas këtaj na vjen bejari, pa na nxirr të tjerë . . .	But summer will come once again and you will give birth to new ones . . .

Although the "singer" most often lapses into falsetto on the word *bilbil* ("nightingale"), I was assured that this technique was not being used to imitate a birdcall, but rather to evoke a sense of longing similar to that to which the song's text alludes.[12]

Like women, men also interpolate exclamatory words into the texts of their songs. A few men's songs contain a variety of embellishments that are a set part of the text. One is a *këngë të shtruar* that chronicles the demise of a woman's unpopular husband. As recited, the song begins as follows:

EXAMPLE 3.9. Men's Singing "With Crying": Second Verse of *Rëzonet bilbili*

Moj syzezë, syzezë e vogël	O small, black-eyed one,
burrën tënd ta kanë plagosur,	they have wounded your husband,
ta kanë plagosur, goditur në ballën.	they have wounded him, struck him in the forehead.
Mirë ja bënë se nuk shkonte me mejalën . . .	They did the right thing, for he didn't get along with the neighbors [his lineage group].

It is sung, however, in the following manner (ex. 3.10; CD #14):

> // *ajde* moj syzez' *edhe moj* syzez' *edhe moj* e=o e vogëlë //
> // *ajde* burrën tënd *o moj* ta kanë *edhe moj* pla=o plagosurë //
> // *ajde* ta kanë plagosur *moj* goditur *edhe moj* në=o në ballënë //
> // *ajde* mirë ja bënë *o moj* se nuk shkonte *dhe moj* me=o mejalënë// . . .
>
> (Wedding in Krani, 1972)

As with similar women's songs, one of the aspects of this song that particularly appeals to performers is the complicated way in which the text is declaimed.

In most men's songs, as with the women's repertoire, there are standard places where singers may insert exclamatory words of their choice. For songs that are sung in *shtruar* style, men tend to choose the same words that women use: *ajde, aman, moj,* or *mor(e)*. In *këngë të lartëra,* however, they also draw upon a range of exclamations that are not used in women's singing. For the song cited in ex. 3.8, for example, there are customary places at the beginning of certain lines where each soloist may add exclamations (indicated below with parentheses):

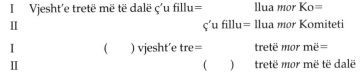

In the performance cited, the first soloist generally sang *aman aman o-i,* followed by *mor* (sung to initiate the text), while the second sang simply *e* or *o lele*. But a survey of a number of performances of this type of song yielded a great variety of interpolations—by the first soloist: *o o-i, o-i o-i, aman o-i, aman aman o-i, aman o-i o-i, aman aman aman aman (aman aman), ajde o-i (o-i), ajde ajdo, o bilbil bilbil, o bir (o bir) o-i, ajde bir aj o-i, o lele lele le-i, o lele lele lele lele, o lele o bir, o lele lele lele o bir o mos qani,*

orig. pitch

EXAMPLE 3.10. Men's Song with Verbal Interpolations: *Moj syzezë e vogël*

o lele lele le aman; by the second soloist: *o o-i, e, o lele, o-bo-bo, aman (aman)(aman), o bilbil.* More rarely, a singer might tack such exclamations onto the end of a line of text or insert them into the middle of a line. In one performance, for example, the second soloist sang the lines:

Dëllëndyshe ju që shkoni,	O swallow, as you pass by,
do t'ju jap një porosi . . .	I will ask a favor of you . . .

as:

Dëllëndyshe ju që shkoni
do t'ju jap *bo-bo o-i o-i o-i o-bo-bo* një porosi . . .

(Dinner in Toronto, 1985)

As with the elaborate melodic ornamentation that characterizes this style of song, such extensive textual interpolation pulls the song out of any steady rhythm.

Presparë use virtually all these sounds in speech with specific meanings. The words *lele* and *aman,* when reiterated, imply that one is undergoing something difficult or painful, and that one is suffering. *O-i* and *o-bo-bo* are intensifiers used to express a very strong reaction to something, whether positive or negative. Thus one might hear, on the one hand:

O-i!
O-bo-bo! } What [tragedy] has befallen us?!

but, on the other:

O-i!
O-bo-bo! } What a beautiful girl!

In comparison with *aman* (said only once) or *more/mori,* these two sounds indicate far more intense emotion. *O bilbil,* the one exclamation used only in singing, means "O nightingale!" *O bir* means literally "O my son!" and *mos qani,* "don't cry!" Together with the exclamation *o-i,* which is used in women's funeral lamenting, these phrases suggest that the exclamations in *këngë të lartëra* may have originated as commentary on the tragic events that these songs often recount, although this is not how present-day singers interpret them.[13]

Men have different associations with songs that they designate as *shtruar* and *lartër.* One is generational. Ideally, any man who sings in *lartër* style should have a strong and flexible voice. Several singers alluded to a need for such songs to be sung *me fuqi* ("with strength/ power"):

> Not every man can sing songs with a *lartër* melody. A man must have more voice. He must have a "stronger" [*më i fuqishëm*] tone, he must have more *fuqi*. And he must have a clear voice, so that he can lift his voice high. (Interview in Toronto, 1986)

Such phraseology suggests that the resonant, "thick" vocal quality associated with the best of the younger male singers is apprehended implicitly as indicative of the strength and virility of men in their prime of life, thus rendering it particularly suitable for the more rousing heroic songs of the Prespa repertoire.[14]

As a man ages he may continue to sing *këngë të lartëra*, but his voice gradually loses much of the resonance and physical strength associated with that repertoire. For this reason, many singers who mastered this style when young eventually switch to *këngë të shtruara* once their voices are past their prime. *Këngë të shtruara* are therefore associated with the older generation of men, just as *këngë të lartëra* are associated with younger adults.[15] *Këngë të shtruara* may also be chosen by men of any age who are less experienced or accomplished singers.

A second association is geographic. Several of the *këngë të shtruara* are commonly referred to as *këngë myzeqare*, that is, as having originated in the region of Myzeqe in Albania. Indeed, at least two *shtruar* songs, including that in ex. 3.7, mention this area. *Këngë të lartëra*, in contrast, are associated with the Korçë region lying just to the west of Prespa.[16] In my experience, *këngë të lartëra* are sung far more commonly in the lower villages of Prespa, particularly Krani and Arvati. It is singers from these villages that speak of having learned songs such as that in ex. 3.8 "from the elders" (*pe pleqve*), although they also know radio versions of some of the same songs. Among families from the upper villages, as well as among Kolonjarë, men speak of having learned *këngë të lartëra* more recently from the radio. This distribution of types of songs is consistent with the claims made by families in the lower villages that they formerly maintained particularly close ties with communities in the Korçë region.

A third type of men's song is sung boisterously in a more rapid, strictly metric style with little ornamentation. Most such songs are ebullient love songs or humorous comments on male-female relations (ex. 3.11; CD #15):

EXAMPLE 3.11. Men's Rapid, Metric Song: *Kjo shtëpi e plakës*

Kjo shtëpi e plakës thurur me purteka . . .

Ngre, moj çup' [bij'] e nënës, se na zuri drekë!

Të na bësh lakrori me nja dyzet petë . . .

se na vjen një djalë, ajde vetë i tretë . . .

This old lady's house made of planks and mud . . .

(Get up, mother's daughter, for lunchtime has caught up with us!)

Make us a cabbage pie with forty leaves of dough . . .

because a young man is coming, accompanied by three others . . .

ajde me daulle, ajde me   with drums and with
gërnetë . . .   clarinets . . .

(Krani, 1980)

Singers have no specific designation for songs in this style, apparently because many were learned in recent years from Albanian radio. They seem to have replaced the older dance songs, also rapid and metric, that once ended long evenings of men's social singing.

Each of these three types of songs—*këngë të shtruara, këngë të lartëra,* and rapid, metric songs—represents a distinctive style of performance in terms of volume, tempo, degree of metricity, and extent and type of ornamentation. When, in my interviewing, men have cited specific songs in their repertoire as examples of each style, they have chosen songs that would only be sung in that style. In essence, these are songs that stand out within the men's repertoire for their distinctive style of performance.

A great many men's songs, however, were never cited by singers as falling into any of these three categories. These remaining songs are the ones that I found sung most widely in the Prespa district by both Sunni and Bektashi families, and may possibly be the oldest songs in the men's repertoire. All are essentially metric, and many may be classified as based upon the same *melodi*s that characterize much of the women's repertoire. They include love songs, heroic songs, songs about *gurbet* and about daily life, and ritual songs sung at weddings by both men and women (*këngë dasme*). Less accomplished male singers sing such songs in a fairly uniform manner, not unlike much women's singing: somewhat slowly, in a steady meter, at medium volume, and with little ornamentation. More experienced singers, however, have a few options available to them for a more elaborate or rousing performance. One option, favored by older singers but not limited to them, is to perform a song in a *shtruar* manner, that is, still more slowly and with melismatic ornamentation. Such performances are similar to those of the best women singers, although the men might sing at an even slower tempo, and their ornamentation might be so extensive that the meter is relaxed.

A second stylistic option that a singer might choose, particularly for heroic songs, is to incorporate many of the expressive techniques of *këngë të lartëra*. Such performances are generally louder and slower than those that could be called *shtruar,* and may feature the full range of ornamental techniques characteristic of men's singing: portamento, extensive melismas, and frequent interjection of exclamations, as well as perhaps yodeling and lapses into falsetto. As with *këngë të lartëra,* when a man per-

113

EXAMPLE 3.12. Women's *shtruar* Rendition: *Po kjo anë e lumit*

EXAMPLE 3.13. Men's *lartër* Rendition: *Në plepat Bilishtit*

forms a metric song in this way he may prolong individual syllables through his ornamentation to such an extent that a clear sense of the meter is undermined. In Examples 3.12 and 3.13, a women's *shtruar* rendition of a song (3.12; CD #16) is compared with a men's song with the same *melodi* as sung in *lartër* style (3.13; this performance may be heard on Vuylsteke 1981, A1). A third option for men, often chosen for heroic or ritual songs, is a more rapid, boisterous style of singing.

When women's and men's singing are compared, it may be noted

EXAMPLE 3.14. Women's (a) and Men's (b) Performances of *Nëpër limoj*

that men's singing is far more varied, and that men have more expressive options available to them. They may sing in the more subdued manner characteristic of women's singing, or they may sing at the top of their lungs. They may sing rapidly in a strict meter, or much more slowly, with the meter relaxed. As will be detailed in subsequent chapters, their choices as to performance style may be shaped by considerations that arise in the course of a singing occasion.

Three interrelated features distinguish the most highly regarded men's performances from those of women. First is more extensive textual embellishment, including not only the interpolation of exclamatory words, but also more frequent interruption of words and reiteration of syllables. Second is a more relaxed concept of meter. Many of the most celebrated Prespa men's songs are nonmetric. Even for metric songs, however, singers often draw out certain syllables through various types of melodic ornamentation. They may also declaim phrases of the text in an almost conversational manner, so that individual syllables are in fact shortened. A sort of rhythmic elasticity is thus a prominent feature of men's singing, one that gives it an especially spontaneous and dramatic quality. Lastly, men singers may vary the melodic line more extensively than women, often "lifting" the melody (*e ngren zënë*) by extending its range upward to an octave or more above the drone note. All three of these features are illustrated by a men's performance of the ritual song *Nëpër limoj* (b) juxtaposed in ex. 3.14 with a women's performance (a).

"Additions" to Songs

When any individual performs a song, he or she may choose between a variety of stylistic options and types of ornamentation. In addition, a singer may personalize a performance by concluding it with one or more short, rhymed verses. Most such verses are sung to a single *melodi* performed in a triple meter, and may be lightly or extensively ornamented as the singer desires.

In terms of the sentiments that they express, these verses are of two types. First are ones of a complimentary nature: verses that praise the host family's hospitality or refer to the event being celebrated. At a wedding, for example, the following verses might be sung (ex. 3.15; CD #17):

EXAMPLE 3.15. Addition to Song: *Muabet i shtruar*

Muabet i shtruar:	A long, elaborate *muabet:*
gazi, trashëguar!	Be happy and wish the couple well!
[Zotërinjve t'ja kemi ua]	[May we now be obligated to our hosts]

| kujt më djema, kujt më çupa! | to return the favor with [the weddings of] our sons and daughters! |

Second are verses that are meant to tease someone else in the room. If a certain person has not yet sung at a social occasion, for example, another singer might end his song with a verse addressed to him:

| O ZARIF, t'u bëfsha ferrë! | O ZARIF, may you be pricked by a thorn! |
| As ja merr këngës një erë! | You haven't taken up a song even once! |

Most of the time singers choose verses that, like songs, are widely known. In the past, however, it was common for such verses to be extemporized, in the sense that new combinations were created out of commonly used verbal formulas.

Verses of the complimentary sort are sung frequently by both women and men. Those meant to tease, however, are associated more with men's singing. At the end of an evening of singing, pairs of soloists often exchange such verses back and forth as a sort of contest. Even when only preexistent texts are drawn on, it is still a challenge for singers to come up with a suitable retort for a particular verbal jab.

There is no single word that community members use to encompass such verses. Most commonly singers merely say that they "add" (*shtojnë*) to the song. Several individuals, however, used the word *bejte* for teasing verses, a word that is more widely known in Albania. In their form, as well as in the spirit of competition that propels their performance at men's gatherings, *bejte* resemble types of extemporized spoken or sung verses found in many parts of southeast Europe and the Mediterranean.[17]

One point on which singers that I spoke with agreed is that such verses are not *këngë* ("songs"). As one man explained, they must always follow a song. If, for example, a man wishes to initiate a string of *bejte*, he must first sing a song. It is the song that is the obligatory part of his performance, after which the *bejte* are purely optional.

F O U R

The "Order" Of Weddings

Fshat dhe zanat, shtëpi dhe orëndi. Just as every house has its furnishings, so every village has its customs. (Prespa saying)

THE BRIDE IS ADORNED

In the summer of 1986, Memet, a young Prespar living in a community outside Chicago, married Feime, a young Presparkë from Toronto. Feime had been widely viewed as one of the most desirable young women in the community and had been sought by two other families before Memet's had asked for her hand. Those first two times, her parents had turned down the inquiring family without even approaching her about the matter. Then Memet saw her at a gathering at her home, and soon his parents and other relatives had contacted hers. "You know how Albanians are," she explained to me several years later, "they act fast!" Her parents liked Memet and proposed that Feime marry him; but they let her have the final say, and she agreed. The two did not know each other at all. Shortly thereafter, they "exchanged *nishanë*" (tokens of their commitment to each other), and later had an engagement celebration. Feime was seventeen at the time, Memet eighteen. During the next two years they went out together a few times, with Feime's younger brother acting as a chaperone. They then went with their families to the *xhami*, or mosque, where they signed an Islamic wedding contract. A few months later, their wedding was held.

During the first weekend of the wedding period, male emissaries from Memet's family, known as the *sinitorë*, drove to Toronto with Feime's bridal outfit and other gifts for her. There they were served a festive meal at Feime's home and sang with men of her family for most of the afternoon, returning to Illinois the next day. On Monday evening Feime's female relatives gathered to put henna on her hair, for which they sang special ritual songs. Then, on Thursday evening, relatives and friends began to visit her home. While the men gathered in the *odë* to converse and sing, the women performed dance songs in the family room. They then examined the various gifts from the groom while Feime took turns modeling some of the new outfits, standing demurely against one wall. On Friday evening a smaller group of visitors gathered in the *odë* to sing. At Memet's home, evenings of singing began even earlier in the week.

My husband and I were taken to Feime's home on Thursday and Friday evenings on the initiative of a family friend. We were also invited to attend the activities at Memet's on Saturday and Sunday through a close relative we had known in Macedonia. With the encouragement of both families, we filmed much of the wedding and then participated in viewing sessions on both sides. It is from this recording, as well as subsequent conversations with many of the participants, that the following description of the gathering held at Feime's on Friday evening, as well as those of events at Memet's on both Saturday (see chapter 5) and Sunday (chapter 8), are drawn.

The Friday gathering at Feime's home was a particularly small affair. In part this was because her family had to pack that night before departing for Illinois the next morning, and so they had encouraged guests to come the previous night. As a result, men and women congregated together in the *odë,* and they exchanged songs back and forth throughout the evening. In their juxtaposition, the distinction between the women's songs, which directly addressed the wedding taking place, and the men's songs, which focused on concerns bearing no relationship to the event, was particularly striking.

Two couples had come from Australia for the wedding and were at Feime's home throughout the evening: her father's older brother (her *xhaxha*) and his wife, and her mother's parents. In the early evening a second cousin and his wife stopped by, together with another Prespa couple from the neighborhood with the husband's parents. Men and women assembled in the *odë* to exchange conversation and best wishes while, once again, Feime modeled outfits that the *sinitorë* had brought the weekend before. After perhaps an hour and a half, this first group of visitors began to depart just as a second arrived at the door.

This second group consisted of three younger couples: a cousin of Feime's with her husband, and a brother and sister from Feime's father's village together with their spouses. When Feime's relatives opened the door, they found the three couples arranged outside the entrance according to gender: men nearer the door, their wives farther away. Once they entered the hallway the men greeted Feime's family members in order of age: first her grandparents and then the remaining younger people. Their wives repeated the same sequence just behind them.

The women greeted Feime's grandmother with a particularly respectful gesture: kissing her hand and then pressing it to their forehead. With her mother and aunt they kissed on the lips, pressed their left cheeks together, and then repeated that sequence twice more. The men greeted Feime's grandfather by kissing his hand, and then shook hands with her father and *xhaxha*. As each two people greeted each other the member of the host family exclaimed, *Mirë se ardhe!* ("Welcome!"), to which the visitor responded, *Mirë se ju gjeta!* ("Well met!") and then *Të trashëgoet!* ("Congratulations on the wedding!").

The guests were then ushered into the *odë* (fig. 4).[1] Feime's grandfather and *xhaxha*, together with an older man from Albania who had arrived earlier, took seats on the couch opposite the doorway. The husband of Feime's cousin, together with another of the younger men, sat on the floor, while the other younger man chose an armchair. After Feime's father had greeted each guest a second time, he seated himself on the floor facing the older men. The women sat in much this same formation at the other end of the room. Feime's grandmother and aunt and the wives of the other two guests sat on another sofa or on chairs set to its side. Both my husband and I initially sat on the floor in order to film, although later I was asked to sit with the other women and to sing. When all were seated, Feime's female relatives brought in cigarettes, beer, and whiskey for the men, which they placed on a coffee table in front of the elder men's sofa. Her mother then seated herself on the floor, facing the women guests, while the cousin sat in a chair. To one side of the women, "at the end of the room" (*në fund të odës*), stood the bride. Feime was wearing a pale lavender dress trimmed with lace and ruffles, the sort of dress that she might wear to other wedding celebrations later in the summer. Her hair was hennaed and coiffed, her face impeccably made up, her nails carefully polished. In her clasped hands she held a white handkerchief (*shamiçkë*) trimmed with small metal sequins. Several large gold coins glistened from chains around her neck, gold earrings sparkled below her ears, and gold bracelets glittered on each wrist. A sequined decoration (*lulkë*) was fastened to her forehead, and long streamers of silver wire (*tel*) hung from her temples. She stood erect and dignified, breathing almost imperceptibly, eyes cast downward. As those around her moved to and fro, dispensing refreshments and greeting guests, she remained motionless.

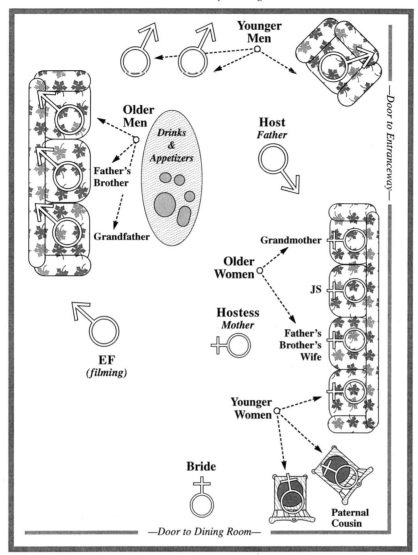

FIGURE 4. The Bride Is Adorned, Toronto, 1986

Once all the guests were seated, Feime's cousin began circulating around the room with a plate of *llokume*, or "Turkish delight." She approached each guest in descending order of age, offering him or her a piece of *llokume* on a cocktail napkin. As the guest took the candy he or she announced, *Të trashëgoet!* or *Me jetë të lumtur!* ("May they have a long and happy life!") or perhaps *Të na trashëgoet për gjithërisht!* ("May they have a happy life forever!"). Immediate members of Feime's family responded with sentiments such as *Arrifshi edhe më djemtë!* ("We look forward also to your sons' weddings!") or *Arrifshi më evladërit tuaj!* ("We look forward to the weddings of your children!").

While the *llokume* was being distributed, those gathered also exchanged individual greetings with each other, turning to each person in the order in which they were seated. When a woman greeted a man, for example, she asked him roughly the following sequence of questions:

Si je, NEVZAT?	How are you, NEVZAT?
Si je me shëndet?	How is your health?
Si e ke zonjën?	How is your wife?
Babanë? Nënën?	Your father? Mother?
Djemtë? (Nuset)?	Your sons (and their wives)?
Çupkat?	Your daughters?

She was expected to know the composition of his household and to ask about each individual, or category of individuals, in a set order. To each question he responded "Well, thank you" (*Mirë, faleminderit*), nodding slightly and placing his right hand over his heart. Because this was a wedding gathering, she terminated the exchange by exclaiming once again, *Të trashëgoet!* They then reversed the process, with him inquiring of her in the same manner. After their exchange, she greeted the person next to him, and he the person next to her, and so they each proceeded around the room. Together with the distribution of the *llokume*, this preliminary portion of the gathering lasted for perhaps ten minutes.

The younger man seated in the armchair is very much *të këngës* ("of the song"): someone for whom singing is a major preoccupation. He once told me in an interview that there were three things that were important to him in life: singing, fish and chips (he and his wife had a small fish-and-chips restaurant at the time), and family. He is also widely considered to be one of the best singers in the Toronto community. When it seemed that the men might simply converse all evening, he became more and more agitated and began to coax the others to sing. *Dasmë pa këngë s'është dasmë!* ("A wedding without singing isn't a wedding!"), he exclaimed several times, citing a common saying, and then, *Dasmë pa këngë nuku bë'et!* ("It just doesn't do to have a wedding without singing!"). Suddenly, as the conversation momentarily trailed off, Feime's father at last felt convinced. He launched into a spirited historical song, which the younger man accompanied. All other men in the room droned (CD #18):

Pashë një ëndërr shumë me ratali . . .	I had a terrible nightmare . . .
mos durofsh, moj perëndi!	(May you not stand this, O Lord!)
Djegur Shqipëria, djegur, bërë i . . .	Albania was burnt, burnt and leveled . . .
Djegur e tërë, gjer në kufi . . .	entirely burnt all the way to its borders . . .
t'ardhtë keq, moj perëndi!	(You should feel sorry, O Lord!)
Gjysmë Kolonjës shkojnë në Itali . . .	Half of Kolonjë is fleeing to Italy . . .
Po thërresin gra, burra, qajnë çilimi . . .	Women and men cry out, children weep . . .

This is a metric song, but the two sang in elaborate, *lartër* style. The host sang in a resonant baritone voice and injected exclamations such as *bubu!* ("alas!"), *lele!,* and *asaman o-i!* ("O my!") into the text, while the second soloist sang exaggeratedly slow portamenti at the end of each phrase as he descended to the drone pitch. The evening's singing was off to a strong start. When the host finished he exclaimed, *ajde Gëzuar e mirë!* ("Happiness and well being!"), to which both men and women called out in praise: *Të këndoftë zëmbra!* ("May your heart sing!"), *Si goja e zëmbra!* ("May your heart be as happy as the sentiments you have uttered!"), *Arrifshi edhe dhëndër!* ("Toward the wedding of your son!"). The host then shook hands all around with the other men.

Here it would have been customary for the other men present to sing in descending order of age, followed by the hostess and then the other women by age. Instead, a more casual singing order was observed. Next to sing was Feime's female cousin, a woman in her thirties, who chose to lead the same north Albanian radio song that had been sung at the women's gathering described in the previous chapter (*Bien tri daire*). Because it depicts a young woman on the night before her marriage, it was a particularly appropriate song for this evening, even though it is not from the Prespa repertoire. Other younger women joined in. When the song was finished, the singer was praised and congratulated by the other women. During her singing, Feime, having disappeared a few minutes before, had reappeared wearing another ruffly, dressy dress, and had resumed her bridal pose. She now stepped forward to kiss her cousin's hand, and then the two kissed each other's cheeks.

I was asked to sing next. As others around me broke into conversation, various thoughts began racing through my mind. Of the songs that I felt confident singing "in public," most were more suitable to the groom's side. I could sing one of them here but, since this was a gathering of the bride's side, I would be expected to insert the name of Feime's brother in place of the groom's name. Having just met the family, I wasn't sure of it. Of the songs associated with the bride's side, the one that I knew best is most often sung by the groom's relatives at the moment that they take her, and I wasn't sure that this would be appropriate. I did somehow think, however, that I had also heard the song sung at evening gatherings in Prespa. And so I decided to sing it, piecing together a text from various versions that I had heard in the course of my fieldwork.

When I felt ready to sing I sat politely, waiting for a pause in the conversation so that I could begin. Clearly I did not understand the conventions of beginning a song. Finally the women on either side nudged me. "Just break in whenever you are ready," they urged. And so I did, beginning my performance by intoning the usual *e-o*. Once my voice was heard, the others did indeed stop talking, and the cousin began to accompany me. She sang her line very simply, executing much of it on the drone pitch. All women present, other than the bride, droned (for a more typical version, see ex. 3.6; CD #10):

Në divan të lartër ke dalë e më rri . . .	On the high balcony you've come out and sit for me . . .
vajzë e parritur, pa vënë stoli.	(O young girl not yet grown, with your finery not yet put on.)
Tufkë manushaqe syri jot i zi . . .	A bouquet of violets your black eyes . . .
Si lum ky djalë që do të marr tynë . . .	How lucky that young man is who is going to marry you . . .
Bukuria jote shpirtin ma dogji . . .	Your beauty sets my soul on fire . . .

Midway through the song, one of the women motioned to Feime to sit down and rest for a moment.

When I have watched the video of my performance in recent years, I have been amused to note the lessons regarding Prespa singing that I had not yet learned. First, as I sang, I looked out at others in the room, and I moved my head from side to side or furrowed my brows so as to indicate my engagement in my performance and my sincerity regarding the sentiments expressed in the song's text. The other women, however, including the one accompanying me, sat very still when they sang, and most looked directly downward or focused their gaze on some vague spot on the floor across the room. I must have looked to them like a restless teenager, not yet mature enough to sit in a composed fashion. Secondly, I did not yet realize that I was expected to exclaim something at the end of my performance so as to signal that the song was over. Instead, when I finished the final verse, I simply sat and smiled at the others. There was an awkward pause, and then the other women began to call out various compliments. Feime stepped forward and, eyes still cast downward, took my hand in hers, kissed it, and pressed it to her forehead.

At this point, Feime's *xhaxha* initiated a long historical song. It is about a man named Avni Rustemi who, in 1920, assassinated Esat Pasha Toptani, an Albanian diplomat who was believed to be betraying his country's cause (see Panajoti 1982:144). This is a typical *këngë të shtruar*: a metric song with a small range, sung customarily with little ornamentation. As such it is one of the simpler songs in the men's repertoire, and thus suitable to men who, like the *xhaxha*, are not accomplished singers. As he began the song, he nodded slightly to the younger man on the floor near him to accompany him:

Kjo Libova shumë e mirë,	O excellent Libohovë, [birthplace of Avni Rustemi]
vetëm paska bukurinë,	what beauty [you have]!
vetëm paska bukurinë,	what beauty [you have]:
djalo trim paske Avninë.	you have the young hero Avni.

As the *xhaxha* sang, slowly and methodically, a thought occurred to Feime's father. Why not liven up the rendition by singing the song *me dy kolla* ("in two alternating groups")? After the second verse, he broke in with the first verse, accompanied by the excellent younger singer seated to his side. The *xhaxha* then reiterated the second verse, and the two pairs of soloists continued in alternation:

Or Avni, kë lule e prillit,	O Avni, flower of April,
ç'ia derdhe zorrët qafirit.	you disemboweled the scoundrel.
Or Avni, kë lule e majit,	O Avni, flower of May,
ç'ia derdhe zorrët dushmanit.	you disemboweled the enemy.
Të pyetçi për Avni Rustemnë,	If you should ask for Avni Rustemi:
ay shkojti n'Ingliterë,	he went to England,
ay shkojti n'Ingliterë	he went to England
për fyshekë, për mavzerë.	for cartridges, for Mauzers.
Në jotel kur ante bukë,	In the hotel where he was eating bread,
ante bukë, pinte verë,	eating bread and drinking wine,
ante bukë, pinte verë,	eating bread and drinking wine,
dy lëvorë përmi derë.	with two revolvers above the door.
[Poliçat me vrap ç'u dhanë:]	[The police came running:]
—Kush na e vra Esat pashanë?	"Who has killed our Esat Pasha?"
—Unë e vrava, qerratanë,	"I killed him, the scoundrel,
unë e vrava, qerratanë,	I killed him, the scoundrel,
se punonte prapagandë,	because he was spreading propaganda,
se punonte prapagandë	because he was spreading propaganda
me sërbinë, me junanë.	with the Serbs and the Greeks."

Whereas the *xhaxha* had been singing the melody in a uniform manner, the host began to vary it immediately, at some points extending its range up to a full octave above the drone note so as to heighten the "heroic" affect of the song's text (CD #19). He told me later that he had initiated this format of alternation so that the song would last longer, since there would be so few people singing that evening. At the song's conclusion, the other men congratulated each of the "singers," and Feime stepped forward to kiss her uncle's hand.

He was followed by Feime's grandfather, who likewise chose a heroic song, this time about a young man who is dying in battle. It is one of the oldest songs in the Prespa repertoire, evidently dating from the early nineteenth century. The same young man who accompanied the *xhaxha* continued his supporting role:

Mbeçë, shokë, që në mbeçë	May I leave you behind, my friends,
përtej Urës të Qabesë.	across the bridge of Qabej.
T'i bëni selam nënesë	Bring greetings to my mother
të më shesë të dy qetë,	and tell her to sell the two oxen,
të më shesë të dy qetë	to sell the two oxen
të japë niqa së resë.	so that I can draw up a new marriage contract.
Në pyettë nënja për mua,	If my mother should ask for me,
t'i thuani se u martua.	tell her that I have married.
Në pyetçin se ç'i krushqi vanë:	If they should ask what sort of wedding guests came:
dy dervishë, dy oxhallarë.	two dervishes and two *oxha*s.
Në pyetçin se ç'nuse mori:	If they should ask what sort of bride he took:
shtatë plumba dë kra i mori.	he took seven bullets in the arm.[2]

Now that all the older men who wished to had sung, the *xhaxha*'s wife was asked to sing. She at once tried to refuse, saying that she had a bad cold and that her voice was hoarse. Despite her protestations the other women insisted until she had no recourse but to sing. She chose a short song which she addressed not to Feime but to her brother, who was then in his late teens:

Një limua që nai sjell lumi,	The river has carried us a lemon.
Djalin tonë e zënka gjumi.	Sleep has overtaken our young man.
Mi gadale, djalin mos e zgjoni,	Go softly, don't awaken him,
është i vogël djalin ta ndër-toni/martoni.	for he's still young to be en-gaged/married.

Next, one of the younger women was asked to sing: the wife of the man who is such an avid singer. She was eager to sing a song that she had learned from an Albanian radio broadcast of a festival of village singers. In a break with Prespa tradition, she had learned to perform this song with her husband singing the supporting line. She intoned her initial *e-o* and then checked with him to make certain that the pitch level would be comfortable for him to sing as well. They then sang the song together, their voices bridging the gap between the men's and women's realms within the room. This time both men and women droned. Feime, standing to the singer's left in all her wedding finery, perfectly exemplified the song's opening lines (CD #20):

Vetëtin në fund të odës	There is something shining at the end of the room
po se është diell,	as if it were the sun.
aman aman o moj	
po se është diell.	
Ajo është nusja jonë,	It is our bride,
ne do ta rrëmbemë . . .	and we are going to steal her . . .
Po babai që mban qoshenë,	But her father who is sitting in the corner,
me se ta gënjejmë? . . .	with what shall we bribe him? . . .
Do t'i shtrojmë rakinë, meze,	We'll set out the brandy and appetizers for him
vajzën t'ia rrëmbemë . . .	in order to steal the girl . . .
Po nënja që mban qoshenë,	But her mother who is sitting in the corner,
me se ta gënjejmë? . . .	with what shall we bribe her? . . .
Do t'i mbushim dy erë ujë,	We'll fetch water twice for her,
vajzën t'ia rrëmbemë . . .	in order to steal the girl . . .

As they sang, the wife seemed quite self-conscious. She clutched at her hands and stared nervously into space or down at the floor. Her husband, however, looked out across the room toward her, and moved back and forth easily in his seat. When they had finished, both were congratulated by the others in the room.

Those at the gathering had been awaiting the moment when the husband would lead a song and had already encouraged him to do so at several points in the evening. He had not yet felt in the right mood, however, and had even excused himself at one point by reciting a couplet:

| Për këngë duet shoqëri | For singing one must have pleasant company |
| edhe dy kupa raki! | as well as two shot glasses of brandy! |

after which he had added, as if to qualify such a bravado statement, "but not to the point of being drunk!" Now, however, he felt ready.

In subsequent conversations with him, I was surprised to learn that he had not sung much as a young man. His interest in singing dated from a period while still in Macedonia when he drove a truck for a living. Often he listened to Albanian radio as he drove, and he began practicing his singing along with the radio. As a result he sings somewhat differently from other Prespa men. He feels most at home with the nonmetric *këngë të lartëra* that are characteristic of the Korçë district, and he sings them in a high voice that, while common among Korçë singers, sounds somewhat "thin" to other Presparë. He is best known for a love song sung in that style that he now performed, accompanied by his brother-in-law:

Qaj moj Lule bejar	Cry, my Lule ["flower"] for the summer,
si e motra të vëllanë.	as a sister mourns for her brother.
Mi shtëpi të shkova prëmë:	Last night I went by your house
si bilbil të ndieva zënë	and I sensed your voice like a nightingale's
kur llafosnje me të t'ëmë.	as you were speaking with your mother.
Lule, në të erdhsha pranë,	Lule, if I were to come near you
mos të lënça ty pa marrë.	I would not leave you untaken.
Lule, në mos të marrça,	Lule, if I don't marry you
si lisi më këmbë u thafsha,	may my legs wither like an oak,
më prevshin me tri sapata,	may they be cut with three axes,
më bëfshin kondur për dërrasa,	may they be made into planks,

| më bëfshin koritë mbi krua | may they be made into a trough over the stream, |
| që të lajnë vajzat mbi mua. | for the girls to bathe in me. |

His performance was a tour de force, replete with elaborate melismas, dramatic portamenti, and occasional surges to the octave above the drone. Before many of the lines he injected especially intense exclamations such as *ajde aman a-i!* or *o bir o-i!*, while his partner exclaimed *aman aman!* At times he let his voice break in the middle of ornaments to signal particularly intense feelings. His demeanor was equally dramatic. He appeared to be entirely absorbed by his singing, as he threw back his head and closed his eyes, or swayed back and forth in his seat. When he had finished, he seemed almost disoriented as he pronounced the customary exclamation. The other men shook his hand enthusiastically, and Feime kissed it. With the level of *muabet* having been substantially raised by his singing, the *xhaxha* led a hearty toast among the men.

The final singer was this man's brother-in-law, whom he accompanied. He too chose a song from the radio, a lyric song in *shtruar* style that is popular among the younger generation of singers:

Zura një bilbil me vesë . . .	I caught a nightingale in the dew . . .
more bilbil.	(O nightingale)
në parmak të penxheresë . . .	on the balcony by the window . . .
Unë me të kam lidhur besë . . .	I gave him my word of honor . . .
apa zëmbrën, i bëra folenë . . .	I opened my heart, and made for him a nest . . .

During his song, Feime's female cousin brought out a bowl filled with *kokolinkë,* a mixture of chickpeas, dried fruits, and hard candies that the groom's emissaries had brought the previous weekend. She began distributing a handful of the mixture wrapped in a paper napkin to each guest. With this allusion to Feime's imminent wedding, the evening came to a close.

Prespa Social Occasions

When I first arrived in Toronto in 1985, a close relative of my hosts was visiting from Prespa. On two Sundays in succession, we made the rounds of the families from her village, stopping at each of six or seven homes for an hour or two. At each house we entered and were greeted in a particular order, and sat arranged in order in each living room. We were also served a nearly identical sequence of refreshments: first a piece of candy, upon the receipt of which each guest wished the host household well; then soft drinks and snack foods such as potato chips, peanuts, and roasted chickpeas for the women, and beer with feta cheese, olives, and pickled vegetables for the men; next a plate of various kinds of fresh fruit; and finally coffee, perhaps with cake. To add to the effect of uniformity, the furnishings in the living room of each home were in much the same style: plush carpeting; plush velveteen sofas and matching armchairs; marble coffee- and end-tables with Baroque gold trim, each decorated with a crocheted or embroidered cloth topped by a heavy sheet of clear plastic and then a large bouquet of silk flowers; glass-doored china cabinets with crocheted doilies draped over each shelf; crystal chandeliers and pole lamps; and off-white, floor-length curtains flanked by colored or floral drapes. Displayed prominently throughout the homes, on tables and shelves as well as on all the walls, were two types of decoration. First were Islamic items such as miniature mosques, inscriptions from the Qur'ān, and velveteen hangings picturing the Ka'ba in Mecca. Second were large, framed portraits of young couples in their wedding attire.

Whereas in Prespa I had made a few such social calls over the course of two summers, the proximity in time of these visits brought home to me the centrality of reciprocal visiting within the lives of Presparë. It also highlighted for me both how elaborate and formal their social etiquette can be, and how predictable the structuring of their get-togethers often is. Weddings are the largest and most complex of Prespa social occasions, and their structure is most highly codified. But formality and organization also characterize less elaborate moments in Prespa social life.

Presparë often say that one's family, in the sense of household, should be one's first concern. *Shiko e familjen; shiko e punën tënde,* they often preach: "Look to your family, look to your own work." The affairs of others outside one's household, from those of other community members to the political affairs of the state, should be at best peripheral concerns. Nevertheless, individual households have been extremely reliant on each other. During the time I lived in a Prespa village, for example, it was clear that many economic transactions between households took the form of reciprocal exchanges: selling homemade cheese to a neighbor at a discount in return for intermittent use of his tractor, or volunteering to help with farm chores in return for access to a supply of firewood for the winter. Households also cooperated in such matters as the allocation of irrigation water during the dry summer months and the repair of bridges crossing the river that runs through the village. It is not only economic and logistical concerns that have drawn families together; if Prespare are to survive as a distinct community, then their children's spouses must come from other Prespa families. Prespare thus recognize a need to balance the individualistic concerns of each household with the cultivation of an attitude of good will toward other families.

It is to this attitude that Prespare allude when they speak of *muabet* in its broadest sense. The word *muabet* was introduced to southeast European peoples through Turkish from the Arabic *maḥabbah*, "affection." In Turkish, *muhabbet* has taken on the meaning of a "friendly conversation," and the phrase "to make *mu(h)abet*" is a fixed expression for most south Slavic and Albanian communities: "Let's make *muabet*"—"let's have a chat." Prespare, however, use the word extensively, with a connotation closer to that of the original Arabic.

Prespare see themselves as a particularly sociable, gregarious people. "We live for *muabet*," one man exclaimed to me, and another quoted a local saying: *Ne jemi axhet për muabet* ("*Muabet* is a necessity of life"). To "have *muabet*" with someone means to maintain a relationship of openness and mutual respect: to be, as is said in English, "on speaking terms." More generally, the word *muabet* connotes an approach to life in which a priority is placed on maintaining good relations with others by engaging in constructive social interchange. It thus stands in opposition to the idea of living one's life purely for oneself or one's household, as well as to the excessive expression of any such particularistic concerns. Prespare cite *muabet* as a feature that distinguishes them from north Albanians, who have often dealt with disputes between kin groups through blood feuds. As one man commented, in English, "We're lovers, not fighters."

Consistent with the dichotomy that they recognize between family and community concerns, Prespare make a strong distinction between everyday work activities and time deliberately set aside from them. Work activities are associated with the pursuit of the economically oriented interests of one's household and primarily involve household members, with the occasional assistance of kin and neighbors. Time set apart from work is used to establish and reaffirm ties with other households, so much so that Presparë, whether in Prespa or overseas, spend most of their free time visiting each other.

When I was in Prespa, time set aside for socializing ranged from informal visits between individuals, to evening gatherings of several households, to elaborate celebrations lasting one or more full days. Within a neighborhood, individual adults, both men and women, took frequent breaks during the day to drop in on relatives or neighbors of their own gender and age. On weekends, whole households regularly visited relatives and friends living farther away. In such instances, additional relatives and acquaintances living in the neighborhood would congregate at the host's home for an evening gathering known as a *gosti*. For major events in the life of a household member, or of the household as a whole, a large celebration or commemoration was held. These included events such as the birth of a child, a son's circumcision, a child's betrothal or wedding, a funeral (*xhenaze,* Tk. *cenaze*), or the construction of a new house. Even though families in North America often live farther from each other, most of these types of visiting continue to take place.

During the time I was in Macedonia, two features distinguished Prespa social life from that of Christian Macedonian communities. First, the social life of Christian villagers was closely connected to the church calendar. Major social events occurred on holidays such as Christmas, Epiphany, Easter, and St. George's Day, with smaller celebrations occurring every few weeks on one or another saint's day. These events were financed by contributions made to the village church, organized by church officials, and celebrated in and around the church grounds, and they involved everyone in the community. In addition, each village celebrated its patron saint's day, and families gathered each Sunday at church. All such community events were held in addition to family celebrations and commemorations.[3]

In contrast, Prespa men went to the *xhami* or mosque on Fridays, but this was regarded as a religious rather than a social occasion. Families also visited each other for coffee and sweets on the two *bajram*s, or Muslim holidays (Tk. *bayram,* Arab. *'īd*). But there was no type of Prespa social occasion that drew together the entire village or regional community. Even today in North America, the great majority of occasions continue to revolve around events that are important to a particular household. Celebrations are held in individual homes and are hosted by individual households, and those who attend are there because of the express invitation of the host family. The roles of host and guest have therefore been, and continue to be, intrinsic to all types of Prespa social occasions.

Secondly, the social life of Presparë in the lower villages has been distinctive in that there has not had to be a specific occasion to commemorate in order for a family to host a social gathering. Like most villagers in the former Ottoman territories, village Presparë traditionally distinguished between two major seasons, demarcated by St. George's Day (Shëngjergj) on May 6 and St. Dimitrius' Day (Shënmitër) on November 8. *Bejar* ("spring-summer"; Tk. *behar*), extending from May to November, was a period of intensive agricultural activities, when little time was available for socializing. During *dimër* ("winter"), however, which extends from November to May, there was in the past very little to be done around the household compound, and virtually every evening was set aside for socializing. As one Prespa acquaintance in Chicago explained in English, summer was "work time" while winter was "party time."

In the days before families began to emigrate, and before the men spent much of the winter selling apples in northern Yugoslavia, small groups of families would congregate virtually every evening during the winter at someone's home. Sometimes Albanian families would gather together with neighboring Macedonians for a work bee held for the purpose of husking corn or preparing tobacco for sale. But most often Albanians would assemble by themselves for an evening devoted exclusively to the "making" of *muabet*, in the sense of social intimacy. At these smaller, less formal gatherings, *muabet* was "made" through any of several types of good-natured social interaction: storytelling, recounting funny anecdotes about village families, singing, playing the shepherd's flute *kavall*, or dancing to singing or *kavall*. Gatherings held for no other reason than this were known simply as *muabet*s:

> When I was married, my father-in-law had seven daughters-in-law—there were fifty people total in the family. And they weren't scattered about on *gurbet*. I was married in 1952, and everyone was at home. We would gather after dinner and then there was just singing and *muabet*. . . . We'd bring out fruit and coffee and we'd make *muabet* until midnight or one in the morning. People would sing or tell about the old days. (Interview with an older woman in Chicago, 1986)

Most often, a household would go to the home of a nearby relative or to a close friend in the neighborhood for a *muabet*. In the dead of winter, there would likely be several such gatherings in each village in a single evening, and families could visit two or three in succession. *Muabet*s are still held, both in Prespa and in North America, although much less frequently.

Albanians from the lower villages are quick to point out that both the frequency of their social gatherings and the number of people that would come to a *muabet* or *gosti* were features that distinguished them both from Albanians in other Prespa villages and from their Macedonian fellow villagers:

> Macedonians didn't come to a *muabet*. Sometimes they came to help with tobacco or corn. But for *muabet* they didn't come. When a Macedonian came to one of their houses, they made *muabet*, but no, not like us. The Macedonians didn't have that custom. But us—if one person came, the whole village would rise up and come to visit him. (Interview with a younger man in Toronto, 1986)

Because of the structure of Prespa Albanian social life, one cannot really speak of a united community that functions as a whole. Rather, the Prespa community consists of an array of interconnected networks of individual households that are established and maintained through bonds of mutual aid and support. This might be material aid, in the form of goods and services, or it might be moral support offered in times of celebration or mourning. It is through the ongoing honoring of such reciprocal obligations that any household retains its right to be considered as part of the elaborate network that defines the community as a whole.

The "Order" of Weddings

One of the features that has distinguished Prespa gatherings of whatever sort has been the formalized character of individual behavior (see Moore and Myerhoff 1977; Irvine 1979). With "formalized" I refer primarily to two attributes. First, individuals behave in a more consistent and predictable manner, rather than in the more improvisatory way they might interact with other members of their households or during casual interchanges at work or on the street. Second, their more stereotypic ways of interacting are premised on assumptions as to what constitutes proper behavior for a person of their gender and age. In short, individuals in social situations act more as members of a particular social category and less as idiosyncratic individuals. In so doing, they are not merely following customary rules of behavior. Rather, they are presenting themselves as exemplary members of that social category, in a context where their actions are closely scrutinized by others. Social behavior for Prespare is thus a self-conscious performance in a way that everyday behavior is not.

The degree to which Prespare formalize their behavior varies according to the size, duration, and perceived intimacy of the occasion. For brief visits between relatives or close friends, those present often assemble in a single room, where they loosely observe spatial segregation by gender and age. Their dress and refreshments are informal, their greetings are more spontaneous, and their conversation is relatively unstructured. For a similar visit between households that are not on close terms, individuals pay greater attention to the refreshments served and the dress worn, and they sit more strictly segregated by gender and age. Formulaic verbal exchanges pave the way for unstructured but often self-conscious conversation. For gatherings that bring a large number of households together for a full evening, usually in connection with a family celebration, refreshments are more extensive and follow a strict menu, clothing is often more dressy, men and women usually gather in separate rooms and sit strictly according to age, flowery verbal formulas are exchanged throughout the evening, and singing replaces conversation as the primary means of social interchange.

Singing for Prespare is thus one aspect of their more generalized formal social behavior. It is most common at occasions where there are more individual personalities to accommodate and when activities must be organized over a longer time-frame. Singing may therefore be regarded in part as a device that helps to shape the course of a social event and channel the interaction of participants toward a desired outcome. At a large family occasion such as a wedding, singing serves as a form of crowd control, coordinating the many participants into orderly configurations of, as Blacking so cleverly put it, "soundly organized humanity" (1973:89).

Prespare explain the pervasive formality of their behavior at social occasions by referring to their *radhë*, or "order." In their view, there is a specific *radhë* or *rregull* ("rule" or "regulation") for every domain of activity: the right way to do things, or simply, the way things are done. Prespare speak of a *radhë* of singing, by which they mean the conventions of the polyphonic structure of their songs and the styles of singing that are appropriate to men and women. Likewise, there is a *radhë* for greeting guests, as well as a *radhë* for serving them. In addition, every type of Prespa social event, from a short visit between households to each stage in a large event such as a wedding, has its *radhë*.

When overseas Prespa families make preparations for a wedding, they refer back to a core *radhë* of activities that they remember from their days in Prespa as a sort of model of a "Prespa wedding." When I was in Prespa in the early 1980s, I attended several such model weddings. So similar were they both in their activities and in their timetables that I commented in my field notes at one point that you could probably set your watch according to the major ritual actions. In fact, I came to realize, two major *radhës* could be identified for these weddings: one for the ritual actions that the two host families observed, and another for the evening gatherings that they hosted. I describe the two *radhës* here in a sort of "ethnographic present," not because all phases are still observed in Prespa villages, but because of their status as a reference point for present-day diaspora weddings.

The "Order" of Ritual Activities

If the different stages of a Prespa wedding of the early 1980s struck me as unusually predictable, so that participants seemed at times like players in an elaborate theatrical piece, this was in part because they were realizing a script of long standing. Each of the two model *radhës* of a Prespa wedding is a variation of practices found widely in the eastern Mediterranean. Most of the ritual activities that might be included, for example, are common to weddings held by north and south Albanians living both in Albania and in adjacent areas. Many features are also shared with other east Mediterranean communities, whether Slavs, Greeks, Turks, or Arabs. As weddings have been celebrated in recent decades in Prespa, they seem to be an elaborate layering of older southeast European elements, practices that became common throughout the Ottoman territories in more recent centuries, and a few contemporary additions drawn from Western practices.[4]

Of the many activities that make up a village wedding, the focal point is the taking of the bride. Most older Presparë refer to the day on which this happens, and the celebration associated with it, as the *dasmë* or "wedding." In recent decades that day has most often been a Sunday, with specific rituals occurring for a full week beforehand. Singing, by men or women or both, accompanies each step in the ritual sequence:

Ja vënë kënanë nuses ("They put henna on the bride"). One week before the wedding day, emissaries from the groom's family bring henna to the bride's home, together with a few articles of clothing. In recent years, commercial hair coloring has sometimes been substituted for henna. On the following day, women of her family, and particularly her young relatives, congregate at the bride's home to watch and sing while the henna or coloring is put on her hair.

E nisin nusen ("They adorn the bride"). Three evenings before she is taken, the bride *bë'et nuse:* she "becomes a bride."[5] In the presence of female relatives and family friends, she models some of the clothing given to her by her family, as well as the jewelry given to her by the groom at their betrothal. Remaining items are displayed for the women to inspect and admire. Throughout the course of the evening, the women sing songs drawn from a large repertoire that can be sung at any such gathering on the bride's side; or they sing songs characteristically addressed to the groom, inserting the bride's brother's name. Male guests may also gather, usually in a separate room, to socialize through either conversation or singing. Such gatherings continue at her home each of the two remaining evenings before she is taken.

E rrain qeshqeknë ("They crush the wheat"). Activities at the groom's home also intensify three days before the wedding. Male relatives and family friends assemble in the family's courtyard during the afternoon to crush wheat berries. These will later be boiled with meat for a dish known as *qeshqek* (fr. Pers. *kešk*), which is served to the groom's party on the day of the wedding. Often long tables are set out in the courtyard for the male guests, and liquor and appetizers are provided. Women remain in the house and do not participate in the activities.

The wheat berries are first poured into a wooden trough, and then broken up using two long, T-shaped wooden poles. Traditionally it is a male relative with living parents who initiates the crushing, followed by various younger relatives who are close to the groom. To the side, other male relatives address him with ritual songs (plate 2):

ZARIF bej, yll i shënuar,	ZARIF *bey*, special star,
sh'të zu BABAI për të martuar.	your FATHER has undertaken to marry you off.
Qoftë me air, me të trashëguar!	May you have good fortune, may you live a long and happy life!
ZARIF bej, yll i shënuar,	ZARIF *bey*, special star,
sh'të zu NËNJA për të martuar.	your MOTHER has undertaken to marry you off.
Qoftë me air, me të trashëguar! . . .	May you have good fortune, may you live a long and happy life! . . .

In such songs the same short verse is repeated over and over, with the kinship terms of different relatives inserted in order of their age and closeness to the groom.

Many families also hire Rom musicians to play and sing for the crushing of the *qeshqek.* The most usual configuration during the 1980s was a group consisting of two clarinet (*gërnetë*) players, an accordion (*armonikë*) player, and a man who played a two-headed bass drum (*daulle*) with a snare over one skin. The two clarinets most often play melodic lines structured like Prespa polyphonic songs, with the accordion playing a chordal drone. These musicians are known most commonly as the *daulle,* or "drums," because the noise that they make serves as an announcement to the rest of the village that a wedding is taking place. One of their tunes, serving as a sort of fanfare, is used to greet guests as they arrive (CD #21). Another, based on the same melody as most of the men's ritual songs, may be played interspersed with the men's singing. When not involved in either of these activities, they may also play music for listening or for the accompaniment of line dances. Whether or not they are hired for the *qeshqek* ceremony, they are almost always hired for the final two days of the celebration.

Sinitorët ("The emissaries"). The day before the bride is taken, a group of adult men from the groom's family, known as the *sinitorë,* parade to the bride's home, led by the *daulle,* to bring her an array of gifts. Neither the groom nor his father serves as *sinitorë,* who are generally uncles and cousins of the groom. The gifts that they bring include various items of clothing and jewelry, together with the outfit that the bride will wear on her wedding day. The *sinitorë,* together with the men in the bride's party, assemble for an elaborate gathering that lasts for most of the afternoon. This reception given in honor of the *sinitorë* is often thought of as the "wedding" on the bride's side.

On the groom's side, women guests assemble on that morning or during the evening before to pack the *rroba,* the clothes that are to be sent to the bride with the *sinitorë.* One or more women place a suitcase in the middle of the floor and carefully lay each item of clothing inside, while the remaining women sit on couches surrounding them. Both those who pack and those who look on sing as the clothes are packed, often inserting the groom's name into the texts of their songs:

Ç'ditë erdhe nga Stambolli	What day did you arrive from Istanbul,
ASAN bej, yll i shënuar?	ASAN *bey,* special star?

141

Unë erdha ditën e Shënmitrit,	I arrived on St. Demetrius's Day,
moj nuse, ënë e shkruar.	O bride, colorful moon.
Tinë kur erdhe, mua ç'më solle,	When you came, what did you bring me,
ASAN bej, yll i shënuar?	ASAN *bey*, special star?
Unë të solla veilo me lule,	I brought you a veil with flowers,
moj nuse, ënë e shkruar.	O bride, colorful moon.
Po e idh, vallë të ka ije,	Put it on and see if it becomes you,
moj nuse, ënë e skhruar.	O bride, colorful moon.
Të djelën kur do vij atije,	I will on Sunday when I go "there,"
ASAN bej, yll i shënuar.	ASAN *bey*, special star.
	(wedding in Grnčari, 1983)

Once the *rroba* have arrived at the bride's, the women on her side gather in a side room to sing as they unpack them, inserting the bride's name in appropriate places:

Kë nishan që të dërguam,	That gift that we sent you,
PERIJAN, vallë je gëzuar?	are you happy, PERIJAN?
Për kokën tënde, sa jam gëzuar!	Upon your head, I swear that I am so happy!
Tër natën e natës kam qenë zgjuar,	All night long I have remained awake,
tër ditën e ditës unë kam kënduar.	all day long I have sung.
	(wedding in Chicago, 1987)

As they sing, one woman slowly draws each item of clothing from the suitcase, holding it up and twisting it from side to side so that all may admire it. Particularly dressy outfits are handed to the bride, who then puts them on and models them for the assembled women (plate 11).

At the end of the day, the *sinitorë* return triumphantly to the groom's home, bearing gifts prepared by the bride that are distributed to each member of the groom's family.

E marrin pajën ("They fetch the dowry"). On the morning of the wedding, the bride is dressed in her wedding attire by her female relatives and spends much of the day resting quietly and anticipating the arrival of the groom's party. Meanwhile, her relatives carefully display her dowry items in the courtyard of her home. The dowry generally includes clothing, furniture, blankets, cushions, rugs, cooking implements, and decorative items for her new home.

At the groom's home, the *daulle* arrive early and begin to play dance music in the courtyard (plate 3), interspersed with listening music addressed to the male guests (plate 4) and with the fanfare music that they use to greet arriving guests. Around midmorning, a party of guests from the groom's side departs for the bride's home to fetch the dowry, led by the *daulle* playing their fanfare tune. If the two families live close enough for the procession to go on foot, children from the groom's party may be chosen to parade smaller pieces of the dowry back to the groom's house in their arms (plate 5). Larger items are taken by truck. Once at the groom's house, the dowry is exhibited in one of the bedrooms.

E lajnë dhe e rruajnë dhëndrin ("They bathe and shave the groom"). In the late morning, after the dowry has been fetched, the groom is bathed in the kitchen of his home. Outside the door, various relatives congregate to sing (plate 18). In Prespa, preference is given to male relatives, who often have the *daulle* play between the verses of their songs. Very close female relatives may also sing.

Once he has bathed, the groom is dressed in a suit or tuxedo and led outdoors into the courtyard of his home. There he is shaved by the *berber* or "barber," one of his adult male relatives. The groom selects a young male relative of whom he is particularly fond, usually the son of a sibling or cousin, to hold a mirror before him as he is shaved. The mirror has been draped with a red kerchief. The little boy then circulates through the assembled crowd, collecting tips on the mirror which are split between him and the "barber." While the groom is being shaved, his male relatives resume their singing (plate 6), often augmented by or alternated with melodies played by the *daulle*:

Ka ije baça me lule . . .	It becomes a garden to have flowers . . .
ka ije.	(it is becoming)
Si SHEFQET bej ku nise dhëndër . . .	So it became SHEFQET *bey* to set out as a groom . . .
ku rrinin krushqit përpara . . .	with his wedding party before him . . .
ku rrinte edhe nusja prapa . . .	with his bride behind him . . . (wedding in Chicago, 1987)

E darovitin dhëndrin ("They give gifts to the groom"). Shortly after he is shaved, the women of the groom's family join him in the courtyard. Each presents him with a *boçe,* items of clothing such as a shirt, tie, and socks wrapped in a white, embroidered cloth (plate 1). They may also take turns combing perfume into his hair, savoring their final moment with him before he attains adulthood (plate 7). One by one they step forward, take the comb, and sing to him as they comb his hair, often fighting back tears as they do so:

Atje lartë në gur i verdhë	Up there on the golden rock
njëzet e pesë bejlerë	twenty-five *bey*s
nisnin dhëndër ARIF benë.	were sending off ARIF *bey* as a groom.
ANAJA ç'i rrinte pranë	His GRANDMOTHER, sitting next to him,
ia krinte leshkat mënjanë.	was cutting his hair to one side.
E ËMA ç'i rrinte pranë	His MOTHER, sitting next to him,
ia ndante leshkat mënjanë.	was parting his hair to one side.
I ATI ç'i rrinte pranë	His FATHER, sitting next to him,
ia dridhte leshkat mënjanë . . .	was curling his hair to one side . . .

(wedding in Nakolec, 1980)

E marrin nusen ("They take the bride"). After the midday meal, all those who have assembled at the groom's home, except for his mother, walk or drive in procession to the home of the bride, once again led by the *daulle.* The adult women are ushered into the *odë* of the bride's home, while the men adjourn to a nearby house. Young, unmarried guests usually remain outside to listen, or dance, to the music of the *daulle.* At the men's gathering, the groom's party is welcomed by the bride's closest male relatives. Coffee and cigarettes are offered to the guests, and then men of each side offer shot glasses of homemade brandy (*raki*) to those on the other side. After some initial conversation, which is often stiff and self-conscious, one or two songs are sung by relatives of the bride and are answered by one or two sung by the groom's relatives.

The women of the groom's party are met outside the bride's house by her female relatives, who exchange greetings with the guests and sprinkle perfume into their hair. All then enter the *odë*. After some initial greetings, women of the bride's family initiate a sequence of songs, which they sing while dancing in a line (see ex. 3.4; CD #8):

Duallë dy spai në lëmë . . .	Two *sipahi*s [Ottoman over-lords] have come out onto the threshing floor . . .
nën' moj nën', bij' moj bij'.	(O mother, O daughter)
E kërkojnë çupën tonë . . .	They are asking for our young girl . . .
Çupa jonë s'është bërë . . .	Our girl isn't ready yet . . .
duart në brumë s'i ka vënë . . .	She hasn't yet put her fingers into the bread dough . . .
pe, gjilpërë me dorë s'ka zënë . . .	she hasn't yet taken a needle and thread in hand . . .
	(wedding in Krani, 1980)

After six or eight songs, the bride is led into the room and is greeted by the groom's relatives with special songs reserved for that moment. After only a few minutes, she retires to make final preparations for her departure. Once she has left, it is the turn of the groom's relatives to perform a series of dance songs:

Me llambë në dorë më gjezdis divan . . .	With lamp in hand you stroll along the hallway . . .
Bandill s'gjen si mua të kërkosh dynjanë.	(You'll never find a man like me if you search the whole world.)
Pesë napolonë ta bleva gjerdan . . .	For five napoleons I bought you a necklace . . .
Dy lira e gjysmë ta bleva fustan . . .	For two and a half lira I bought you a dress . . .
	(wedding in Grnčari, 1983)

Finally, when the bride is ready, the groom is brought to the doorway of the bride's home to take her (plate 8). If his home is distant from hers, the couple are ushered to a waiting car for the procession to the groom's home (plate 9); otherwise the new couple, together with the groom's party, returns to his home on foot. There a number of ritual actions are carried out to incorporate the bride into the household. Following these actions, the groom's party goes out into the courtyard, where they perform a dance known as the "bride's dance" (*valle e nuses*). This is a custom that was evidently adopted by Prespare in recent decades from Macedonians (cf. Mac. *nevestinsko oro*), in which relatives of the groom take turns leading the bride in a six-measure line dance (plate 10).

I mbyllin dhëndrin me nusen ("They close in the groom and bride"). Shortly after nightfall, the bride is taken to the room in the groom's house where the dowry has been displayed, and is joined by the groom. Outside in the courtyard the *daulle* strike up a particularly lively tune, and all dance in celebration of the marriage's impending consummation.

Following the wedding night, attention focuses on the new bride. In the morning she is brought refreshments in bed, including a plate of *bukëvale*, a dish of cubes of bread that are soaked in butter and then baked in the oven. On the third day of the wedding (Tuesday if she was taken on Sunday), she is already put to work. Very early in the morning, she is awakened and taken to the neighborhood spring or fountain with the other women, who sing to her as she washes their hands and fetches water for the household. Later in the day she makes her first loaves of bread, called *kulaçka*, for the groom. Somewhat later in the week, the young couple visits her parents' home for the first time, where a formal dinner is held in their honor. With this dinner, the intense period of celebration surrounding the taking of the bride comes to a close.

When in all of this does the couple become "married"? The civil marriage license is generally obtained privately by the couple and their parents, often long before the wedding day. A more important event to the families themselves is the signing of the *niqa* (Tk. *nikâh*, Arab. *nikāḥ*), the Islamic marriage contract, which involves a monetary commitment to the bride by the family of the groom in the event that he should later divorce her. This is generally observed as a private ceremony between the bride- and groom-to-be and the *oxha*, or local religious leader, either at the time the bride is taken or on some day beforehand.

The "Order" of Social Gatherings
In the course of a wedding celebration, the sequence of ritual activities detailed above is interwoven with gatherings of a more social character. Early in the week of the wedding, guests gather at the groom's or bride's home after the evening meal or *darkë* (table 4). They remain there for two or three hours and depart before midnight (type A). A similar gathering takes place on the day after the bride is taken. These gatherings have essentially the same format as a *muabet*, the most informal type of Prespa

TABLE 4 Activities at Prespa Village Weddings in the 1980s

Day[a]		Bride's Home Social Gathering[b]		Ritual Activity	Ritual Activity	Groom's Home Social Gathering[b]	
		Men	Women			Women	Men
Su	D			henna brought to bride		X	
	E					A	A
Mo	D		X	henna put on bride's hair			
	E					A	A
Tu	D						
	E					A	A
We	D						
	E					A	A
Th	D				qeshqek crushed		X
	E	A	A	bride "is adorned"		A	A
Fr	D						
	E	A	A	bride models trousseau		A	A
Sa	D				women pack clothes for bride	X	
	B			sinitorë take rroba to bride			
			X	women unpack clothes			
	E	A	A	bride models rroba			B
Su	D			groom's party fetches dowry			
					groom bathes	X	X
					groom shaved		X
					women give gifts	X	
		A	A	groom's party takes bride			
		(abbreviated)			"bride's dance" danced		
	E				dancing in courtyard		B
Mo	D					A	A
	E						
Tu	D				bride fetches water	X	
					bride makes kulaçka	X	
	E						

a. D, during day; E, during evening.
b. A, short social gathering; B, long gathering with meal; X, ritual gathering

gathering, although in the past *muabet*s not connected with weddings often continued until one or two in the morning.

As the day of the taking of the bride approaches, two gatherings of a more extended type are held (type B). One is the reception hosted by the bride's family for the *sinitorë* on Saturday afternoon. The other, known as a *konak*, is held only by the men on the groom's side of a wedding, on both Saturday and Sunday nights. The reception for the *sinitorë* generally begins in the late morning and lasts almost until dusk. Similarly, the *konak*s held on the groom's side begin shortly after nightfall and are expected to last until daybreak. In either case, the men are served a multicourse meal just before departing. These more formal occasions are similar to the dinners (*gosti*s) that families host when relatives or friends visit from out of town, except that only men take part in the extended gatherings associated with weddings.

Like the sequence of ritual activities that constitutes the wedding proper, social gatherings connected with weddings also have a very specific *radhë*, one which, as with the wedding ritual, betrays historical connections to events held elsewhere in the eastern Mediterranean and beyond. Throughout this large region, it has been common for men in particular to host gatherings known by terms such as *majlis* (Arab.; Tk. *meclis*) or *bazm* (Pers.; Tk. *bezm*). Usually these have involved some type of performance activity, be it poetry recitation, singing, instrumental music, and/or dancing. Participants speak of the goal of such gatherings as the attainment of some sort of elevated emotional state (e.g., Arab. *ṭarab*, Pers. *ḥāl*, Tk. *hâl* or *keyif*, Greek *kefi*), which they induce in themselves primarily by participating in or observing whatever performance activities are featured.[6]

Both the phraseology surrounding Prespa gatherings and the ways in which they are structured suggest their affinity to such Near Eastern forms. Members of Sufi orders, for example, use the Arabic word *maḥabbah* ("love, affection"), or the Turkicized *muhabbet*, to describe a mystical state in which one is "penetrated with love of God" (Rouget 1985:268, citing al-Ghazali; see also Nurbakhsh 1987:15–18). Albanian Bektashi in fact refer to their social gatherings as *muabet*s (Baba Rexhep, personal communication). Similarly, Presparë explain that the goal of their gatherings is the attainment of a state of *muabet* by those assembled, although they use the word in a secular sense to mean social "openness" or "intimacy." In the course of an especially successful event, male participants in particular expect eventually to be transported into a more agitated, elated state of *qejf* (Tk. *keyif*, from Arab. *kayf*).

148

Occasionally, Prespare also refer to a social gathering as a *mexhelis* (cf. Arab. *majlis*), such as when they use the phrase *dë mexhelis* ("at the gathering") to refer to their experiences singing "in public" as a child. Other contexts in which they sang as children, such as at home with a relative or during play with a peer, are regarded by them as "practicing" for such events rather than as "singing." Such usage underscores how closely community members associate singing with large social occasions.

Among the features that link Prespa gatherings to a broader Near Eastern tradition is their extensive formal etiquette (cf. Eickelman 1981: 192–95). Many aspects of Prespa etiquette involve an ordering or sequencing of personnel in such a way as to articulate each person's age relative to others in attendance, and perhaps also his or her gender. Prespare refer to this practice as doing things *me radhë:* "with order." When guests first arrive at a gathering, for example, they enter the house and greet the members of the host family *me radhë:* first older adults greet each other, then younger adults greet older ones and then each other, and finally children greet adults in order of age.

For most occasions, male guests are then ushered into the *odë* (the Ottoman term for "room") or the *dhomë e pritjes* (literally, "room for receiving guests"). Female guests are taken to another, side room such as the kitchen, the family room, or a bedroom. After exchanging a second round of greetings, the guests take their seats around the room *me radhë.* Those who are oldest generally sit on couches placed opposite the entrance, with younger adults flanking them on both sides. Any remaining adults and unmarried persons who are present seat themselves on the floor near the doorway. One man explained to me that this seating arrangement dates from the days when most social events took place in the coldest winter months, and when rooms were heated by open fireplaces located in the center of the wall facing the entrance. Under this arrangement, those who were oldest were seated closest to the heat. Today, although other systems of heating are used in both Macedonia and North America, the arrangement is retained essentially unchanged. If the head of household and his wife are relatively young, they each take a seat on the floor facing their respective guests, a gesture that conveys their solicitousness and their readiness to offer hospitality. If they have grown children, they sit with other older adults at the point of the ell, and their oldest son and his wife assume this position on the floor. At wedding gatherings held at the bride's home, the bride herself stands *në fund të odës* ("at the end of the room"), with the youngest of the guests.

Another Near Eastern feature characteristic of Prespa gatherings is the serving of particular types of refreshments. Once guests have been seated, more extensive greetings are exchanged, not only between hosts and guests but also among the various guests. Immediately thereafter, a variety of beverages and foods is brought out. Men are offered alcoholic beverages, either homemade fruit brandy (*raki*), whiskey (also referred to as *raki*, and used as a substitute for the homemade brandy when none is available), or beer. They are also presented with an assortment of appetizers, referred to as *meze*, that might be quite extensive. The most common items include salads of fresh or pickled vegetables, feta cheese, olives, and chunks of fried or roasted meat. Women are often not served refreshments, or they might be offered juice or soft drinks with light snack foods.

Despite what are often interpreted as sanctions against wine in the Qur'ān and Ḥadīth, the association of alcohol with men's gatherings of both a secular and a spiritual character is an old and consistent one in the Near East.[7] Presparë in particular excuse their drinking of alcohol by explaining that it is wine alone that is forbidden them. Nevertheless, alcohol is not served at weddings held during Ramazan (Arab. Ramaḍān), the Muslim month of fasting. The rather substantial appetizers (*meze*) that are served the men with their alcohol are explained as its logical accompaniment: something to stave off, for a time at least, the onset of excessive intoxication. Since women are not offered alcohol, they are not served *meze*. Again, this pairing of a type of distilled liquor with various appetizers is typical of Near Eastern and southeast European men's events (cf. Arab. *araq* and *maza*; Tk. *rakı* and *meze*).

In his account of gatherings held in Turkey in Ottoman times that were devoted to the performance of the song-form *ghazal*, Andrews (1985:148) draws attention to two individuals who figured prominently in such occasions. First was an older man who served as the ceremonial host and focus of the group's attention, whom Andrews designates by the Sufi term "beloved." The second was a younger man known as the *saki* (Arab. *saqī*), who poured wine for those present. Both such roles were apparent until recently at Prespa men's gatherings, in the form of the *kryetar* and the *sak*.

The *kryetar* ("leader") or, if an older man, the *kryeplak* ("head elder"), serves even today as the ceremonial leader of the event. He may be the head of the host household or another older relative. Generally he sits opposite the entrance to the *odë* with the other older men. It is his duty to lead off the singing that dominates the evening's socializing, and to see to it that the occasion proceeds in a convivial but orderly manner. He should be both well versed in the community's etiquette and an experienced and confident singer.

Formerly at Prespa occasions there was also a *sak*, a young man from the household who began the evening's events by circulating a bottle of homemade *raki* and a shot glass around the room. Each man was poured a shot and drank at least part of it. When all had drunk, there was a group toast, after which one of the men led a song. When the song ended, the *sak* again circulated the *raki* and glass, another toast was made, another song sung, and on and on until each man had sung at least once. This practice was referred to as *një kupë, një këngë* ("one shot, one song"). Like the *meze* (appetizers), it was intended to mitigate the effects of the alcohol so that the men gradually became pleasantly *qejfli* ("elated") without becoming unpleasantly drunk.[8]

Today each man drinks from his own glass or bottle of beer, but the sequence is maintained in spirit in that the *kryetar* leads a toast after each song (plate 14). Although there is no longer a designated *sak*, younger men of the family still spend much of the evening pouring drinks for the family's guests. At women's gatherings, individuals perform these same functions, although there is no verbal designation for them. The oldest woman of the household or another older relative generally serves as the hostess, and younger women of the household bring light refreshments to the guests. Since no alcohol is served, there is no formal toasting.

The remainder of the gathering is devoted to singing. Whether at a men's or women's gathering, it is the *kryetar* or the female hostess who leads off the singing. When this first song is finished, there is a pause for conversation. In the case of a men's event, the *kryetar* initiates a toast. Each guest then sings *me radhë* or, as is sometimes said, *pas pleqësisë* ("in order of age"), from oldest to youngest. The singing continues until each married adult present, and any older teenager who wishes to be included, has led one song. This practice of singing in a specific order recalls the medieval Arabic *nawbah*, in which singers in the 'Abbasid court performed in the order of their stature as performers (Sawa 1989: 166–67).

Lengthier Prespa gatherings follow a slightly different order. At the reception held for the *sinitorë*, the men of the bride's side of the wedding customarily sing in descending order of age, followed by those of the groom's party. At the Saturday night *konak*s that were held until recently on the groom's side, the groom, together with his father and another male relative, visited each *konak* in turn toward the beginning of the evening. First the men at the *konak* sang, and then the groom's father and other relative responded. Although the precise ordering varies, all such events have in common that the hosts, in the sense of the host group or hosting side of the wedding, initiate the singing.

Once each person present who is capable of doing so has sung one song, the obligatory part of the occasion is over. Often, women cease to sing at this point. Those who are more eager singers may wish to continue informal singing, or the women may simply converse quietly for the remainder of the evening. Sometimes women sing a round of seated songs followed by dance songs, or vice versa. For men, however, the choice of how to proceed is more complicated. If they need to go to work early the next morning, or if they have not succeeded in attaining sufficient *muabet* among themselves, they may curtail the event. Otherwise they may continue to sing until close to midnight.

The reception given for the *sinitorë* and any *konak*s that are held at the groom's are expected to last substantially beyond this point. Presparë tell stories of the days when a live rooster used to be brought into a men's *konak* sometime after midnight. While one man restrained him, another poured a shot glass of *raki* down his throat. If he crowed, he was let go. The gathering was ended and the men went home. If he was unable to crow, he was slaughtered and roasted for the men, who continued their singing "until dawn" (*gjer më saba*), when the cocks outside crowed. For today's Presparë, the notion of continuing to sing "until dawn" is still an ideal for men at their *konak*s, one that is often reiterated in a popular *bejte:*

Do pijmë ca nga ca,   We're going to drink a bit at a
                                               time

  do vazhdojmë gjer më saba!   and continue until dawn!

And roasted chicken may still provide a delectable accompaniment to late-night singing.

Activities at longer men's gatherings are directed toward sustaining the *muabet* that the men have established earlier on and channeling it toward an emotional climax. The men's goal is the coordinated attainment of a state of "elation" (*qejf*) that enables them to break down the social barriers that otherwise divide them and to experience a surge of communal affection. It should not be surprising that those occasions that are expected to last the longest are those that involve the greatest number of men. While *muabet* is to a great extent assumed among the family members and friends who gather in the early days of a wedding, it must be actively created at the more formal occasions that bring large numbers of unrelated men together.

In the later hours of a gathering, the order of singers is no longer a consideration, nor do men feel that they should sing a more serious song to honor the host. It is at this point that those who particularly like to sing might perform a second time, either by request or because they feel overcome by an urge to do so. Eventually, many of the better-known historical and love songs have been sung, and their serious themes may not be thought to suit the more elated, intense atmosphere that the men, often extremely intoxicated by this point, have created among themselves. And so, at this point, men may begin to sing more exuberant or humorous songs.

In Prespa, one contribution to the nurturing of *muabet* at the men's evening *konak*s has been the visit made by the Rom *daulle*, who have entertained each group of guests for an hour or more. The *daulle* sing their own repertoire of polyphonic songs, provide instrumental accompaniment for the men's singing, and play music for dancing. The highlights of their performances, however, are long, nonmetric improvisations known as *kaba* (from the Turkish word for "low-pitched") or *me të qarë* ("with crying"). These are said to be imitations of women's funeral lamenting, and they resemble the men's *këngë të lartëra* in both style and melancholy affect. Generally they conclude with a dance-like melody in duple time that releases the emotional tension induced by the *kaba*. The appearance of the *daulle* at each *konak* has been eagerly anticipated by the guests and has often provided the climax of the evening. (CD #22 features a performance by Prespa *daulle* of a polyphonic song followed by a *kaba*.)[9]

At their more extended gatherings, men expect their interaction to build to a state of ecstatic abandonment. As the event reaches its peak of activity, the "order" that was so pervasive at its beginning is largely undermined. Often the men group and regroup themselves in these late hours, leaving their seats to sit closer to those with whom they are singing, or to sprawl on the floor if they are more comfortable. Occasionally the session may end with dancing, accompanied either by the *daulle* or—in rare instances—by the men's own singing.

At any type of gathering, once the singing has concluded, an additional round of food may be offered. At the lengthier men's gatherings, it is obligatory to serve a full dinner at the event's conclusion. For an after-dinner gathering that is attended by guests other than the closest kin, the hosts might bring out some fresh fruit or a sweet, together with cups of Turkish coffee. The coffee is an unequivocal signal that the guests should begin to think about leaving.[10]

During the period when today's younger adults were growing up in Prespa, guests at social gatherings, even those not connected with an elaborate celebration such as a wedding, also set out for home in a particularly orderly manner. The following is one man's description of the way in which guests used to depart from the informal winter *muabet*s that were held in his village of Arvati when he was a boy:

> The men would send a child to the women's room to summon first the women from the homes which were furthest away. If the gathering was [in Arvati], then those from Krani [the village down the mountainside from Arvati], or those from [the most distant] neighborhood would be called first. Those women would then wait for the men of their households and all would leave as a group. The women from the next most distant neighborhood would then be summoned, and on and on until each group had left for home. (Field notes, October 1986)

In this way any gathering ended as it began: *me radhë.*

The Prespa "System"

In Yugoslavia we honor the son more, because we say that he is "of the house." A girl grows up and her husband takes her, but a boy brings a bride into the household. . . . [When a boy is born] we say, "[My son] has made a son. *T'i rrojë me ymbër, t'i rrojë!* May he live a long life!" We're happy that he had a son. If he's made a girl, we still say, *"T'i rrojë me ymbër, me kësmet të jetë!* May she live a long life, may she have good fortune!" But a girl is, as we say, "the doorway to the world." A boy is "the foundation of the house." (Interview with a grandmother in Chicago, 1986)

MEN'S SINGING AT THE GROOM'S

The previous chapter began with a gathering of men and women held on a Friday evening in Toronto in 1986, when a young woman named Feime "adorned herself as a bride" in anticipation of her upcoming marriage to Memet. Early the following morning, Feime, her parents, and other close relatives drove from Toronto to a small town outside Chicago, where they rented several rooms in a motel near Memet's home. On his side of the wedding, Memet's relatives gathered at his home on Saturday evening to sing in separate groups of women and men. The men's gathering held that evening provides a range of insights into the more personal factors that prompt men to choose the songs they perform at such gatherings and the variety of performance styles that they adopt. It also illustrates the sorts of interpersonal dynamics that determine whether an evening of singing will be an uncomfortable or pleasurable experience for those involved.

Of the families who assembled at Memet's home, virtually all were close relatives. One *xhaxha* (father's first cousin in this case) had come with his family from Australia, while a female cousin and her family were visiting from Scandinavia. Most of the others lived close by in surrounding towns. While in Prespa the closest neighbors of the groom's family would most likely have been his father's male brothers and cousins, here the nearby relatives were mostly women of Memet's father's family. Many of the women who gathered to sing had grown up together, whereas many of the men were in-laws. Memet's mother was particularly disappointed that her brother and his wife were not present, and in fact did not attend the wedding at all, although they live nearby. As is happening increasingly among overseas Prespare, their two households had had a falling out and no longer "had *muabet.*"

The weather this evening was particularly hot and humid. In the early evening, the men set a card table in the backyard and sat around it chatting, smoking, and drinking beer or *raki.* The women laid out an array of appetizers for them on small serving plates: thick chunks of feta cheese, pieces of roasted meat, kebabs of ground meat, slices of tomato, and pickled cucumbers. They then gathered to sing inside, in the *odë.* Once the women had sung one song each, they broke into casual conversation. At this point Memet's father, serving as the evening's *kryetar,* initiated the men's singing. He chose a formulaic ritual song in which relatives of the groom are designated *me radhë:*

Mirë bërë, bukur bërë . . .	Well done, nicely done . . .
O bej, O MEMET bej,	(O MEMET *bey*)
që gëzove BABANË tënd . . .	you've made your FATHER happy . . .
Mirë bërë, bukur bërë . . .	Well done, nicely done . . .
që gëzove NËNËN tënde . . .	you've made your MOTHER happy . . .
që gëzove GJITHË MIQËSINË . . .	you've made ALL OUR FRIENDS happy . . .

The most experienced singer among the younger men accompanied him, and the other men droned.

The two sang slowly and softly in *shtruar* style, ornamenting the melody with melismas that pulled the song somewhat out of meter. At the song's close, the father exclaimed "Happiness and well-being!" to which the others responded with various phrases of praise. As they congratulated him, each man reached forward to shake his hand. The man who had accompanied him then initiated a round of toasts. At this gathering, the first few toasts were formal and extensive. As each pair of men clinked glasses, they exchanged several complimentary phrases each, exclaiming *Të trashëgoet!* ("Congratulations!") and then alluding to the weddings of the other man's children.

Once the toasting had died down, the men decided to move into the *odë.* Seeing that they were to be displaced, the women rose to bring the men's food and drinks in from the back yard and to set them inside on the coffee table. They then retired to the adjacent family room, where they chatted quietly and listened to the men's singing. As the men entered the *odë,* they arranged themselves very properly *me radhë.* So closely did their seating arrangement parallel that of the earlier women's gathering that several men took the exact seat that their wives had just vacated. My husband positioned himself "at the end of the room" to film (fig. 5).

Since the *kryetar* had already performed, the men now sang *pas pleqësisë:* in descending order of age. The oldest man there, a man in his fifties who is the groom's mother's cousin, led off the singing, accompanied by the host. He sang an abbreviated version of a well-known song about the regiment of the famous hero Çerçiz Topulli, who fought against Greek forces in the early twentieth century. This is a metric song that can be sung either more simply, or more elaborately in *lartër* style. This singer chose a quiet but rapid, sparsely ornamented style of performance:

Ku do ta bëjmë dimrin sivjet?	Where are we to spend the winter? . . .
O Riza medet!	(Alas poor Riza!)
Dë një dimër, dë një kjamet . . .	In the middle of winter, in a blizzard . . .
Kur erdhi dimri, tynë më s'të gjet . . .	When winter came, you could not be found . . .
Të kërkon Çerçizi breg ore me breg . . .	Çerçiz searches for you from peak to peak . . .

At the end of the song, he too exclaimed "Happiness and well-being!" placing his right hand over his heart in a gesture of humility. The others congratulated him. As Memet reached to shake his hand, he said in English, with a smile, *"ajde* Good luck!" Another prolonged period of toasting followed.

At this point the next older man should have sung, but instead a young cousin of the groom broke in. He is the son of Memet's father's brother and mother's sister (i.e., brothers married sisters); in other words, he is both a paternal and a maternal first cousin. The family, however, refers to him as Memet's *djali i xhaxhait,* "son of father's brother," emphasizing the paternal relationship. As the cousin explained later, he

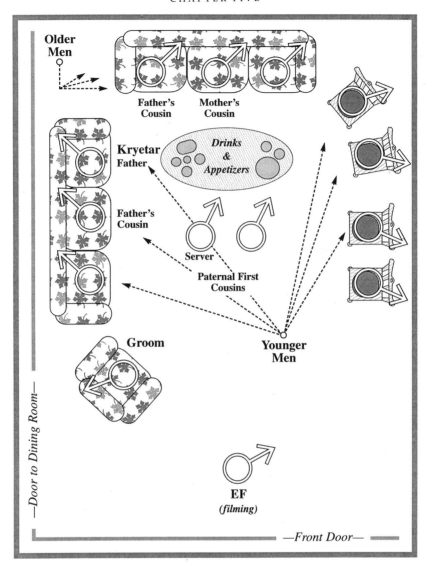

FIGURE 5. Men's Singing at the Groom's, Chicago, 1986

felt that this was an appropriate place for a particularly close relative to sing. Indeed, were this a ritual point in the wedding, then he would have been correct, for at those moments relatives sing *me radhë* in order of their closeness to the bride or groom. At a social gathering, however, he should have waited to sing with the other younger men. Despite his breach of etiquette, he was not cut off but continued his song, accompanied by the groom's father.

The cousin had only learned to sing in the previous few years, although he is an enthusiastic performer now. For this occasion he chose a metric song more often sung by women, but he sang it more slowly and freely than any woman would have. As is customary in such songs, he inserted Memet's name into the text, as he said, "to kid him":

Sh't'është nxirë vetulla
    tynë? . . .
edhe moj, ajde dhe moj.
	Is it that your eyebrows have
	    been blackened? . . .

Mos ja ke shtënë mazinë? . . .	You haven't put on makeup, have you? . . .
Jo e jo, për perëndinë . . .	O no, in God's name . . .
Bandilli në fshat të uaj . . .	The young man is in a far-off village . . .
mollënë në xhep ç'ja ruaj . . .	I keep the apple in my pocket . . .

T'u kalp molla, u gëris
    xhepi . . .
	If the apple rots, the pocket
	    tears . . .

MEMETIT ç'i erdhi lezeti . . .	MEMET's time [to get married] has come . . .

At the end of this and each subsequent song, more exclamations and congratulations were exchanged, followed by a round of toasting.

After some conversation, the proper order of singers resumed with another older man, a cousin of Memet's father. He sang the same song about Avni Rustemi that had been sung by Feime's *xhaxha* the evening before (see CD #20). This is a typical men's *këngë të shtruar,* sung metrically with little ornamentation. Nevertheless, as the song progressed, the "singer" gradually became more absorbed in his performance, singing louder and injecting more exclamations such as *Ajde moj!* into the text.

At the song's end, an effort was made to convince the one remaining older man to sing. Once known for his spirited performances, he had recently had heart surgery and felt weak, and so he declined. Since the momentum of the gathering was faltering somewhat, Memet's father, as the *kryetar,* took up another song. This time he chose a *shtruar* song that he had recently learned from an Albanian video. The man who had just sung accompanied him. As the accompanying man did not know the song, he fudged the words of the verses, taking his lead from the "singer." Eventually, however, he learned the refrain well enough to perform at least that part of the song with confidence. The song refers to the eagle on the Albanian flag, alluding to the country's name Shqipëria, which is often translated as "land of the eagle": [1]

Ç'ke bilbil që po vajton? . . .	Why are you lamenting, nightingale? . . .
edhe o bilbil more,	(O nightingale)
aman, aman edhe o bilbil more.	
Unë vajtoj për një shqiponjë . . .	I am lamenting for an eagle . . .
Plumb i zi seç e qëlloi . . .	A black bullet struck her . . .
Shoqja tonë nuk vdes kurrë . . .	Our young woman will never die . . .
se u bënja me flamur . . .	because I have made myself into a flag . . .

Now the group's attention turned again to the older man who had refused to sing, but he held fast: he did not wish to sing. The *radhë* thus passed to the next generation of younger married men. First in this group was an in-law of the family, an accomplished singer from the lower village of Arvati. He chose a wedding song to address to the groom, but one that—as he once explained to me—has special significance for him as well, since it was the first song that he learned as a child. With its various references to bachelorhood, he had hoped as a boy that singing it would cause the young girls to notice him:

Kur shtira sytë, nëne, n'atë mal . . .	When I lifted my eyes, mother, to that mountain . . .
qaj moj nënja ime, qaj.	(Cry, my mother, cry)
Them ta marr, moj nëne, them të mos e marr? . . .	Should I say I'll marry him, my mother, or should I say no? . . .
Ç'e pashë, nëne, një djalë beqar . . .	I saw, mother, a young bachelor . . .
Them ta marr, moj nëne, them të mos e marr? . . .	Should I say I'll marry him, my mother, or should I say no? . . .
Merre MEMET bej, merre, mos iu ndaj . . .	Marry MEMET *bey,* marry him and never leave him . . .

Më thonë shoqet: "Pi raki,	My girlfriends tell me: "He
duan" . . .	drinks brandy and
	smokes" . . .
Ashtu pinë burrat, raki e	That's how men are, they
duan . . .	drink brandy and smoke . . .

Like the songs sung before it, this is a metric song, but the singer chose to elaborate it in *lartër* style. He sang in full voice, inserting various exclamations into the text and pulling the song out of meter with extensive ornamentation. It was by far the most stirring performance thus far. When those droning did not also intensify their singing, the groom's young cousin intoned on the drone note: *Asaman aman! Iso bëni!* ("Come on! Come on! Do a drone!"). As the singer continued in an animated fashion, the others became more energized and the evening's *muabet* began to "take," as men often explain it. Accompanied by shouts of enthusiasm from the other men, the singer capped off his performance with couplets addressed to the host family (ex. 3.15; CD #17):

Muabet i shtruar	A long, elaborate *muabet:*
gazi, trashëguar!	Be happy and wish the couple
	well!
[omitted line: Zotërinjve ja pa-	[May we now be obligated to
çim ua]	our hosts]
kujt më djemë, kujt më çupa!	to return the favor with [the
	weddings of] our sons and
	daughters!

The praise that greeted his performance was especially animated. One elder exclaimed that he was *bilbil të Arvatit!* ("a nightingale of Arvati!").

Now that the men were beginning to feel "elated," the one elder who had declined to sing at last agreed, and initiated a heroic *këngë të lartër*. Not wishing to agitate his physical condition, he sang softly and at a relatively low pitch level. Nevertheless, he performed the song in a way that conveyed heartfelt emotion, singing out of meter and beginning each line with highly evocative exclamations such as *o-i o-i, ajd' ajde!*, or *o-bo-bo o-i!* This song too had special significance for its performer, who had been afraid that he might die in his recent surgery. Its text, together with his restrained performance, reminded all present of his recent brush with death:

Se ç'u errë e se ç'u nxi.	It got dark and everything turned black.
Mentova se bie shi:	I thought that it was raining,
Ato qenkanë lot e mi.	but it was my tears.
I sëmurë në spitalë	Lying sick in a hospital,
asnjeri as vjen më pa	no one came to see me
përveç dashnores ç'e kam.	except my beloved.
Dëllëndyshe, që po shkoni,	O swallow, when you go,
do t'ju jap një porosi:	I will ask a favor of you:
Vendin tim kur ta afroni,	When you reach my home,
thuani, vdiq një djalë i ri.	tell them that a young man has died.

It was now his brother's turn to sing. The brother is considerably younger and not nearly so experienced as a singer. In this period he often managed not to perform at all, so the others were surprised that he even took part. He started to sing a simple love song learned from a recent recording, but the others interrupted him. The song was more suitable for children, they insisted, not adults. And so his brother suggested a heroic song in *shtruar* style, surely one of the easiest in the Prespa repertoire. It is about a partisan, a man who fought with the Communist forces in World War II:

Tetoria më të dalë . . .	At the end of October . . .
bir Sadush, bir o djalë.	(O son Sadush)
Sadushi shkoi partizan . . .	Sadush went as a partizan . . .
Se ç'e ra murtaja pranë . . .	A bomb landed next to him . . .
se ç'e mori këmbën, kranë . . .	it took his leg and arm . . .
Se ç'e shpunë në spital . . .	They took him to the hospital . . .
në spital në Tiranë . . .	to the hospital in Tiranë . . .

Among those gathered was one older man who had been a partisan in the Yugoslav forces, and another who for years staunchly opposed the Communist regimes in both Yugoslavia and Albania. The singer had sung an especially simple song, as Presparë often say, *ta kapërcejë radhën:* "to get through one's place in the *radhë,*" not to make a political statement through its text. Nevertheless, its sentiments did not go unnoticed. As he sang, the one older man with opposing loyalties sat politely but pointedly refused to drone. How could he "honor" the choice of such a song? His action was evident to the others. Once the song was over, his feelings did not subside. Although he shook hands with the singer, he turned away to avoid his gaze. For a moment the *muabet* of the evening had been "broken" (*prishur*).

Three younger men now remained who had not yet sung, and who do not know how to sing. No one wanted the evening to end so quickly, however, and particularly not on such an awkward note. So at this point my husband and I were summoned to perform for the men, while the women crowded into the doorway to listen. As I stepped into the *odë* amidst the men and took my seat on the floor, I suddenly became very self-conscious and very aware of how unusual my presence there was. In that moment I had my greatest first-hand experience of the *turp* ("shame") to which women often refer when they speak of singing "in public." As I began my song, I found myself staring at the floor and adopting the same stiff and self-effacing posture that I had often seen women my age assume. In so doing I discovered that I felt much as they had often remarked to me that they do: that it helped me in overcoming my sense of embarrassment to cast my eyes downward like a quintessential young woman, avoiding the gaze of others.

Despite my nervousness, our performance was warmly received. Once we had finished, attention returned to the holdouts among the men. Although the two in-laws of the family could easily decline to sing, the situation was more embarrassing for the one who was Memet's *xhaxha*. How could he not sing at his nephew's wedding? As the men conversed, the younger cousin who had earlier interrupted the evening's *radhë* volunteered to sing a song to represent his father, who had not been able to attend the wedding. As Memet's father's brother, his father would have been one of the most important guests. Seeing his way out of a predicament, the recalcitrant *xhaxha* conceded to the cousin.

The cousin selected one of his father's favorite historical songs. It narrates events surrounding the Congress of Berlin held in 1878, when the patriot Abdyl Frashëri beseeched Bismarck to declare Albania an independent country (see Skendi 1967:43–53). One of the older men began to accompany him:

Ipe tren, shkove Gjermani . . .	You got on a train and went to Germany . . .
Avdyl bej nga Frashëri . . .	(Abdyl *bey* from Frashëri) . . .

Although metric, this song is usually performed in *lartër* style. The young singer did indeed sing it loudly and with the appropriate exclamations, but he pitched it well below where men usually sing. After one verse, the second soloist interrupted him. "Sing it higher!" he suggested. The cousin resumed singing, still at the same pitch level, only now he was accompanied by Memet's father:

Aty në Berlin mbaeshte bisedim . . .	There in Berlin they were holding a conference . . .
Ishin mbledhur gjithë kombësi . . .	All the nations were gathered . . .

At such a low pitch level the other men were having trouble droning. As their voices faded, the cousin called out in frustration, "Do a drone!" At this the older man who had first accompanied him interrupted again. First of all, he explained, the other men did not understand why the cousin was singing a second time. Should not the *xhaxha* have tried to sing a song? The *xhaxha* explained that he had let his nephew go ahead, and so it was agreed that the cousin should continue. But now Memet's father interceded, explaining to the cousin that he had a nice voice but that he was singing too low.

Immediately the cousin launched into the next verse. This time, however, he raised the pitch level by a fourth. In a voice that suddenly rang out with the resonance that is so esteemed for heroic songs, he finished the remaining verses. His singing sounded enormously better:

As më jep një lejë të flas unë tani? . . .	"Won't you give me permission to speak now?" . . .
Se ç'u odh Bismarku, pyeti: Kush je ti? . . .	Bismarck spoke up and asked: "Who are you?" . . .
Unë jam Avdyli, ne ma Shqipëri! . . .	"I am Abdyl: give me Albania! . . .
Pesë qind vjet neve o në robëri . . .	For five hundred years we have been enslaved . . .
rrinim nëpër malet me libra në gji . . .	We were living in the mountains, clutching our [Albanian language] books to our hearts." . . .

As soon as he raised the song's pitch, the other men broke into surprised but approving laughter. The older man who had first accompanied him was absolutely delighted. As one rousing verse followed another, he reached into his pocket, pulled out a small revolver, and carefully loaded it. Just as the singer began a new verse, he raised his arm and shot a round into the ceiling, spraying bits of plaster in all di-

rections. Hearing the commotion, the women of the house quickly gathered in the doorway and, when they understood what had happened,
began to applaud. Once the revolver was put away, the other men
reached forward to congratulate its owner heartily. Clearly, the evening's *muabet* had been restored. So pleased was the gun's owner by this
turn in the evening's events that he initiated one final song, another metric song with a historical theme sung in *lartër* style.

The hour was drawing late, and a full day of activities lay ahead of
them, so the men decided to conclude their singing at this point. The
women ushered them to the basement where a long table was set out for
their dinner. There they took their seats *me radhë* and were served a sequence of courses that is standard for wedding meals: chicken noodle
soup; a stew of white beans with meat; roasted chicken served with rice
and tossed green salad; and lastly a Turkish-style pastry, in this case one
called *sheqerpare.* As they ate, Memet's mother and *allo* (father's paternal
female cousin) sang a ritual song for such meals:

Ani mirë edhe pini mirë	Eat well and drink well
mos përpiqni buzat	so that your lips don't even touch,
se nai thyeni lugët.	so you don't bend our spoons.
Lugët pe mergjani s'ka	After all, these are not spoons of silver,
zgjatni duart edhe a.	so stretch out your arms and eat!

At its close, they could not resist teasing the *xhaxha* by adding a *bejte*
intended to cajole him into singing the next time:

Kaq e dita, shumë ja thashë.	I knew only so much, but with that I said a lot [meaning: I'm not a great singer either, but I sang anyway].
Merr e, AZIZ, se ta lashë.	Take up the song, AZIZ, be-cause I leave it to you!

The Prespa "System"

Shortly after we began studying the Albanian language, my husband
and I spent an afternoon with our teacher and his wife in their small

apartment in Skopje. He had been born to a father from southern Albania and a Kolonjar mother and was at that time a graduate assistant in the Macedonian language at the University. His wife is a north Albanian who was then working as a lawyer in the courthouse building. The two of them shared all the duties of childcare for their extremely restless baby daughter, who was then about six months old. As the parents spoke with us, they took turns walking around the room bouncing their baby up and down to keep her from crying; and before they put her down for her nap, they placed her in a blanket and rocked her insistently in the hopes that she would fall asleep. Clearly, her tireless energy was wearing them both out. Once she had fallen asleep and the parents had seated themselves at the dinner table with us, our teacher explained her behavior as best he could. "She has double *inat*," he sighed—*inat* being a much-used Turkish word to describe the obstinacy of children— "Albanian *inat* and Prespa *inat*."

My teacher's comment illustrates a phenomenon that I noticed among many of my Prespa acquaintances: that they speak of themselves as noticeably distinct from other Yugoslav Albanians. Within the context of southeastern Europe, Albanians are particularly notorious for their fierce sense of ethnic pride. But Prespa Albanians augment their close identification with Albanian ethnicity with an emphatic sense of regional identity. As another Prespa friend once commented to us, "It's not to say that I'm not an Albanian, but I'm a Prespar: we're big localists." Most commonly, this localism is summoned up by a word or phrase that refers to the Prespa region. Individuals refer to their community as *presparë*, as *njerëz nga Prespa*, or as *populli tonë të Prespës*, all of which translate as "(our) people from Prespa." It is only for the sake of brevity that I have favored the first term in this study.

Prespa localism is based on a number of perceptions held by community members. First is a recognition of the unusual demographic position of their community within the former Yugoslavia. Prespa families grew up as members of a Muslim Albanian minority within a country that was largely Christian and Slavic. Among that minority, they comprised one of only three small islands of south Albanian culture in a sea of northerners. Their community thus lived as a minority within a minority. Because of their complicated ethnic, religious, and national situation, individuals from Prespa have found themselves identifying at times with collective labels that have united them with a wide variety of other, larger groups: as *shqiptarë* ("Albanians"), as *toskë* ("Tosks"), as *muslimanë* ("Muslims"), as *jugosllavë* ("Yugoslavs"), as "Yugoslavians" or "Yugoslav-Albanians" or "Yugoslav-Canadians" (in North America), and some even as *maqedonë* ("Macedonians"). The term Presparë, then, has designated a group of people united by the confluence of these other, broader designations, at the same time distinguishing them from all other groups with whom they have shared partial affinity.

Presparë also recognize, at some level, that their families are intricately interrelated, to the extent that it is probably possible to identify some sort of kinship tie between any two Prespa households. For this reason, individuals often use the term Presparë to include only those families who commonly intermarry and who interact socially on a regular basis because of marriage ties established in the past. Families from the lower villages, for example, might use "Presparë" to denote only Albanians from those villages, excluding both Kolonjarë families and the Albanian-speaking Muslims of villages to the north.

The strongest source of Prespa localism, however, is their sense of themselves as a moral community defined by a distinctive set of shared discourses and practices. Presparë often allude to these by speaking of their *sistem* or "system," a word that has clearly been introduced only recently into their speech. Individuals might also characterize them by the word *besë* (roughly "credo"), which in literary Albanian refers most commonly to one's "faith" or "religion." Presparë do at times use *besë* to refer specifically to Islamic tenets, but it seems to me that they also often use it when speaking of features of community life that have no direct connection to Islam.

Over the years I have come to see the "system" of Presparë as a complex and at times contradictory blending of discourses and practices that developed during different historical periods and, in some cases, originally among other population groups. First are those elements common to virtually all Albanian communities, whether Christian or Muslim, and whether northern or southern. Here it is significant that Presparë evoke the word *besë*, which carries great resonance in north Albanian speech in its meaning as a man's "word of honor." Second are elements shared with other Muslim communities. Many of these, even ones not directly associated with religious observance, seem to have developed initially within Arab society. They were then introduced into southeast Europe during the Ottoman period, where they were adopted by many communities, especially Muslim ones. Some were associated with secular, urban Ottoman culture, others with aspects of Ottoman Islam, particularly Sufism. The Prespa "system" thus resembles those of other eastern Mediterranean communities in part because many elements have a common source, although there has been considerable local modification. Less in evidence, but still important, are discourses and practices associated with the majority societies in which Presparë have lived in recent decades: those of post-war Yugoslavia and of late twentieth-century North America.

Presparë intuitively recognize those commonalities when they refer to their *sistem* or their *besë* as the basis of their affiliation with larger social entities. First and foremost, they see their "system" as their birthright as Albanians. Secondarily it is their *besë*, in the sense of "religion," that connects them to all who share the Muslim faith, regardless of ethnicity. Finally, many of the practices that exemplify their *sistem* are shared by virtually all ethnic groups in southeast Europe. Much of the *radhë* of their social gatherings, for example, is commonly observed by all groups in the Prespa region, most particularly by Muslims.

Presparë cite certain aspects of their "system," however, such as the relatively high regard in which women are held and the more temperate, less belligerent tone that characterizes interfamilial relations, as distinguishing them as Prespa Muslim Tosk Albanians from other groups with whom they share an ethnic or religious affiliation, and particularly from north Albanians. These they attribute, first, to the teachings of local Muslim leaders and itinerant holy men. It is my suspicion that Sufi precepts, and particularly those of the Bektashi order (see Birge 1937), have formed a substantial part of their exposure to Islam, although that "faith" was never embraced officially by Presparë other than the Kolonjarë. Second, they commonly refer to their having been "outside" (*jashtë*), that is, to their having traveled and lived in North America, western Europe, and Australia. It is because of their greater experience with the world beyond Kosova and Macedonia that Presparë often speak of themselves as the most "progressive" (*përparuar*) Albanians of the former Yugoslavia, in the sense of their having accommodated their "system" somewhat more to a Western view of society. At present, it is mainstream North American society that is providing the most significant challenge to the "system" of immigrant families living there, but it is also the richest source of new discourses and practices that might successfully be accommodated within it.

Notions of Social Identity

The Prespa community's "system" consists, in part, of a set of understandings as to the organization of Prespa society and an individual's place within it. When I first visited Prespa villages, it was the strong division recognized between males and females that initially caught my attention, and so it might seem logical to begin an exposition of community notions of social identity with a discussion of gender. I have come to believe, however, that Prespa understandings of gender, like those of most other Mediterranean communities, derive from a more fundamental view of society as composed of kin groups related through patrilineal descent. Such a view inevitably shapes the ways that individuals of either gender, of various age groups, and of different family units are perceived and come to perceive themselves, and informs the sorts of relationships that they establish and sustain between each other.

The "House"

Presparë who are related through their father's line proclaim themselves to be "one lineage" (*një fis*) or "one blood" (*një gjak*), or to be "of one house" (*pe një shtëpi*). Phrases such as these would seem to derive from a view of procreation that was once widespread among Albanians, not to mention throughout Europe and the Near East. In this view, a child is formed from the father's substance alone, while the mother's body provides a nourishing medium during the fetus's development.[2] Durham, for example, discusses the north Albanian belief that "the child is the descendant of his father only. He merely, as it were, passes through his mother" (1928:147). Reineck confirms such attitudes among present-day north Albanians in Kosova: "A knowledge of modern genetics notwithstanding, many Kosova Albanians state that, indeed, their 'blood,' their essence, derives from their father and his agnatic line. Children 'belong' to the patriline" (1991:47). Although present-day Presparë are familiar with the medical concepts of semen and ovum, much of their parlance regarding kinship keeps the older view alive at some implicit level. As is detailed in subsequent chapters, so do many of the ritual practices that are crucial to wedding celebrations.

In line with this view of procreation, an individual's sense of social identity centers on the interconnected notions of lineage and "house." In one meaning, the word *shtëpi* ("house") refers to a single household: the individuals who reside in one building or complex of buildings. Most typically, such a household has consisted of a married couple, their married sons with wives and children, and their unmarried daughters. These households have been the basic units of Prespa society. In old ethnographies and "geographies" of the area, the population of villages was most frequently given in terms of "houses" rather than individuals.

Even today, Presparë speak of how many *shtëpi* make up their villages, or how many *shtëpi* of Presparë live in Toronto or Chicago.

The principal representative of any household within the community is its *zoti i shtëpisë*, literally the "lord" or "master of the house." Most often this term denotes the oldest male member. For community members who do not know the family well, his name is synonymous with the household. If his name is Asan, for example, his son's wedding will be referred to as "Asan's wedding," rather than the son's. Even when his sons are in their thirties or forties, they might still be alluded to by others as "Asan's boys" (*djemtë të Asanit*), and their wives as "Asan's brides" (*nuset të Asanit*). Children learn early to define themselves in terms of their family's patriarch. Whereas I might ask a child in my North American neighborhood, "Who are you?" a Prespa child is asked, "*Whose* are you?"

The word *shtëpi* may also indicate a patrilineal unit larger than a single household: a person's lineage group. In Prespa such lineage groups comprise clusters of households whose male ancestors are said to have formed a single household at some point in the past. Generally they have names consisting of the Turkish plural form of the personal name of a man who was *zoti i shtëpisë* at some prior point in time. If his name was Memet, for example, then they are known as the Memetllarë, or "Memet's people." Members of a lineage group generally live in a distinct neighborhood or *mejallë* (from Arab. *mahallah*) of the village that is known by their family name. People speak of taking the oxen out past the Memetllarë on their way to pasture, or fetching water from the spring over by the Ramizllarë. Likewise, Macedonian extended families, who live intermixed with Albanians in the lower villages, occupy their own neighborhoods identified according to Slavic patronymics such as Petkovski or Stojanovski. Patrilineality is thus inscribed on the landscape of each Prespa village, and an individual grows up with a sense of self and a sense of place that are intimately intertwined.

In most cases, the name that designates the lineage group of Albanian families refers to the father, grandfather, or great-grandfather of Presparë who are still alive; in other words, to the *zoti i shtëpisë* of an extended household that existed within living memory of the oldest generation. The names of such groups therefore summon up, for that generation, images of village society as it was when they were young. In some cases, however, families claim that their lineage designation refers to the patriarch of an extended family that came to settle in Prespa from

Albania several centuries ago. At present there is no way to verify such claims. The legends associated with such groups are one of the means through which Prespare establish their legitimacy as Albanians and, more particularly, as participants within the larger world of southern Albanian history and culture. Similar claims to "authentic" Albanianness also seem to motivate the use by the *bejlerë* families of the ascription "Kolonjarë," which emphasizes their direct tie to the Albanian homeland and particularly to prominent Bektashi families from Kolonjë.[3]

Patrilineality is likewise at the basis of the legal surnames that Prespare now use, which are formed from their grandfather's or great-grandfather's name. In the period following World War II, these were formed with a Slavic suffix: for example, the descendants of Memet were known as Memetovski. Within the last few decades, however, in line with greater recognition of their distinctiveness as Albanians, most Prespa families have replaced the Slavic suffix with an Albanian one: from Memetovski to Memeti. In some cases this legal surname was formed from the name of the same progenitor whose name was given to the lineage, so that the families known as the Memetllarë, for example, took the surname Memeti. In most instances, however, this was not the case; a family might instead have taken the name Aliu, after a son or grandson of Memet named Ali. Even today Prespare rarely know the surnames of other families, but they frequently use lineage designations in conversation to identify lesser known individuals within the Prespa community: "You know her—she's from the Memetllarë!"

Male and Female

Because of the primacy of patrilineal descent, an individual's ongoing relationship to his or her household is ordained at birth. A son is hailed as *temeli i shtëpisë*, "the foundation of the house."[4] His birth signals the continuity of household and lineage and is cause for a large celebration. He will remain within the family home, providing labor and income for his family and eventually bringing home a bride who will help with women's chores. For those families that continue to place their incomes in a common fund, as used to be customary, their household's wealth lies in its number of sons.

A daughter, in contrast, is considered to be the family's *dera e botës*, "doorway to the world," in that she will eventually leave the household and establish ties of kinship and obligation to heretofore unrelated families. Until perhaps twenty years ago, a daughter left her family home and entered her husband's on the basis of a marriage contracted by the couple's parents and other relatives. Thereafter she lived with him, his parents, and his brothers and their families in a single household. She was regarded as the "bride," or *nuse*, of the household and addressed by that title by all of her husband's kin of her generation and older.

Today, young people have some say in the choice of a marriage partner, and couples move out to live on their own at a younger age; but the ways in which a young married woman is regarded within her household, and the expectations that are placed on her, have not much changed. From the point of view of her in-laws her principal duty within the family is to bear children, preferably male heirs to the family line.[5] Secondarily, she is expected to add to the household's work force. Her virginity at marriage is insisted on, as is her chaste behavior as a married woman, in order to insure that her offspring are genuinely of her husband's "blood." As du Boulay has remarked of Greek brides, she is expected to "bring to her marriage a chastity that reaches far beyond sexual fidelity and involves, without exception, all areas of her behavior" (1986:163). In particular, it is her responsibility to avoid any intimate contact with men outside her household and to suppress any hint of sexuality in her demeanor.

In the sense that society is seen as comprised of male-defined kin groups, it may be said that society itself has been construed as male. For families living in Prespa, it is the men who have been charged with the "public" realm of economic transactions and community-wide concerns and who have represented their family group ceremonially at large events, such as weddings, that bring various households together. As Ortner (1978:24) has pointed out, women are "interstitial" within such a schema: they provide the glue that links men of different generations together into an ongoing lineage. I received confirmation of this view of female identity during a conversation with a young Prespa woman. Having been married at that point for a few years, she volunteered to me that she felt very lucky with the choice of husband that her parents had made for her and detailed the many things that she liked about him. When I asked if he too felt lucky to have married her, she replied simply, "Well, I gave him his children. I'm sort of an in-between person." Her statement alludes both to her primary role as child-bearer and to unilineal views of procreation. Consistent with such beliefs, the role of women has been to preside over a "private," family-centered realm that includes domestic activities as well as the sexual relations of those within the family.[6]

The Cycle of Generations

Within any Prespa household, individuals refer to each other with designations that unite gender, marital status, and generation. A male is considered to be a *djalë* ("boy") until he marries, when he becomes a *burrë* ("man"). When his first child of either gender marries, he becomes a *plak*, or male "elder." Similarly, a female is a *çupë* ("girl") until she marries and leaves the family home. At this point she becomes known, not as a "woman," but as the "bride" or *nuse* of her husband's household. When her first child marries, she then becomes a *plakë*, or female "elder" (table 5). These six designations are the only categories of rank that Prespařë recognize among themselves. One's category within one's household thus serves as the criterion for one's inclusion within the social hierarchy of the Prespa Albanian community as a whole.

One older woman, as she explained these designations to me, moved her hands in a circle and exclaimed, "This earth is always spinning!" as if to emphasize their cyclic character. Indeed, the age designations for each gender seem to be experienced not in terms of each individual's biological cycle, but rather as a progression of stages that is synchronized with that of other household members. In particular, adults speak of themselves as attaining elder status when the next younger generation displaces them. The most common response of women to my questioning as to when they became an "elder" was that they ceased to be a *nuse* either when they had a *nuse* or when their daughter became a *nuse*.

One striking feature of this system of age-grades is that it assumes a household consisting of no more than three generations, and this was generally the case until recently. A household typically consisted of a

TABLE 5 Categories of Gender and Generation

Household	1st Generation	2nd Generation	3rd Generation
1	djalë / çupë	burrë / nuse	plak / plakë
2	djalë / çupë	burrë / nuse	plak / plakë
3	djalë / çupë	burrë / nuse	plak / plakë

married couple of the elder generation, their married sons with wives and children, and any unmarried sons and/or daughters. By the time the first grandsons were teenagers, the youngest daughters had already married and were no longer part of the household. At this point or even before, most households "separated": each married son established a household, and the elderly parents went to live with the youngest son, whose children were usually still young. By the time that his sons married and his first grandchildren were born, his parents had most often already died.

Before World War II, it was not uncommon for married couples to have six or eight or more children apiece, so as to provide an ample work force and to guard against infant mortality. Households grew significantly with each generation, with the result that most of today's elders were born into relatively large households. In the early 1950s, one household in Krani, at the point when its members separated, was made up of seven brothers with their wives and children (the brothers' parents had died), as well as the wives and children of the oldest grown sons, and totaled almost fifty individuals. Such a family was referred to as a *kallaballëk shtëpi* (from Tk. *kalabalık:* "crowd, throng, confused mass").

A few families have continued to maintain this type of extended household, even in North America. At the time one family in Chicago separated in 1989, for example, nineteen individuals—an older couple, their three married sons with their wives, and eleven grandchildren—occupied most of the apartments in a large, family-owned building. A married daughter with her husband, his parents, and their two children had lived in the one remaining apartment until the year before, but were regarded as a separate "house." In most instances, however, both in Macedonia and abroad, household sizes have decreased dramatically in the past few decades, and young couples hope to move into their own home only a few years after marriage. It is nevertheless still common for a son and his wife to live with his parents at least in their first few years of married life.

Some of the most commonly used kinship designations can be understood with reference to the situation that used to exist in the large patrilineal households. Most notably, individuals generally refer to all agnatic male kin of their father's generation—men who in English would be distinguished as one's father's "brothers" or "first cousins"—by the term *xhaxha* (probably from the Slavic root *djadja*). Collectively, these men are referred to as the *xhaxhallarë* (lit. "uncles"), a word which, by extension, may be used to include all the men of one's father's lineage.

The wives of all such "uncles" are referred to by the term *xhaxhicë*, formed with a Slavic suffix. Agnatic female kin of the parental generation, both the father's sisters and his first cousins, are known as *allo* (Tk. *hala*, Arab. *khāla*; "father's sister"), while their husbands are called *enishte* (Tk. *enişte*) or *dhëndër* (used for many types of male "in-law"). Likewise, both first and second cousins of one's own generation are most commonly referred to as the "boy" or "girl" of one's *xhaxha* or *allo* (for example, *djali i xhaxhait, çupa e allos*). The more general term *kushëri* ("cousin") is used far less frequently.[7]

A second feature of the system of age-grades is its relationship to issues of sexuality and procreation. By linking stages of adulthood to both marriage and the bearing of children, the generational cycle constructs any individual's gendered identity around the imperative of reproducing for the sake of the lineage. Since adulthood is conceptualized as being attained through marriage, there is no slot within the system for a person who chooses not to marry at a young age. For males, who might marry considerably later than females, this situation is mitigated somewhat by the use of the word *beqar* or "bachelor" (Tk. *bekâr*, from Pers. *bīkār*, lit. "unemployed, idle"), but no such term exists to describe an unmarried adult female. There is also no slot for a person who pursues ongoing sexual relations, whether heterosexual or homosexual, outside marriage; nor for a person who does not pursue the goal of having children. Since social life is organized on the basis of these categories, individuals who pursue alternative life strategies are generally ostracized from community occasions and risk being disinherited by their families.[8]

Likewise, it is sexual activity and the bearing of children that distinguish adults of the parent and grandparent generations. Young married adults are regarded as the generation responsible for producing children. Sexual activity is expected of them, but only as a means of procreation. Most brides hope to bear their first child within the first year of marriage; indeed, a bride is not considered to be a "woman" (*grua* or *zonjë*) until she does so. In giving birth she achieves womanhood and can henceforth claim legitimacy and authority within the household by virtue of that experience.

The years of a woman's young adulthood are marked in part by her dress. Once a girl approaches marriageable age, her mother begins to dress her in a manner that, without any implication of sexuality, highlights her physical attractiveness and her ladylike bearing. After marriage, as a new "bride," she is expected to present herself publicly as a most attractive and prized acquisition of her husband's family, and so she dresses in an even more eye-catching manner, one that expresses both her fertility and the economic standing of her new household:

> My father-in-law had been in America and he brought me a dress with flowers at the hem. When I wore it, people would say, "Where is your beautiful dress from?" And I would say, "My father-in-law brought it to me from America!" He brought it for my mother-in-law but he gave it to me because [my husband] was the oldest son. (Interview with a woman elder in Chicago, 1986)

Particularly in public, but even within the home, a present-day "bride" characteristically wears bright, "open" colors (*boja të apura*) such as red, white, pink, royal blue, or spring green. For more formal occasions, she may wear elegant fabrics such as satiny polyester or velvet, often interwoven with metallic threads or covered with sequins or beading. She is expected to have her hair styled fashionably and to wear makeup. In the words of innumerable wedding songs, she is a *lule*—a flower in bloom:

Lule e bukur me bojë allit	Beautiful, bright red flower
duke dalë për rrëzë malit	blooming at the edge of the mountain
gjer e zgjodhe bashnë e djalit.	until you found the best possible young man.
Lule e bukur me bojë allit	Beautiful, bright red flower
duke dalë për rrëzë fushës	blooming at the edge of the field
gjer të zgjodhë bashnë e çupës.	until you were found to be the best possible young lady.
Ruaju, lule, se mos të shkelin!	Be careful, flower, that they don't trample you!
Jo, more baba, nuku më shkelin	Oh no, father, they won't trample me
se më kanë nuse, më përkëdhelin.	for I am their bride, and they pamper me.

(Women's wedding song, bride's side; Krani, 1972)

As a couple's children approach the age of marriage, both husband and wife begin to mark their transition to "elder" status with a shift in their dress that I interpret as denoting a progression beyond the period of procreation. Female elders typically begin to wear dresses of dark, "closed" colors (*boja të mbyllura*): dark brown, navy blue, or forest green.[9] They may choose to cover their hair with a scarf and may cease to wear much makeup. Men may begin to wear a dark-colored shirt. In becoming elders, a couple in essence passes on reproductive responsibility within the household to its children's generation. No longer expected to be sexually active, it is considered inappropriate for them to dress in a way that would call attention to their appearance. As one woman commented on the change in attire that would be prompted by her daughter's marriage: "People would say, 'Her daughter has come out as a bride, and she's still dressing like a bride!'"

In the days when large patrilineal households were the norm in Prespa, work activities were also structured in terms of gender and generation, in ways that were still evident when I lived there in 1981. On the one hand a strict division was observed by most households between women's work within the home and men's outside it:

> At that time the women didn't go out to work in the fields; they just stayed at home. We had a four-day work cycle (*radhë*) for making food, with three or four women working together. . . . My father-in-law with one of his brothers ran the store. Another brother went with the sheep. Two or three brothers worked the land. Of the sons, one went with the lambs, one with the cow. We were quite a crowd (*kallaballëk*), but we were very well-to-do. (Interview in Chicago with a female elder, 1986; speaking of the early 1950s)

Men performed the agricultural work in the fields, cared for livestock, and took charge of all business transactions, whether with fellow villagers or at the market in town. In addition to these subsistence activities, many families also raised tobacco and, more recently, apples as cash crops, both of which were maintained and harvested by the men. Men were thus most active in the open, "public" spaces surrounding household compounds, as well as in the world beyond the village. In contrast, women's chores included cooking, preparing clothing for household members, maintaining the house and its courtyard, and caring for children. For those households that raised tobacco as a cash crop, they also spent much of the summer and fall stringing it in the courtyard of their homes and packing it for sale. Women were thus most active in the "private" realm of the family compound and its immediate environs. In the past, if there were an insufficient number of adult males to handle the heavy farm work, the household temporarily hired outside laborers, usually Roma. Only in cases where a family had almost no adult males was it seen as acceptable for women to do some work in the fields. In recent years, however, as household size has decreased, women have frequently worked in the fields, harvested tobacco, and tended the apple orchards together with their husbands.

On the other hand, different sorts of chores were assigned to different generations. For each gender, those involved in the greatest amount of physical labor were the members of the young adult generation, who were seen as being at their physically strongest. Men had the greater number of backbreaking tasks to perform, such as plowing and harvesting. Young women, however, had to knead troughfuls of bread dough, scrub family-sized loads of soiled clothing, and fetch large buckets of water from distant springs or fountains. Whether a teenage girl exhibited the physical stature and endurance necessary for heavy work was, in fact, an important consideration for parents when choosing a bride for their son.

As adults passed into "elder" status, they gradually withdrew from such tasks and took on a supervising role within their appropriate sphere. At the other end of the cycle, children were viewed as apprentice or assistant laborers. In the family with whom I lived in Prespa, the children assisted their parents in chores appropriate to their gender and in addition were assigned simple tasks to perform on their own. By their early teens they had gradually been put in charge of a range of specific household or farming tasks, such as laundering the clothes for girls or caring for certain livestock for boys. By their mid-teens, they were expected to have mastered the full range of activities necessary for them to take on the adult responsibilities that went along with their impending marriage.

Kin and Friends

When today's immigrants were living in Prespa, their daily lives revolved around work activities carried out with the members of their household, as well as with their *xhaxhallarë* living nearby in the neighborhood. Despite the emphasis placed on patrilineality, however, close ties were also maintained with the households of the *zoti i shtëpisë*'s blood relatives through the female line. These might have included his sisters; his father's sisters and female cousins; his mother's sisters; and his mother's brothers and male cousins, these last known collectively as his family's *daillarë* (from Tk. *dayı*, "mother's brother"). Because relatives through the female line often lived in distant neighborhoods or in other villages, they did not commonly engage in joint work activities. Except in rare instances, however, households thus related did socialize frequently. A similar situation existed with the households of a man's wife's kin, most notably her parents and siblings, but also her cousins. In many instances, affinal ties were reinforced with agnatic ones through marriage patterns in which related females were married to related males: for example, marriages of two sisters, or of an aunt and niece, to two brothers.

Presparë refer to individuals related through any such ties as their *soj* (Tk. *soy*), that is, of their "breed." They might also allude to them as their "people" (*njerëz*) or simply as "ours" (*tonë*):

Do you have *njerëz* in Chicago? (Do you have *people* [relatives] there?)

Which Sami? Oh, Sami *tonë*. (Oh, *our* Sami.)

Soj are spoken of in terms of their "closeness" to a household. Usually it is aunts, uncles, and first and second cousins who are considered to be "closest" to (*më të afërt*) or "innermost" within (*më të brëndshme*) the family. In the case of the *xhaxhallarë* and their wives and children, these are often individuals who, at some point in the past, lived in a single extended household or in neighboring households, and who therefore share a lifetime of common memories and experiences.

Any individual can usually describe quite precisely his or her connection to another relative to the distance of third or fourth cousin. For more distant relatives, that same individual may only be able to explain the relationship in vague terms. One man explained to me his relationship to a range of men of different generations simply by saying, of each, "He is my *dai* (lit., 'mother's brother')," meaning that each was related to him in some way through his mother. This vagueness can be explained in part by the commonly expressed belief that one should not marry a relative on either the paternal or maternal side who is a fourth cousin or closer. As Prespa families intermarry more and more, it is harder for parents to find potential spouses for their children who meet that criterion. One prominent role of female elders in the community is to keep track of such matters, both to assure that kin do not marry and to be alert for appropriate pairings among the current crop of young people of marriageable age. It is primarily for this purpose that families maintain a notion of a genealogy, rather than from a desire to legitimate their place in society through their descent from a distant ancestor, as is often the case among north Albanians.

Families commonly speak of those who are not *soj* as *njerëz të uaj*: "foreigners" or "strangers." Among many Mediterranean communities, such phraseology betrays the antagonistic and competitive stance that has often been maintained between agnatic groups that have functioned largely as self-contained economic units. As has already been remarked, however, Prespa households have relied heavily on each other for exchanges of goods and services, for spouses for their children, and for economic and social support at times of family celebrations or crises. They have thus functioned as a community through a network of reciprocal relationships that, for each household, extends considerably beyond those families recognized as being *soj*. Families refer to those nonrelatives with whom a household maintains ongoing close relationships as their "friends" (*miq;* sing. *mik*). Friends have very often included neighbors (*komshi;* Tk. *komşu*), whose proximity makes them convenient candidates for daily exchanges. Other friends have included the neighbors of close relatives or, more generally, families that they have come to know through years of social interchange.

Presparë commonly speak of friends with reference to kinship designations. A man will often refer to a long-time friend as being "like a brother"; or a woman will be spoken of by another woman as being "like a sister." Likewise, children are taught to address adult friends of their household by the titles *xhaxha* ("father's brother") for a man, and *teze* ("mother's sister") for a woman, followed by the person's name. I was, for example, addressed as *"teze* Xhejn" by many children. In informal situations, young people often address any older woman simply as *nëne* ("mother"; vocative form). And all older men are referred to within the community by the title *Xha,* a shortened version of *xhaxha;* for example, an elder named Naim would commonly be known as *Xha* Naim. Often in Mediterranean communities, usages such as these enable families to bridge the gap of antagonism and distrust that separates one's kin from all others within one's social world. Among Presparë, for whom they are particularly pervasive, they point out the interconnectedness that community members feel as a small and distinctive social group.

The overwhelming majority of the friends of any household have been other Prespa Albanians. Each household may, however, have had a few friends from other ethnic groups. In the upper villages, households have had friends who are Turkish-speaking Muslims, and it has been even more common for Albanians in the lower villages to count a few Macedonian families among their close friends. In these villages there was a widespread custom in the past whereby adolescent boys from a Macedonian and an Albanian household would become "blood brothers" (Alb. *vëllam*, Mac. *pobratim*). The two would each prick a finger and then drink a bit of the other's blood, thereby entering symbolically into the other's lineage group. To this day, blood brothers customarily attend each other's family celebrations, help each other with major household tasks, and even provide financial assistance if needed.[10]

A family's economic standing has also been a factor in forming friendships. In prior historical periods, relations between Prespa households were characterized by varying degrees of economic disparity. In the Ottoman period, most villagers were *çifçi*, that is, indentured workers on land belonging to the *bejlerë* or to a few other landholders who had attained wealth and position in the Ottoman administration. In the period between the wars, under a capitalist system, some households were able to amass considerable wealth and to acquire large landholdings. In some instances one or more of the men of the household had earned money abroad that was then invested in the village. In other instances, families with several sons were able to bring in supplemental incomes from livestock, cash crops, or maintaining a store or inn. These more well-to-do families often hired other villagers as workers in various capacities. It may be assumed that the wealth of such families enabled them to attain certain privileges, at least within the district, as well as to bring other households into a position of financial obligation to them.

With the establishment of socialism in Yugoslavia, the amount of land that any household could own was limited, as was the size of any private enterprise. Economic discrepancies between families lessened, but it is still possible to derive some status within the Prespa community through membership in one of the former wealthy lineages. Kolonjarë families, descendants of the former overlords, have used their distinctive religion and their more "authentic" Albanian-ness as justification for maintaining a community separate from that of other Prespare. Likewise, members of formerly wealthy and powerful families who are not Kolonjarë have tended to associate primarily with each other. As a result of such patterns, most of the friends of any Prespa household are from families that had roughly the same economic standing in pre-war Yugoslavia.

These patterns are in turn enforced by marriage practices. Kolonjarë most often marry their children to other Kolonjarë, or to the children of Bektashi families from Albania. The only exception might be to a child of one of the formerly wealthy and prominent Sunni lineages. For these latter families, a child's marriage to a Kolonjar or Kolonjarkë is a means of paving the way for the family's entry into the world of the Prespa elite, and children of such marriages inevitably identify themselves as Kolonjarë. In the upper villages, marriages between Albanian- and Turkish-speaking families are fairly common, since the two groups are both Muslim. Often both languages continue to be spoken in such households. In the lower villages, however, marriages between Muslim Albanians and Christian Macedonians are the great exception. I have heard of only one such match, and the couple in question immediately moved out of the district.

Honor and the Moral Order

Within the Prespa community's "system," aspects of social identity such as household and lineage, gender and generation, kinship and friendship, are linked together by discourses and practices that outline how individuals within the community should behave in the company of others, as well as the degree of respect or deference that they should show toward or expect from others within the community. These, in turn, imply certain assumptions as to the innate nature of males and females and the roles that members of each gender are expected to play within society as they move through the cycle of generations. Such assumptions serve to articulate and legitimate the degree of power and autonomy that members of each gender and generation may expect to command within the household and, by extension, within the community as a whole. They center on the question of what it means to be a "person" within Prespa society, and the "honor" that accrues to one's personhood.

Personhood, Mindfulness, and Potency

One of my Prespa acquaintances in Toronto is a man who grew up in one of the few Albanian households in an otherwise Macedonian village. During one of my visits with him, he spoke fondly of some of the Macedonians with whom he grew up and complained of the prejudice that people in the former Yugoslavia have often expressed toward other ethnic groups or kombë (lit., "nations"). "Even if a person is from another kombë," he exclaimed, "I was born of a mother and he was born of a mother. There is only one God." To which his mother added, "There is only one God. There is only one sun."

Phrases such as these are commonly recited by Presparë and were evidently instilled in them by religious teachers when they were grow-ing up. They have held Presparë in good stead in their relations with other linguistic and religious groups, both in the former Yugoslavia and abroad. In North America, Presparë often reconcile their necessary in-teractions with other groups through the stock phrase, "They too are people" (*Edhe ata janë njerëz*). I suspect, however, that the sentiments expressed in such phrases are significant for Presparë, not because they represent their most deeply felt beliefs, but because they temper a much more fundamental assumption among community members: that their distinctive "system" renders them morally superior to the other groups among whom they live.

The stock sayings of Presparë would seem to imply that "all men are created equal," regardless of the social group into which they are born. In everyday parlance, however, the word *njeri* ("person" or "human be-ing") is not a descriptive term for any person, but rather a moral ascrip-tion that must be earned. According to this view, all humans have the potential to be good and moral individuals, but the attribution of "per-son" is reserved for an individual who demonstrates his or her adherence to the community's moral code through acceptable social behavior.

If an individual behaves in an improper, antisocial manner, then he or she risks being called an "animal" or *ajvan* (more specifically, "beast of burden"; Tk. *hayvan*, Arab. *ḥayawān*). When, for example, one of my Prespa friends in Toronto complained about her Italian neighbor, who consistently refused to acknowledge or greet her when they met on the street, she exclaimed (in English): "That's not a person, that's an animal!" What distinguishes a *njeri* from an *ajvan* is *mënd*, literally "mind."[11] A *njeri*, or a person who is *i mënçëm* (lit. "mindful," fem. *e mënçme*), has learned to overcome his or her animalistic aspects in order to act as a social being. This theme of mastery over one's animal nature was evi-dently also a part of Muslim religious teaching in the villages:

> On Fridays in [the village] they would read [the Qur'ān] in the mosque, and the *imam* or *oxha* would instruct the people. He taught a person how to be a *njeri* and not an *ajvan*, what was sinful, what was shameful, hon-orable, good, evil. (Interview with an older woman in Detroit, 1986)

One important aspect of "mindfulness" is a person's capacity for emo-tional self-control. In this sense *mënd* can be thought of as an equivalent for the English notion of "reason." Being "mindful" also involves being cognizant of the extent to which one's behavior affects others within one's social world. As one man pointed out, "A *njeri* who thinks only of himself isn't a *njeri*."

Children are born human, but are not yet socialized humans. The period of their childhood is seen as one in which they gradually become "mindful," in the sense of "socialized." When they misbehave, they are not told that they are "bad," but that they are animals of various sorts. "You're a monkey!" an exasperated parent will yell at a child, "You're a donkey and a pig!" With marriage and the birth of one's first child, one becomes an adult man (*burrë*) or woman (*grua* or *zonjë*), terms that in this context designate members of both the parent and grandparent generations. At this point one is expected to have been socialized to a manner of behavior that is appropriate to a member of one's gender, and one is fully accountable to the society at large for one's actions.[12]

Not all adults, however, are considered to be equally "mindful." Presparë regard the acquisition of knowledge through experience in the social world as a lifelong process. As a man gains experience within the public sphere, his esteem within the community increases to the point where, once he has achieved a position of seniority, he may be consulted on a range of matters by younger members of the community and asked to mediate when disputes between households arise. Likewise, while relatively lacking in knowledge of community politics, adult women are nevertheless in charge of domestic matters, and here too esteem increases together with experience. As a woman bears children and takes a greater part in the management of the household, she establishes her legitimacy within the family and is viewed as less of an outsider. Once she has daughters-in-law, she supervises their domestic activities and, like her husband, may be consulted for her knowledge on a range of matters such as social etiquette, ritual observance, and family genealogies. It is the maturity and discretion that come with age that Presparë, together with all other Albanians, salute through their use of a separate designation for "elders" (masc. *pleq*, fem. *plaka*).

Presparë speak of degrees of social knowledge, and thus of "mindfulness," through metaphors of aurality and orality. When they wish to indicate that an older person is particularly knowledgeable in some realm, they will say that he or she *ka fjalë*: "has words." Worldly wisdom is manifest through the ability to speak well, to articulate one's knowledge. Indeed, like other Albanians, they distinguish two different ways of saying "to understand": *kuptoj*, which means to grasp the logic of something; and *marr vesh*, literally, "to seize with one's ears," which can mean both to comprehend what is being communicated and to come to an agreement with someone. A person, for example, *kupton* a mathematical equation, but *merr vesh* something that has just been explained to him or her.

At any gathering, lines of communication between those present are ideally drawn according to such perceptions of relative degrees of social knowledge. Elders are entitled to dominate any discussion, although they may choose not to do so, and children in particular are expected to "listen to" (*dëgjojnë*), in the sense of "obey," all adults. This conversational hierarchy was evident in my first contacts with north Albanian families in Skopje: if I visited a friend of roughly my own age, I was expected to converse primarily with the friend's parents, while the friend and other siblings sat and listened politely.

Likewise, men and women cannot be said to be equally "mindful." In many strongly patrilineal societies, the emphasis placed on the man's role in decision-making regarding his household has been legitimated in part through the belief that men by nature are more capable of rational intelligence than women. Women are seen to remain closer to their natural, animal selves, and thus to be less "rational" and more "emotional." As anthropologists have paid more attention to the women within such societies, however, they have found that women often counter such notions by attributing a man's greater "intelligence" to his more extensive experience in and knowledge of the public sphere. They therefore grant him his right to make decisions by viewing the realm of interfamilial relations, economic matters, and political concerns as his domain of responsibility.

In my conversations with Presparë, I have found them to be especially sensitive about such issues. Having lived within predominantly Christian societies in both Yugoslavia and North America, where discourses circulate widely that label Muslims as culturally "backward," community members have grown reticent about gender relations, and a number have spoken to me critically of their "system" with regard to the status and treatment of women. No Prespa man has openly made any claims to me as to the intellectual superiority of men. Prespa women, in turn, have expressed no doubts as to their own intellectual capacities, which many were able to demonstrate to themselves and others as children by excelling in their schoolwork. Because of a belief on the part of most parents that young women should be kept close to home, however, most adult women did not go to school beyond the eighth grade, while many men went to high school and even college. Women therefore frequently defer to their husbands' opinions because they associate their more substantial education with greater knowledge.

During the period of my fieldwork, I received clearer indications of the men's view on such matters when, on several occasions, I visited married couples in order to interview them about weddings and singing. In some cases the husband assumed that I came to speak with him; in others he was the first to proffer an answer, regardless of whether we were speaking of men's or women's activities. One explanation for these responses would be an adult man's assumption that it is his duty to serve as the household's spokesman when dealing with an outsider such as myself. In other instances, however, husbands questioned the usefulness of any points that their wives could contribute to the conversation, and several men suggested to me that it was really only the men's song repertoire that was worthy of my scholarly attention, because, in their view, it is more difficult to perform. The wives often deferred to their husbands during such interviews, waiting until the end of the session, or until their husband had gone out, before eagerly adding their own remarks. I did notice, however, that men often seemed more willing to have me interview their mothers, sisters, or aunts: their agnatic kin with whom they grew up. And so it is possible that, for Prespa men, it is not so much women in general who are regarded as less "mindful," in the sense of knowledgeable and experienced, as it is women who have come from outside the kin group. If we now relate notions of "mindfulness" back to being a "person," there are two implications. First is that one becomes more and more "human," in the sense of attaining the moral ideals of the Prespa community, as one ages. Second, even in old age, males have a greater capacity to attain those ideals than do females.[13]

Gender relations are also understood with reference to the word *fuqi* ("strength" or "potency"), which denotes a man's innate capacities in a number of domains of action. More than any other factor, it is the perceived physical strength of men that legitimates their greater autonomy within society and their association with the public realm. The men of the family are seen as forming a protective layer between the inner world of the family, peopled by the weaker women and children of the household, and the larger world of the village, the district, and the state. Man's greater *fuqi* also implies—as does being *i mënçëm* or *e mënçme*— greater mental acuity, as well as a greater capacity for emotional strength and, hence, the courage to face adversaries. Finally, it seems to me that, on an intuitive level, *fuqi* is associated with sexual potency or virility, and thus with the creative, life-giving abilities of man, within a "system" in which procreative activities and a heterosexual orientation are viewed as intrinsic to masculinity. By virtue of his *fuqi* the *zoti* or "lord" of the household is charged with the care of his progeny and of the women of his household in a manner homologous to the role of *Zoti,* or God, in creating and caring for the people of the world.[14]

The notion of *fuqi* may be seen to lie behind the traditional desire on the part of Prespa families to produce many sons, who have been viewed as evidence both of the virility of their father and of the overall "strength" of their lineage.[15] It also provides the single greatest justification for the primacy granted to patrilineal kin. Whereas *mënd* is something that is acquired during the course of one's life, *fuqi* is an innate property. By virtue of their *fuqi*, males have an inherent claim to precedence within Prespa society.

Honor and Shame

Early in my stay in Toronto, I began to visit one woman elder to learn about the community's etiquette. When I asked why certain things were said or done in certain ways, the response was invariably the same. *Atë e kemi si për nder,* she would say, "We do this out of honor." So frequently do Presparë invoke the notion of "honor" in conversations regarding social behavior that the word *përnder,* which means literally "for honor" (*për nder*), is also used to denote a "custom." Thus her response could just as well have been translated as, "We do that because it is our custom."

Among Presparë, the discourse that centers on the concept of *nder* or "honor" serves as the principal idiom for speaking about social relations, both between members of individual households and between households. This discourse may be thought of as their version of what scholars of the Mediterranean often refer to as a "code of honor."[16] Nevertheless, as several scholars have noted, members of each Mediterranean community have come to conceptualize "honor," and what Friedrich (1977:290) has termed "honor-linked values," in distinctive ways that are not entirely paralleled in any other Mediterranean ideology (cf. Herzfeld 1980; Wikan 1984).

For Presparë, "honor" in its basic meaning refers to the esteem or respect that is accorded to one by others within the community and that one comes to recognize in oneself. It may be thought of as a person's sense of self that develops largely through one's perception of how one's actions are received by others. In the course of becoming an adult, any individual is expected to develop a "sense" of honor, as Bourdieu has worded it (see especially 1979:95–132), entailing both a cognizance of the moral qualities that are expected of a member of the community, and the ability to behave in such a way as to embody those qualities. In short, a person becomes "honorable" by acquiring a practical, lived mastery of the Prespa *sistem*. It follows that to be a *burrë* ("man") or a *grua* ("woman") is to be a moral person: for each word the qualification of "honorable" is implicit. It is therefore highly complimentary to say of an adult male, *Ay është burrë!* ("He's a man!"), or of a female, *Ajo është grua!* ("She's a woman!") This is also true for the designations Prespar (masc.) and Presparkë (fem.).

Conversely, to behave in a way that runs counter to community expectations of propriety and appropriateness is *turp*, a word that is heard as ubiquitously in Prespa speech as is *nder*. *Turp* may be used in the sense of social embarrassment or self-consciousness, but its most general meaning is the "shame" that one feels when one behaves in a way that could be deemed to be socially inappropriate. In feeling *turp*, an individual senses that his or her action has the potential of meeting with community disapproval, and thus as being judged to be dishonorable.

If an individual consistently behaves in a "shameful" manner, not only that individual but his or her entire household runs the risk of being ostracized by members of the community. It is thus possible to speak of a household's, as well as an individual's, "honor." In the event that a man becomes head of household, he also becomes the symbol of that household's honor, and his behavior comes under particular scrutiny. The word "honor" may therefore be used to encompass attributes that are associated more particularly with the male realm. But, as is outlined in the following discussion, women and younger men also play a crucial role in the maintenance of family honor, and some of the attributes associated with "honor" are expected to be demonstrated by all adults.

Female Modesty

In its general meaning of "shame," Presparë use the word *turp* most often as the opposite of *nder*. Each of these terms, however, has more specific connotations with reference to the conduct deemed appropriate for each gender. In this context, *turp*, best translated as "modesty" or "propriety," may be seen to be the female counterpart to male *nder*.[17] As with the more general meaning of *nder* as "honor," both terms in their gender-specific usages imply that a person is "mindful." But here, it seems to me, this concept refers less to matters of intelligence than to one's capacity to effectively control the distinctive type of emotionality that is seen to characterize members of one's gender, specifically during the period of young adulthood.

A young Prespa woman is expected to preserve her virginity until she is married, a stipulation that ensures that her offspring will indeed be heirs of her husband's lineage. At first it is adult family members that monitor her activities once she reaches the age of puberty. Some families restrict a daughter's activities as much as possible to the immediate environs of her home, and do not allow her to venture anywhere alone:

S'më lë nënja të dal në porta . . .	My mother won't let me go out to the gateway . . .
kjo nënja s'më lë.	(My mother won't let me.)
se më shonë gjithë bota . . .	because the whole world will see me . . .
S'më lë nënja të dal në shkallë . . .	My mother won't let me go out on the stairway . . .
se më shonë gjithë mejallë . . .	because the whole neighborhood will see me . . .
S'më lë nënja të dal në vija . . .	My mother won't let me go out to the millstream . . .
se më shonë djemurlia . . .	because the young men will see me . . .
S'm'i kanë fajet djemurlia . . .	It is not the young men who are to blame . . .
Fajet m'i ka bukuria . . .	It is my beauty that is to blame . . .

(Women's wedding song, bride's side, Toronto 1986; another version may be heard on Vuylsteke 1981, A4)[18]

The strictest of parents may also require that their daughters dress in the least revealing of clothing, with long sleeves, a skirt below the knee, and a high neckline. Gradually, as a girl becomes more "mindful," she is expected to develop her own sense of *turp*—"modesty" or "propriety" in the sense of a deliberate avoidance of potentially "shameful" behavior—which she will demonstrate in any type of social interaction for the duration of her childbearing years.

The notion of female *turp* is closely linked to attitudes regarding sexuality. Male sexuality is treated practically as inherently positive, for it is equated with virility and represents a man's ability to father offspring and thus continue the family line. But a woman's unrestrained sexuality is dangerous, for it threatens the patriarchal order. This is particularly true both before and outside marriage, when a woman's sexual relations with a man other than her husband would risk her bearing a child that was not of his "blood." Even within marriage, however, too close an emotional attachment between a wife and husband threatens the solidarity of the men of the agnatic group. In order to be viewed as an honorable and trustworthy member of her household and of the community, a woman in her childbearing years must demonstrate her capacity for controlling behavior that, when unchecked, would be clearly antisocial. She does this by adopting forms of behavior in social situations that deflect any attention to her body or sexuality.[19]

Ideally, a girl or younger woman is expected to congregate with other women at all social occasions and to avoid any private interchange with any male of her generation or older. If seated in a raised chair, she is expected to sit with knees together and with her legs dangling from her seat; if on the floor, with her legs stretched out before her or tucked demurely under her. She should keep her hands folded in her lap and refrain from making any large gestures. She is also expected to avoid speaking either too often or too loudly, and to cast her eyes downward, avoiding direct eye contact with others.

A young woman's physical display of *turp* has been a major factor that adult women have considered when choosing a bride for their sons. It has also been a central component of a woman's demeanor during the celebration of her marriage and in the first months of her residence in her new home. In the past, a newly married woman was expected to behave in a particularly stiff and subdued manner that conveyed not only her propriety, but also extreme deference and self-effacement before her new in-laws:

> Before, a bride had a lot of *turp* to speak: just enough to rush the words out of her mouth. She had a lot of *turp* to speak and to sing. At one time she had *turp* also when she sat down to eat: they would give her meat to eat and she wouldn't eat. They would say, "The bride doesn't eat meat." For as long as she knew *turp* they would take the meat and the elders would eat it. That's what we've heard from the elders. . . . For her first week as a bride she kept her eyes closed. Afterwards, during her first year as a bride she was expected to remain . . . very quiet, not to speak much, not to move much, not to laugh. (Interview in Chicago with a mother- and daughter-in-law, 1986)

Only gradually did a new bride relax such behavior.

A young woman was also expected to convey her deference to members of her new household, as well as to relatives and friends of the household, in the ways that she spoke to or about them. Her father-in-law, the head of the household, was to be addressed and referred to simply as *bej* (Tk. *bey*), an Ottoman honorific term. Other men in the household and its circle of acquaintances were addressed by name, as ASAN *bej* or NEIM *bej*. Her husband, however, was addressed simply as "You!" or referred to as "Him." Such practices serve to undermine any sense of a special tie between husband and wife (cf. Denich 1974: 253). Similarly, a bride addressed her mother-in-law as *anëm nëne*, literally, "lady mother" (from Tk. *hanım*). Other women in the household, including her husband's sisters and his brothers' wives, as well as women within the family's social sphere, were addressed as *anëm* FA-TIME or *anëm* MAZES (Ottoman parlance would be FATIME *hanım*).[20]

Until the end of World War II, non-Bektashi women also conveyed their *turp* through their clothing. Women past the age of puberty were expected to wear a black overcoat (*ferexhe* or *xharxhe*; Tk. *ferace*) and a white headscarf (*jashmak*; Tk. *yaşmak*) that covered their hair and mouth whenever they left the family compound. Such garments effectively veiled them from the gaze of unrelated males. Since that time, both because of the enactment of laws in Yugoslavia forbidding the veiling of women, and because of their emulation of Western practices, Prespa women have abandoned these forms of dress.

Today, both in Prespa and in North America, women are gradually renegotiating the notion of "modesty" and are allowing themselves to deviate more and more from what were formerly its ideals. Such changes are most noticeable among younger "brides" at social gatherings, who no longer feel hesitant to speak out or to act in a more animated fashion. Many women also choose not to use the Ottoman terms of respect, and many men in fact encourage women to eschew them. Nevertheless, a younger woman is still expected to convey an air of deference and propriety throughout her years as a bride.

When a woman's children have married and she has become an "elder," however, she can in all confidence act in an outspoken and even boisterous fashion, although not all older women choose to do so. On the one hand, her loss of fertility has freed her of the need to be ever mindful of her demeanor. On the other hand, through her bearing of children, through her work, and through her proper conduct she has proven herself to be a trustworthy and responsible member of her household and can now command considerable authority, at least in matters pertaining to the domestic sphere.

Male Honor

Expectations for male behavior contrast strikingly with those held for girls and women. Innate male qualities of "strength" (*fuqi*) and greater "mindfulness" give boys a charter for unrestricted behavior and freedom of movement (cf. du Boulay 1986:151). Young boys have the run of the village in Prespa, or of the neighborhood in North America. In their late teens and early twenties, as "bachelors," they are expected to do their share of "adventuring" (*gjezdis*; from Tk. *gez*). Before the breakup of Yugoslavia, for the sons of apple-growing families in Prespa this adventuring involved selling apples in various towns in northern Yugoslavia during the winter months. For many men now in their forties and fifties, it included traveling overseas to North America or Australia in search of work.

Young men in their teens and early twenties often behave in a reserved manner in public, still very conscious of the need to defer to men of their fathers' generation (cf. Erlich 1966:64–65). Away from the older men, however, they begin to cultivate the air of male bravado that they have witnessed among somewhat older men, accompanied by such marks of masculinity as smoking and drinking:

Kur shtira sytë, nëne, n'atë mal . . .	When I lifted my eyes, mother, to that mountain . . .
qaj moj nënja ime, qaj.	(cry, my mother, cry)
ç'e pashë, nëne, një djalë beqar . . .	I saw, mother, a young bachelor . . .
Them ta marr, moj nëne, them të mos e marr? . . .	Should I say I'll marry him, my mother, or should I say no? . . .
Merre NN bej, merre, mos iu ndaj . . .	Marry [the groom] *bey*, marry him and never leave him . . .
Më thonë shoqet: "Pi raki, duan!" . . .	My girlfriends tell me: "He drinks brandy and smokes!" . . .
Ashtu pinë burrat, raki e duan . . .	That's how men are, they drink brandy and smoke . . .

(Men's wedding song, groom's side, Chicago 1986)

As males marry and become "men," they often take on a particularly lively demeanor in social settings, characterized by large movements, frequent hand gestures, and equally frequent verbal exclamations such as *o-bo-bo!* or *o-i o-i!* that inject energy and emotion into their speech. They are also said to speak—just as they sing—in a "thick voice" (*zë të trashë*): loud, resonant, and emphatic; in contrast to the softer, more nasal "thin voice" (*zë të ollë*) of women. In every regard they display their physical and sexual *fuqi* ("potency") through their boisterous behavior. In their prime of life, men need not be concerned with masking their sexuality through their stance or movements. Any allusion to it is seen as demonstrating their *fuqi* rather than as suggesting promiscuity. They thus experience their behavior as being "free": as not being subject to the same sorts of strictures as is a young woman's. But it is accepted that one component of a young man's energy is a volatility of temper that carries the potential of propelling him into a heated argument or even a physical confrontation with other men. Hence, from a community perspective, it is not within the realm of male–female relations that a man is called upon to demonstrate his "mindfulness," in the sense of exhibiting his self-control, but rather with regard to his capacity for violence, as well as for physical excess, within the context of all-male interaction.[21]

Once men become elders, they often retire into a state of dignity and tranquility, speaking more softly and moving in a more circumscribed fashion. On the one hand, their period of greatest *fuqi*, in the sense of physical strength, emotional forcefulness, and virility, is seen to have passed. But on the other, they can now command greater authority within the family group or the community at large based on their ever increasing understanding of the ways of the world. If expansiveness to the point of aggressiveness is an acknowledged aspect of a younger man's nature, it is expected to mature into a sense of reason and measured conciliation by the time a man is an elder.[22]

Such attitudes regarding the different stages of a man's life are informed by a cluster of attributes subsumed in the notion of male "honor." Many of these attributes are valued by all Albanians, whether northern or southern. Within north Albanian society, a man's "honor" is intimately bound up with his role in the blood feud (see especially Durham 1909; Hasluck 1954). Young northern men served in the past as a "warrior" generation that was expected to defend the primacy of the clan in any feuds with other clans, risking and perhaps losing their lives in the process. Their generation has often been referred to by the term *trimë*, literally "warrior-heroes." The qualities that younger men have been expected to exemplify as upholders of clan honor include physical strength, fearless courage, and an aggressive, often confrontational stance vis-à-vis other men of their generation who are outside their kin group. Here we see a more elaborate version of the volatility associated with younger men by Prespare.

The role of mediator is central to the position of elders within northern society, as they have been the ones who have negotiated settlements between feuding clans. As the primary representatives of their household or clan honor, elders have also been expected to exemplify other qualities that can be related to the institution of feuding. These include trustworthiness, exhibited in a man's commitment to *besa* (the "word of honor" or "oath of peace") that is sworn to suspend feuding; and an unflinching hospitality that may be expected to extend even to members of a rival clan that might enter his domain.

Prespare, with no known history of institutionalized feuding, at least in the recent past, nevertheless identify strongly with the image of male honor that north Albanian highlanders epitomize and do not hesitate to conjure it up in their discussions of proper behavior. One of the surest ways that a man can be said to lose "honor" in the community, for example, is to renege on a commitment, for a "man" (*burrë*) "stands upon his word" (*rri me fjalë*). Aspects of behavior such as showing oneself to be generous to a fault, unswervingly loyal to a friend, and hospitable to all who enter one's home are also highly prized. It is not unusual for a Prespa man to underscore the extent of his hospitality by reciting a saying that relates far more to customary law among northern mountaineers than to the comparatively tame tenor of life in Chicago or Toronto: "Any man who enters my home is a friend (*mik*); even my enemy (*armik*), when he enters my home, is a friend!"[23]

Prespare assume that the moral rectitude symbolized by such behavior develops in a man as he is socialized to the Prespa "system," and that it forms an important part of his legacy as an Albanian. This is particularly true of individuals from the lower villages of Prespa, who regard themselves as more purely "Albanian" than the Muslims in upper Prespa. As with such terms as *njeri* ("person") and *burrë* ("man"), the concept of male "honor," in the sense of punctilious behavior in the public realm, is for them implicit both in being an "Albanian" (*shqiptar*) and in being from lower Prespa.

An angry outburst addressed by a friend from a lower village to my husband illustrates many of the components of one Prespa man's sense of "honor." His words were prompted by the actions of two other men in the community: one from an upper village who had gone back on a prior commitment, another from a lower village who had distinguished himself as a gracious host. Note that the friend excluded the upper villages from the designation "Prespa":

> People (*njerëz;* plural of *njeri*) from Prespa—from Krani, from Arvati, from Nakolec—they give their word one day, they give the same word the next day! Those from [the upper villages] . . . they aren't men (*burra*), they're wild beasts (*të egër*) [even less "mindful" than *ajvanë*]—you can't come to an agreement with them! . . . But QAZIM: he's a man! He's from Krani! (Conversation in Toronto, 1986)

Family Honor

Because a man is the representative of his household in the public sphere, the honor that he is expected to embody through his behavior is not merely his personal sense of honor, but the combined honor of the members of his household. Those honorable attributes that he is expected to exhibit, such as trustworthiness, loyalty, generosity, and hospitality, pertain to all aspects of his relations with other families: economic exchanges, marriage agreements, and the interactions that take place at social occasions.

If a man is seen by others as acting in a manner inconsistent with those attributes, then he may be judged to have "lost" his honor, or to have brought "shame" (*turp*) upon himself. When, for example, a family in Toronto returned to Yugoslavia to live, taking with them a daughter who was scheduled to be married in Canada two weeks hence, the father's "shame" became the talk of the town. *Nga frika mund të ikësh, ama nga turpi jo!* exclaimed one female elder: "You can run from fear, but never from shame!" Any demonstration of lack of "mind," in the sense of self-control, may also be judged as shameful. Showing too much emotional weakness toward any woman, including one's wife, meets with disapproval, as does abuse of any of the male pursuits such as drinking and gambling. Likewise, it is "shameful" for any man, young or old, to behave violently toward another person in the community. For an elder any such behavior is particularly inappropriate, because excessiveness is something that a man should forsake as he ages. Finally, a man risks "shaming" himself by impugning the honor of others, such as when a host is not perceived as behaving in a manner sufficiently solicitous of his guests.

Although "honor" is associated most with the head of a household, the role of other members in the maintenance of family honor is crucial.

If any of the women of the household, or any younger men, are judged as behaving in a manner that is immodest or disrespectful of others within the community, then the whole household may be shamed. In effect, the head of household is shamed because he has been shown to be incapable of maintaining discipline within his family. As Abu-Lughod has noted for Egyptian Bedouins, who maintain similar notions of "honor" and "modesty," the honor of a household is sustained through the coordinated effort of all its members, male and female:

> Honor and modesty are dialectically related in the establishment of family or lineage honor. A family has honor when its men are "real men," embodying the ideals of Bedouin society, including supporting and protecting their dependents, and the women and dependents are modest, deferring to their providers and thus validating these men's claims to their high positions in the hierarchy. If the men fail, their women lose honor, and if the women or other dependents fail, the men lose honor. Thus, all members are responsible for the honor of all those with whom they identify as kin. (1986:166)

A young woman's capacity to dishonor her family continues even after she leaves the family home. Within her new home, her "modest" demeanor is not forced on her by her in-laws but is, rather, seen as something she adopts voluntarily. Nevertheless, it may be orchestrated from her natal home. One young woman in Chicago recounted to me that her mother had threatened never to visit her once she was married if she heard anyone speak critically of her daughter's demeanor as a "bride." Whenever her mother did come to visit after her marriage, she would stop outside the door and ask her in-laws how her daughter was behaving before entering the house. A married woman contributes to her new household's honor by attending scrupulously to her demeanor, by keeping a meticulous household, and by serving as a gracious and responsive hostess whenever guests visit her home.

Within the Prespa "system," then, men and women can each attain a sense of honor by developing expertise and knowledge within specific domains of activity, and by acting in such a way as to earn the trust of others both within their household and in the community at large. Those individuals who carry out their prescribed social roles with particular rectitude and aplomb are praised as being *i zoti* or *i zotëruar* for a man (from the word for "master") or, for a woman, *e zonja* or *e zonjëruar* (from "mistress"):

N'atë mal ngreur një qoshk,	On the mountain stood a kiosk:
por sa mirë, sa bukur shtruar.	How nicely, how beautifully decorated.
Atje qenka nusja e NN beut	There [the groom]'s bride stood
me veilo mbuluar,	covered with a veil
me florinj ngarkuar.	and laden with gold coins.
I ati që i rrinte pranë	His father, standing beside her,
fortë një zot i zotëruar.	is a most honorable man.
Nënja që i rrinte pranë	His mother, standing beside her,
shumë një zonjë e zonjëruar . . .	is a most honorable woman . . .

(Women's wedding song, groom's side; Chicago, 1986)

A woman may also be extolled as a *trime* ("heroine"), a female counterpart to a male "hero" (*trim*), if she excels in her duties within the domestic sphere.

For Prespare, it is only when members of two households regard each other as honorable that it is possible for them to relate with the openness and affection that they designate as *muabet*. To say that two households "have *muabet*," therefore, does not simply mean that members note positive features in each other; rather, it confirms that each household has proven itself worthy of the other's friendship through its ongoing recognition of social obligations and the upstanding behavior of all its members. Honorable behavior, on the part of all household members, is the precondition for membership in the moral community of Prespare and for participation in the various social occasions that perpetuate their community.

Tensions within the Prespa "System"

Taken together, the discourses and practices that comprise the Prespa "system" construct three major axes of social differentiation. First is a distinction between "males" and "females," enforced through a range of beliefs as to the innate natures of both as well as the social roles and domains of concern that are considered to be appropriate to each. It is the emphasis placed on male precedence and patrilineal descent that

197

warrants the designation of their "system" as a patriarchal one. Second is a delineation of three distinct generational categories for each gender, highlighted by practices that give precedence to older members of the community over younger ones: to "elders" over younger adults, and to all adults over children. As Bourdieu (1977:232) and others have noted, Mediterranean communities are "gerontocratic" as much as they are patriarchal. The sharp divisions that Prespare recognize between members of different generations militate against a social hierarchy formed exclusively around issues of gender. The last axis is that between individual households, in which an egalitarian ethos prevails.

In a community with as complex a history as that of Prespare, however, the nature of power relations along any axis is rarely so unambiguously clear. And so it is important to ask, Is the Prespa "system" really so systematic? Ortner (1990) has argued recently, with regard to gender relations, that communities often live in a state of tension in which hierarchical assumptions governing certain domains of activity conflict with complementary ones governing other domains. She also suggests that such conflicting tendencies may represent different periods of historical experience. In her view, it is necessary to survey the range of both ideological constructions and on-the-ground relations within any given community so as to appraise whether it is hierarchical or egalitarian tendencies that are hegemonic.

Put somewhat differently, it is in the nature of social formations to be characterized by internal contradictions and disjunctures, however much those living within them experience them as internally consistent. In the case of families living in Prespa villages, it is only within the realm of age distinctions that hierarchical assumptions would seem to have prevailed unambiguously, although these too are now being challenged. In the realms of both interfamilial and gender relations, contradictory tendencies have been clearly evident. One consideration in any social analysis should be the means through which such contradictions are mediated or masked, so that members of communities come to experience their "system" as forming a coherent whole.

Honor versus Economic Standing

One of the points of tension evident within the Prespa "system" is the relationship between the ascription of "honor" and other types of status based upon economic factors. In order to be considered honorable, a Prespa head of household must see to it that his family is able to sustain itself economically, and thus to be autonomous within the community.

Beyond that minimal requirement, however, "honor" is not bestowed with respect to economic factors. Contemporary Prespa households may derive a certain sense of self-regard either from the legacy of a lineage that was successful within an earlier socioeconomic order, or from their elevated economic standing at the present time. Neither genealogical precedence nor wealth, however, guarantees them the ascription of "honorable."

In general, the performance of any household within the social sphere is judged in terms of the means it has available to it; no one expects a poorer household to give as extensive a display of hospitality as a richer one. In this regard, the notion of "honor" might even be interpreted as having favored those families who have been poorest in material resources, for it has assured that they can participate with dignity even in situations where they are interacting with individuals of far greater economic standing. Herzfeld (1980:342), speaking of similar notions of "honor" among Greeks, has suggested that a man's honor depends on "his ability to live up to the expectations which he creates about himself." Those heads of household who, through economic means, make the greatest claims to precedence within the community therefore have the most to lose if they, or any members of their household, are seen to have lost honor.

It is tempting to conclude, therefore, that the principle of "honor" works to level economic distinctions by requiring that wealthier households return more wealth to the community in the form of more lavish hospitality. But such a conclusion, I think, would be simplistic. By living their lives in accordance with discourses and practices that emphasize the notion of "honor," Presparë are encouraged to experience their community as operating on an egalitarian basis and to view discrepancies in economic standing, while real, as relatively unimportant. In so doing, they in fact allow such discrepancies to persist unchallenged. Egalitarianism is not so much the reality of interfamilial relations among Presparë as it is an aspect of a lived ideology: one to which most families, regardless of their economic situation, have remained firmly committed.

Gender Complementarity versus Hierarchy

A similarly vexing issue is how to regard tendencies toward gender complementarity within a "system" that otherwise seems to favor males over females. Parallel constructions in Prespa speech, such as the pair *trim* and *trime* (for male and female "hero") or the terms *i zoti* and *e zonja* (for "master"-fully carrying out one's household duties) would seem to suggest that men and women regard the contrasting concerns of men and women, and their distinct spheres of activity, as granting them a status of "separate but equal." Indeed, the pervasive observance of gender segregation by Presparë, in both work activities and social situations, can be seen as encouraging such a view of gendered relations. Without the fear of men overseeing their activities, women at smaller segregated gatherings may feel quite free to speak among themselves of some of the foibles and dilemmas surrounding gender relations and to behave with less reserve than in other situations. But more fundamentally, by spending so much of their time within a segregated sphere, both men and women are encouraged to experience social hierarchy primarily along the axis of age. In many respects, younger women come to regard female elders, rather than the men of their household, as those who exert power over most aspects of their lives. Certainly, it is at the "elder" stage of life that men and women achieve greatest social parity, signaled here again through the parallel terms of *plak* and *plakë*.

There is also a suggestion that women represent the "power behind the throne" in many Prespa households. When I lived in Skopje, a Macedonian woman quoted to me a saying to the effect that "The man is the head of the household, but the woman is the neck that determines which direction the head turns." This is not a Prespa saying, but my host during my stay in Prespa nodded in bemused agreement when I told it to him. A substantial degree of behind-the-scenes influence by women over their husbands seems to be the reality, if not the expressed sentiment, of an increasing number of Prespa marriages, particularly for couples living in a nuclear family arrangement.

Such complementary tendencies mitigate but do not override, and may in fact deflect attention from, a more pervasive hegemony of male precedence within Prespa social life. This precedence is evident in the array of forms of etiquette that grant men a privileged status at any communal occasion. It is evident also in the many forms of self-control that women are expected to exhibit in their dress, speech, and demeanor, as well as in their refraining from extramarital sexual relations or activities such as drinking and smoking. Men are granted precedence intrinsically by their possession of *fuqi* ("strength"/"potency") and by their close association with the notion of *nder* ("honor"), while women demonstrate their capacity for honorable behavior through practices that both allude to and mask their inherent "shame" (*turp*). As a number of gender theorists have pointed out, the separate sphere of women, however much it is experienced as complementary to that of men, may also be interpreted as encompassed by the male domain, in that men bear ultimate political and economic responsibility for the household as a whole. Women require the presence of a man within their household—a husband, father-in-law, father, or son—throughout their lives, and cannot choose to live on their own. Most fundamentally, the pervasive practice within Prespa social life of distinguishing between male and female qualities, activities, and concerns has the effect of encouraging men and women to see themselves as innately very different, as opposites who need each other to exist. In this way, as has also often been pointed out, the division of labor helps to construct heterosexual relations as the norm (cf. Rubin 1975:178–80).

In speaking to Presparë about family relations, it would seem that male control over women was more marked in the past. A generation ago the practice of the levirate, in which a widow was automatically remarried to a kinsman of her deceased husband, seems to have been customary. Wife-beating was certainly also practiced, as it still is in some households, and the threat of male violence exists today even when it is not so often a reality. Women are severely constrained from speaking to others about any harsh treatment they receive, or about problems in their relationship with their husbands, because of the common attitude that such statements would exhibit their disloyalty to their family. There is thus no adequate forum for them to develop an effective form of resistance to problematic aspects of family life. Often a woman's only hope in dealing with serious misconduct by her husband, such as abusive or addictive behavior, is that some of his male relatives and friends will take notice and jointly confront him to insist that his behavior change.

I was visiting once with several Prespa women in Toronto while their husbands were out for the evening. When the men returned, unusually inebriated, they began to joke about gender relations in the community. One of them announced quite flamboyantly that women are intrinsically more dangerous than men: you can tell because, when they die, they are buried deeper in the earth! At the time I took his remark as an example of Prespa humor, but I have since come to understand that this has indeed been the practice in some regions of Albania.[24] Moore (1988:37–38) has pointed out that gender stereotypes such as this may be wielded strategically as a means of exerting power over others. It is such patterns of teasing, as well as ultimate threats of physical force, that serve as reminders to Prespa women that whatever sense of autonomy they experience, and whatever degree of responsibility they exercise within their household, are granted through the grace of its male members. The question is not, then, whether gender relations among Presparë are to be characterized as wholly "hierarchical" or "complementary." As with many other communities in North America, the question is, rather, how it is that women have been encouraged to experience their position as complementary to that of men, to staunchly defend it, and ultimately to participate in its reproduction in succeeding generations. It is to such questions, as well as to those surrounding the egalitarian basis of interfamilial relations, that I return in subsequent chapters as I analyze the role of weddings and singing in the ongoing reinscription of the Prespa "system."

A Family's Social World

When Prespa families host a wedding, both the structure of their guest list and the pattern of attendance of guests may be understood with regard to the notions surrounding interhousehold relations that are central to the community's "system." During the course of a wedding, each of the two host households gathers around itself all those families with whom it recognizes ongoing social ties: all those among its kin (*soj*) and friends (*miq*) whom it regards as honorable, and with whom it therefore currently "has *muabet.*" In so doing it constitutes, as it were, its individual social world.

Guests are invited to a wedding, and in turn plan their attendance, in accordance with perceptions as to their closeness to one of the two families. Usually a household is seen as more closely related to one of the two families and therefore attends only one "side" of the wedding. Until very recently, invitations were issued orally to prospective guests three days before the taking of the bride. Those guests who felt particularly close to that family might then begin to visit the appropriate household on that day to participate in ritual activities: on the bride's side, her being "adorned" in the evening; on the groom's side, the *qeshqek* ceremony during the afternoon. Additional guests with less close ties to the family, or those unable to arrive earlier, would go to the groom's for the final two days of the celebration or to the bride's for the final day. Nowadays, both in Prespa and overseas, printed invitations are mailed to guests several weeks beforehand, but patterns of attendance are much the same. In North America, those guests more distant from the host families attend only the final evening celebration held in a banquet hall and do not attend home events at all.

Some individuals are so close to the host household that they are not even issued invitations. These are the family members and, more rarely, friends who interact so extensively with the host household on such a regular basis that their attendance is assumed. Bourdieu (1977:33–38) has termed such relatives a household's "practical kin," in that mutual ties are maintained through daily, practical interaction rather than more intermittent, ceremonial gestures of reciprocity. In their case, a formal invitation would imply some social distance between them and the hosts and would in itself be a snub.

At village weddings, the family's *xhaxhallarë*, who live in their neighborhood and cooperate regularly in household chores, fall most readily into this category. As extensions of the host household during the preparation, arrangement, and celebration of the marriage, it is their wedding as well. But it is also their wedding in that the child who is getting married is seen as theirs. On the groom's side, as members of his lineage, the *xhaxhallarë* are in effect the party that takes the bride. During the wedding they are referred to specifically as the *krushq* ("groom's party"), in contrast to the much larger group of *dasmorë* ("wedding guests"). On the bride's side, they are the larger lineage that gives her away. It is the "practical kin" who are charged with many of the behind-the-scenes activities that assure the event's success, such as preparing and serving refreshments, moving furniture, and buying supplies. And, as Memet's *xhaxha* Aziz was continually reminded, it is the *xhaxhallarë* who are expected to participate with particular prominence in the ritual observances and the singing that occur throughout the wedding period, including those that take place early in the week of the wedding before most other guests have arrived.

The differentiation observed between various types of wedding guests, together with the structure of ritual activities, constrained my access to different portions of wedding celebrations and thus my ability to write of them from first-hand experience. During the period in which I conducted intensive fieldwork, I did not ever attend a wedding gathering held more than three days before the taking of the bride, although I was eventually given copies of community recordings and videos of some such events. As non-kin, my presence at such gatherings would have been highly unusual. Although my husband and I came to be considered *miq të ngushtë* ("close friends") of several families—as they said of us, *njerëz tonë* ("our people")—none of those families hosted a wedding during the period of my most intensive fieldwork.[25] When I did not know a family well, I attended only the final day or two of a wedding. With rare exceptions, it was only in the case of families with whom I had established relationships well before the wedding period that I was able to attend ritual gatherings held on earlier days.

In most instances, I was acquainted with only one of the two host families, and hence only attended activities on one side of a wedding. The exceptions were one wedding in Prespa, where by chance I received invitations from both the bride's and groom's families; and the wedding of Memet and Feime, where a last-minute invitation to attend gatherings at the bride's home supplemented a prior invitation from the groom's side. I return to the culmination of this wedding in chapter 8.

11. The bride is adorned. Three nights before she is taken, female relatives and friends of the bride's family gather at her home to sing and to admire the gifts (*rroba*) sent to her by the groom. Female elders, dressed in dark colors, are seated on the sofa with the bride, who is resting while modeling an outfit sent to her by the groom. Younger women, wearing brighter colors, sit on the floor. (Toronto, 1986; photograph by Jane Sugarman)

12. "Honoring" the elders. The bride kisses the hand of an older relative as a show of deference and respect. (Toronto, 1986; photograph by Jane Sugarman)

13. Singing at a women's gathering. Although this photograph was taken at a circumcision celebration, it captures the dignified atmosphere of women's gatherings that take place during the wedding period. (Toronto, 1985; photograph by Jane Sugarman)

14. Men's toasting. At a small gathering at the groom's home, men toast each other between songs. (Toronto, 1994; photograph by Jane Sugarman)

15. Men's singing at the groom's. At a gathering on the groom's side, men raise their voices in a rousing song. Cigarettes and alcoholic beverages have been set out on the table. (Bridgeport, Conn., 1985; photograph by Jane Sugarman)

16. Entertaining the guests. Young Albanian musicians play for men of the groom's party on the wedding morning. Male elders sit on the couch closest to them, younger men on the other couch. Drinks and appetizers line the table in front of them. (Chicago area, 1986; photograph by Jane Sugarman)

17. May he have *bereqet!* As guests arrive at the groom's house on his wedding day, they are offered a mixture of roasted chickpeas and candies (*kokolinkë*) so that his marriage will be blessed by both fertility and prosperity. (Bridgeport, Conn., 1985; photograph by Jane Sugarman)

18. Bathing the groom. As the groom showers in the bathroom of his home, his relatives line up in the hallway to sing ritual wedding songs. (Chicago area, 1986; photograph by Jane Sugarman)

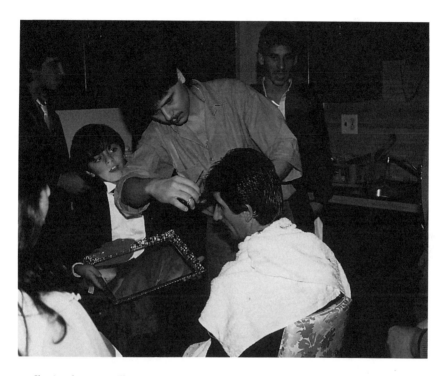

19. Shaving the groom. The groom is shaved and has his hair cut while a young relative holds the mirror. Because of space limitations, he was shaved in the kitchen rather than outdoors. (Bridgeport, Conn., 1985; photograph by Jane Sugarman)

20. Taking the bride. The groom and his relatives lead a smiling bride to the car just before they depart for the banquet hall. (Bridgeport, Conn., 1985; photograph by Jane Sugarman)

SIX

Singing and the Discourse of Honor

> ... One's face, then, is a sacred thing, and the expressive order
> required to sustain it is therefore a ritual one. (Goffman 1967:19)

A MEN'S *KONAK* AT THE GROOM'S

Two years after the wedding of Feime and Memet, another family in
the Chicago area invited my husband and me to come to film the
wedding of their son. I was unable to go, and so my husband attended
alone. The groom, Nuredin, was marrying Emine, a north Albanian
woman from Yugoslavia who had already arrived in the United States
and was staying with his family. On a Saturday evening, a large number of guests assembled at Nuredin's home. Then, during the next day,
he bathed and was shaved by his male relatives and had his hair
combed by female relatives before all set out for a larger celebration at
a banquet hall.

In contrast to the men's gathering at Memet's home two years earlier, the Saturday evening gathering at Nuredin's included a number of
guests in addition to the family's close relatives. Once the first guests
had arrived, the women gathered informally in the family room. There
Emine modeled clothes given her by Nuredin's family and demonstrated her initiation into Prespa culture by singing a well-known wedding song with his mother. Early in the evening the women danced to
cassettes of north Albanian music from Kosova. Later there was some
singing by the other women.

The men's gathering proceeded much like the *konak*s that were held
until recently at weddings in Prespa, beginning with hours of singing
around a table laden with refreshments, and ending many hours later
with a full meal. For the early stages of the gathering, two tables were
placed end-to-end in the home's large living room. Homemade *raki* as
well as commercial beer and whiskey were set out for the men. There

was also an impressive array of traditional appetizers: grilled liver, roasted chicken, pickled cucumbers, pickled red and green tomatoes, sliced tomatoes smothered in grated feta cheese and decorated with black olives, slices of hard-boiled eggs in vinaigrette, and chunks of feta cheese; to which a few American touches had been added: carrot slices, onion dip with cauliflower florets. Nuredin's father and *xhaxha* (father's brother, in this case) took their places at the head of the table, flanked by those elders who were present and younger men who were outsiders to the family circle. Closer relatives among the younger men were seated at the far end. Nuredin's older brother and the husband of his cousin sat near the doorway and served refreshments (fig. 6). Nuredin himself, together with other unmarried men, did not attend the gathering at all, but congregated elsewhere in the house.

Once the men were seated, they began to sing *me radhë,* led off by Nuredin's father. He was followed by the oldest man present, who thereafter served as the *kryeplak* of the gathering in that he led the toasting. The men's choice of songs covered the full range of subject matter: ritual wedding songs, heroic and love songs, a song about nature, and one about working abroad. After subdued, *shtruar* singing by the first two men, subsequent performances were in a more animated, *lartër* style. A number of the more distant guests did not sing, either because they chose not to or because they did not know the tradition.

Once each man who wished to had sung one song, several men sang a second time. First of these was Nuredin's *xhaxha*, a particularly outgoing and good-natured man. He chose a wedding song to address to Nuredin, which he sang in *lartër* style. During his performance the younger men at the table's far end, having become somewhat inebriated, began to interact in a more lively manner, and two of them rose to link arms in the spirit of friendship and to empty their glasses. They, at least, were beginning to feel *qejfli*.

The uncle was followed by one of the younger men. He led off a boisterous love song from Albanian radio that has become extremely popular among Prespare:

Do marr sharrën,	I'm going to take my saw
do sharroj selvinë . . .	to cut down the cypress tree . . .
Fëllënxë moj, gushë e bardhë moj,	(O partridge, white-throated one,
se s'na flet me gojë?	why won't you speak to us?)

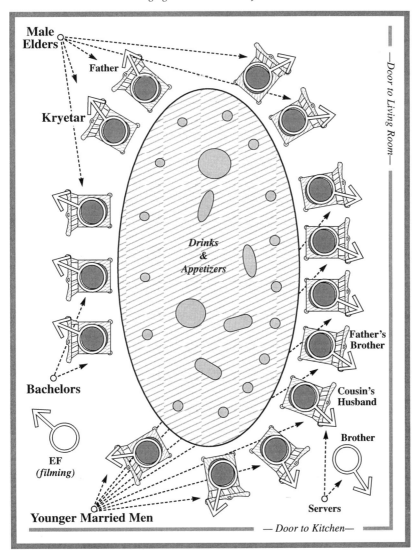

FIGURE 6. A Men's *Konak* at the Groom's, Chicago, 1988 (initial seating)

ta sharroj selvinë	to cut down the cypress tree
[ty të bëj seir . . .	[so that I can watch you . . .
ty të bëj seir]	so that I can watch you]
ku mbledh trëndafilë . . .	where you are gathering
	roses . . .

Accompanying him was another young man, an equally ardent but less experienced singer. Before certain lines the "singer" imitated the particularly exuberant radio performance by injecting lively exclamations such as *o-po-po-po-po-po!* into the text.

After only two verses he left off this song, perhaps because he had omitted a verse crucial to the song's meaning (indicated above in brackets). Rather than complete the song, he began another humorous one that is closely associated with late-night singing:

Laju, zbardhu,	*vajzë*	me sapun	Wash and whiten your face with soap, girl,
se do shkojmë		në katund	because we're going to the village,
në katund	*o moj*	të plakave.	to the village of lady elders.
Plakat e		katundit-e	The lady elders of the village
si zhabat		pas lumit-e.	are like the frogs by the river [old and wrinkled]
Laju, zbardhu	*vajzë*	me sapun	Wash and whiten your face with soap, girl,
se do shkojmë		në katund	because we're going to the village,
në katund	*o moj*	të nuseve.	to the village of brides.
Nuset e		katundit-e	The brides of the village
si peshkët		pas lumit-e.	are like the fish by the river. [slender-waisted]
Laju, zbardhu	*vajzë*	me sapun	Wash and whiten your face with soap, girl,
se do shkojmë		në katund	because we're going to the village,
në katund	*o moj*	të çupave.	to the village of girls.
Çupat e		katundit-e	The girls of the village
si pëllumbat		pas lumit-e.	are like the doves by the river [gentle and demure].[1]

During the course of this second song, the singer became increasingly involved in his performance. He began gesturing to the others as he sang and, every so often, brushed his hands together in a show of enthusiasm and called out *Ha-ha-ha!* At the song's conclusion he added some couplets addressed to Nuredin and Emine. The verses are taken from a well-liked song that the *daulle* are known for singing:

O Xhinxhile, Xhinxhile,	O Xhinxhile [girl's name],
kam sevda të çupës-e.	I have the love of a young woman.
O Xhinxhile, Xhinxhile,	O Xhinxhile,
kam sevda të djalit-e.	I have the love of a young man.

During his singing, the men, becoming more jovial, raised their glasses in a communal toast.

To cap off his performance, the singer then added two *bejte* commenting on the gathering and the conviviality of drinking. In the second he inserted, not the host's name, but rather that of Nuredin's uncle who had sung before him. The implication was that the uncle, whose son was then among the community's most eligible bachelors, should consider hosting a similar gathering in the near future:

Do të pijmë ca nga ca,	We're going to drink little by little
ta vazhdojmë gjer më saba!	and continue until dawn!
Pini, shokë more, pini,	Drink up, my friends,
de ISMAIL na mburon mburimi!	for the spring gushes forth at ISMAIL's!

With the singer's long performance over, the others shouted out congratulations and reached out to shake his hand. As the bustle of activity began to die down, the uncle decided to respond to the younger man's final *bejte* by deflecting the obligation for a future gathering onto him. He was accompanied by another older man, so that the verbal duel that ensued was in part a generational one. In this case, both singers drew entirely on preexisting verses, but selected ones suitable for the particular men at the gathering:

O FEIM aman o-i,	O FEIM, my-my-my,
u mbledhshim më shtëpi!	may we gather next at *your* house!

The younger man responded with a feigned apology:

Unë s'të fola nga inati,	I didn't speak to you out of spite,
nga dashuria, nga akikati.	but out of love and sincerity.

to which the uncle responded in a conciliatory manner:

Ashtu vërtetë, me të vërtetë,	You're absolutely right,
ç'jemi mbledhur për muabet.	after all, we've gathered for *muabet.*

Now the younger man renewed his teasing of the uncle:

Fletë-fletë mollës,	Leaves of an apple tree:
të keqën të gojës!	your mouth is evil!

and the uncle teased him in kind:

Fletë-fletë dardhës,	Leaves of a pear tree:
të keqën të fjalës!	your words are evil!

This time the younger man brought up the uncle's eligible son by name (CD #23):

Këjo odë me tavan:	This *odë* with a roof:
ARIF e kemi si kapedan!	ARIF is our captain!

Now it was the uncle who feigned an apology:

Unë s'të fola nga inati,	I didn't speak to *you* out of spite,
nga dashuria, nga akikati.	but out of love and sincerity.

and so the younger man became more specific about his son:

Kush nai foli këtë fjalë?	Who spoke those words to us?
Ia martofshim atë djalë!	May we marry off his son!

The uncle now deflected attention onto the present gathering:

Do të pijmë ca nga ca,	We're going to drink little by little
do ta vazhdojmë gjer më saba!	and continue until dawn!

At the mention of drinking, others around the table, who were following the battle of wits with eager attention, began to shout and hoot in falsetto. The younger man's teasing resumed:

Ajde mor ISMAIL, more pikë,	O ISMAIL, my-my-my,
më t'u mbledhshim më shtëpi!	May we gather next at *your* house![2]

The uncle continued to focus attention on the present gathering, saluting the *kryeplak:*

Pini, shokë more, pini,	Drink up, my friends, drink up,
de NEIM mburon mburimi!	for the spring gushes forth at NEIM's!

And so the younger man backed off:

Ashtu vërtetë, me të vërtetë,	You're absolutely right,
jemi mbledhur për muabet.	after all, we have gathered for *muabet.*

The uncle responded by praising the host's hospitality:

Muabet i shtruar!	An elaborately laid-out *muabet!*
Gazi, trashëguar!	Be happy and wish the groom well!

Now the second young man, who had been accompanying the first, broke in with his own congratulations to the bride and groom. Rather than traditional verses, however, he sang two couplets learned from the radio, ones he had already sung earlier in the evening:

Ne këndojmë si nga mali,	We sing as if from the mountain:
na u trashëgoftë djali!	May we congratulate the young man!
Ne këndojmë si nga fusha,	We sing as if from the field:
na u trashëgoftë çupa!	May we congratulate the young woman!

The uncle could not resist a chance to tease the novice singer for reiterating the same couplets:

Ajo është e vjetër,	Oh, that's an old line:
foli na ndonjë tjetër!	tell us a new one!

At this the young man paused a moment, and then decided to respond with a song rather than a *bejte*. He sang another Albanian radio song that had recently swept through the community, accompanied by the man whom he had been partnering. The first of the younger singers then resumed the lead and sang yet another radio song. From this point the men's singing continued with two pairs of soloists performing a heroic song in two alternating groups (*me dy kolla*).

Meanwhile, in the adjoining room, the women's gathering was disrupted by the sudden entrance of two costumed figures. The first was a mustachioed "elder" wearing jeans, a suit jacket, a straw hat, and an eye patch, played by a lively older woman with a stocking over her face. The second was a busty young "bride" wearing a leopard-print dress and a white prayer scarf draped modestly around her face, played by the tall young husband of Nuredin's sister. As the women howled with laughter, the "elder" accosted a young man who was passing through on his way to the kitchen, asking him if he was interested in marrying his "daughter." The young man responded with some disparaging remarks about the "daughter"'s appearance, which produced more laughter. As the two proceeded to exchange banter with the women, they fidgeted with their costumes, the "elder" pulling his jacket closed, the "daughter" adjusting her bustline. Slowly they made their way through the crowd of women and children toward the living room.

Entering the men's gathering, the two first approached the older men seated closest to the doorway, looking for a prospective father-in-law. The men took turns calling out comments about the "daughter" while all in the room giggled. From the direction of the kitchen, one young man pinched the "daughter's" behind. Finally Nuredin was located in a side room and dragged into the doorway, where the "daughter" began to check out his physique by tweaking his chest and reaching threateningly for his crotch. The assembled crowd roared with laughter. During one moment that the "daughter" was distracted, Nuredin returned the advance by goosing her from the behind. The "elder" and his "daughter" then retreated into the family room, where they joined a dance line that had been formed by the women. After a short while the "daughter" continued her advances on various younger men who passed through. As she reached for the crotch of one, another stepped forward to bargain for her, speaking in Macedonian. She turned him down flat, in Albanian. "He's a pauper!" she exclaimed haughtily. "He has no Mercedes!"[3]

A Community in Honor

When I first attended wedding gatherings in Prespa, with the vantage point of an outside observer, I came to regard them, through a familiar ethnographic trope, as presenting a sort of grand tableau of Prespa society. Despite the occasional diversion of premarital mumming or other bits of tomfoolery, the behavior of individuals in most instances, from where they stood or sat to the clothing they wore, from their gestures and postures to the ways they sang or danced, provided an overwhelming impression of social and moral order. As participants grouped and regrouped themselves me radhë, they produced the effect of a community sorted and color-coded by gender and age. This is essentially the vantage point of Prespa children, who are not yet full participants at weddings but for whom weddings offer a potent, multisensory lesson in their community and its "system."

Prespa adults do not simply watch a wedding unfold from the sidelines, however; they participate actively in all its phases. As they experience it, a wedding is not a static depiction of social order but a dynamic process through which they simultaneously constitute themselves as a community and assert their individual places within it. Throughout the course of a wedding, participants are constantly mindful of where they fit within the whole: by physically placing themselves within an appropriate slot, and by behaving in ways that affirm their sense of who they are and how they are connected to all other persons there. By acting in terms of the basic categories that they see as comprising their community, they also establish those categories through a range of tangible means.

It is not merely a society as a collection of discrete social categories that is constructed through wedding gatherings; it is also a moral community. Prespare understand and explain the *radhë* of their gatherings by alluding to their "system," and particularly to their discourse of "honor." For them, *radhë* is an embodied performance of their "system." The observance of *radhë* defines each individual at a gathering as related to others in specific ways. It outlines both how individuals should interact with others and how they should expect others to interact with them. As individuals carry out the various practices that comprise their *radhë*, they construct themselves as honorable persons, and their social world as a "community in honor."

Reciprocity

One of the types of relationships that Prespare constitute through their observance of *radhë* is that of reciprocal obligation. As Prespare see it, each of the two host families invites its guests to the activities on its side of the wedding as a way of "honoring" (*nderoj*) or "respecting" (*respektoj*) them. These are the families who have included the hosts in their family celebrations in the past, and so the hosts have a "debt" or "obligation" (*ua*) to return the favor. Likewise, guests attend the wedding to "honor" the host and to return obligations accrued by them in the past. It is assumed that, when their children marry, they will reciprocate with an invitation to the wedding that they host:[4]

Muabet i shtruar!	A long, elaborate *muabet!*
Gazi, trashëguar!	Be happy and wish the couple well!
Zotërinjve ja paçim ua	May we now be obligated to our hosts

kujt më djemë, kujt më çupa!   to return the favor with [the
weddings of] our sons and
daughters!

Since weddings are an occasion for each of the two families to be punctilious in its hospitality, most families in the past few decades have felt compelled to invite as many guests as they can afford to entertain. If they fail to invite any household related through kinship or friendship, they convey a clear message that the uninvited family has in some way acted dishonorably, and that a state of *muabet,* in the sense of friendly relations, no longer exists between the two. The most common reason for hosts to omit a family from their guest list is its refusal at some point in the past to have "honored" them by acknowledging a reciprocal obligation, either by not attending an earlier event sponsored by the same hosts or by not issuing an invitation to the present hosts to attend one of their family events. Another reason might be an individual family member's "shameful" behavior at recent community events, such as excessive drunkenness or argumentativeness on the part of one of the men. Conversely, when an invited household refuses to attend a wedding, it communicates to the hosts the same message of a rupture in mutual regard.

In short, for the host family, the guest list for a wedding represents both its indication to its guests of their standing in its eyes, and its assessment of its current place in the elaborate network of relationships that define the Prespa community. Likewise, the assembly of attending guests is a statement on the part of a substantial portion of the community of the host family's standing in their eyes. A wedding thus provides its host with perhaps the most tangible measure of the esteem in which he and his household are held: a reading of his and his household's present "honor."

Hosts and guests continue to "honor" each other through reciprocal gestures throughout each wedding gathering. Hosts "show honor" to their guests by initiating each of the lengthy exchanges of greetings that occur at the event's beginning. As one younger man explained:

> If you just remain seated and say, "Hi, how are you?" [the guests] don't get a "good feeling." They don't know how much you care for them and what sort of respect you have for them. . . . Your host greets you to honor you, to say to you that he loves you *me gjith zëmbër* ("with all his heart"). (Interview in Toronto, 1986)

Hosts "honor" their guests by being attentive to their needs for food, drink, and comfort, signaling their solicitude by seating themselves literally at the feet of their guests. They also "honor" their guests by providing a pleasant ambience for the nurturing of *muabet*, in the form of a tidy, well-appointed home and active encouragement of whatever type of interaction—conversation, singing, or dancing—comes to the fore. In return, guests "honor" the hosts by bringing a gift, by dressing in a festive manner, by consuming at least a healthy portion of whatever refreshments are offered them, and by contributing to the making of *muabet* by participating in an engaged and lively manner in whatever type of interaction develops. For both host and guests, an essential aspect of being honorable is being *muabetli*: exhibiting a willingness, and perhaps a predilection, to participate in the making of *muabet*.

Hierarchy and Equality

Individual guests also bring themselves into a relationship "in honor" through wedding gatherings. On the one hand, individuals are expected to demonstrate their "mindfulness" throughout the event by exhibiting an appropriately "honorable" or "modest" demeanor, and by dressing in a manner suitable to someone in their stage in life. On the other hand, each individual is expected to interact with others at a gathering in a way that accords them "honor" or "respect" on the basis of their presumed degree of "mindfulness." Older individuals are entitled to be "honored" by any younger persons by being granted spatial or temporal precedence. Elders are further "honored" through hand-kissing (plate 12) and especially solicitous complimentary exclamations. Men are "honored" in similar ways by women. Rappaport (1979:193) has argued that participation in ritualized practices compels individuals to behave in ways that imply both a recognition of the principles that underlie the order that the ritual constructs, and a public endorsement of those principles. Viewed in this way, the observance of *radhë* on the part of Prespare compels them both to embody and to publicly endorse the specific relations of power that underlie their community, as well as to lay claim to and assert their specific place within the hierarchy that they have thereby constructed.

Observance of *radhë* may also constitute a relationship of equality between two persons of the same social category. In an analysis of Yemeni men's greetings that are similar to those of Prespare, Caton (1986:293–95) suggests that when one man "honors" another through a reciprocal form of greeting, he simultaneously acknowledges the other as his social equal: his equivalent within the moral order. The second man's greeting is, in turn, a demand for a show of respect for his honor, so that the first man is compelled to respond to him in a respectful way. An exchange of greetings between two men not only constructs each as an honorable individual, but also constitutes their relationship on an egalitarian basis. The greetings exchanged by Prespa men and women may be seen to follow this same logic, although they are particularly important for the adult men, as their households' ceremonial representatives. Through the various reciprocal exchanges that the men observe, the households that make up the Prespa community are recognized as "equal in honor," despite what might be great disparities in their economic standing.

At any wedding gathering it may be assumed that the host family and its guests do indeed "honor" each other: that they "have *muabet*." Not all guests, however, are presumed to feel the same sort of regard for each other. At the largest events it is inevitable that some of those attending may be experiencing strained relations and may not feel comfortable interacting. This is especially true of *konak*s held for the men on the groom's side, and for the two particularly awkward gatherings that bring the men of both sides of the wedding together: the reception for the *sinitorë*, and the moment when the bride is taken.[5] The strict etiquette that is observed at these large gatherings provides a preordained structure through which those attending may establish sufficient *muabet* among themselves for the event to eventually take on its own momentum. In particular, the various exchanges of "honor" that occur throughout the gathering's initial phase serve as a pledge on the part of all parties present that they will interact with each other in a manner that is at least outwardly respectful, even if they never succeed in shedding their feelings of discomfort altogether, and even if they do not truly regard each other as honorable. If any guest refuses to act in such a way as to "honor" another, his or her behavior is an affront not only to the snubbed individual, but also to the host family. By impugning the host's "honor," a guest risks dishonoring himself or herself.

An individual's "honor," in the sense of the reading of his or her position within the community that emerges from participation in a social occasion, is thus negotiated through an interaction between personal demeanor and shows of deference toward others. Here Goffman's analysis of similar forms observed in middle-class American society, and of their role in the construction of a person's sense of self, is particularly useful. Phrased in his terms, if demeanor is the means through which individuals present themselves as honorable, while deference is the recognition of an individual's "honor" on the part of others, then "each individual is responsible for the demeanor image of himself and the deference image of others" (1967:84).

Goffman notes, however, that the two aspects do not work in an identical way. In terms of Prespa practices, one is required in a social situation to "honor" others, not on the basis of the moral attributes one believes them to possess, but purely in terms of their position within the social hierarchy: in other words, in terms of their gender and age. One's own demeanor, however, is a demonstration that one does indeed possess the moral attributes expected of a member of one's social category: that one is truly worthy of being deemed honorable. Through demeanor one presents not so much how one inwardly feels about oneself, but how one wishes to be perceived by others. This performative aspect of social demeanor has been astutely captured in the definition of "honor" given by the authors of the foremost dictionary of the Albanian language: "a person's social skin, which he guards with pride and which he does not allow to be violated" (Kostallari 1980:1204).[6]

One's sense of self as a social being is thus built up reciprocally through interaction with others. When one "honors" others through one's polite demeanor, one both confirms for them the esteem that is due them and brings honor or esteem upon oneself. One is said to *nderoet*, "honor oneself," by acting in an appropriate way. If one behaves in such a way as to impugn another's honor, then one runs the risk of "shaming" oneself. An appropriate show of deference is therefore a required component of proper demeanor. Conversely, by maintaining an honorable demeanor, one shows one's deference not only to other individuals, but to the "system" of the Prespa community as a whole.

Goffman's observations on the nature of forms of deference may suggest one reason for the elaborate, highly redundant quality of much Prespa etiquette. Because these forms are based solely on social category, they cannot of themselves indicate the degree of esteem or "honor" in which an individual is held. Being extremely formulaic, they run the risk of coming across as empty gestures, performed as a matter of course with no feeling and no real judgment behind them. How can individuals know where their family actually stands in the community if they are always received in the same polite way? Wikan's observations about men's social occasions in Oman seem apt also for Presparë:

To be a man in a society where sanctions are discreetly expressed, if at all, and everyone is provided with a public that in a sense "honours" him, does not make life all that easy. The man must steer a deft and elegant course with very few signals from that public who are his judges. He can never be sure that his value is what he thinks it is, as he observes his bland reflection in his polite spectators. (1984:646)

The notion of interacting with another person "with all one's heart" (*me gjith zëmbër*), as proposed by the man quoted earlier, implies that there are ways for an individual to make an otherwise formulaic exclamation seem sincere and "heartfelt." One can embellish one's verbal message by uttering it in an energetic manner, perhaps accompanying it with a gesture of the hands or head, or by adding more and more phrases of good will to the basic message. But these additions, too, eventually become standardized. It is perhaps out of this desire to convey the sincerity of one's message that Prespa forms of etiquette have gradually become more elaborate and lengthy.

Another aspect of Prespa gatherings that is central to the constitution of social relations is the serving of refreshments. Men are in fact singled out as the spokesmen for their household through the refreshments that they are offered. In the early stages of a gathering, men are served alcoholic beverages and extensive appetizers, while women are served light snacks or nothing at all. If a formal dinner is served later in the event, male guests are not only urged by their hosts to take a healthy portion of each course and to finish it, but feel obligated to do so. Women guests are free to take only a sampling to taste their hostess's skills as a cook, or even to skip a course altogether. What such practices imply is that the men are the true guests at the event, while the women are auxiliary.[7]

Refreshments also underscore the "equality in honor" of the men who participate in a gathering. Formerly, men consumed the brandy that was offered them at the event's beginning by drinking from a single glass. Still today, appetizers are arranged on serving plates placed in the center of the table, from which the men help themselves with individual forks. By taking from a common store, men signal both the egalitarian premise of the gathering and their individual "mindfulness" in not taking more than their due. These have been common practices at men's events throughout southeastern Europe. As a north Albanian friend once commented to me, only dogs are served food on individual dishes, while men take from a common plate.

The emphasis placed on egalitarianism between men is most pronounced at weddings that preserve the custom of *konak*s, such as the gathering held at Nuredin's home. These gatherings are in essence a form of commensal meal through which the men of the community affirm their solidarity, with the extensiveness of both the refreshments and the singing serving to highlight the importance of the congregation of men on the groom's side. After a long night of singing, and perhaps some clowning, each man takes his place at table *me radhë* for a festive meal. Through his participation he both signals the "honor" with which his household regards the host and affirms the "honor" that others in the community accord his household. No such larger resonances accompany the women's meal, served hastily and informally many hours earlier in the evening.

Singing for Honor

The aspect of wedding gatherings that most comprehensively constitutes Presparë as a "community in honor" is the activity of singing. In my earliest fieldwork, I began to regard Prespa singing as a form of heightened speech: a sort of stylized conversation between the two soloists. In part this was my reaction to the insistent explanations of community members that "song is *muabet*," where I took *muabet* to mean "conversation." I was not alone in perceiving their singing in this way. In an article surveying various types of south Albanian polyphony, Kruta has described one type of Tosk singing by saying that, "like all Albanian polyphony, it resembles a mutual conversation between two or more persons" (1980:54). It is certainly correct to say that Presparë regard singing as a form of relaxed and good-natured interchange. One man in Toronto, for example, translated the terms used for the two solo lines as if speaking of a game of catch:

I	*këndon*	"he sings"
	merr:	"he takes/grabs the song"
II	*pret:*	"he catches the song"
	mban:	"he holds the song"

Within the framework of any but the most intimate gathering, however, Prespatë tend to regard singing as the very antithesis of conversation, and as symbolizing intentions and values opposed to those expressed through speech.

This attitude is especially true with regard to the singing that takes place at life-cycle celebrations. In such instances, all individuals present are expected to be particularly attentive to the event being celebrated. As Presparë view them, the topics that come up most frequently in conversation, such as where one works, how much one makes per hour, or how much one's new house cost, are simply too mundane for an auspicious occasion. Because such topics tend to revolve around the economic concerns of an individual's household, they may even hinder the establishment or maintenance of *muabet,* in that their competitive tone may challenge the egalitarian basis of the gathering. Through speech, individuals may also bring up a personal problem or allude to a point of conflict with another person present. In so doing, they make themselves and their concerns the focus of everyone's attention, drawing the thoughts of others away from the hosts and the occasion at hand:

> . . . at a wedding I don't make *muabeti i punës* or *i liqenit* [talk about work or matters down at the lake] or whatever: at a wedding we've gathered for a wedding. Nevertheless, people do converse. If you err and start talking about something else, if you stray from that [wedding] *muabet,* then someone will intentionally begin a song, so as to cut off the conversation. Something lively, whatever, so as not to offend you by saying, "Leave off that work *muabet!*" If I talk like that, it's "no good" [said in English]. So I'll sing a song for the host, I'll praise him, and the other conversation will be forgotten. Because you've gathered for a wedding. (Interview with an older man in Detroit, 1987)

Even when it is not divisive in its message, conversation may prompt a large assembled group to break up into a number of small factions, so that each person relates only to those present whom he or she knows and likes best. For all these reasons, Presparë often associate conversation with the mundane and competitive interests of individuals and families that threaten to undermine social cohesion.

Several community members pointed out to me that the very structure of their songs is unlike that of conversation. In conversation, one speaker may respond to another in a variety of ways. He or she may agree with the first speaker, or may challenge his or her point of view, even to the point of initiating an argument. But no such retort is possible within the format of a song.[8] Rather, the second soloist repeats and affirms the sentiments expressed by the first in his or her text. As one younger man volunteered spontaneously to me, in English:

> You know how I always think about these songs? When I sing and somebody else "comes from behind" [his translation of *vjen pas*] it's like I say

something and then he says, "OK, it *is* like that. That's the way it is!" (Conversation in Toronto, 1985)

It is only through exchanges of *bejte* that Prespa singing moves closer to both the structure and the improvisatory quality of conversation. Some community members in fact recognized this distinction between songs and *bejte* when they referred to the latter as being "said" (*thënë*) rather than "sung" (*kënduar*).

Another way in which singing is unlike conversation is that it draws on a corpus of preexisting texts that are not merely the expression of the individual who performs them. In any polyphonic performance, the first soloist's choice of text may draw attention to some aspect of his or her life and may therefore be regarded to some extent as a personal statement. The songs, however, are seen as part of the south Albanian singing tradition, and the sentiments that they express are presumed to be shared by all present. When the second soloist repeats and completes the first soloist's text, he or she is confirming the communal nature of the song's sentiments.

Those performing the drone also contribute to a type of interaction that is distinct from speech. Although only one person "sings" or leads a song, all present perform it, with those providing the drone serving simultaneously as participants in the song and as audience for the soloists. Droning provides an assurance that no one in the room will be lured into conversation, for a mouth that is occupied with droning cannot also be speaking. The requirement that all in the room drone serves as a reminder that everyone is expected to be attentive both to the performance taking place and to the occasion. Through its inclusion of a choral drone, Prespa singing thus establishes what Irvine (1979:779) has called a "central situational focus": a focal activity that automatically relegates all other types of interaction, such as subdued conversation, to a secondary status. By involving those present in an alternative form of vocalizing, droning restricts the extent to which conversation, with its message of particularism, is allowed to challenge the sociability of the occasion. In this regard, the stipulation that everyone present should drone does not require that all individuals actually be vocalizing at all times. A few individuals even explained to me that, when they had particularly enjoyed a performance in the past, they had stopped droning just to listen. In such instances, one's silence is at least as great a show of esteem for the soloists as one's droning would otherwise be.

An alternative way to view the distinction that Presparë make between speech and song is in terms of communicative "frames," a concept originally proposed by Bateson (1972) and taken up by both Goffman (1974) and Bauman (1977:15ff). Prespa song may be distinguished from everyday speech by various features, including the organization of textual elements by poetic meter and rhyme, and the intoning of that text within a polyphonic format. These features provide a "frame" around whatever sentiments are expressed in a song's text, signaling that it should be interpreted as contrasting in important respects with utterances that are spoken. Singing is thus a type of metacommunication: its format transmits certain messages over and above those communicated through its text. When Presparë choose to socialize through song rather than through speech, they automatically signal the communal nature of the sentiments expressed in their songs and emphasize that the event taking place is one in which precedence is given to shared concerns over particularistic ones. Singing in effect marks the activities that take place through it as dedicated to the fostering of solidarity. The polyphonic structure of Prespa songs not only encourages, but also embodies the sort of attentive, unselfish, coordinated interaction between individuals that Presparë regard as optimal at their social events: all those qualities that are implicit in their notion of *muabet*.[9]

The egalitarianism that singing constructs through its structure is reinforced through the ordering of song performances. As Presparë interpret their song structure, each individual may articulate his or her participation in a wedding gathering at specific points by performing the first solo line of a song. This is particularly true at the beginning of an event, when each person leads one song. As with other aspects of *radhë*, Presparë explain this first round of songs in terms of "honor." First of all, singing "honors" the host family because it is considered to be auspicious and its presence at the occasion calls attention to the event being celebrated. Any song or added couplet referring specifically to the occasion or to a family member reinforces this connection and further "honors" the hosts, just as allusions in women's songs to the sons of other women "honor" their families. Any such gestures, whether directed to the host family or to individual guests, in turn single out the singer as particularly honorable and solicitous. In response, the others present "honor" the singer by droning, a sign that they are attentive to the performance. It is in fact even possible to register one's small displeasure with the singer by pointedly refusing to drone, as Memet's uncle did on the night before Feime was taken (see chapter 5). When the singer has finished, the others "honor" him or her with their praise, realizing that a person often has to overcome considerable embarrassment to perform "in public." Singing thus constructs a relationship of reciprocity among those attending a wedding gathering on several levels simultaneously, providing a framework within which they can present themselves and recognize others as honorable members of the community.

At any social gathering, the point in time of a person's initial song performance is determined not by any individual qualities that that person might possess, but by his or her place within the social hierarchy. Gender and generation are the only aspects of status that are recognized; neither economic standing nor the prominence of one's lineage is in any way relevant. In this regard, the practice of acting *me radhë*, regardless of the specific activity, establishes a firmly egalitarian stance between members of different households by suggesting that, on a moral plane, all households are equal, and that age, life experience, and exemplary conduct are the sole criteria through which one gains prestige within the community. The egalitarianism of *radhë* is most pronounced with regard to the singing order, however, precisely because singing is the main activity and the main form of communication at wedding gatherings. By regulating access to the forum that singing provides, the practice of singing *me radhë* assures that no individuals, no matter how excellent their singing or how commanding their presence, are allowed to dominate the occasion.

The egalitarian ethos that pervades wedding singing is particularly striking as a contrast to the various ways that families involved in wedding gatherings may allude to their household's economic well-being as a means of vying for prestige. Such displays, which may provide a genuine or highly deceptive reading of financial standing, are evident in the effusive rococo decor of the host's homes, in the extensive refreshments that are served, in the elegant dress of both men and women, and in the women's opulent gold jewelry. Prespa singing, however, is a form of expression that is virtually impervious to the representation of economic distinctions. As interpreted by Prespari, it is in the very nature of singing to override elements that might divide individuals and to bring them together in a common pursuit. Through both its structure and its ordering, then, the singing that dominates weddings and other community celebrations encourages participants to overlook the hierarchical tendencies that are otherwise evident within community relations, so as to experience their society as one founded on egalitarian principles.[10]

Singing and the Discourse of Honor

As children, adult members of today's Prespa community were socialized to their "system" in two sorts of ways. The first was through observation of and participation in various social practices. In their interactions with others, they learned not abstract concepts such as "mind," "honor," or "modesty," but rather distinctive, formulaic ways of acting in the world. These are the practices that Presparë refer to when they speak of their *adetë* ("customs"), their *ligjë* or *zakonë* (also "customs"; literally "laws"), or their *radhë* ("order"). Although such practical learning took place in every type of interaction, it was at large social occasions that children were called on to interact with the greatest number of other people, and thus to master the greatest range of appropriate behaviors. At wedding celebrations, young girls attended all the various ritual activities, as well as evening gatherings, in the company of their mothers. Young boys did likewise until they reached an age when they were encouraged to quietly observe all but the most lengthy and formal of the men's events. In their elaborateness and complexity, weddings thus served as a privileged forum for this type of practical socialization.

Second, at less formal gatherings that brought together two or three households, those present often devoted much of the conversation to evaluations of recent instances of their own behavior and that of others, so as to determine whether particular actions upheld and exemplified, or undermined and challenged, aspects of the community's "system." As children listened to such conversations, they became familiar with individual concepts such as "mind" and "honor," together with the discourses in which they are embedded, as they were applied to specific domains of action. As major events in the life of the community, weddings often prompted particularly lively conversations and offered a particularly broad range of activities to be appraised. Gradually children acquired a set of verbal discourses with which to interpret the actions of others as well as fashion their own subsequent actions. Aspects of practical socialization that were instigated at occasions such as weddings were thus complemented by the subsequent rounds of conversation that inevitably followed, and processed, those larger events.

As adults, those same individuals renegotiate the terms of their "system" at present-day events through a similar process. In the weeks and even months following a wedding, whether in solitude or at smaller gatherings, they think back over their own behavior during the course of the event and scrutinize the actions of others, framing their interpretations in the terms of their community's honor-based discourse. As they do so, they refine or revise their understanding of what precisely constitutes "honorable" or "shameful" behavior, or which qualities one should have to be considered "mindful." In this way the community's moral discourse is continually revitalized, and individuals continually reframe their sense of self within its terms.

The two contexts within which this process unfolds through time are related, not as a linear progression nor as a cycle, but as a dialectic through which verbal discourse and social practice are mutually and continuously constituted. As subsequent generations of young Prespare have begun to participate in the ongoing whirl of community social occasions, they have become folded into that dialectic and have helped to propel it, learning in the process to understand themselves, and their community, through the terms that they have also helped to construct. Through their attendance at occasions such as weddings, and their subsequent participation in conversations evaluating those occasions, they have simultaneously contributed to the ongoing constitution of the community's moral code and of their sense of subjectivity.

Singing, of course, is precisely one of the practices that has been central to Prespa social occasions and is perhaps the most patterned and stylized aspect of the community's *radhë* that any Prespar or Presparkë has traditionally learned. As such, it has served the community as an activity that integrates and embodies their various understandings of "honor" perhaps more succinctly than any other. For me to have offered an interpretation of Prespa singing as developing out of community discourses would thus have addressed only one side of the dialectic. It has been at least as important for me to point out that dialectic's other phase: to present singing as one of the major sites within which Presparë have developed and transmitted their notions of morality.

In this respect there exists no separable Prespa "social ideology" outside the realm of scholarly abstraction. Ethnographers are prone to locating a community's ideology within a set of shared moral discourses. But ideology is, no less importantly, embedded within realms of social practice: internalized as "habitus" within each individual's experiencing of self and community. As the practice of Prespa singing exemplifies, activities such as music-making are not to be regarded merely as reflections or articulations of some more primary aspect of a social formation. They are fundamental factors in any formation's constitution, maintenance, and transformation.

Singing as the Practice of Patriarchy

Since the time when, thanks to Prometheus, grains no longer grow by
themselves, it has been necessary to bury seeds in the belly of the
earth and then watch them disappear in the form of *sitos,* grain food,
into the bellies of women. From the day that Zeus' will determined
the existence of women, men, like wheat, no longer grow by
themselves out of the ground. Men must put their seed in the belly of
their wives so that it may germinate; and when the time comes,
legitimate children who can extend their father's lineage will emerge
from it. (Vernant 1989:67; interpreting Hesiod's account of the legend
of Prometheus)

THE GROOM BATHES AND IS SHAVED

In the fall of 1985 I attended a one-day wedding in Connecticut at
which Merita, a Presparkë who had grown up in the United States,
married Fatmir, a Prespar who had recently arrived from Macedonia.
The couple were already legally married and had taken an apartment
together several weeks before the celebration. Of Fatmir's family in Macedonia, only his mother came for the wedding. He did, however, have
assorted relatives and family friends living in various cities in the
United States, and these congregated at a house in a town near where
he was living, together with some neighbors from Prespa who were, in
fact, distant relatives of Merita's rather than his. In the absence of close
family, this group of people, who in Prespa would probably never have
been gathered together for such an event, served ceremonially as his
"kin" during the wedding celebration. Likewise, the house served as the
site for the ritual activities that took place on the day of the wedding.

I rendezvoused with the couple early Sunday morning at their own
apartment. From there I drove with Fatmir's party to his ritual "house."
Soon after we arrived, his cousin's wife began to circulate through the
assembled guests, handing each a handful of *kokolinkë,* the same type of

roasted chickpea mixture that was distributed to the guests at Feime's home on the night that she was "adorned" (see chapter 4). Fatmir then excused himself and went into the bathroom to "bathe," that is, to take a leisurely shower and to dress for the wedding. As is customary, his relatives followed and stood outside the door in the hallway, where they began to sing to him.

First to lead a song was a *xhaxha* (father's first cousin) of Fatmir, who sang one of the most popular of the songs customarily addressed to the groom at such ritual moments. In it he inserted *me radhë* terms for the groom's closest relatives and then finished off with a general term that included all others who were present:

FATMIR beu nëpër limoj . . .	FATMIR *bey* under a lemon tree . . .
moj nëpër limoj.	(under a lemon tree)
ç'e zu gjumi, djalën e qëlloi . . .	Sleep by chance overtook him . . .
Nai erdh' BABAI ME NËNËN ta zgjojë . . .	His FATHER came with his MOTHER to awaken him . . .
FATMIR beu nëpër limoj . . .	FATMIR *bey* under a lemon tree . . .
Nai erdh' GJYSHI ME GJYSHEN ta zgjojë . . .	His GRANDFATHER came with his GRANDMOTHER to awaken him . . .
FATMIR beu nëpër limoj . . .	FATMIR *bey* under a lemon tree . . .
Erdh' VËLLAI ME MOTRËN ta zgjojë . . .	His BROTHER came with his SISTER to awaken him . . . [their names were inserted in the repeat]
FATMIR beu nëpër limoj . . .	FATMIR *bey* under a lemon tree . . .
Erdhë FAREFISI nga gjumi ta zgjojë . . .	ALL HIS RELATIVES came to awaken him from his dreams . . .

The *xhaxha* launched into the song in a full-voiced, animated style, singing rapidly and accentuating the song's duple meter. Fatmir's maternal grandfather, an elderly man with a deep, booming voice, accompanied him. At the end of their spirited rendition, those who were gathered around congratulated the singer heartily and shook his hand.

The grandfather then began a song, one that would not generally be considered appropriate for this point in the wedding. It addresses a theme that, while rare in the Prespa repertoire, is common in the wedding songs of many neighboring communities: the sad lot of a young bride within her husband's home. The grandfather sang in much the same rousing style as had the first singer, who now accompanied him:

Të rriti nëna me naze shumë . . .	Your mother raised you to be very coy . . .
bij' e nënës.	(O mother's daughter)
Të rriti, të bëri nuse . . .	She raised you, she made you a bride . . .
Të rriti, ty të porositi: . . .	She raised you and instructed you: . . .
Dolloman të bardhë, të mos e nxjerrç kurrë . . .	Don't ever take off your white [bridal] gown . . .
Që sa vajta unë, dolloman ma muarë . . .	As soon as I went [as a bride], they took my gown . . .
Thuai u nënës!	(Call out to your mother!)
Shtëpi e madhe me kunata shumë . . .	A big house with many sisters-in-law . . .
Tërë natën të natës unë vete, mbush ujë . . .	All night long I go to fetch water . . .
Tërë ditën të ditës doçet dë brumë . . .	All day long my hands are in the [bread] dough . . .
Shtëpi e madhe me punë shumë . . .	A big house with much work . . .

He too was roundly congratulated at the end of his performance.

I have heard the grandfather sing this song on other occasions as well—not, it seems, because it relates to the moment in the ceremony being observed, but simply because he likes it. In instances such as this, those who are present find their own explanations for why a song has been sung. Fatmir, for example, told me later that Merita's mother had been deserted by her husband when she was a small child and had had an unhappy life as a wife and mother. The song, he explained, had been sung with Merita in mind.

Next to sing was a man living in the same town who is married to

Merita's distant cousin. He also chose a ritual song in which he named Fatmir's close relatives. The "short time" mentioned in the first line is said to refer to the fact that the wedding was arranged within a short time period. Another of Merita's relatives accompanied him. In contrast to the previous performances, the two men sang relatively softly and slowly in *shtruar* style, drawing their melodic lines out so as to obliterate any sense of meter:

Ç'është ky gaz kaqe dë një çast? . . .	What is it that is making us so happy in such a short time? . . .
O bej O FATMIR bej.	(O FATMIR *bey*)
Gëzove BABANË TËND . . .	You made YOUR FATHER happy . . .
Gëzove NËNËN TËNDE . . .	You made YOUR MOTHER happy . . .
Ç'është ky gaz kaqe dë një çast? . . .	What is it that is making us so happy in such a short time? . . .
Gëzove GJYSHIN TËND . . .	You made YOUR GRAND-FATHER happy . . .
Gëzove GJYSHEN TËNDE . . .	you made YOUR GRAND-MOTHER happy . . .
Ç'është ky gaz kaqe dë një çast? . . .	What is it that is making us so happy in such a short time? . . .
Gëzove FAREFISNË TËND . . .	You made ALL YOUR RELA-TIVES happy . . .

Now the women were invited to sing. First was the wife of the man who had just sung the second line, accompanied by another of Merita's younger cousins. She chose the same song that the *xhaxha* had sung, a frequent occurrence at such ritual moments. She did, however, select different verses from among those that are widely sung, and she mentioned his relatives in a different manner:

FATMIR beu nëpër limoj . . .	FATMIR *bey* under a lemon tree . . .
moj nëpër limoj.	(under a lemon tree)
ç'e zu gjumi e ç'e qëlloi . . .	Sleep by chance overtook him . . .

Vai BABAI edhe e zgjoi . . .	His FATHER came and awakened him . . .
Ngreu FATMIR, të të martoj . . .	Get up, FATMIR, so I can marry you off . . .
Vai NËNEJA edhe e zgjoi . . .	His MOTHER came and awakened him . . .
Ngreu FATMIR, të të martoj . . .	Get up, FATMIR, so I can marry you off . . .
me një nuse të të gëzoj . . .	and make you happy with a bride . . .

The two women sang softly, in *shtruar* style, although the first soloist performed her line with almost no ornamentation. The second soloist, however, is an experienced and admired singer. By entering each time with assurance and delicately embellishing her melody line with turns and glottal ornaments she was able to "regulate" the performance, transforming a very simple rendition of the song into one that the others found highly pleasing.

At this point the second soloist assumed that she should lead a song. Turning to the women around her, she asked under her breath, "Now, which song should I sing?" Before she could decide, Fatmir's grandmother initiated yet another ritual song, and so the younger woman once again accompanied:

FATMIR beu, filis i shkruar, as na jep lejë për të martuar?	FATMIR *bey*, slender sapling, won't you give us permission to marry you off?
Ç'e kam vënë dorën në zëmbër	I swore with my hand on my heart
kur ta bëjë NËNA, BABAI embër.	that I would [marry] whenever my MOTHER and FATHER gave the word.
Ç'e kam vënë dorën në zëmbër	I swore with my hand on my heart
kur ta bëjë VËLLAI, MOTRA embër.	that I would whenever my BROTHER and SISTER gave the word.

Now Fatmir's mother came forward to sing. She too performed *Nëpër limoj:*

FATMIR beu nëpër limoj . . .	FATMIR *bey* under a lemon tree . . .
moj nëpër limoj.	(under a lemon tree)
ç'e zu gjumi e ç'e qëlloi . . .	Sleep by chance overtook him . . .
Vai BABAI edhe e zgjoi . . .	His FATHER came and awakened him . . .
Ngreu mor BIR të të martoj . . .	Get up, SON, so that I can marry you off . . .
me një nuse të të gëzoj . . .	and make you happy with a bride . . .
FATMIR beu nëpër limoj . . .	FATMIR *bey* under a lemon tree . . .
Vai VËLLAI, NUSJA e zgjoi . . .	His BROTHER AND HIS WIFE came and awakened him . . .
Ngreu mor VËLLA të të martoj . . .	Get up, BROTHER, so I can marry you off . . .

Once again the song was sung in *shtruar* style. This time, however, the second soloist was unsure of her part. Occasionally she entered late, breaking the momentum of the singing, and was thus not able to hold the performance together.

At this point Fatmir appeared in the doorway of the bathroom, dressed in a tuxedo. Because the house was in the middle of town, with no yard to speak of, he was led instead into the kitchen to be shaved. This task was entrusted not to one of Fatmir's close relatives, as would be usual, but rather to one of Merita's male cousins who is a professional hairdresser. He first shaved Fatmir and then trimmed and dried his hair. With the sound of snipping shears and then a whirring blow-dryer in the background, the women's singing continued.

For Fatmir's shaving, the women shifted from ritual wedding songs to songs that are also commonly sung at evening gatherings. The first singer was his mother's sister, accompanied by his mother:

Ungju, rri në fron t'ërgjëntë . . .	Sit down on the silver throne . . .
ore bej, O FATMIR bej.	(O FATMIR *bey*)
Unë ungjem, s'mund të ungjem . . .	I sit down, but I can't stay seated . . .

se ma shajnë nusen . . .	because they are making fun of my bride . . .
Le ta shajnë për inat . . .	Let them make fun of her out of spite . . .
Si nusja jote s'ka në fshat . . .	There's not another bride like yours in the whole village . . .

Next was the wife of the *xhaxha* who had initiated the singing, also accompanied by Fatmir's mother:

FATMIR beu i Shkodrës,	FATMIR *bey* of Shkodër [a town in northern Albania],
pse s'na del pe odës?	why won't you come out of your room?
Ç'kam nuse të vogël	Because I have a young bride
veshur në të bardhë:	dressed in white:
lulëzon si dardhë.	she blooms like a pear tree.
FATMIR beu i Shkodrës,	FATMIR *bey* of Shkodër,
pse s'na del pe odës?	why won't you come out of your room?
Kam nuse të vogël	I have a young bride
veshur në të ollë:	in a slender dress:
lulëzon si mollë.	she blooms like an apple tree.

At long last came the turn of the younger woman who had accompanied the first women singers so well. She chose a radio song which has become enormously popular among Prespare, one that is a close textual variant of a local song. Accompanying her was her sister. The song is always sung in a particularly animated, rapid style with no ornamentation:

Ç'ke bilbil që po këndon? . . .	Nightingale, why are you singing?
edhe o bilbil more, aman edhe o bilbil more.	(O nightingale)
Unë këndoj për djalërinë . . .	I sing for bachelorhood . . .
Djalëria s'vjen më kurrë . . .	Bachelorhood will never come again . . .
se të thonë burrë me grua . . .	now that they call you a man with a wife . . .

Ç'ke bilbil që po këndon? . . .	Nightingale, why are you singing? . . .
Unë këndoj për vajzërinë . . .	I sing for maidenhood . . .
Vajzëria s'vjen më kurrë . . .	Maidenhood will never come again . . .
se të thonë grua me burrë . . .	now that they call you a woman with a husband . . .

Finally the two women switched musical roles, and the sister led one of the most frequently sung songs associated with the groom's side of a wedding. In contrast to the preceding performance, this song, as is customary, was performed in a particularly drawn out, ornamented style:

Djalë FATMIR beu qysh e bëmë fjalën	Young man FATMIR *bey,* since we gave our word
të piqemi bashkë pa mbushur javën,	that we should see each other before the week was out,
letër të dërgova, letër s'ke këthyer.	I sent you a letter, but you didn't send one in return.
A më ke dër ment apo më ke arruar?	Are you thinking of me or have you forgotten me?
Unë dër ment të kam, s'të kam arruar.	I am thinking of you, I haven't forgotten you.
Sheqer e llokume bashkë janë gatuar.	[Like] sugar and *llokume* [we are] bound together.

With the shaving finished, Fatmir was led out into the living room, where the men had congregated. A male cousin brought out a large *bakllava* (baked pastry made of filo dough filled with chopped nuts and soaked in sugar water) decorated with candies and served a small portion to each guest. For a few minutes the older men, fueled by some Yugoslav liquor, sang informally. The entire party then set out to "take" Merita from the couple's apartment.

Weddings and Subjectivity

In my early days of living with a Prespa family in Toronto, I was watching one day as Beti, the family's five-year-old daughter, helped her mother to tidy up the *odë* by running a damp rag over the surfaces of the room's two low tables. Whenever the family had guests, a table was placed in front of each of the room's two couches, which sat in an ell opposite the entrance. As she wiped the first table, Beti explained to me, "This is where the women put their coffee." She then moved on to the second table, explaining, "This is where the men put their beer." I asked if men always sit on the one sofa and women on the other. She and her older sister responded, "Yes."

At age five Beti already saw the *odë* in her home as divided into female and male domains and was learning to identify herself with particular sets of gendered spaces and activities. As in any community, that process of learning was taking place less through verbal instruction than through Beti's observation of and participation in the usual round of social activities. In short, she was becoming socialized to community notions of gender, and of social order more broadly, by attaining a practical mastery of the intricacies of *radhë*.

Beti's comments provide the most dramatic illustration that the extensive structuring of community social occasions has a profound effect on any Prespar or Presparkë's sense of gendered subjectivity. Weddings are by far the largest of community occasions, and so participants are called on to behave in ways that are more stereotypic for persons of their gender and generation than is the case in other situations. Weddings are also most comprehensively about a gendered self: about the progression of a female and a male from childhood to adulthood, about the nature of courtship and marriage between woman and man, and about the roles that each will play as adults within their household and community. Considerations of gender are not addressed in isolation by the rituals that make up the core of the celebration, however, but rather as one component of a far more pervasive, interwoven vision of social order. As they participate in weddings, Presparë are called on to reinscribe not only their sense of a gendered self, but also that self as embedded within a particular form of patriarchal society.

Realigning the Social Order

The majority of the marriages of today's adult Presparë were celebrated in their home villages in Prespa. These were elaborate, lengthy affairs that began with the sending of henna to the bride by the groom and the dyeing of her hair, culminated with the taking of the bride and the consummation of the marriage, and continued through the new couple's first visit to her natal home. Despite the fact that the individual customs that had been combined to form the wedding ritual might be diverse in their origins, they had coalesced by the mid-twentieth century into a highly cohesive symbolic construct that exemplified community notions of self and social order in a particularly powerful and comprehensive manner.

Most of the weddings that I saw celebrated in Prespa villages in the early 1980s conformed closely to that same wedding format. At the weddings that I have attended since then in North America, families have most often attempted to retain as much as is feasible of the skeletal structure of a village wedding and to observe many of the smaller customs that embellish it. For any Prespare old enough to have memories of village weddings, it is this prototypic village celebration that informs their experience even of North American weddings, catching up bits and pieces of ritual observance into a coherent structure and endowing the event as it unfolds with its symbolic import. In this chapter I focus on that prototypic format, highlighting those aspects of Prespa wedding practices that represent a direct continuation of weddings as celebrated in the 1970s and early 1980s in Macedonia. This analysis is then complemented in chapter 8 with attention to the sorts of changes in practice that are beginning to take place among overseas families.

Any Prespa wedding, above all else, is a celebration of the taking of a woman by a patrilineal group so that its line may continue into the next generation:

Ra vesa, vesojti dhenë.	The dew fell and moistened the earth.
Ku jemi nisur ne të vemë?	Where have we set out for?
Jemi nisur për dë Kranjë	We have set out for [the village of] Krani
ta bastisim FIKRI benë,	to fall upon the house of FIKRI *bey,*
t'ja marrim të bijën,	to take his daughter,
atë më të mirën,	the nicest one,
atë ballëkartën,	with a forehead as smooth as paper,
atë gojëmjaltën.	with a mouth as sweet as honey.

(Women's wedding song, groom's side; Krani, 1972; CD #5)

This is the literal meaning of the phrase uttered ubiquitously by relatives of the bride and groom throughout the celebration: *Të trashëgoet!* Although community members think of this phrase as meaning "May they live a long and happy married life!" or simply "Congratulations!" it in fact derives from the verb *trashëgoj*, "to inherit," and thus means something like "May it be inherited!"

In the course of a wedding the bride is transferred from her natal home to that of her in-laws, an action that effects a profound transformation in her status within the social order. The transformation that takes place, however, is not limited to her. In most instances, two unrelated or distantly related lineage groups, comprising at times dozens of members, become "kin" or *soj* and are brought into a relationship of reciprocity and mutual obligation. Since adulthood is regarded as being attained through marriage, and the status of "elder" through the marriage of one's children, a wedding also accomplishes the progression of the bride and groom, and often of their parents, to the next phase of the cycle of generations. In short, a wedding effects a major reordering both within and between the two host households and their extended families. In so doing, it contributes incrementally to the reordering and reproduction of the Prespa community as a whole.

The core of a wedding celebration consists of a basic sequence of ritual activities that dramatizes these transformations. As the rituals are carried out, the bride and groom, together with their immediate family and closest friends, are prompted to redefine themselves as individuals and their place within family and community. Through their participation in the wedding, their subjectivity is fundamentally realigned. But a wedding also has a major impact on those less closely connected to the two families. Through their collective participation in all phases of the ritual, the wedding guests sanctify the individual transformations that the wedding effects on the part of the larger Prespa community. And as the sequence of rituals unfolds, their stereotypic actions evoke, juxtapose, consolidate, and provide a rationale for many of the tenets of the Prespa "system." In short, weddings provide all participants with a tangible, lived representation of their shared views of social order.

The most important of the transformations that are accomplished in the course of a wedding is the transferral of the bride from her home to that of the groom. The bride is taken, not so much by the groom or his immediate family, as by the whole lineage group, the *krushq*:

Ç'u mbush mali plot me dushk?	How is it that the mountain has become dense with foliage?
S'janë dushk, por janë krushq.	It is not foliage, but the *krushq*.

Dë janë krushq, të dalin	If it is the *krushq*, may they come out
SADETNË ta marrin.	to take SADET [the bride].
Ç'u mbush lëmë plot me duaj?	How is it that the threshing floor has become filled with sheaves?
S'janë duaj, por janë kuaj.	They are not sheaves, but horses.
Dë janë kuaj, të dalin	If they are horses, may they come out
SADETNË ta marrin.	to take SADET.
SADETI tonë qan me lot:	Our SADET cries with tears:
e ka babanë s'e lë dot.	Her father won't give her up at all.

(Men's wedding song, groom's side; Arvati, ca. 1969)

Until perhaps thirty years ago, the groom in fact remained at home while his father and other adult relatives fetched the bride and brought her back to the house. He stood in an upstairs window watching the party approaching and then came out into the courtyard and fired a rifle shot into the air.

The incorporation of the bride into the lineage group is enacted most graphically in the dancing of the "bride's dance," or *valle e nuses*. Shortly after her arrival at the groom's home, the bride is led out into the courtyard amid all the guests. To music played by the *daulle,* all members of the groom's party who are considered to be close to his family take hands and form a long dance line, with the bride, followed by the groom, at the head. One by one each relative or family friend steps to the head of the line in front of the bride, takes her handkerchief (*shamiçkë*) or bouquet in his or her right hand, and leads or "dances" the bride for a few moments, as all perform the same six-measure pattern of footwork that is used for the women's dance songs (plate 10). The full sequence of the dance may last for a half hour or more, as each important guest takes his or her turn.

Once all appropriate guests have led the dance, the groom steps to the head of the line in front of his bride and dances at the lead. With this gesture, he takes his place symbolically both as an adult member of the community and as the bride's husband. One younger man in Chicago in fact singled out the "bride's dance" as the moment in his long and complicated wedding celebration when he finally felt "married." It was "the moment of truth," he remembered thinking, "There's no turning back now!"[1]

Këndona bilbil i vesës . . .	Sing to us, nightingale of the summer . . .
këndona.	(sing to us)
ZARIF, ç'i mentonesh besës? . . .	ZARIF, what are you thinking about? . . .
I mentonesh djalërisë . . .	You're thinking about boyhood . . .
se djalë mos bënesh kurrë . . .	because you'll never be a boy again . . .
Kur të gjejnë shokët mb'udhë . . .	When your friends find you on the street . . .
Xh'bën? Si je? s'të thonë kurrë . . .	they'll no longer say, "Whatcha doin'? How are ya?" . . .

(Women's wedding song sung to the groom; Chicago, 1986)

The groom's coming of age is also signaled earlier in the celebration with his shaving and the cutting of his hair (plates 6, 19). It is likely that in the past the wedding was in fact the first time that the groom had been shaved (Dojaka 1978:126). This is only one of several allusions to the hair and head that signal the progression of one of the individuals in the wedding party through the stages of the generational cycle. The bride's progression is marked by the dyeing of her hair with henna, as well as by her adornment as a bride on each of the three nights before she is taken (plate 11). Each of these practices establishes a sense of discontinuity between two stages of life that would otherwise form an unbroken continuum and thus helps to construct discrete categories that separate childhood from adulthood.

As for the groom's parents, the headscarf of the groom's mother, or the hat or shirt of his father, is often set on fire and waved jubilantly in the air during the dancing of the "bride's dance" or at another point shortly after the bride's arrival at the groom's home. Symbolically, with their arrival at his home, the bride and groom have replaced his parents as the young adults of the household: the generation of fertility and procreation. Henceforth, the groom's mother in particular will wear a dark-colored headscarf to signify her new status as an "elder" (*plakë*). As with the actions performed on the groom and bride, the practices through which older Prespare distinguish themselves by their dress serve to constitute "elders" as a distinct social category.[2]

The groom is constituted as a "man" in the course of his wedding and he gains a wife, but he remains within his family home and his daily activities do not much change. The bride's life, however, is radically altered by her marriage, and the wedding is often a traumatic event for her. In essence, she ceases to be a member of her natal family and becomes a part of the groom's family. For a bride whose new home is in a distant locale, her marriage may mean long years of separation from her closest kin. But the separation can be hard even for those who remain close to their parents' home:

> Sometimes you leave your family—you never see the family again. That's the worst. I was married "in town" [in the same village], so I could go [home] every day. But still . . . you know, when you first get married, you have to go back [to your family] for a *gosti:* three days later, or five, or seven. I couldn't wait three days. I wanted to go and see my family. When my cousin came [to invite the couple for the *gosti*] . . . I cried. I had missed him so much, for two days! I couldn't wait to see him. When I went there, when I left that night, I cried again. "I was so many years over here, now I gotta come here for awhile and go back?" It feels—you know, you feel so bad. (Interview, in English, with a young woman in Chicago, 1987)

Both because of the transformation that she undergoes during the wedding, and because she is the prized object of the wedding, the bride is the single most prominent figure in the celebration. Among all the wedding participants, she stands out both through her characteristic bridal attire and through her demeanor. In the period before World War II, a Prespa bride wore a Western-style dress, usually of pastel or floral fabric. Long strands of silver wire (*tel*) were draped on either side of her face, and special decorations of beads, sequins, and metal foil, called *lulkë*, were custom-made for her to wear on her forehead, cheeks, and chin. In her hand she clasped a small kerchief with a sequined, crocheted edge. When she left her home for the groom's, she wore a black velvet coat and a tube-shaped head covering (*duvak*) made of red or pink satin that covered her head and extended down at least to her waist. When she arrived at the groom's home, the groom was brought forward to throw back her *duvak* and thus to see his bride for the first time. Shortly after the war, men working overseas began to bring back American white wedding dresses and white wreaths and veils for their sons' brides to wear. Since that time it has become standard for a bride to wear a white outfit made in Turkey or North America. Modern brides often retain both the *tel* and the face decorations. In addition to their handker-chief, they often carry a large bouquet of flowers.

Even more striking than her attire is the bride's demeanor. Beginning with the first evening that she is "adorned," a bride-to-be adopts a stance that she is expected to maintain throughout the wedding period, whenever she is in the presence of other than her immediate family. She is expected to stand very still, eyes cast to the ground, unsmiling and almost unmoving (plate 8). In the past, brides shut their eyes entirely, or even had their eyelids glued together with sugar water. During the evenings before she is taken, as she models her new wardrobe, the bride stands for ten or fifteen minutes, maintaining this stance. She is then encouraged to sit and rest for a few minutes before resuming her pose.

On the day of her wedding, as soon as guests of her family begin to arrive at her home, the bride again assumes her stance. Once the groom's party arrives, she does not move unless physically escorted, either by her own relatives or those of the groom:

Të djelën që më saba . . .	On Sunday in the morning
t'u bëftë mamaja.	(I, your mother, will sacrifice everything for you!)
do gëdhiet, do bënet saba . . .	the sun will rise and morning will break . . .
do vijnë krushqit e do shkosh me ta . . .	The *krushq* will come and you will go with them . . .
rrugës do shkojnë e do bëjnë shaka . . .	As they go along the road they'll joke with you . . .
e ti, moj vajzë, mos qeshç me ta . . .	but you, young girl, must not laugh with them . . .

(Wedding song sung by the *daulle*, Nakolec, 1980; for a version of this song, see CD #22)

Until very recently, no member of the bride's family accompanied her from this moment forward, as she set out for the groom's home. For her family and all those who had gathered at her house, the wedding ended at this sorrowful point, with her leave-taking.

The bride is taken directly to the groom's home, where she is asked to perform a variety of ritual actions. She is then brought into the court-yard and retains her stiff, expressionless pose while she is "danced" in the "bride's dance." Afterward she returns inside, where she stands in the *odë* or a bedroom on display for the remainder of the afternoon. As guests of the groom's party approach her, she stands with eyes cast downward, taking each guest's hand, kissing it, and then pressing it to her forehead in a sign of deference. She retains her unmoving stance until she is "closed in" with the groom after nightfall.

When I have spoken with community members about various wedding customs, they have offered three types of explanations for particular actions. For some they have ready explanations, ones that I have learned are highly consistent from one person to the next. A second type of answer is more idiosyncratic and is usually an individual's attempt to provide a rational explanation for something that he or she has probably never before discussed with others, or even privately considered. Most commonly, however, individuals respond with a single word. *Adet,* they answer: "That's the custom." Or *Ka mbetur që ndonj'erë:* "That's the way it has been done."[3]

I have received all three types of responses in asking about the bride's characteristic stance. A classic anthropological interpretation, in the spirit of Victor Turner (1969), would propose that it exemplifies her "liminal" status during the wedding, as she passes from one family group to another. Scholars of east European folklore might also point out that, in many communities, marriage and death are viewed as parallel stages, in which an individual leaves one world and enters another. The bride thus signifies her "death" within the world of her family and her entrance into the world of the groom's family by adopting a corpselike pose.[4]

Although Presparë may sense such meanings implicitly, they have offered me a range of different explanations. The most formulaic, and the briefest, is that the bride behaves as she does *për turp:* out of "shame" or "modesty." In this regard, the bride's stance is a highly stylized form of the demeanor that is expected of a young woman in any social situation. Just as older girls and younger women are asked to demonstrate their *turp* by behaving demurely and quietly, so the bride conveys through her stance her capacity for sexually proper, modest behavior. She conveys as well her self-discipline and her physical and emotional stamina, for she must maintain that same stance for twelve or fourteen hours on the day that she is taken. Most importantly, she demonstrates through her stance her deference both toward her natal family, who arranged her marriage and chose her husband, and toward the groom's family, which she is entering as its most subordinate adult member. In so doing, she also confirms the "honor" of each family: of her own, by demonstrating that they have raised an obedient daughter; and of the groom's, by showing that they have acquired, as many wedding songs say, "the best possible young woman" (*bashnë e çupës*). In all these respects, a "good" bride—that is, a bride who takes care to maintain her stance throughout the wedding celebration—embodies all the most prized qualities that one would hope to find in a young woman. Richly attired in her white dress, standing in deference and modesty, she presents the quintessence of female "shame."

Several women pointed out to me that the bride's downcast gaze has the practical effect of keeping her from seeing her new husband until they are closed in together that night. "All that I saw of my husband on my wedding day," one older woman pronounced emphatically, "was his socks!" A few suggested that their demeanor as brides had enabled them to keep their composure as they found themselves thrust into a group of strangers:

> Well, actually, if you keep your eyes open, who are you going to see? . . .
> You can't look at everybody. You feel embarrassed. . . . Even now if I look
> at somebody I would be embarrassed, somebody that I don't know. 'Cause
> at the weddings they invite everybody, especially on your husband's side.
> You don't know nobody. How're you going to look at everybody and
> smile? (Interview in English with a young woman in Chicago, 1987)

Throughout the wedding period, the establishment or reaffirmation of relationships of mutual obligation between participants is brought about, as in other social situations, through acts of reciprocity. Most important of these is the gift-giving that joins together the bride and groom and their families. The groom gives gifts to the bride at three points in the wedding sequence: at their betrothal, when the henna is sent, and through the *sinitorë*. In each case, the bride reciprocates. At the betrothal she gives gifts to the groom, while on the other two occasions she presents gifts to his emissaries: a kerchief for the boys that bring the henna, and a decorative towel (*rizë*) for each *sinitor*. She also sends a *boçe* of gifts to the groom and each of his close relatives, which the *sinitorë* bring when they return to the groom's home.

In addition to the gifts that the bride and groom exchange, gifts are presented to each of them by their own relatives, a gesture that expresses the obligations of kinship and hence reaffirms the solidarity of each lineage. Household items are contributed to the bride's dowry by close relatives, who also present items of jewelry to the bride on the morning of her wedding before the groom's party arrives. The groom's female relatives present him with gifts of clothing after he is shaved.

The bride is taken, in large part, through the giving of gifts. She is first presented to the female relatives of the groom in the *odë* of her parents' home. Once she has entered the room, an older relative of the groom pulls back her veil and places some money on her head. Other relatives then begin to place over her head the strands of gold coins (*florinj*) that indicate her status as a married woman. Meanwhile, at the men's gathering in a nearby home, the groom's father formally pays the brideprice to the bride's father as part of the Islamic marriage contract. Once the ceremony at the bride's house is concluded, the bride is brought into the doorway, and other relatives of the groom step forward to place still more jewelry on her. Finally, the groom joins her and the two exchange gold wedding bands before the party sets out for his home. Henceforth, the bride will wear this gold jewelry at all major social occasions, as a sign of the groom's economic responsibilities toward her and of the economic standing of his family. As elsewhere in Europe and North America, their wedding bands will signify their acceptance of the mutual obligations inherent in marriage.

Naturalizing Patriarchy

In addition to practices that realign social relations, Prespa families also include a number of subsidiary *adetë* ("customs") or *traditë* ("traditions") in their wedding celebrations. Each wedding is thus rich with layer upon layer of symbolic practices. Most often, the explanation family members give for specific customs is that they insure a successful outcome for the wedding. But a number of these customs may also be seen as naturalizing the particular view of social order that the wedding celebration projects.

Among those customs that are meant to assure an auspicious outcome for the wedding are those that are structured around odd numbers. It is an odd number of young boys, usually one or three, that take the bride her henna; and an odd number of *sinitorë*, anywhere from one to fifteen, that take her clothing to her. When henna is put on the bride's hair, it may also be put on one or three other young women, usually her sisters or sisters-in-law. The major ritual days of the wedding also fall three days apart: the bride is adorned and the *qeshqek* is crushed three days before the bride is fetched; the bride's henna is put on three days before that. On the third day of the wedding, the bride makes her first bread loaves. And the young couple first visit the bride's family an odd number of days after the wedding day.[5]

Customs are also carried out for which community members have no ready explanation, but which are nevertheless consistent with practices throughout the Mediterranean region concerning the warding off of the "evil eye" (*syri i keq*). These include placing metallic materials such as *tel* and sequined face decorations around the face of the bride. The red color of the bride's hennaed hair, and of the *duvak* that she formerly wore, is also associated in many Mediterranean countries with the warding off of evil, although it may also have been intended to signify the bride's menstrual blood, and hence her fertility.[6] Today most Prespar explain that henna is put on the bride's hair "for beauty" (*për bukuri*).

One custom that seems intended to insure the new couple's fertility is the mumming that some families stage on the night before the bride is taken, in which copulation or other erotic actions are simulated (see chapter 6). The cross-dressing that generally occurs in conjunction with the mumming might seem to present a challenge to binary notions of gender, but I see it as confirming them. It is invariably met with uncontrolled laughter, as if no individual could possibly take on any of the qualities that are associated with another gender. Cross-dressing would seem to serve a practical purpose here, since it assures that the miming of erotic actions takes place between individuals of the same gender, for to have such things enacted by a male and a female would be "shameful." At a south Albanian wedding that my husband and I attended in Bitola, the mumming was in fact performed by a group of women at the women's gathering, and a separate group of men at the men's gathering.[7]

The greatest number of subsidiary wedding customs revolve around various foods: grain and grain products, legumes, sugar or honey, candies, and fruits. Three days before the bride is taken, wheat berries are crushed by men of the groom's party (plate 2). The man who initiates this must have living relatives, yet another assurance that the wedding will be a success. The wheat berries are later boiled with meat and served on the wedding day and evening at the groom's home. On the day that the *sinitorë* take the bride's clothing to her, the women of the groom's family prepare a mixture of roasted chickpeas, dried fruits, and hard candies that they call *kokolinkë* (or sometimes *pemë*, lit. "fruits"), which they then distribute to each guest on the groom's side (plate 17). The remainder of the mixture is packed in with the bride's clothing that is sent to her with the *sinitorë*.[8] On the bride's side, the women of her family wait until the *sinitorë* have left. They then distribute the *kokolinkë* to each guest on the bride's side, as well as to those who gather at her home each evening before she is taken. On the day of the wedding, a

bakllava baked by his sister or another close female relative and decorated with flowers or candies (plate 1), is served to the men of the
groom's party after the groom has been shaved.[9]

Such practices intensify in the hours surrounding the taking of the
bride and her incorporation into the groom's household. When the
women of the groom's party fetch the bride, and/or when she and
the groom leave her house, a mixture of rice or chickpeas, hard candies,
and coins is thrown over their heads, which children then scramble to
collect. As she rides in the car that takes her back to the groom's home,
the bride has a large mirror held before her, draped with a red kerchief.
The wedding party always returns to the groom's by a different route
than that taken to the bride's. As they arrive at the groom's home, his
mother watches the bride's arrival through a ring held within a sieve.
The bride is given two loaves of bread baked with chickpea flour (*peshnikë me qiqra*) to be placed under each arm. She then kicks over a copper
water vessel (*gjymkë*) in the doorway of the home before entering it.
Once inside, she may be asked to perform any of a variety of actions.
She may be given a glass of sugar water (*sherbet*) to drink. Or she may
be asked to dip her fingers in *sherbet* and then touch her fingers to the
doorway of the house. She may kiss a male child, or sit and rise three
times over a chair on which the felt hats (*fesa*) of three boys have been
piled. She may also be asked to touch her forehead three times to the
hearth (*oxhak*) in the reception room of the home.

Prespare have standard explanations for some but not all of these
customs. Rice is thrown on the bride *që të jetë e shtuarë, të ketë fëmijë:* so
that she may have many children. A different route is taken by the returning party in order that no harm may befall them: perhaps a remnant
of an earlier practice of bride-stealing (see Dojaka 1978:131). The loaves
of bread are put under the bride's arms *që të ketë bereqet shtëpia:* so that
the bride may bring plenty, both human and agricultural, to the household. She kisses male children, or sits an odd number of times on their
hats, so that she will have many sons. She drinks the sugar water *që të
jetë e ëmbël:* so that she will be sweet to the other members of the family,
and particularly so that she and her mother-in-law will not quarrel. And
she touches her head to the hearth *të rri më sh'pi, të mos gjezdis shumë:* to
stay at home and not to wander about much (see Dojaka 1978 for similar
customs throughout Albania). The mirror held before the bride was perhaps intended to ward off evil, although in some parts of Albania it is
said to be done to shed the sun's rays upon the bride, in order to under-

score the saying that the bride *i ndrist shtëpia:* "lights up the house" (ibid.:132).[10]

Many Mediterranean ritual practices operate by establishing a homology between the cycle of human reproduction and the agricultural cycle. In Prespa ritual, this homology is captured most succinctly by the word *bereqet* (from Arab. *baraka* or "blessing"), which refers at once to human fertility and to agricultural abundance.[11] In his structuralist analysis of Algerian Kabyle practices, including rituals strikingly similar to those of Prespari, Bourdieu presents perhaps the fullest interpretation of wedding symbolism in terms of that homology (1977:96–158). His reading can suggest much of the implicit logic behind Prespa customs as well, and their role in the reproduction of gendered relations.

Bourdieu proposes that dry grains and grain products such as the wheat berries crushed by the groom's male relatives, the roasted chickpeas brought by the *sinitorë,* the baked *bakllava,* and the rice or chickpeas thrown over the couple by the groom's relatives are apprehended implicitly as representing the "seed" of the groom. When man's dry seed is planted in the moist womb of woman, she swells and gives forth children. The moistening and swelling associated with the union of groom and bride are represented by cooked foods such as the loaves of bread placed under her arms and the boiled *qeshqek* served on the wedding night. The sieve is a prominent aspect of wedding customs throughout the Mediterranean and may be interpreted as the bride's hymen through which the groom's seed passes. Other symbols of "male sprinkling" and of semen suggested by Bourdieu also appear among Prespa wedding customs: the firing of a rifle by the groom, the sweets decorating the *bakllava* and the sugar water in which it is soaked, the candies included in the chickpea and rice mixtures, and the sugar water that the bride drinks when she arrives at the groom's.

Most of these customs are interpreted by Prespari as insuring that the bride will be fertile, and particularly that she will bear sons who will carry on the groom's line. But they also provide a symbolic account of the nature of procreation. By framing the union of the bride and groom in agricultural terms, they set forth a view of woman as a nourishing receptacle into which man's seed is planted and from which his offspring, the heirs to his line who are of his "blood," will eventually emerge. Through metaphoric means, the wedding ritual thus provides a model for Prespa patriarchy, as a society of males who reproduce through the medium of women. More fundamentally, it constructs an image of society as composed of two polarized genders, whose natural propensity it is to achieve union and to reproduce. With each celebration of a wedding, participants evoke and confirm this vision, albeit on an implicit level, through practices that frame their roles as men and women as consistent with natural processes.

A second pervasive aspect of wedding symbolism is that which links the bride to interior spaces and the groom to exterior ones. Throughout the wedding, those activities that involve the bride, including the henna ceremony, the packing and unpacking of the *rroba* and her modeling of them (plate 11), her reception by the groom's relatives, and her incorporation into the groom's household, take place indoors and involve only women, whether of her own or of the groom's family. Until World War II, she and the women who came to fetch her were not even visible in the procession that came to her home and then returned with her to the groom's; all were driven in an ox-drawn cart in which they were enclosed within a canopy fashioned from woven rugs. It has only been in recent decades that the bride has then been permitted to appear in the courtyard of the groom's home to be danced in the "bride's dance" before returning inside his house.

In the course of her wedding, the movement of the bride through interior spaces defines them as the domain of women and, by extension, as the private world of family life. It is significant that the bride does not actively claim these spaces, but is led through them by her kin or in-laws. As the wedding proceeds, she is transferred from one sphere of women to another, leaving the private world of her family and then entering the private domain within the groom's household, where she will interact primarily with his female relatives. Although her acquisition by the groom's family is a public celebration, the emotional journey that the wedding entails for her is not highlighted as an official concern of male family members or of the larger group of wedding celebrants.

In contrast, the groom's actions during the course of the wedding trace a movement from interior to exterior spaces, as he traces his progression from childhood to adulthood. At the crushing of the *qeshqek*, the men of his family hold an outdoor ceremony in preparation for his coming of age (plate 2). Often the groom himself is barely noticeable among the crowd whose activities center on his older male relatives. On Sunday morning, he is bathed indoors in an activity that commemorates his last moments as a child within the private realm (plate 18). He then goes out into the courtyard where a male relative shaves him (plate 6). As an adult male, he will serve as a spokesman for his household in community affairs, and so his attainment of adult status is recognized publicly, before the men of the village. Finally, just before his departure to take his bride, the women of his family present gifts to him and comb his hair in the courtyard, thereby acknowledging his entry into the public sphere of men (plate 7). Unlike the bride, the groom moves into and through exterior spaces as a free agent and, in so doing, claims them as his proper domain.

In the ceremony marking the closing in of the groom and bride, these two sets of oppositions converge as the male, symbolized by dryness and the exterior of the house, meets the female, symbolized by moisture and the house's interior. Once it has become dark, all the male guests on the groom's side fill the courtyard of his home, while all the women crowd into the hallway of his house. Three or five small piles of sand are laid out in a row stretching away from the door, doused with kerosene, and lighted. The groom, flanked by two male relatives and / or the village *oxha*, walks through (or around) the fires, carrying a candle in each hand. When he reaches the door, the *oxha* or an elder from the party recites a verse from the Qur'ān. At this point the groom kicks over a vessel of water, spilling the water in the doorway. He then dashes through the hallway and up the stairs, as the women inside the house try to slap him on the back. Finally, he bursts into the upstairs room to meet his waiting bride.

Although Prespare with whom I have conversed do not make the conscious association, I interpret the "closing-in" ritual as a symbolic enactment of sexual union. Here the exterior/interior dichotomy emerges as homologous not only to the characteristic domains associated with members of each gender, but also to the configuration of male and female genitalia. As with the dry/wet opposition established through agricultural symbolism, the interior/exterior opposition that is consolidated through the "closing-in" ritual naturalizes the polarization of the genders as well as their roles within Prespa society. At the same time, by virtue of the active participation of all guests in the consummation ritual, the association of men with public concerns and of women with private ones is at once extended beyond the personages of the groom and bride to all community members and presented as the inevitable outcome of human anatomy.

Cooked grain products symbolizing the union of the groom and bride dominate the rituals that follow the consummation of the marriage. The following morning, the young couple are served a dish known as *bukëvale*, which has been made from the loaves that the bride held under her arms the day before.[12] Then, on the third day of the wedding, the bride is taken to a spring or fountain to fetch water for the family. Upon her return to the house, she is set to the task of making several small bread loaves (*kulaçka*) for the groom. In order to make the dough, she spits into a bowl of flour, to which water that she has fetched is then added. Women of the household mix the dough, and the bride places her hands in it. They then knead the dough and she shapes the loaves, which she shows to the groom for his approval. He is supposed to punch them and tell her that they are not yet good enough. They repeat this sequence a total of three times before he accepts them and they are baked. The bride's first household task in her new home is thus the baking of bread. It is the most quintessential female activity, one that symbolically reproduces her primary role within society as the bearer of her husband's children.[13]

Duallë dy spai në lëmë . . .	Two *sipahi*s [Ottoman overlords] have come out onto the threshing floor . . .
nën' moj nën', bij' moj bij'.	(O mother, O daughter)
E kërkojnë çupën tonë . . .	They are asking for our young girl . . .
Çupa jonë s'është bërë . . .	Our girl isn't ready yet . . .
duart në brumë s'i ka vënë . . .	She hasn't yet put her fingers into the bread dough . . .
pe, gjilpërë me dorë s'ka zënë . . .	she hasn't yet taken a needle and thread in hand . . .
	(Wedding in Krani, 1980)

During the lengthy progression of activities that demarcate the wedding period, the individuals that participate in the celebration move through an elaborate series of ritual practices. As with all such ritual events, the formulaic, predictable sequence of actions that they carry out, together with the stylized behavior that participants adopt in executing them, universalize the individual transformations that the wedding effects and cast the experience of the core protagonists as an archetypal one for all members of the community. The bride, standing motionless in her white dress, is not merely Feime or Merita or Aiten; she is all brides and, by extension, all Prespa women in their years of young adulthood. Her mother-in-law, presenting herself to the community in the subdued dress of an elder even as the *shami* (headscarf) of her younger days is set ablaze, is all Prespa women as they advance into their later years. Through the formalization of behavior that the wedding enforces among its participants, the progression through life that the protagonists experience and the relationships that they exemplify through their actions, including mutual regard between kin, the subordination of women to men and of youths to elders, and the association of each gender with specific domains and concerns, are crystallized as fundamental tenets of Prespa social life and reaffirmed as basic to the functioning of the community.

The Prespa wedding ritual also achieves its universalizing effects through metaphoric means. As participants carry out their various prescribed activities, they reinscribe a view of their community, and particularly of their roles within it as men and women, as ordered in ways consistent both with the configuration of their bodies and with the yearly cycle of agricultural activities that historically formed the basis of their existence. Through their actions, the particular form that their society has taken, with all its gendered implications, emerges not as an arbitrary construct but as an essential and inevitable component of the natural order.

Engendering Song

Do të marr, bardhonja e
     bardhë, do të marr.
	I am going to capture you, O
	     fair one, I am going to cap-
	     ture you.

Do të marr këtë bejar,	I am going to capture you this summer:
pa marrë s'të lë.	I won't leave you untaken.
Do të bënem ënë, do të ryj në re'at, nuk më merr dot.	I will turn into a moon and go up into the skies; you won't catch me.
Do të bënem yll, do të vij pas teje, pa marrë s'të lë.	I will turn into a star, and I'll come after you; I won't leave you untaken.
Do të bënem ngjalë, do të ryj në det, nuk më merr dot.	I will turn into an eel and go into the sea; you won't catch me.
Do të bënem peshkë, do të vij pas teje, pa marrë s'të lë.	I will turn into a fish, and I'll come after you; I won't leave you untaken.

Do bënem fëllënxë,	I will turn into a partridge,
e do fluturoj,	and I'll fly away;
nuk më merr dot.	you won't catch me.
Do bënem bilbil,	I will turn into a nightingale,
do të vij pas teje,	and I'll come after you;
pa marrë s'të lë.	I won't leave you untaken.

(Women's song sung on bride's side; Dolna Bela Crkva, 1981)

Like the wedding ritual, the songs that Prespa women perform at weddings often portray the bride and groom metaphorically as elements of the natural world. In many songs, the bride is a flower or fruit waiting to be picked. In others, she is a fair-faced "moon" (ënë), while the groom is a resplendent "star" (yll); or she may be a slender "eel" (ngjalë), while the groom is an agile "fish" (peshkë). Most often, however, the two are symbolized by various kinds of birds. The groom, as an ardent young suitor, is depicted as a "nightingale" (bilbil), a bird known for its rapturous singing. The bride is occasionally a "swallow" (dëllëndyshe), an industrious nest-builder. Far more frequently, however, she is a "partridge" (fëllënxë) or a "turtledove" (guguçe), birds that are thought of as beautiful, vulnerable, and quiet in demeanor and song. Like the allusions to agricultural processes and to human anatomy that lend coherence to wedding rituals, the ubiquitous metaphors of wedding songs naturalize aspects of Prespa gendered identity. In particular, the figures of the "nightingale," the "partridge," and the "turtledove"—combining as they do attributes of physical appearance, bodily demeanor, and vocal quality—present these particular features as inextricably related, and as natural for young men and women as for birds.[14]

Throughout a wedding celebration, men and women gather to sing in ways that strongly differentiate them by gender. Almost without exception, they sing in segregated groups, and most commonly in different locations. Their songs address different sets of themes, and their vocal qualities and styles of singing contrast markedly, contributing to the evocation of entirely different types of atmospheres at their gatherings. While women sing softly and "thinly" of courtship and marriage, sitting with great composure deep within the host family's house, men sing loudly and "thickly" of heroism and romance, drinking and toasting boisterously in the family's odë or courtyard. If the women's singing embodies the demure cooing of partridges and turtledoves, the men's evokes the flamboyant songs of the nightingale. Singers perform in these ways because they are consistent with shared beliefs regarding gendered relations, but in the process they also constitute those beliefs. For Prespare, in a very real sense, to participate in wedding singing is to engage in a process of "engendering."

Song Texts and Spatial Arrangements

One of the ways in which participants are engendered through their singing is through the texts that they sing. Virtually all the songs that women sing at a wedding, whether at evening gatherings or at ritual moments, center on courtship and marriage and are sung with the young people of their families in mind. Many of the women's songs explore dilemmas and sources of tension that are involved in arranging and realizing a marriage: the compatibility of the bride and groom, the bride's sorrow at leaving her family, her acceptance within her new home, and her duties within the household. In the song text, the young person who is the focus of the song often sorts through these issues in conversation with his or her mother. The mother might also serve as an intermediary between the two young people:

Shkova mbrëmë asaj ulice	Last night I went along the street, mother,
e pashë, nëne, një të bukur.	and I saw a beautiful young woman.
Ajo e bukur, kur më pa mua,	When she saw me
edhe rendi, rendi, mbylli derën.	she ran inside and closed the door.
Sheqer e mjaltë, mos mbylli derën!	O sugar and honey, don't close the door!
Se vjen NN beu, vjen i lodhur,	Because NN *bey* is coming,
i lodhur, i kapitur:	tired and exhausted:
Amerikën e tërë ç'i ka gjezdisur.	He has traveled across all of America.

(Women's song on groom's side; Chicago, 1986)

Within Prespa households, it is the women who are charged with dealing with such important familial issues: by instructing their children in their responsibilities as adults, or by facilitating the adjustment of a bride to her new family. Those women who take part in wedding singing are also those who have played by far the largest role in raising the two young people who are getting married. While the taking of a bride is an event to be celebrated before the community at large, the mechanisms that have brought the couple together and that will establish them as functioning adults within society are ones that are worked out largely within the women's family-centered domain. Through their songs, women acknowledge and claim their precedence within that sphere, even as it is constructed through their singing as a female one.

The women's repertoire also instructs children in the expectations that the community has for them. Young children, both boys and girls, spend their first several years of life attending the women's side of any social gathering, and so they hear this repertoire sung constantly as they are growing up: not only at every wedding, but at every *muabet*, every *gosti*, every circumcision, and every betrothal. The messages that the women's songs hold for them are very clear. On one level, the details of courtship follow certain prescribed patterns. It is the young male, always addressed with the honorific *bey*, whose role it is to pursue the female:

Moj fëllënxë, bijë beu . . .	O partridge, daughter of the *bey* . . .
bijë beu.	(daughter of the *bey*)
Kushdo shkoi, ty të pëlçeu . . .	Whoever went by pleased you . . .
Shkoi një djalë si NN beu . . .	NN *bey* went by . . .
Zgjati dorën, të rrëmbeu . . .	He put out his hand and grabbed you . . .
Vallë me se të gënjeu? . . .	With what did he deceive you? . . .
Me një sërëzë flori . . .	With a string of gold coins . . .
mystekil për gjoksin tënd . . .	made especially for your throat . . .

(Women's song sung on bride's side; Toronto, 1986)

In response the young woman, like the flower or game bird in whose metaphoric image she is portrayed, should expect to be pursued or snatched away by suitors as she is growing up.[15] She does, however, have the power to refuse a young man's suit through her parents, a decision that they might also make themselves. Or she may confide to them her interest in a particular young man:

Lonin në një sërë djem . . .	Some young men are dancing in a row . . .
eja moj lonin.	(come, they are dancing)

në një shesh, në një lëndinë . . .	in a clearing, in a field . . .
Cili të pëlçen, moj bijë? . . .	Which of them pleases you, my daughter? . . .
NN beu, ay floriri . . .	NN *bey*, the golden one . . .

(Women's song sung on groom's side; Krani, 1980)

Nevertheless, a young woman's role in courtship is presented as a more passive one than that of a young man. Girls learn from songs not only how they should respond to suitors, but also how they are expected to comport themselves, both in their family's home before marriage and in their husband's thereafter:

Dëllëndyshkë e malit ta prishnë folenë . . .	Little swallow of the mountain, they destroyed your nest . . .
ta kesh dashurinë edhe muabetnë.	(may you find love and *muabet* [in your new home])
Beu i madh në derë, ti me vrap shiltenë . . .	When the great *bey* appears at the door, you run to bring him his pillow . . .
Anëm nënja në derë, ti me vrap kafenë . . .	When the lady of the house appears at the door, you run to bring her her coffee . . .

(Women's song sung on bride's side; Krani, 1984)

A more fundamental lesson that children learn from women's songs is that the route to adulthood and to membership in Prespa society is to be traveled through the pattern of courtship and marriage that the songs detail. By constructing this pattern as the norm, the corpus of songs casts any alternative into the realm of the "unspeakable." To choose such a route would represent the most basic challenge possible to the Prespa community's "system" and would be an unforgivable affront both to one's family and to the community at large.

The most quintessential men's songs, in contrast, bypass personal and familial concerns to address issues pertaining to south Albanians in general. These are the historical songs that recount an illustrious moment in recent Albanian history or a man's tragic death in the struggle for Albanian independence. The men in such songs are not legendary figures, but actual individuals who contributed in some way to recent local history and who are usually identified in the songs by name. Women, if they are mentioned at all, are alluded to only through their relationship to the men portrayed. Generally they appear in these texts not as individuals but as character types who serve to heighten the tragedy of the male hero's death and to emphasize his centrality to the well-being of family and community. The lesson of such texts is that history itself is the domain of men:[16]

Në plepat Bilishtit ranë dy martina,	In the poplars of Bilisht [a town near the Albanian border with Greece] two rifles went off,
u vranë dy trima, Maloa me Selmanë . . .	two heroes were killed, Malo and Selman . . .
Bir-o, djemt' e nën[ës] kë të qaj më parë?	(O son, O sons of a mother, which shall I mourn first?)
Njëri përtej lumit, tjetri më këtë anë . . .	The one across the river, the other on this side . . .
Që të dy që ishin kushërinj të parë . . .	The two of them were first cousins . . .
Nënësë së zezë ku vanë e i thanë	Wherever people went they said to the grieving mother:
t'u vranë dy trima, Maloa me Selmanë.	Your two heroes were killed, Malo and Selman.

(Song about the death of Selman Rakicka and Malo Ago; see ex. 3.13; Panajoti 1982:90 discusses the background to this song)

By emphasizing historical subjects in their songs, men assert their position within Prespa society as spokesmen for their families in affairs of the community, district, and state, much as women claim the concerns of the private sphere through their repertoire.

The texts of historical songs encapsulate and enshrine many of the qualities associated with the *trim*, the hero-warrior and man of honor who battles courageously even unto death:

Malet e Gramosit qajnë,	The mountains of Gramos are weeping,
një zi të madh e mbajnë.	they are observing an extended period of mourning,
Gani Butkën e vajtojnë.	they are lamenting Gani Butka.
Gurë e drurë po vajtojnë,	The rocks and the trees weep,

Gani Butkën e kërkojnë.	they are searching for Gani Butka.
Trim i mirë, luftëtar,	A good hero, a fighter,
i vinte lufta mbarë	he battled successfully
me gjermanë, me junanë.	against the Germans and the Greeks.
Ato male kush i shkelte	Those mountains, who was able to conquer them
veç Ganiu me shokë të tij!	other than Gani and his comrades!

(Song about the death of Gani Butka in 1914, as sung at a *gosti* in Arvati, 1980; see Panajoti 1982:95–96 for background to the song)

Several men mentioned to me that, when they first began as teenagers to learn men's songs, they particularly liked ones such as those quoted above because they identified with the heroic qualities of the songs' protagonists. In this regard, heroic songs have been instrumental in socializing young Prespa men to the concept of male "honor," with its emphasis on assertive, fearless behavior. It should be noted that historical songs such as these are not unique to Albanian communities but form part of a larger tradition of southeast European men's songs concerned with the territorial struggles of the nineteenth and early twentieth centuries, during which the national identities of most present-day groups in the region were consolidated. As such, historical songs have played a crucial role in socializing several generations of peoples within that area to specific national loyalties and in binding them emotionally to those loyalties: often to the extent of encouraging among them the fierce and uncompromising nationalism that has made of the region such a fractious political arena.[17]

As in neighboring communities, Prespa men also have a smaller repertoire of songs about romantic love, a genre that is sometimes attributed to the influence of urban Ottoman culture:[18]

Gjysmën të ballit ta zuri stolia,	Your bridal jewelry covered half your forehead
më s'ta pashë dot . . .	so that I couldn't see it at all . . .
Tërë natën e natës të bëra seir.	(All night long I watched you.
Më le pa ment, ore guri xhevahir.	You drove all thoughts from my head, O precious jewel)

Gjysmën të gushës të zunë floritë,	Your gold coins covered half your throat
më s'ta pashë dot . . .	so that I couldn't see it at all . . .
Gjysmën të belkë[s] ta zuri kollani,	Your belt covered half your waist
më s'ta pashë dot . . .	so that I couldn't see it at all . . .

(Men's song on groom's side, Chicago, 1987)

The love depicted in men's songs is a romantic, even erotic feeling that is not always constrained by expectations of marriage, and females in the community should not necessarily draw lessons from these songs as to how to behave. Even when sung in the wedding context, they are not meant to allude to the celebration taking place. Rather, as is detailed below, they are one of many elements used by men at their social gatherings to transport themselves into an elated state.

The customary locations where men and women sing serve to reinforce the division between male and female concerns that is articulated in song texts. As already detailed for ritual activities connected with the wedding, singing to the bride takes place indoors, out of sight of all but close family members and performed exclusively by women. Singing to the groom, however, generally takes place outdoors in front of the village at large, performed in most cases by men of his family. For the crushing of the *qeshqek* and for the groom's shaving, the *daulle* may also be called on to augment the men's singing with their boisterous drumming and swirling clarinet melodies. Here instrumental music plays an important role in proclaiming the public nature of the groom's coming to adulthood.

This same spatial patterning is observed at evening social gatherings. If the men congregate to sing outdoors in the courtyard, then the women are free to gather in the *odë* of the house. More often, however, the men choose to sing in the more public *odë*, while the women retire to a more private room such as the kitchen, the family room, or a bedroom, reproducing as they do so the exterior/interior opposition consolidated in the "closing in" ritual. Only in the case of a particularly small gathering (as in chapters 2 and 4) do men and women assemble together in the *odë*. In such instances, older men are offered the seats of greatest honor facing the door, while women fit themselves in as best they can.

Women and men sing songs with specific themes and in specific locales because of long-observed practices that define where it is appropriate for them to gather and which sorts of concerns are their appropriate focus. But by continually and consistently placing themselves within clearly contrasting spaces, they also inscribe those spaces as their domains of authority; and by addressing markedly different subject matter, they lay claim to the discrete sets of concerns that their particular repertoire of songs emphasizes.

Embellishments of Texts

When Prespa men and women sing at a wedding, they draw on a corpus of songs whose texts and melodies are both fairly set. They are, to build upon a phrase suggested by A. L. Becker (1979:213), "singing the past": performing songs that, because they are part of the local repertoire, convey the accumulated authority of past generations of south Albanians.[19] By virtue of their status as preexistent, communally sanctioned entities, these songs sanctify the rituals that are carried out through them and thus help to bring about the act of marriage that the wedding celebrates.

Any performance of a wedding song also contains elements of "singing the present": aspects through which the "singer" comments in some way on the event at which the performance is taking place, and even on the moment of performance, as well as on her or his experiencing of that moment. Women in particular connect a song with the occasion at which it is being sung, in part through alterations to the song's text. At evening gatherings on the groom's side, they customarily insert the groom's name into their songs and then list the names of his unmarried male relatives in the final verses. On the bride's side, they most often insert her name and/or that of her oldest unmarried brother in the appropriate places. Women may also "add" one or more rhymed couplets to the end of the song to further personalize their performances. At times the most accomplished singers, such as Aiten's cousin in chapter 3, may even create new lines spontaneously in the moment of performance, so as to adapt a song's text more precisely to the life situation of the bride and/or groom.

For the songs that men and women sing to the groom at ritual moments, such naming practices are absolutely required, for the basic texts of the songs provide merely a skeletal framework on which the name of the groom and the terms for different classes of relatives are hung. Such songs cannot be performed without the addition of personal names and kinship terms:

Mirë bërë, bukur bërë,	Well done, nicely done,
bir o NN₁ bej.	O [name of groom] *bey*.
Gezove NN₂ tënd . . .	You made your [type of relative] happy . . .

The practice of name insertion has the seeming effect of personalizing the songs that are sung to the bride and the groom, so that they are set apart from other wedding participants as the focus of the celebration. What it accomplishes, however, is more their depersonalization. At every step in the long wedding ritual, the transformation that each undergoes from "girl" to "woman" or from "boy" to "man" is marked through the invocation of a traditional repertoire that highlights their continuity with all past brides and grooms. As they are summoned by name, their individuality is not so much saluted as it is merged with the legions of brides and grooms to whom those same songs were sung at prior celebrations.

For the women who participate in wedding singing, the naming of the bride and groom provides a means of focusing and expressing the emotions that arise in them as the event progresses. This effect is heightened by the way that performances at a wedding build on many earlier ones that took place as the two young people were growing up. In the years preceding any wedding, whenever female relatives of the bride or groom attended any sort of evening social event that involved singing, they sang many of the same songs about courtship and marriage that are sung prominently at weddings, particularly those associated with the groom's side. Most often they personalized their songs by inserting the name of the oldest unmarried male in the host household—the host's son or grandson—into the texts of their songs, in the place that the groom would be mentioned during a wedding. At the end of their song, they enumerated the unmarried sons of other women present:

Merr gjergjefnë edhe aj të rrimë . . .	Grab your embroidery hoop, let's sit for a while . . .
more trëndafil.	(O rose)
Unë vij po s'të kam ngenë . . .	I would come but I don't have time . . .
se martojmë JETON benë . . .	because we're marrying off JETON *bey* . . .
arrifshi më ZIA benë . . .	and we look forward to the wedding of ZIA *bey* . . .

They followed a similar practice at the weddings of the boy's sisters, when they inserted his name in the songs customarily sung on the bride's side.

At gatherings held in conjunction with a boy's circumcision, and again at his betrothal, the women focused on him even more specifically in their singing. Often they changed lines that would otherwise refer to his marriage:

se *martojmë* JETON benë . . .   because we are *marrying off* JE-
                                                        TON *bey* . . .

to refer instead to his engagement:

se *ndërtojmë* JETON benë . . .   because we are *betrothing* JE-
                                                        TON *bey* . . .

so that the song conformed more closely to the stage in the life-cycle that he had reached.

By the time family members gather to sing in celebration of a young man's marriage, they have thus already been singing about it for years. This does not mean, however, that the performances of songs during the evening gatherings that initiate the wedding period have the same effect as those taking place at prior gatherings. Between the time that a young man was last sung about and the beginning of his wedding, much has taken place. The family has found a bride for him and has made extensive arrangements for the celebration of his marriage. They have bought gifts for him and the bride, decided on a guest list, planned the many meals involved, and prepared for the event in myriad other ways. As the evenings of singing begin at his home, the songs sung about him signal to all present that the day so long anticipated has finally come, and that he is indeed the young man who is to be "married off," as the songs say. The very sound of one of these songs, with the groom's name inserted into the text, generates both joy and satisfaction among the women who have been close to him as he was growing up.

The situation is somewhat different on the bride's side of a wedding. As a daughter, songs are addressed specifically to her only at her betrothal ceremony and again at her wedding. She is thus always the "bride" mentioned in the songs. Because the majority of songs sung by women at other types of social occasions are ones associated with the groom's side of a wedding, those sung at evening wedding gatherings on the bride's side have more specific associations with weddings. When sung in the evenings preceding a young woman's departure for her new home, they therefore summon up those associations in a particularly powerful manner. At the moment when her relatives finally hear her name inserted into a wedding song, with her standing demurely by in her bridal pose, they are forcefully reminded that it is their particular young woman who has come of and is to be married.

Women's songs on both sides of the wedding become even more evocative as they are transposed from evening social gatherings to a ritual point during the final days of a wedding. The song *Në divan të lartër* provides a particularly good example of this process:

Në divan të lartër ke dalë e më rri . . .	On the high balcony you have come out to sit for me . . .
Vajzë e parritur, pa vënë stoli.	(O girl not yet married, with your wedding finery not yet put on.)

When sung at gatherings on the bride's side before she is taken, it draws attention to the arrival of the bride at the point of marriage. That effect is even stronger whenever the singer inserts the bride's name into the refrain in place of the word *vajzë* ("girl"). At the same time, however, she is still a "girl," enjoying her last days of maidenhood.

More than any other song, however, this one is associated with the taking of the bride. I have, in fact, never been to a Prespa wedding when it was not sung to the bride by one of the groom's relatives as she was about to depart from her natal home. For her immediate family there is probably no moment that more powerfully signals her transformation from girl to woman than when she steps into the *odë* of her home to greet the groom's relatives and the first words of that song are heard. As the groom's relatives place over her head the "finery" (*stoli*) that marks her new status as a married woman, the song acknowledges that she is no longer a "girl," and that her days of maidenhood in her family home are forever at an end. At such ritual moments, what has been anticipated in the many songs sung during the evenings leading up to that point—and on the groom's side, for years beforehand—becomes reality.

As with the formulaic texts of wedding songs, the practice of inserting children's names into songs can contribute profoundly to the subjectivity of both the women who sing and the children whom their songs address. For a family's son, who hears his name continually reiterated at the many gatherings that he attends as he is growing up, there is little doubt either that he is the focus of his household's aspirations or that it is his destiny to marry. For a daughter, her very omission from the listing of her family's children reminds her of the temporary nature of her ties to her household. Once she reaches the point of betrothal, however, her destiny too is proclaimed. For their mother, she will spend a good portion of her social life as an adult singing about her sons, about her daughters to a lesser extent, and in later life, about their children. But her songs will rarely address any other theme. Together with the spoken greetings enumerating family members that guests exchange throughout social gatherings, and the compliments addressed to singers after a performance that allude to their offspring, social singing constructs the subjectivity of women around a set of family-centered concerns: the marriage of their children, particularly their sons, and the continuity of their husband's lineage group. These practices are particularly instrumental in binding new brides to the lineage of their husband, since with each song they are asked to articulate their newly constituted relationship to the male children of all of his extended family. Through their singing, women continually reaffirm both their role as bearer of children and the primacy of the patrilineal group within their community's view of social order.

Performance Style

A second way in which a singer may connect a song to its moment of performance is through the style in which she or he performs, involving such options as volume and vocal quality, extent of melodic ornamentation, and degree of metricity. Certain stylistic features are associated with good singing regardless of a singer's gender or of the particular song being sung. The most minimal requirements are that a singer perform in tune and get through the song without forgetting the words. But good singing also involves an unhurried rendering of the text, some degree of textual and melodic embellishment, perhaps some variation in the melodic line, and a focused vocal quality that has been achieved without straining. It is these features that are summed up in the notion of singing *shtruar*, in its most general meaning. Together they convey an image of a person who is "mindful": able to maintain dignity and composure in a social setting.

These are also the features that transform a text as it might be recited into a song, a transformation that Presparë refer to when they say that a good singer "doesn't just say the words." Implied in this phrase is a view that a song is itself impersonal and that it only serves as a vehicle for personal expression when it is properly sung. By singing a song *shtruar*, an individual signals that he or she is not merely rendering the words but is cognizant of them and means them. As one man explained, "When you know the words"—by which he meant, when you understand what the song is about—"it comes from the heart. Then you are *really* singing." A perfunctory performance of a song neither conveys the singer's sincerity, nor does it move those listening. But a performance infused with a balanced range of expressive techniques both puts across the text more powerfully and wraps it in embellishments that signal the singer's personal connection to it.

The greatest compliment that can be paid to either of the soloists in a song performance is that he or she sang *me gjith zëmbër:* "with all his / her heart." This is a phrase that has already been discussed with reference to social etiquette, but it is used even more frequently for singing. In general terms, to execute an action *me gjith zëmbër* means to do it sincerely, with unqualified good will. When used to describe singing, it indicates above all else that a singer has been able to set aside feelings of self-consciousness and become so fully involved in the performance that it comes across as spontaneous and heartfelt.

Prespparë explain "heartfelt" performances in two very different ways. On the one hand, they may feel that the singer was transported by the occasion into a state of heightened emotion:

> To sing *me gjith zëmbër* means that the singer is happy. . . . Such as someone who has a wedding in the household, a brother or nephew is getting married. She sings *me gjith zëmbër* because she's happy—because they're going to take a bride. (Interview in Chicago, 1987)

On the other hand, the intensity of the performance might be attributed to the experience and/or skill of the singer, who is able to perform confidently in any situation:

> . . . there are people who sing that way *nga natyra* [because it is their nature]. Whether they feel happy or not they sing that way. Others sing that way when their feelings are greater, when they are happy. (Interview in Chicago, 1986)

In the first instance, the performance is viewed as indicating the true feelings of the singer, whereas in the second it is viewed as the artful embodiment of sentiment. Prespparë see both types of performance as producing the same effect: singing that conveys feeling evokes an emotional response in those listening and draws their attention to the emotional richness of the moment.

Singing *me gjith zëmbër* involves something different from simply singing well. An individual may, for example, sing in an exemplary but somewhat self-conscious manner. This has been the case particularly when singers have performed outside a community social occasion, such as for Macedonian radio or for a commercial recording. Performances cited by community members as *me gjith zëmbër*, however, show evidence of particular spontaneity or emotional agitation on the part of the performers. For a woman this evidence might be in the form of extensive melisma, more frequent glottal ornamentation, or somewhat more verbal interpolation. The singer might also add her own extemporized lines to those customarily sung, or conclude her performance with rhymed lines that honor the hosts. For a man, performances might involve even more extensive use of these techniques than is true for women, as well as greater elasticity in the song's meter and perhaps upward extension of the melody line. A man might also call out verbal exclamations between lines of the song or follow it by initiating a sequence of *bejte*. Other factors, such as pitching a song particularly high, singing with a somewhat animated demeanor, or simply singing more than usual, might all be taken as signs of a singer's greater involvement in the occasion at hand. The corpus of expressive techniques that characterizes Prespa singing may thus be seen as the aural counterpart to the flowery aspects of their etiquette.

What Prespare are suggesting when they speak of singing in these ways is that certain aspects of musical style serve as a form of "metacommunicative commentary" (Irvine 1982:39) upon the basic song. Each of these stylistic features may be taken as signaling the actual emotional state of the singer, or merely the level of emotionality that is appropriate for a singer of that person's social category to express on such an occasion. In good *shtruar* singing, the performer is conveying a sense of emotional restraint, even tranquility. That restraint is signified musically both by singing more softly and by confining the various expressive techniques available to the singer within the song's meter. Singing *me gjith zëmbër*, on the other hand, presents an image of "mindfulness" as challenged by an emotionality and spontaneity that could undermine it. These attributes are also signified musically: by extensive manipulations of the text, what might be termed "broken syntax"; by shifts in vocal register; by elaborate melismas and exaggerated portamento; and by unexpected variations in the melody line.[20] Let me phrase the contrast between these two types of singing in a slightly different way.

Shtruar singing implies that the singer is rendering the song in such a way as to focus the listeners' attention on the song's text. A highly elaborate performance *me gjith zëmbër*, however, calls particular attention to the emotional state of the singer at the moment of performance, even to the point of overshadowing the text of the song itself.

Seen from this point of view, the contrasting singing styles of women and men imply very different levels of emotionality. In women's performances, even the most extensive ornamentation is expected to be confined both by a more subdued type of vocal production and by an overriding sense of meter. By singing in this manner, a woman assures that she does not draw undue attention to her own feelings but rather places emphasis on the song that she is performing. In contrast, a man may break through such confines, both by using a louder, more focused type of vocal production and by drawing on a range of expressive techniques that relax or even undermine any sense of a steady pulse. In so doing, he draws attention to his own emotional state in a way that would be inappropriate for a woman.

If slower, ornamented singing conveys a singer's sincerity and concern for the occasion at hand, then rapid, unornamented singing may convey a contrasting sort of message: that the sentiments expressed in the song's text are of a playful nature. Virtually all the humorous songs in the men's repertoire are sung in this manner, as are those women's wedding songs, on both the bride's and groom's sides, whose intent is to tease some member of the wedding party. The women's song *Ra vesa, vesojti dhenë* may serve as one example:

Ra vesa, vesojti dhenë.	The dew fell and moistened the earth.
Ku jemi nisur ne të vemë?	Where have we set out for?
Jemi nisur për dë Kranjë	We have set out for [the village of] Krani
ta bastisim FIKRI benë,	to fall upon the house of FIKRI *bey,*
t'ja marrin të bijën,	to take his daughter,
atë më të mirën,	the nicest one,
atë ballëkartën,	with a forehead as smooth as paper,
atë gojëmjaltën.	with a mouth as sweet as honey.

Characteristically sung while the groom's party processes to take the bride, it describes the wedding party "falling upon" the house of her father and "taking" the bride, in language appropriate to the description of a military operation. If women were to sing the song slowly and emphatically, their style of delivery could imply a seriousness of purpose and a view of the bride's family as a true adversary to the groom's. The lively, boisterous manner in which it is commonly sung, however, indicates that it is sung playfully, and that the attitude of the groom's relatives toward the bride's family is in fact one of respect and affection.[21]

In this regard, *bejte* are of particular interest. Unlike songs, and regardless of whether they are extemporized, they are openly addressed to individuals present at a singing occasion and are meant to be interpreted as the personal expression of the individual initiating them rather than as the communal pronouncement of those gathered. Furthermore, they are always meant to be taken in fun, no matter how offensively they are worded. The switch in frames of reference that occurs when a singer moves from a song to a *bejte* is accomplished not only by shifting into a rapid, metric style of performance but also by singing the words to a particular melody type performed in triple time. Even when the text of a *bejte* cannot be clearly heard, that musical formula alerts all present to a shift on the part of the singer to a more personal, and especially playful, form of utterance.

Demeanor and Emotionality

Through both its textual and its musical components, the activity of singing plays a central role in binding participants emotionally to a wedding as it unfolds. By attuning the texts of their songs to the progression of the event and by juxtaposing various performance styles, singers are able to chronicle their emotional peaks and valleys at each stage in the celebration, and to communicate their emotional state to others. As they do so, they incite those around them to match their own degree of engrossment. As the celebration progresses, the emotional level of social and ritual gatherings rises in tandem with the intensity of participants' singing, reaching a climax in the final hours of the celebration. The ways women and men represent their emotions through their singing, however, are strikingly different, as are the ways they physically signal their emotional state and even the ways in which they come to conceive of their own emotionality. As participants plunge deeper and deeper into a wedding celebration, members of each gender find themselves inhabiting markedly different affective worlds.

When I questioned community members about the contrasts that I observed between women's and men's singing occasions, their responses were stereotypic. *Ndryshe kanë gratë, burrat ndryshe,* commented one: "Women have one manner, men another." Another remarked, *Tjetër sistem e kanë gratë:* "Women have their own system"; while a third phrased it as *Gratë kanë tjetër muabet:* "Women have their own *muabet.*" Singing is a means of "making *muabet.*" Once *muabet* is achieved, singing can then be a vehicle for the attainment of a state of elation, or *qejf.* But just as the innate natures of women and men are thought to differ in fundamental respects, so the emotional atmosphere that develops at their gatherings should be expected to contrast. In the minds of community members, the subdued and mellifluous singing of women, and the restrained tenor of their gatherings, are as natural for them as the men's rhythmically elastic singing and abandoned behavior are natural for them.

Women's song texts, both those sung at evening gatherings and those reserved for ritual moments, are designed to highlight the poignancy of each stage of the long and elaborate ritual. Some songs are phrased as a conversation between a young man and a young woman, in which each expresses his or her feelings for the other. At other times, the sentiments are portrayed as those of the person singing, or the song might speak of the feelings experienced by other close relatives of either young person. Although some songs speak directly in terms of affective states, others merely suggest them through the actions that they portray:

Mëngova me natë shumë që në t'errët,	I got up very early, in the darkness,
t'errët, moj xhanja, natën.	in the darkness, O my soul, at night.
Erdhça dhe të pashë baçen,	I came to see your garden,
vallë të kishin bërë pemët,	whether the fruits had ripened,
pemët, moj xhanja, mollët.	the fruits, O my soul, the apples.
E apa xhevrenë dhe t'i mblodha,	I opened my kerchief and gathered them
djalë NN beut se ç'ja dërgova,	and sent them to [the groom] *bey*,
se ç'ja dërgova me mashalla,	sent them to him with God's blessing,
se është djalë i vogel, ka sevda.	for he is a young man and is in love.

(song sung to the groom by his sister; Grnčari, 1983)

Regardless of which personages are "speaking" in a wedding song, its performance serves to draw the attention of those gathered to the emotional richness of the moment in the ritual sequence at which it is being performed. This effect is substantially heightened whenever the two soloists perform the song in a particularly evocative manner, *me gjith zëmbër*. It may very well be that a singer genuinely feels that the text she sings or the way she performs the song expresses the sentiments she is experiencing, but this connection is not necessary for the performance to have an evocative effect. The women's songs are better seen as prescriptive than as descriptive: they prescribe which sentiments are appropriate to any given moment, even if not everyone is experiencing them.

At each point in the event, women express and generate very specific affects as they sing, ones that are assumed to be shared by all who are present. On the groom's side, there is much to celebrate: his coming of age and the family's acquisition of a new bride. The predominant affect associated with the moments of singing on his side is one of virtually unrestrained joy. On the bride's side, feelings are more mixed: joy at her coming of age, but also sorrow at her imminent departure. Any of these sentiments may be evoked through the choice of an appropriate song. On either side, women may also be experiencing other intense feelings of joy and perhaps also sorrow because of the presence or absence of relatives and friends that they have not seen for some time, or for other reasons. Such sentiments may find indirect expression in the texts of their songs, although song texts do not address such subjects directly.

A younger woman may emphasize a certain sentiment not only through her choice of a specific song but also through her rendering of its melody line. Through a louder, more high-pitched, and more rapid *lartër* performance, she may indicate joy and excitement. Or she may convey her concern and sincere good wishes through the delicate melismas, glottal ornaments, and relaxed tempo of a *shtruar* performance. As she sings, however, she is expected not to allude unduly to her personal emotional state, either by adopting an excessively evocative style of performance or through her demeanor. In most contexts she is expected to sit very still, not exchanging glances with those listening or even with her singing partner, not gesturing with her hands. To behave in any other way would be considered "shameful" (*turp*). If she were to act out her feelings by strongly establishing eye contact with her listeners, adopting a particular facial expression, or using dramatic gestures, she could be accused of drawing too much attention to herself, or even of performing in the sexually provocative manner of a professional songstress.[22]

Even women who are otherwise quite lively or demonstrative during a wedding celebration generally revert to a subdued and self-effacing pose when they sing, one that, in its stiffness, resembles that characteristic of brides. In every regard they present themselves as the idealized image of a "modest" young woman. Through their stance they express their deference toward those older women who are present and demonstrate their ability to subordinate whatever feelings they are experiencing to the dominant affective atmosphere of the occasion. The one time it is acceptable for them to relax this physical restraint is on the groom's side during the final hours of a celebration, when those singing *lartër* songs might wave their arms in the air. Again, this motion is not to be taken so much as an indication of their personal feelings, but as a stylized gesture exemplifying the joyous nature of the occasion.

The very composed manner in which young women sing is often referred to by the same adjective, *shtruar,* that is used to describe moderately ornamented metric singing. A young woman's singing style is thus the aural counterpart to her visual presentation of herself. Just as a singer is expected to subordinate any outward show of feelings to a modest and respectful demeanor, so a *shtruar* performance subordinates the emotionality of ornamentation to the restraint of the song's meter. In this regard, the women's *shtruar* singing style is iconic of community ideals for feminine behavior, where meter and voice quality provide a veil of "modesty" constraining the expressive possibilities of the performance.[23]

Although singing is a way for women to highlight the sentiments inherent in a wedding, it may also enable younger women to check what would otherwise develop into an unseemly display of emotion. At one wedding that I attended, the groom's sister burst into tears in front of her whole family at the moment that she was supposed to sing to her brother as she combed his hair. In addition to the touching quality of that moment, she was suddenly overcome by sadness because of the absence of one of her sisters who was living overseas. Immediately some of the male elders began to chide her. "Why are you crying?" they called out. "Do you expect him to remain a bachelor forever?!" At this she dried her eyes, took a deep breath, and sang through her song without interruption. More rarely, a woman's delight in the wedding occasion might be so great that she begins to laugh during her song performance, as did a relative of the groom in chapter 2. In either case it would be shameful for any younger woman to let her feelings overtake her composure and interrupt her song. At such times, singing provides a young woman with a means not only of demonstrating her self-control, but also of enforcing it.

In contrast to the expectations of restraint placed on younger women, older women can exercise considerably more expressive freedom in their performances as singers, and they need be far less attentive to their demeanor. As they approach the end of their reproductive years, they may begin to behave, and sing, in a more evocative manner, closer to that characteristic of men. It is women elders that I have seen break off a song performance at the height of a ritual moment because they were too moved by the occasion, as with the bride's aunt at the gathering described in chapter 3; or sing in the more evocative style associated with the men's *lartër* repertoire, as was the case for the groom's aunt at the gathering in chapter 2. As in the latter instance, elders may also choose to sing a song that draws attention more to their own thoughts and life situation than to the event at hand. In all these ways, older women assert and lay claim to their more authoritative position with Prespa society through the manner in which they sing.

I once asked a mother- and a daughter-in-law in Chicago why the women do not drink and become rowdy at their gatherings. *Gratë të mënçme janë!* the daughter-in-law exclaimed mischievously: "Women are 'mindful'!" Another woman expressed a similar sentiment as she watched a videotape of a wedding celebration: "We women have such nice, quiet *muabet*s. We don't stand up and wave our arms around like the men" (Toronto, 1986). Despite the expressive license permitted women elders, it is extremely important for women of all ages to remain sufficiently "mindful" throughout the course of a wedding. If constant proof of self-control is their route to achieving "honor" within their household and community, then it is crucial that they maintain their dignity and composure as they sing, not allowing themselves to become either too silly or too overcome with grief. For them, maintaining a composed demeanor is not experienced as an unwelcome degree of restriction, but as a source of pride (plate 13). Through it they are able to demonstrate—at least to themselves and each other—great restraint in the face of a powerful emotional experience. In so doing, they affirm their capacity for honorable behavior despite the volatility and weakness that others might attribute to them.

At any wedding, the women's role as singers, whether in a social or a ritual context, is to sing about the impending marriage: in fact, to bring it about through their songs. All of their singing can thus be seen to be of a "ritual" character. The ritual emphasis of women's singing is evident in the number of their songs that can be sung in either context, and in the fact that women are the predominant, although not the exclusive, singers at ritual moments. As a wedding celebration progresses from intimate gatherings to larger ones to days filled with ritual activities, women find themselves swept up in a continuous flow of singing that moves seamlessly between social and ritual settings. Just as the feelings that are generated in them by the event intensify, so does the emotionality of their singing.

For most women, the wedding reaches its peak during Sunday's activities, particularly at the time the bride is taken. When I have listened to recordings of this moment made at many different weddings, the excitement and tension surrounding it have been evident in the extremely rapid, high-pitched manner in which the dance songs were performed by both the bride's and groom's relatives, as well as in the performance of ritual songs such as *Në divan të lartër* (CD #10 as well as #8, both recorded at this moment). Here stylistic features such as pitch and tempo serve as indices of the women's emotional agitation. The sense of elation that carries them through these final hours has been generated primarily by the event. They have then both expressed and enhanced that elation through their singing.

Men's wedding singing, in contrast, is more sharply divided between social gatherings and moments when ritual songs are sung to the groom. These moments are the major context in which men sing songs that relate to the event. Unlike the women's songs, theirs do not detail the sentiments involved in the occasion. Rather, they convey to the groom in approving tones that, in marrying, he has agreed to do what his family has long expected of him. The ritual songs that men most often choose to perform are sung in the name not of the singer, but of the groom's extended family and friends, who are most often enumerated *me radhë* during the performance:

NN₁ bej, yll i shënuar,	[Groom's name] *bey*, resplendent star,
as na jep një lejë për të martuar?	won't you give us your permission to marry you off?
Ç'e kam vënë dorën në zëmbër	I swore with my hand on my heart

| si ta bëjë NN₂ embër . . . | that I would whenever my [kinship term /s] gave the word . . . |

A singer may express affection and pride in the groom by performing the song in a sincere, *shtruar* manner or even in a more emotional *lartër* style. The dominant message of the performance, however, is that expressed through the song's text: the authority that the groom's family commands over him in ordaining when he will marry and in choosing his bride. In response, the groom is expected to behave during his wedding as he is depicted in several of the women's wedding songs: as a quiet and obedient "dove" (*pëllumb*) whose demeanor during the wedding is almost as deferential to elders as that of the bride:

Filloi babai dasmën për të martuar . . .	Father began the wedding to marry off . . .
djal' i vogl' i babait, pëllumb i shkruar.	(father's young son, speckled dove)
për të martuar, për të trashëguar . . .	to marry him off, to wish him a long and happy married life . . .
Janë mbledhur shokët për të juruar . . .	His friends are gathered to congratulate him . . .
për të juruar, për të trashëguar . . .	to congratulate him, to wish him a long and happy married life . . .

(Women's wedding song, as performed on Leibman 1974, B5)

These ritual moments represent the groom's introduction into adult, male society, with the men of his close family officiating.

The public, more "social" character of men's singing extends to the context in which by far the greatest portion of their singing takes place: their social gatherings. The immediate focus of women at their gatherings is the marriage of their young relative or family friend. Ultimately, however, the men's goal is the cultivation of an atmosphere of good will among the heads of household who are gathered, so that their families may continue to relate in a constructive manner. The wedding taking place, and the young people involved, are of secondary concern to all but the most immediate kin.[24]

When I first sat in on men's *konak*s in Prespa, they struck me as a sort of game where the goal was to make the event last as long as possible with as much singing and as little unstructured conversation as possible. To whatever extent they could, the men conveyed messages to one another *me bejte* ("with a *bejte*"), rather than saying them *me fjalë* ("with words"). Even the requisite spoken exchanges at the ends of songs were phrased as preexisting formulas, so that almost no spontaneous conversation took place. By way of contrast, I was present at a women's gathering in Toronto that was striking in its informality. Neither seating nor singing was strictly *me radhë*, and song performances were separated by long intervals of conversation. As my husband later reported, however, the husbands of the same women, singing in an adjacent room, sat stiffly and self-consciously *me radhë* and conversed very little between songs. The *kryeplak* of the evening, the host's uncle, led lengthy toasts after each song performance and addressed formulaic sayings or *bejte* to the other men to goad them into singing.

At men's events there is an expectation that those gathered might feel greater antipathy toward each other than would be the case for women. Men's gatherings are often larger than women's, and they involve more men who do not otherwise socialize with each other. But even at more intimate men's events, it is expected that this antipathy might manifest itself in open aggressiveness. A few individuals commented to me that women can be expected to attain a state of *muabet* almost automatically at their gatherings, simply by virtue of the celebratory event taking place. For men, however, *muabet* must be systematically induced. This view of the contrast between the natures of men and women can suggest why sustained singing is so much more important at men's gatherings, why men observe various forms of etiquette so much more rigidly, and why the consumption of alcohol is considered indispensable. Both the participatory structure of their songs and the formulaic quality of their *radhë* militate against unstructured conversation and keep the men's progression toward a state of *muabet* on a steady course, while alcohol helps to break down the affective barriers that men see as being erected between themselves.

One potentially divisive element that is avoided at men's gatherings is too great an emphasis on familial matters. During their nights of social singing, only the children of the host family are mentioned in song: by members of the family as a means of emphasizing the nature of the occasion being celebrated, and by guests as a way of showing respect toward their hosts. Otherwise, the great majority of songs sung bear no relationship to the event at hand, and in most cases do not even concern issues that men face in their day-to-day lives.

At the beginning of their gatherings, men sing songs that focus on themes of great emotional resonance for all men of the community: heroism, patriotism, and love. Those droning and listening have heard most of these songs hundreds of times in the course of their lives. To the extent that they focus their attention away from the performers and onto the texts, their thoughts may be drawn away from present company into the heroic past or a timeless, non-specific present. Men have commented to me that, in the course of an event, they are often reminded of individuals who sang these songs when they were growing up, or of gatherings in the past that were particularly memorable. Although such associations are often idiosyncratic and disparate, the songs help to establish a sense of common ground among those present by dwelling on subject matter that, while highly evocative, is neither controversial nor personal. The simultaneous evocation of enduring communal themes and memories of past events reminds the men of their commonalities with others and thus fosters sentiments of solidarity among them.

The repertoire of historical songs is particularly interesting in this regard. Were these songs to depict events that took place in recent decades, in and around the Prespa district, they would most certainly keep alive political antagonisms that have at times deeply divided the Prespa community. Such was the case with the song about a partisan in World War II that temporarily derailed the night of singing detailed in chapter 5. The great majority of songs, however, date from now-distant historical periods and portray the deeds of men who are regarded as Albanian patriots by all Prespa men, regardless of their current political leanings. In some instances, the songs are so old and/or the wording is so vague that community members do not know any of the particulars of the event described, and so the songs present little more than an abstracted image of heroism. For today's Prespa men, the greatest attraction of these songs lies not in the historical intricacies that they describe, but in their glorification of values with which most men identify strongly as important components of male honor. Only a small number of men respond to the historical repertoire out of any partisan sentiments.[25]

As the men sing this more serious repertoire, a gradual progression usually takes place in the level of emotionality of individual performances. At the beginning of a gathering, the elders sing, soberly and sedately, in *shtruar* style. Such singing conveys, and prompts in return, only the most subtle, and often inward, expression of emotion. By the time the younger men begin to sing, all in the room are becoming more intoxicated and the atmosphere in the room has begun to build. It is at this point that more singers take up songs in *lartër* style, ornamenting their vocal lines with elaborate melismas and interjecting highly evocative exclamations. Men have explained to me that they sing in this emotional manner, not as a commentary on the tragic texts of many of their songs, but rather to express the sense of elation and conviviality that they are feeling, and to "lift" (*ngrejnë*) the emotional level of the others. In essence they are presenting an aural representation of their own emotional state, with the intention of inducing a similarly heightened state in the others. As one performance follows another, the men urge each other on through song, using their singing to coordinate a gradual intensification of their sense of arousal. At first the performances are somewhat studied, since even the best singers monitor their performance as it unfolds, conscious of the others listening. But if an atmosphere of *muabet* has indeed permeated the gathering, singers may eventually reach the point when they shed their reserve and sing *me gjith zëmbër* ("with all their hearts"): confidently, resonantly, and spontaneously. In that moment they become the personification of the nightingale and are often praised as such by listeners whom they have moved. *Ajde bilbil!* other men may call out, "Come on, nightingale!" In the parlance of many men, it is at this moment that the *muabet* has "taken."[26]

As singers begin to feel less self-conscious, they throw back their heads and close their eyes (plate 15), or they gesture emphatically toward those around them. It is a dramatic and forceful manner of performance that, like their *lartër* singing, demonstrates their *fuqi:* their strength and virility as men. In response to their stirring singing, others in the room affirm the elation that they hear in the soloists' performances by calling out phrases such as "May your voice be praised!" or "Come on, *muabet*, come on!" Or they express their approval through stereotypic gestures of physical release such as clinking bottles with another man, slamming their hand down on the table, or firing a loaded gun toward the ceiling. In every way, their extroverted demeanor and physical interaction contrast with the reserved and self-contained behavior characteristic of women's gatherings.[27]

Once such an atmosphere of *muabet* has been established, the men at a longer gathering might then move on to songs that deal with less lofty sentiments or with subjects closer to their everyday experience: ebullient love songs, humorous commentaries on marital relations, or exchanges of teasing *bejte*. At this point in the event, subjects such as these can be broached because of the spirit of openness and affection that prevails. Performances of this repertoire often have a particularly interactive quality.·If the men choose to sing in two alternating groups or to exchange *bejte,* then a greater number of men are actively incorporated as soloists. In both types of singing, it is common for each pair of soloists to address themselves physically to the other pair or pairs, looking them squarely in the eye and gesticulating emphatically.

It is fine for men to get inebriated at their gatherings, as indeed they do, and it is fine for them to act in an emotionally unrestrained manner, provided that they continue to "make good *muabet."* As men feel particularly moved by the occasion, they may begin to embrace or kiss each other, hook arms as they drink, or continue their gestures of physical release. At the most successful of such occasions, only the most senior and dignified of the elders refrain from such boisterous behavior. As an event progresses, however, the situation becomes increasingly volatile and the *muabet* can easily be "broken." If any man should become so rowdy as to begin to spill drinks or scatter food, then the host, together with relatives of the offending man, will try to subdue him or remove him to another room to sleep. Even worse, and more rarely, two or more men may get into an argument. In such an event it is customary for an elder to assume his role as a mediator by initiating a song, hoping to draw the attention of the others away from the disruptive individuals and to involve them in a communal activity. Singing can thus not only preclude an outburst of antagonism, but also thwart it once it has been initiated.[28]

In order to avoid such unpleasant digressions in the course of the event, each guest is expected to maintain a minimum standard of propriety and sociability, to remain *i zoti* (lit. "gentlemanly," or "master of his behavior"). No one wants an event to end in disarray and ill will, since all recognize that this would be disappointing for the host and would ultimately dishonor him. In most instances it is possible to put an event back on course, even if this entails one or two hours of sensitive diplomacy on the part of the host and certain guests. It is precisely because of the increasing volatility of the situation as an event proceeds that the dusk-to-dawn *konak* represents an ideal for men. If an occasion does indeed continue "until dawn" (*gjer më saba*), it brings credit both to the host, who created the proper atmosphere, and to the guests, who managed to tread a fine line between abandon and propriety.[29]

At the most successful gatherings, the men's continued singing together with drinking eventually brings about in them a prolonged and intense experience of nurturing their emotional capacities to the very

brink of self-control and then releasing their energy in socially sanctioned ways. Although they cannot permit themselves to risk the col-
lapse of the *muabet* that prevails by totally losing their self-control, they
are able to set aside the bounds of customary propriety far more than
women do in any context. It is clear that the *qejf* of these final hours
has been generated neither by the subject matter of their songs nor by
the wedding that they are celebrating. Unlike the definable sentiments
evoked and then contained by women through their singing, men use
singing to induce a transcendent experience, one that is beyond affect.

Any effective performance of a men's song in *lartër* style, even in a
ritual context, evokes for men the progression of emotional intensification and release that they experience at their gatherings, together with
the sense of camaraderie that such events generate. At the first notes of
such a performance, male listeners often reach spontaneously for their
drinks and begin to pound the table and yell. For them the *lartër* style of
singing both embodies and evokes the euphoric state that is the goal of
their gatherings. It is a state that is viewed as expressly, even quintes-
sentially male, since only men have the *fuqi* to induce it in themselves
and then gain mastery over it. Just as the *shtruar* style of singing con-
solidates community ideals of femininity, so the men's *lartër* style of
performance—combining dramatic behavior with resonant, overtly
emotional, and rhythmically elastic singing—constructs an image of
masculinity in which emotion stretches the bounds of propriety.[30]

Muabet *and Flow*

The nature of *muabet*, and the experience generated through singing at
men's gatherings, have been a favorite topic of conversation for virtually
all the Prespa men that I have interviewed. In their accounts, they have
often stressed the openness and warmth that they have experienced
with regard to others and the loss of self-consciousness that the experience has induced in them:

> Alcohol stimulates you to become elated. When you don't have alcohol you
> remain subdued, you think more. . . . When you think too much, you're
> not ready for *muabet* (*ti s'je për muabet*). Like when you go to a "party"—if
> there's no alcohol it's no fun. Why? Because you're "bounded" (*i kufizuar*).
> You think about what you're saying. Once you've had two shot glasses of
> brandy (*dy kupë raki*), you don't think about what you're saying. . . . Once
> you start to think, you can't make *muabet*. Once you start thinking about,
> "I better not make a mistake and say that"—forget it! There goes the *mu-*

abet! (*Shkoi muabeti!*) You have to be quiet, to be free. If you're free and quiet (*i lirë, i qetë*) and are not engrossed in your thoughts, then alcohol is a stimulus. You forget those things. And when you forget those things, then the *muabet* begins. In *muabet* you're free with each other, you're more open with people. You don't need to equivocate (*dyshosh*)—you don't have time to think, to be of two minds. (Interview with a younger man in Toronto, 1986)

Men's comments about *muabet* suggest that the ultimate goal of a singing gathering is the experience itself: the "peak experience" that it provides. For men who are "good singers" and who enjoy singing, those moments when they found an ideal singing partner and sang better than they thought themselves capable of stand out as high points in their lives, and their performances live on as well in the memories of all who attended. Men also remember vividly the gatherings at which they achieved the most profound degree of *qejf*.

Such descriptions closely resemble those that the psychologist Csikszentmihalyi (1975, 1990) has identified as typical of what he terms "flow states": mental states characterized by a loss of ego, a "merging of action and awareness," a "narrowing of consciousness," and a heightened sensation of control and awareness of one's physical self. Such "flow states" are often induced by "flow activities" that, like Prespa social gatherings, provide both established rules for action (*radhë*) and a clear form of feedback to participants (the level of emotionality of each man's singing). Csikszentmihalyi refers to the relationship among those engaged in a "flow activity" as a "social system with no deviance" (1975:42), and indeed this seems to be the image that Prespa men take away from the most successful of their gatherings: a fleeting vision of themselves interacting as a close and cohesive community.

When women have spoken to me about their singing at weddings, they have been far more apt to emphasize its obligatory aspect and to focus on considerations such as their rationale in choosing a specific song. Indeed, their repertoire would seem to encourage this perspective, since many of the texts are intended to be taken as an expression of sentiment by the singer toward a central figure in the wedding. When they have spoken of their emotions during the course of wedding gatherings, it has been largely in terms of feelings of "connectedness": the closeness that they have felt to particular relatives and long-time friends at particular points in the celebration. When they have sung particularly well, or felt transported by the occasion, for example, they have attributed this to the "happiness" or *gëzim* they were feeling because of the presence of some specific individual. And yet I have encountered at least as many women as men who have spoken of a great interest in and "passion" (*merak*) for singing since their childhood. Moreover, the intensity and fluidity that women achieve in their singing at climactic points in a wedding suggest that singing for them is also a type of "flow activity." Women, however, would seem to experience their relations with others as generating the sense of elation and "flow" that singing then embodies.

The comments made by men and women on their experiences at weddings and on their performances of particular songs suggest that singing prompts in them fundamentally different views not only of their role within their community, but also of their own emotionality. Women are never the protagonists of their own songs; rather, they sing songs that express their relationship to the bride or groom, or to another important family member in the wedding. Through their singing they explore their relationships to others, and they come to experience themselves as having an emotional life that is socially grounded: inextricably bound to the concerns of others. Here the very emotionality of their repertoire helps to "wed" them to familial ties.

Men, in contrast, choose songs that they identify with personally and only rarely sing songs that are meant to depict the groom. They are thus the protagonists of their own songs. Through their singing they explore their sense of their individual identity, and in so doing constitute themselves as more autonomous individuals, often casting themselves in the masculine ideal of the warrior-hero. Although men share with women concerns for close relatives, they reach beyond such earthbound sentiments in their singing to achieve a state of transcendence. If the state that men induce in themselves is made possible through their possession of *fuqi*, then it is the emotionality of their singing that provides evidence of that attribute. In so doing, it provides justification as well for the social and expressive precedence of men within the Prespa "system."

Singing as the Practice of Patriarchy

There is a common cliché in studies of folk song that singing allows members of a community to "sing what cannot be said": to express thoughts and feelings that are not usually permitted in everyday conversation. Within the Mediterranean area, scholars have been motivated in recent years to seek out and confirm the existence of vocalized genres that might give voice to the views of those with lesser power and autonomy: women primarily, but also younger males.

Several types of genres have been singled out in this regard. First is women's funeral lamenting, through which women are often able to express more general frustrations with their status in society and to create a view of reality that in some ways challenges that presented by more hegemonic practices (see particularly Auerbach 1987 and Caraveli 1980 and 1986 for Greece; Kacarova 1969 for Bulgaria). Second is the extemporized couplet. Caraveli (1985) has shown how both men and women on the Greek island of Karpathos have addressed the constellation of issues raised by overseas emigration and, in fact, reconstituted a sense of community identity through their exchanges of sung couplets in the late hours of all-night gatherings. Abu-Lughod (1985, 1986) has analyzed the Bedouin genre of recited or sung *ghinnāwa* as allowing those more disenfranchised segments of the community to express sentiments such as longing and vulnerability that are denigrated by the community's "code of honor." Although parallel genres are performed by Prespare, neither serves as an effective "alternative discourse" either for younger men within the community or for women of any age. On the one hand, funeral lamenting is very much restricted as an activity, due to the strictures of Islam. On the other, *bejte* are much more the domain of men than of women and are today so rarely extemporized that they can only obliquely refer to the everyday dilemmas faced by those who sing them.

Notably, each of these is a type of vocalizing in which the text is extemporized at the moment of performance, rather than one that draws on a corpus of set texts as is the case with most of the Prespa repertoire. But songs with set texts can also serve as forms of resistance and protest. In his study of Bulgarian music-making, Rice presents a number of songs sung by one woman in her years of young adulthood whose metaphoric language focuses on particularly fearful and ominous aspects of gender relations. He notes that women in her village often sang such songs "in times of stress" to mask their feelings of powerlessness or outrage over mistreatment (Rice 1994:119). Songs dwelling on unhappy aspects of marriage are also sung occasionally at Prespa weddings, often by elders of the family (see the beginning sections of chapters 2 and 7 for examples); and I have heard women perform a few lively dance songs in which feelings of sorrow or frustration on the part of the bride or of her family are alluded to through oblique humor:

Loje, loje vallen!	Dance, dance the dance!
Si ta loz viranen?	How can I dance?
Unë mando nuku kam.	I don't have a nice coat.
I them beut i beu s'më ble.	I told my father-in-law, but he won't buy me one.
Desha të hiknja natën:	I wanted to run away during the night:
Ankoa ma dha datën! . . .	My mother-in-law suggested the date! . . .

(Wedding in Grnčari, 1983)

The *gurbet* songs that Prespare cultivated in past decades also deal specifically and unsparingly with a troublesome aspect of community life of that time: the separation, desertion, and physical danger that were often associated with men's long forays abroad (CD #1 is one fairly recent example).

The repertoire of *këngë* or polyphonic songs that dominates contemporary Prespa weddings and other social occasions, however, has a very different relationship to ongoing social relations than has been surveyed for these other types of vocal practice. In present-day social situations, it is through conversation, through "everyday" speech, that Prespare address the mundane affairs and thorny issues that they are facing in their daily lives. Speech, as the behind-the-scenes mode of communication at large events such as weddings, is the form of expression that allows Prespare to "say what cannot be sung." Singing, as the community's most public form of utterance, is precisely the cultural form that most upholds their "system," with all its implications for gendered relations. Singing, one could say, is for Prespare the discourse par excellence of patriarchy.

But singing is not a discourse in the sense of being a strictly verbal medium, nor should its verbal component be given precedence in analysis. Although the texts of Prespa wedding songs construct patriarchal relations in a variety of ways, much of the construction of patriarchy that singers bring about through their performances is accomplished through nonverbal means: through the ways singers execute the melody, through their demeanor and vocal quality, through the point in time and space at which they choose to perform. In this respect, singing has operated as a site of social reproduction very much as has the wedding ritual: by structuring human actions in such a way as to suggest a homology between gendered individuals and aspects of the natural world. It is thus more aptly regarded as the quintessential practice of Prespa patriarchy.

The activity of singing presents gender relations to community members in a particular way. Just as the *radhë* of social occasions and the structure and ordering of singing emphasize egalitarian relations between family groups over the hierarchy of economic distinctions, so the segregation of wedding activities into gendered domains, and of song repertoires into gendered sets of concerns, encourages male and female participants to view their roles within their community as parallel and complementary, rather than as hierarchical, thus casting gender relations in an especially acceptable light. Singers at a wedding come to experience their participation as highly personal, in that they may exercise a great range of options in terms of the song that they choose to sing and the manner in which they execute it. The very flexibility allowed within wedding singing in fact seems to mask the degree to which participation in it is profoundly constrained by considerations of gender.

Presparë have also come to understand the gendered implications of their singing through a different process than they have those aspects of their singing that relate to their notions of "honor," "obligation," and *muabet.* The contrast is apparent in the different sorts of answers I have received in interviews to questions about various aspects of wedding singing. When I have asked individual members of the community why they sang at a wedding, for example, they have answered readily, "out of honor" (*për nder*), or "in order to make *muabet.*" When I have asked why they sang well at a wedding, they have answered, "out of happiness" (*nga gëzimi*) or "because the *muabet* was good." When I have asked why they sang at a certain point in the occasion, they have explained that they did so in order to "honor the elders." For each of these aspects of singing, individuals can call upon a well-worn phrase from the discourse that surrounds their notion of "honor."

But in instances when I have asked why men sing with a "thick" voice, for example, or why they sing outdoors, I have received one of two types of answers. Individuals have responded either with the familiar phrase "it is our custom," or they have offered an answer such as "because that's the way men sing," or "because that's where men sing." Those questioned have often seemed stupefied that I would even think to ask. When I have posed similar questions about the conventions of women's singing, I have received similar answers:

JS: When men sing, they might move around a lot while they sing . . .

husband: Oh yeah. There's one singer who, while he sings, sitting down, moves from here all the way to the door during one song. He sings *me gjith zëmbër* ("with all his heart") . . .

JS: When women sing, they don't do that. They sit . . .

husband: . . . in place.

wife: They listen and drone.

JS: But they don't move much.

husband: No, no, no.

JS: What do the other women say if one woman moves around a lot while she sings? Do they think it's good, or not good?

wife: Well, it isn't good, is it?

husband: It's not good for women, that's the way it's been.

JS: Why isn't it good?

wife: Someone can do it out of spite, to wreck the song by talking or conversing.

JS: What about the woman who is singing, if she moves or looks around?

husband: They don't move around. That's how it's been.

wife: I haven't heard of anyone doing that, or seen it. In Prespa the "culture" is different, the "discipline." You don't move around.

husband: There are men who, when they're singing, dance around. Like our [here he named a relative]. Whenever he sang, he moved around. . . . Women aren't like that.

JS: Is he a very lively person?

husband: Yes.

wife: That's his *tabiet* ("nature") . . .

JS: Are there women like that?

husband: No.

wife: Men are different.

JS: Is it just . . .

husband: . . . *nga natyra* ("because of their nature"). That's right.

(Excerpt from an interview with an older couple in Detroit, 1987)

It has been largely from younger women who have had more exposure to North American notions of gender that I have received answers that clearly suggest some distance from Prespa norms: some sense that they are, as I would say, constructs:

> . . . there are those [women] who *nga natyra* move their hands or their whole body. It's better for a person to move *nga natyra*, but among us, we say that it is more *për turp* ("shameful"). For men it's better, but for women it's considered "shameful" to move your hands. For men it's not "shameful." (Interview with a young woman in Chicago, 1986)

In short, the honor-related aspects of singing are understood by Presparë with reference to an explicit verbal discourse. But singing as a gendered activity is apprehended by them largely through the convergence of bodily practices and a symbolically structured environment. Precisely because there is no explicit language to explain them, the gendered aspects of Prespa singing are experienced by the majority of its practitioners as beyond explanation: not as types of behavior that allow deliberate strategies on their part, but as practices that are an inevitable expression of their innate natures. Thus it is that, when asked to explain some aspect of their performance that relates to gender, Presparë will often answer simply *Adet:* "It is our custom."

E I G H T

Emergent Subjectivities

Sillet bota anembanë	The world turns round and round
njerëzia lënë vatanë.	and people leave their homeland.
De po shkojmë më gurbet	As we go off on *gurbet*
e lamë vendin e shkretë.	we leave behind a forsaken place.
Mentuam se përparuam	We thought that we were "advancing" ourselves
gjuhën tonë e harruam.	but we forgot our own language.
Mentoni, shokë, një herë	Consider, my friends, just once:
të vendosim ardhmërinë,	we must decide about our future,
se e humbmë dashurinë	for we have lost our love for each other
do t'i humbim dhe fëminë.	and we risk losing our children.

(Song created by a man in Toronto)

THE BRIDE IS TAKEN

On a Sunday morning in July 1986, a group of young Albanians who sing and play clarinet, accordion, acoustic guitar, and drum arrived at Memet's home outside Chicago (see chapters 4 and 5 for the earlier stages of this wedding). They were to function throughout the day in place of the Rom *daulle* who play and sing for weddings in Prespa. The musicians spent much of the morning performing improvisations and songs in the *odë* for the men. The women busied themselves bringing refreshments to the men and preparing themselves and the house for the activities to take place later in the day. Eventually, however, the music became too infectious for them, and they gathered in the family room to dance while the band played popular north Albanian tunes. The atmosphere at the house was charged in anticipation of the day's events, and with a strong sense of family and of nostalgia for Prespa prompted by the presence of close relatives assembled from distant locales. At one point, two of Memet's female cousins broke into a series of songs as they washed the breakfast dishes in the kitchen. One of them said later that she is not much of a singer and does not usually enjoy singing at weddings. On that day, however, she sang "out of happiness" (*nga gëzimi*) at seeing a cousin of whom she is so fond.

Around noon, male and female relatives lined up outside the bathroom in Memet's home and, while he showered, sang songs for the bathing of the groom. Most of those who sang were his paternal relatives: his oldest *xhaxha*, his father, and a male first cousin; then his mother, one *xhaxhicë*, and several female first and second cousins. He told me later that he took an especially long shower "just to see if they could sing for that long." When he had finished, his male cousin went into the bathroom to help him dress in his tuxedo. He was then taken by the men into the backyard and shaved by his cousin, while the cousin's son held the mirror. The musicians sang and played instrumental tunes for most of the time, although Memet's oldest *xhaxha* led one ritual song. Throughout the groom's shaving, the women remained inside and watched through the glass door.

After the shaving was over, the women went into the yard and began to present *boçe*s of gifts to Memet, singing as they did so. This activity was quickly curtailed, however, since the bride's family was expecting them. And so the entire party dispersed into their cars, each decorated with crepe paper and flowers, and set out for the motel where Feime and her relatives were staying. Memet's mother was the only person to remain behind. Upon their arrival, the women went immediately to the suite of two bedrooms where Feime was waiting with her female relatives. The men of the two parties greeted each other outside and then congregated in a lounge area. Following behind them were the musicians, playing the standard fanfare tune for wedding processions.

Once inside the lounge, the men of Memet's family took seats and were greeted by those of Feime's, who shook hands and offered each guest a cigarette. When these initial greetings were over, older relatives of Memet responded by offering cigarettes to Feime's relatives. As the men sat and conversed, the clarinetist began a long improvisation, or *kaba*. Men on each side then began to offer brandy or whiskey to those on the other side. Each man was handed a shot glass, which he downed and then returned to the server. Most men raised the glass in a short toast.

At this point it would have been customary for the men on Feime's side of the wedding to initiate some singing, but the men chose not to sing at all. I suspect that they were discouraged by the presence of the musicians, who in Prespa would have remained outside. The men therefore chatted quietly and a little stiffly while they waited for the women to be finished. After what seemed to them to have been ample time, they telephoned the bride's suite, only to learn that the women's activities were just getting started. Eventually Memet's cousin began a dance line and was quickly joined by other men from both parties. When the line became too long for the room, they danced out the door and into the parking lot, where they continued to dance until the bride was ready to depart.

At the women's gathering, Memet's family members seated themselves on the beds of the suite's outer room, with elders furthest from the entranceway. Feime's mother remained with her in the inner room, making last-minute adjustments to her outfit so that she would look the perfect bride when she appeared. In the outer room, one of her aunts circulated among the groom's party, welcoming each woman and offering her a piece of *llokume*, for which she was tipped a small sum of money. Three women from Feime's family then formed a short dance line. One *xhaxhicë* chose to begin the singing with a song that draws a succinct portrait of the duties of a young girl within her family's home. In its last line she inserted Feime's brother's name:

Çupa jonë anedanë	Back and forth goes our young girl,
e vogël si protokallë.	little like an orange.
Beu i madh ashu ç'e do	The great *bey* [her father] likes her
për kafe e për liko,	for the coffee and sweets that she brings,
për të shtruarë odat,	for the way she arranges the *odë,*
për të pritur zonjat,	for the way she greets the ladies,
zonjat e mejallës,	the ladies of the neighborhood,
që t'i lonin, t'i këndonin,	when they dance and sing
SAMI benë ta ndërtonin.	to betroth SAMI *bey* [her brother].

Standing at the head of the dance line, and holding aloft a small hand-kerchief (*shami*) in her right hand, she led the customary six-measure dance as she sang. A cousin of Feime's mother, who was dancing next to her in line, sang the second solo part, while Feime's great-aunt droned and danced at the line's end.[1]

Immediately after this song, the great-aunt moved to the head of the dance line, took the *shami* in hand, and began another song, again ac-companied by the mother's cousin, who danced next to her:

Dy tufka me lule	Two bouquets of flowers
dalur nga xheneti.	come down from heaven.
Të martoi babai	Your father married you off
si çupa të mbreti.	like the daughter of a king.
Pajë s'të dha shumë	He didn't give you much of a dowry:
po rafshë sepeti.	just one filled wedding chest.

Suddenly, as the song ended, Feime emerged from the inner room. She was dressed in a white gown and veil and carried both a large bouquet and a small white handkerchief trimmed with sequins. On her forehead she wore a *lulkë* of silver foil, and long streamers of silver *tel* hung from her temples. She stood motionless and expressionless, eyes cast downward. All the women of Memet's family rose to greet her.

At first sight of her, Memet's *allo* (in this case, father's paternal first cousin) began to sing, accompanied by her niece:

Në divan të lartër ke dalë e më rri . . .	On the high balcony you have come out to sit for me . . .
FEIME i parritur, pa vënë stoli.	(FEIME, not yet grown, with your finery not yet put on.)
Tufë manushaqe syri jot i zi . . .	A bouquet of violets your black eyes . . .
Si t'u duket MEMETI që do ta marrësh tynë? . . .	How does MEMET look to you, he whom you will marry? . . .
Bukuria jote shpirtin ma dogji . . .	Your beauty sets my soul on fire . . .

Flanked by an aunt and a young cousin, Memet was escorted slowly through the crowd to the oldest woman of Memet's party, his father's *xhaxhicë*. Three times the older woman threw rice and coins over Feime's

head. She then lifted the veil away from Feime's face and placed a
twenty-dollar bill on the young woman's forehead, which was eventually whisked away by Feime's aunt. Always retaining her modest pose,
Feime was taken to each of the older women in turn so that she could
kiss their right hand and press it to her forehead. During the song's final
verse, the wife of Memet's closest male cousin stepped forward to clasp
a necklace with a gold coin around Feime's neck. She kissed Feime's
cheek, and Feime kissed her hand.

By this time a second song had been begun, led by one of Memet's
cousins and accompanied by his *allo*. The song alludes to the bride's
elaborate wedding attire, provided by the groom's family:

Kush të bëri tynë me pëndë? . . .	Who is it who has given you your feathers? . . .
dëllëndysheja.	(O swallow)
Beu i madh, qoftë me jetë . . .	The great *bey* [her father-in-law], may he live long . . .
që të merr për MEMET benë . . .	who takes you for MEMET *bey* . . .

As the cousin sang, she too reached forward to clasp a gold necklace
around Feime's neck. Her eyes were by now filled with tears, and she
sang with difficulty. She kissed Feime's cheek and had her hand kissed
in return, and then continued her song while Memet's older sister placed
a third necklace over Feime's head.

At this moment one of Memet's more distant cousins began a song
that, in the guise of teasing the bride, compliments her on her beauty:

Sh'të të shaj unë tani? . . .	What can we tease you about now? . . .
me aman, me o-i.	
ma ke undën si qiri . . .	Your nose is like a candle [long and slender] . . .[2]

She was quickly cut off by the other women, presumably because a
closer relative should sing before her. Feime's cousin adjusted the silver
wire that had come unpinned from the bride's hair.

During the taking of the bride, it has become customary for a sister-
in-law, usually the groom's sister or his brother's wife, to sing a particular song learned from Albanian radio. The song praises the bride's
beauty and tells her what a wonderful sister-in-law she will be. In this
case, because Memet's sisters do not know how to sing, his first cousin's

wife led the song. Since she and her husband were at that time living with Memet's family, the song was just as appropriate for her to perform:

Përmbi shtëpinë tonë fluturoi një flutur.	Above our house a butterfly flew.
Të ke qenë kunata, sa qenke e bukur.	If only you were our sister-in-law, you are so beautiful!
Je e ollë, e gjatë, në bel e këputur.	You are slim and tall, and very slender in the waist.
Të ke qenë kunata, sa qenke e bukur.	If only you were our sister-in-law, you are so beautiful!
Vetulla të olla, syrin rrush të zi.	With slender eyebrows and eyes black as grapes.
Të ke qenë kunata, na qenke flori.	If only you were our sister-in-law, you are as good as gold!

As she sang, Memet's younger sister also placed a gold necklace over Feime's head.

Now, with the jewelry in place, the women who had been clustered around Feime stepped back to look at her. Memet's aunt reached down and took from Feime's right slipper a five-dollar bill, sent with her by her family. When it was held up, the others called out with delight and then applauded.

Once these requisite actions have been completed, it is standard for the bride to be led out of the room and for the women of the groom's party to perform a few dance songs. Instead, because of lack of space within the room, Feime remained and the women continued with more ritual songs addressed to her. Memet's paternal second cousin chose the next song:

Si s'të erdhi keq që u bëre nuse? . . .	Why weren't you sad when you became a bride? . . .
buza burbuqe.	(lips like a rosebud)
Erdhë të marrin dyzet e ca krushq . . .	Over forty members of the groom's lineage came to fetch you . . .
Tërë që erdhë me maqinë luks . . .	Everyone who came had a luxury car . . .

Two older women sang the final songs. First was a woman who is unrelated to Memet but a close friend of his family. Her song, which is also closely associated with this point in the wedding ritual, outlines how the bride's in-laws are expected to treat her:

Sh'të vetëtin vëndi ku rri . . .	The place where you sit is shining . . .
moj unda kalemxhiri.	(you with a nose [as slender as] a pencil)
Nuse në preri, nuse në gji . . .	We hold you in our lap, bride, we hold you in our heart . . .
Të prettë ANËM NËNJA me shumë timi . . .	May your MOTHER-IN-LAW greet you with respect and affection . . .

Last was the wife of the oldest of Memet's *xhaxha*s. We have encountered her song before, one whose versatile text renders it suitable to almost any point in a wedding:

Sh't'është nxirë vetulla tynë? . . .	Is it that your eyebrows are blackened? . . .
edhe moj, ajde dhe moj.	
Mos të ke shtënë mazinë? . . .	You haven't put on makeup, have you? . . .
Jo e jo, për perëndinë . . .	Oh no, in God's name . . .
ashtu e kam bukurinë . . .	that is the nature of my beauty . . .

As with several of the other songs, only the first few verses were sung because of time constraints.

Already midway through the women's singing, the sound of drum and clarinet had penetrated the room from the parking lot where the men were dancing. Memet's female relatives now filed out to join the dancing, while Feime made final preparations for her departure. When all was ready, her father and his brother came to the room and led her just outside the doorway. Women of Memet's family gathered around the door and sang as Feime was formally taken by the groom's party.

First Memet's father approached. Feime's aunt reached forward and drew back her veil so that he could see her face. He clasped a chain bearing a large gold coin around her neck, and then embraced and shook hands with her father and uncle. In return, she kissed her new father-in-law's hand and pressed it to her forehead.

Në mes të oborrit mbiu një qershi . . .	In the middle of the courtyard bloomed a cherry tree . . .
fal ma, ne ma, ne ma moj synë e zi.	(Present to me, give me, give me your black eyes.)
Të mbledhim baçes së ëmblat qershi . . .	Let's gather in the garden the sweet cherries . . .
	(led by a cousin and aunt)

Immediately after him, one of Memet's *xhaxha*s came forward and clasped a gold bracelet around her wrist.

Oj nuse, kunata jonë,	O bride, our sister-in-law,
a do t'vish në saraj tonë?	are you coming to our home?
A do t'vish në saraj tonë?	Are you coming to our home?
Atje kemi lum e pata.	There we have a lake with ducks.
Ato pata nuku janë,	Those are not ducks,
ato janë dya kunata.	those are the two sisters-in-law.[3]
	(north Albanian song sung in unison)

Memet was now ready to be brought forward, but first Feime said a final farewell to her relatives. As each one embraced her, she stood rigidly, never once looking up. She kissed the right hand of each and pressed it to her forehead. They approached her *me radhë:* her grandfather, *xhaxha* (father's brother), father, great-aunt, and grandmother, who fervently planted two kisses on each cheek. Her mother, on the verge of tears, remained to one side. When these goodbyes had been exchanged, Feime's veil was once again drawn over her face.

Në divan të lartër ke dalë e më rri . . .	On the high balcony you have come out and sit for me . . .
vajzë e parritur, pa vënë stoli.	(O girl not yet grown, with your finery not yet put on.)
Bë u tufë lule do të marr në gji . . .	Make yourself into a bouquet that I may wear you at my breast . . .
	(led by two cousins of the groom)

Memet now stepped forward, accompanied by his first cousin. He greeted Feime's relatives in a manner almost as deferential as that of a bride, kissing the right hand of each and pressing it to his forehead after they embraced him. The *radhë* was less careful here as he greeted whoever was nearest him: her grandmother, *xhaxhicë*, mother's female cousin, *xhaxha*, father, and great-aunt.

Qershia ç'kullet prej rrënjës,	The cherry tree tears itself from its roots:
a vajza ndaet prej nënës.	the young girl separates from her mother.
Fal ma, moj nëne, fal ma ti,	Forgive me, mother, forgive me,
fal ma, o gjithë miqësi.	forgive me, all our friends.
Gjer tashi dëgjova babanë,	Until now I obeyed my father,
pas kësaj do dëgjoj vjerrin.	from now on I will obey my father-in-law.
Gjer tashi dëgjova nënën,	Until now I obeyed my mother,
pas kësaj do dëgjoj vjerrën.	from now on I will obey my mother-in-law.

(Translation of a Macedonian song, sung in unison by men and women)[4]

Reaching into a small velvet box, Memet pulled out a wedding ring and slipped it over Feime's gloved finger. She slipped a gold band onto his. He lifted her veil, looked at her for a moment, and then took his place beside her to her right. At this his relatives began to call out: *Të trashëgoet!* "Congratulations! May they have a long and happy married life!" For a moment the two stood in the doorway while relatives videotaped them. Then, as the women sang in the background, Memet led Feime to the waiting car. The car had been decorated in modern Prespa fashion, with flowers and streamers of crepe paper, a man's folded shirt under each windshield wiper (to symbolize the gifts given to the groom by the bride), a kerchief tied to the antenna, and two signs reading "Just Married" (in English) on the trunk lid. One of the children had written "Memet + Feime" on the hood in shaving cream.

The couple were seated in the back seat together with Memet's father's *xhaxhicë*, who held in her hand a large mirror wrapped in a red kerchief. Memet's first cousin took the driver's seat. Last came Memet's father. Before he entered the car, he took a large plastic bag filled with a mixture of rice, hard candies, and coins and emptied it over the car. Children ran forward and scampered around the car, grabbing the candy and coins and yelling, "Money! Money!" Once the rice had been brushed off the car's roof, the procession of cars set off for Memet's home. As they pulled out of the driveway, horns honking gaily, Feime's relatives watched solemnly and waved farewell.

The groom's party set out for his home, taking a different route for the return trip. Upon their arrival, the musicians quickly piled out of their car so as to play a processional tune for the arrival of the bride and groom. Memet's mother was there to greet the newlyweds, wearing a bright red kerchief on her head. As the couple left the car, the younger women resumed their singing, adding another layer of sound over the lively melody of the instrumentalists. Their song is a particularly playful one, sung very rapidly:

Moj bel-ollë plot lezet . . .	O slender-waisted one, so very attractive . . .
plot lezet.	(so very attractive)
Maqina n'oborr të pret . . .	The car awaits you in the courtyard . . .
Thuaj BABAIT: Rri me shëndet! . . .	Tell your FATHER, "Remain in health!" . . .[5]
	(sung by two cousins)

One of Memet's female cousins approached Feime and placed a large loaf of bread under each of her arms. She was then taken to the doorway that leads to the kitchen, where she kicked over a vessel filled with water. In the background, the band sang a popular radio song from the town of Vlorë, in southern Albania:

Erdhi koha, çupë, të marto-nesh-o . . .	The time has come, girl, to get married . . .
Dale, bandill, dale, jam e vogël-o.	(Wait, young man, wait, I'm still young.)
Pesëmbëdhjetë vjet, bandill, pa sosur-o . . .	I'm only fifteen, young man, not yet ready . . .
O se jam e vogël, turpëronem-o . . .	I'm still young and ashamed . . .
O se jam e vogël, s'më lënë shoqet-o . . .	I'm still young, my girlfriends won't let me . . .
Pritmë, bandill, pritmë ca të rritem-o . . .	Wait for me, young man, until I've grown up a bit . . .

With Memet at her side, Feime entered the kitchen. There she was given a glass of sugar water to drink, and Memet's young nephew was lifted up so that she could kiss his forehead three times. With the band still singing outside, the women began a north Albanian song, sung in unison:

Në shtëpinë e madhe	In the large house
them të loz një valle . . .	I'm going to lead a dance . . .
Jarnanine, jarnanine	(Jarnanine, jarnanine,
gushën me durmine.	with a throat covered with jewelry.)

Feime was then led into the family room, where she kissed the forehead of another of Memet's nephews, who is crippled.[6] Finally, she was brought into the living room and seated in a chair next to Memet's aunt. His mother approached her and began to straighten her veil and *tel.* Then, spontaneously, she began a song addressed to Feime, who arose on the first notes:

Kush të bëri FEIME me pëndë? . . .	FEIME, who gave you your feathers? . . .
dëllëndysheja.	(O swallow)
Beu i madh, qoftë me jetë . . .	The great *bey,* may he live long . . .
që të merr për MEMET benë . . .	who takes you for MEMET *bey* . . .

At the song's conclusion, Feime kissed her mother-in-law's hand and pressed it to her forehead.

During the song's final verse, Memet had been led to Feime's side. When the song was finished, the two exchanged a few words and he slipped his arm around her, giving her a gentle squeeze. For just a moment she looked up and smiled. Then she resumed her bridal pose, and all set off for the banquet hall.

* * *

During the preceding afternoon, my husband had been present at an animated discussion held among the men. Until that evening, Memet's family had not thought much about how they were going to organize the activities at the banquet hall. Now some specific details needed to be planned. First, how should the celebration in the hall be "regulated" (*rregulluar*)? Who should be in the reception line as people entered? Would people be upset if they were seated too far from the head table? It had already been decided that the bride and groom and their parents and closest older relatives would sit at the head table.

There were to be no bridesmaids and ushers, who were sometimes seated there. Since there would be a few non-Albanian guests (my husband and me, as well as staff from the groom's family's restaurant), should the parents of the bride and groom make toasts in English as well as Albanian? Should any "English" dance tunes be played? Should men and women guests be seated at separate tables, as is often done? One *xhaxha* from Australia felt that it was not "tasteful" for men and women to be seated together.

Next was a particularly thorny issue. What should the bride and groom do if the guests clattered their cutlery against their glasses to signal that the bride and groom should kiss each other? It was known that Feime's father had threatened to walk out if the couple kissed in public, and so it was decided that Memet should hold his glass and make a toast if this happened, and that he and Feime should stand.

More dilemmas followed. Should Memet throw the *lastik* ("garter"), and Feime her bouquet? Memet did not care either way, and was not sure that Feime would be wearing a garter. "I'll look for one and if it's there I'll throw it," he suggested. Should Memet and Feime dance a waltz together? The *xhaxha* from Australia, where Prespa weddings remain much closer to village practice, was very much against many of these "American customs," but he felt that the waltz was "international" and therefore acceptable.

Eventually he burst forth with a speech that got to the heart of the matter: "Are you guys going to have an Albanian wedding or an American wedding? What you guys are doing is saying, 'We like these customs and so we'll keep them. We don't like these other customs and so we won't keep them. We like these American customs and so we'll add them.' In the end you don't have either an Albanian or an American wedding. You can't just abandon certain customs because you don't like them. If you decide you don't want an Albanian wedding, then you can have an American wedding." Most of those who had lived for some years in the United States explained that the guests would expect some American customs mixed in with the Albanian ones: they were becoming part of the *radhë* of North American Prespa weddings. Finally, one of the younger men piped up. "It's going to be an Albanian wedding anyway, because we're Albanians!"

The evening was indeed a blending of the two. Guests ended up seating themselves, mostly in integrated groups of men and women. When they clinked their cutlery against their glasses, Memet and Feime stood and led a toast. All the toasts were made in Albanian, and most of the music was Albanian also. As a nod to the non-Albanian guests, one of the Prespa men sang "Hava Nagilah" with the band.

Shortly after dinner, Memet and Feime went out onto the dance floor. As they swayed back and forth in ballroom position, a slow American pop song was played over the sound system while Memet's two sisters wound streamers of crepe paper around them. Immediately after this, the "bride's dance" was danced, led off by Memet's parents. At first the *radhë* was a bit shaky, as neither parent was sure of the proper order of dancers, and so for a while the groom danced ahead of the bride. Eventually one cousin stepped forward and corrected them. Once each of the groom's party had led the line, however, the entire process was repeated with the bride's relatives leading the groom: a practice now common at overseas weddings that has even been introduced in Prespa. The whole dance went on for almost forty-five minutes. Feime's relatives said later how inappropriate it had felt for them to dance in the "bride's dance," alluding to the close association made between dancing and happiness. "When you take the bride you're happy and so you dance," said her grandfather. The bride's side, however, is not supposed to be happy.

Line dances continued until past midnight to an array of north and south Albanian songs, played by the band on amplified instruments. The exception was one short segment of *denc* (rock-and-roll dancing) for the younger set. Shortly before midnight, Memet and Feime disappeared and then returned in less formal attire. Memet's mother escorted them to the head of the dance line and, one by one, brought each of her family's guests forward to lead it. As the band sang one exuberant song after another, pairs of dancers broke off from the head of the line and danced as couples, waving their arms high in the air in the style of the modern north Albanian dance "Shota." Brother danced with sister, uncle with niece, as the long line spiraled around them. Memet's family members were ready to drop with exhaustion, but they were also immensely relieved. The long days of preparation and celebration were behind them, and the wedding had been a success.

A Changing "System"

A century ago it was only the men of the Prespa community who went abroad, first to towns in the Ottoman Empire and later to North America. A young man left his fiancée or young wife in the village, under the watchful eye of her parents or his. The way of life in those distant places was considered too unruly for Prespa women and children:

Shami kalemqare, *moj kaleshe,*
anës me pampor.

A headscarf decorated (O dark-eyed one) with steamships around the edges.[7]

Ty të shkojti beçja, *moj kaleshe,*
të shkojë në Stamboll.

Your *bey* left you (O dark-eyed one) to go to Istanbul.

Ty dërgojti letër, *moj kaleshe,*
brënda një selam:

He sent you a letter (O dark-eyed one) with a greeting inside:

Dë daç u marto, *moj kaleshe,* dë
daç rri e ve.

If you wish, remarry (O dark-eyed one), if you wish, remain as if a widow.

As nuku martoem, *more beçë,*
as e ve nuku rri,
do t'i lutem Zotit, *more beçë,* të
të sjellë më sh'pi.

I won't remarry (O *bey*) nor will I remain as a widow, I will pray to God (O *bey*) to bring you home.

(*Gurbet* song, Toronto, 1986)

In their years abroad, Prespa men were exposed to new attitudes toward and new practices regarding family life. Even within Yugoslavia, the values associated with rural patriarchy were tested as women began to enter the work force and children of both genders were sent to towns to pursue a higher education. Eventually the views of Prespa men had changed so radically that, beginning in the 1960s, they began to take their families overseas with them and to emigrate permanently. As one elder noted wryly, first it was considered *turp* ("shameful") to take your family abroad, then it was *turp* to leave them behind. Those families who have emigrated to North America now find themselves adapting to life there in ways that have begun to challenge the nature of social relationships, and thus shared views of self and community. In the process, immigrant Prespa families are slowly renegotiating the terms of their "system."

The life experiences of those Presparë who have relocated abroad, now the great majority of village families, have differed radically from those of preceding generations. In choosing to emigrate, families have had to fashion complicated strategies to reconstitute their lives on a new continent. The strategies adopted by two overseas Presparë, Gani and Xhemile, may serve as examples. As a young bachelor, Gani worked in Australia for a few years and then returned to the village to marry. In the early 1970s, he set out for America with his wife and year-old son in search of a new home. First they visited relatives in Connecticut, then his sister and her husband in Detroit. Upon the invitation of the husband of his wife's sister (his *baxhanak*), they then visited Toronto and were eventually able to settle there when his *baxhanak* signed a guarantee for his family. Their two younger children were born soon thereafter. At first the family lived together with the families of the *baxhanak* and of his wife's brother in a small rented apartment. Later, each family was able to purchase its own home.

I met Gani and his wife at a wedding in Prespa in 1980, when they were there for a summer visit. In 1981, when I spent the summer in Prespa, I found that they had returned to their village to live, hoping to invest their savings in some sort of small business. Together with his younger brother, who had lived with his wife and children in Australia, Gani built a large new home, to be occupied by the two men, their wives and children, and their aging parents. Like many of those who had returned, however, Gani and his wife found that they could not live successfully in Prespa: they encountered too many restrictions on private enterprise, and their savings dwindled away on everyday expenses. And so, in 1982, they and their children returned to Toronto and started once again to build a life there. When I lived in Toronto in 1985–86, Gani was working at a car wash, while his wife had a job in a factory that makes paper cups.

Xhemile, a relative of Gani, lived in Australia with her parents and siblings between the ages of 11 and 14. Two years after they returned to Prespa, she was married to a young man from a neighboring village. In the late 1970s, after four years of marriage, Xhemile's husband left Prespa and settled in Chicago with assistance from his brother and other relatives. Xhemile remained in the village with their two small sons. Two years later she joined her husband, leaving the boys with his elderly parents. Like many Chicago-area Presparë, Xhemile's husband worked his way up through the restaurant business from dishwasher to cook. Eventually he bought a family restaurant in a smaller town outside Chicago, where he cooked and Xhemile served as hostess. Ownership of a restaurant proved exhausting for them, and so they returned to Chicago after only a couple of years and rented a small basement apartment. While her husband resumed work as a cook, Xhemile became a salesperson at a clothing store in their neighborhood, leaving a young son born in the United States to be cared for during the day by her husband's niece. In 1986, upon the death of her father-in-law, Xhemile and her husband purchased their own home and brought his mother to live with them, as well as their two older sons. When I last visited them in the early 1990s, Xhemile was working in the office of a hospital, and her husband had recently bought a small diner near their home.

Experiences such as these on the part of immigrant families have begun to affect relationships between family members, and particularly between elders and younger adults. For most of the families that live in North America, it was a younger man and his wife who emigrated first. As a result, the husband found himself functioning as head of household at a young age, struggling together with his wife and with a few relatives and friends to make sense of a complex and demanding way of life. In some instances, these men now have married sons who live at home, and so they can command the same sense of authority and experience that an elder can claim in Prespa. But there are also younger couples who waited until they had their own home and sufficient savings, and then sent for the husband's parents. In these households it is the middle generation that has greater experience of North American society, while the elders are just learning to cope with a new way of life and are usually entirely dependent on their children financially.

Such processes have different ramifications for men and women of each generation. Although a male elder is generally treated with considerable affection, he is often unable to command the respect and authority over interfamilial matters that he would have if the whole family had remained in Prespa. A female elder, however, may still wield authority within the domestic sphere over her "bride." In households in which the husband's parents reside, his wife is expected to wait on them whenever she is at home, showing the same deference toward them that would be expected in the village.

This situation is frequently a source of tension within such households, particularly in view of the otherwise striking changes that have been taking place regarding the role that younger women play in family affairs. It was clear to most Presparë when they arrived in America that both husband and wife would have to work, perhaps more than one job each, in order to reach the economic level to which they aspired. And so, today, most younger women who are physically able to do so work outside the home. In Toronto especially, many work evening or night shift, riding the subway in the late-night hours or driving their own cars. Some work together with their husbands, most often in restaurants. These represent dramatic changes for women who, in the village, might never have been to a large city or seen an airplane. At present, neither men nor women seem uneasy about this situation, since they do not view the women's activities as a break with traditional practices. Whereas in the village women worked around the house and its environs, and to some extent in the fields, now they work in jobs appropriate to an urban setting. For many women, being a dependable worker has become another aspect of being *e zonja* ("mistress" of the house). In fact, most Prespa women in North America now have two jobs: their work outside the home, and all the same housework and care of children that they had in Prespa, with little assistance from anyone but their daughter(s) and perhaps their mother-in-law.[8]

When not at work, women make most of the small household purchases, including items such as food and clothing. For major purchases such as a new house, car, or furniture, they frequently have as much input into the decision as their husbands. In this respect they are gaining responsibility over domains that were once the exclusive concern of men. The entry of women into the realm of decision-making and family finances has come about in part because of their own contribution to the household's income, but also because of changes in a household's composition and social networks. To take one example, Gani lived in Prespa with his parents and his brother and family. Just up the hill lived two of his father's brothers and two second cousins on his father's side. He socialized frequently with his two maternal uncles, who lived in adjoining homes in the village closest to his, and with the families of his sister and his paternal aunt, who lived near each other in yet another nearby village. Among his friends he counted two or three men in his village with whom he had herded livestock as a child.

Whereas patrilineal kin formed the nucleus of his social world in Prespa, in Toronto his family socializes most frequently with the families of his wife's sister and brother. His closest blood relative, a sister, lives in Detroit. Although he has a number of paternal "uncles" and cousins of his generation in the Toronto area, his relations with most of them have become largely ceremonial, except for two rather distant cousins who, with several unrelated friends from various Prespa villages, round out his social circle. In the mid-1980s, he lived down the street from his *baxhanak* who had helped him to settle in Toronto. More recently, he bought a home near a second cousin and three friends with whom he socializes frequently.

Families such as Gani's have had to construct a new social world without the support of the close relatives with whom they grew up. In the absence of an "elder" generation with extensive experience living in North America, and often of close paternal relatives of the husband, young couples have found themselves functioning as partners, jointly planning the elaborate strategies that have brought themselves, their parents, their children, and perhaps other relatives to a new continent. It is hardly surprising that younger women who have contributed so fundamentally to the success of their household in a new environment might feel uncomfortable and even resentful when they are cast in the subordinate role of "bride" by their husband's parents.

The changes that women are experiencing in their role within the family do not prompt them to see themselves as entering thereby into the "public sphere." Women in overseas families take no greater part in community affairs nor in representing their household in public forums than was previously the case. When households get together to social-ize, for example, it is still common for the men to enter into lively dis-cussions of politics and current affairs while the women retire to a back room to watch videos or discuss family matters. Women would appear to regard the many additional responsibilities that they now assume as further instances of family-centered concerns and to continue to look to the men of the family as the protectors and spokesmen for their house-hold in its relations with the outside world.

It is not merely a change in types of social networks that distin-guishes life for overseas Prespärë, but also a change in the tenor of rela-tionships between households. One of the most popular topics of con-versation among Prespärë in North America is their perception of a loss in community cohesion. As one symptom they note that families social-ize less frequently than they did in the village. They attend life-cycle celebrations such as betrothals and weddings, and dinners held in honor of visiting relatives, but they rarely get together just to "make *muabet*." They also refer to frequent fallings-out between households, particu-larly related ones. When I was conducting fieldwork in Toronto, for ex-ample, there were a number of brothers, or cousins, or brothers and sisters, who were not on speaking terms and who pointedly refused to attend each other's social occasions. As far as I could understand, many of these rifts developed because one party did not live up to what the other party regarded as an obligation: they refused to attend a family celebration, or to bring an appropriate gift, or to offer some type of as-sistance. In some cases an elder in the community was called in to try to resolve the dispute, but to little avail, the reason given being that elders no longer command sufficient respect from younger adults. When mat-ters were not quickly resolved, other households found themselves aligning with one or another of the disputing parties, with the result that the community was becoming deeply factionalized.

Presparë cite two main reasons for what they see as their community's "loss of *muabet*." First, their lives seem to them to be much busier and more complicated than they were in the village. In Prespa they worked hard during the summer, but still were able to take time off for visiting and celebrating. During the winter months, they did little else but visit back and forth. But in North America life is *veç punë e gjumë, punë e gjumë*: "just work and sleep, work and sleep." A number of individuals recited to us the same formulaic description of their day's activities: "Go to work, come home, clean the house, go shopping for the kids, go visiting on Sundays. That's it—there's no time for anything else." Those individuals who work six or seven days a week, or hold down two jobs, feel particularly overwhelmed. From my perspective, it is not simply that they have no time to visit each other. On the contrary, for most families hardly a weekend goes by when they do not honor at least one social obligation: to bring flowers or a set of baby clothes to a new mother, to visit a friend who has had an operation, to congratulate a family on their purchase of a new house. But with leisure time at such a premium, visits with other families are often seen not as a diversion but as just one more activity that they pursue out of a sense of duty.

Second, individuals see the community as caught up in a cycle of economic advancement. Unlike the early *gurbet* period, families do not work just to save money to take back to Prespa; now they spend most of their money on themselves and their homes. And they do not work just to subsist, as they did in Prespa; they are determined to advance their standard of living. They may choose to cut short a round of visiting, or to not attend a social occasion at all, because they are shopping or house-hunting or are just "too tired":

> [In the village] it was different. There were a lot of things that we never thought about: to buy a nice house, a car, to make ourselves into this or that kind of person. Everybody had an old house. OK, we thought about building a house, but no "big house"—"*moderno*." Just to build a house to have one. We thought about working to have something to eat. We didn't think about [having] a lot of things. . . . Like now, you have to think about many things. And that's why we don't get together. (Interview with a man in Toronto, 1986)

In short, Prespa families have left behind an economic system that, within the village, operated largely on the basis of barter, in order to embrace North American consumer capitalism. When families do get together, it is such economic matters that often dominate the conversation: how much individuals earn per hour at their jobs, where a family bought its new furniture, how much another family paid for its new house. Such conversation is the very antithesis of *muabet*. As families measure their progress against what other families seem to be achieving, they gradually revise their aspirations upward and thus get further enmeshed in the cycle of conspicuous consumption.

Every year, various fads in decorating and in improving one's living situation sweep through the Prespa community, fueled by the frequent talk of other families' pursuits. The result is that the houses of Prespa families and their decor are remarkably uniform. Most families, for example, have formal living rooms furnished with very similar velvet or brocade sofas and chairs, marble coffee tables, and large credenzas displaying sets of china and crystal. In 1985, many families in Toronto refurbished their basements, usually adding a "family room" that in every way functioned as a second living room, together with a second kitchen adjoining it. In 1986, many of these same families sold their homes to buy much larger ones, all with very much the same house plan, in the suburbs. This flight to the suburbs, into homes that seem to have been designed particularly for extended immigrant families, has continued into the mid-1990s. As soon as one level of attainment is reached, it no longer seems sufficient, and families set their sights on a new goal. As one man reflected, "Look how small the eye is, but it takes in the whole world. The eye is evil, for it wants whatever it sees."

Concrete symbols of economic attainment in the form of a luxurious sofa and love seat combination or a large television set seem to provide justification to Prespare for the many sacrifices they have made in opting for the pressures of life in North America over the more leisurely way of life that they knew in their villages. Families expect not only to fill their own homes with such symbols but also to see similar objects gracing the homes of other Prespare, as if to affirm the priorities that they too have chosen and to project an image of their community as peopled by industrious, successful individuals. One friend in Toronto explained with dismay, in a characteristic mixture of Albanian and English, that he would risk ostracism by other Prespa families were he to choose to live his life differently:

> "*Ne shkojmë njëri pas tjetrit* [we each follow the next guy]—I have to go by the others, I cannot be different. I see that *filani* [so-and-so] has a TV, I have to have one too." If you don't live according to community standards "the

people will go away from you" and you'll have to associate with different
kinds of people who live the way you do. (Field notes, Toronto, 1985)

And so Prespa families find themselves faced by a dilemma. If they
forego a social occasion in order to shop for clothes or household items,
they are seen as placing materialistic concerns over community values.
But if they do not use their scarce moments of free time in this way, they
will be unable to entertain at the level expected of them by other community members when it comes their turn to receive guests. The materialism that they berate has in fact become as crucial to the maintenance
of their "system," as it is developing in North America, as are the more
traditional rounds of visiting.

A third factor in the breakdown of community cohesion, from my
perspective, is a lack of economic ties between households. Despite the
fact that most families in Prespa no longer live in extended households,
those that farm continue to help each other with chores on an ongoing
basis. During the time I stayed in Prespa, for example, my host and his
brother jointly maintained a flock of sheep, and they helped each other,
as well as cousins living nearby, with activities such as harvesting and
threshing wheat, slaughtering livestock for the winter, and picking
apples. It is the need for such types of assistance that has provided
much of the impetus for village families to continue to honor social
obligations.

Among overseas Presparë, such interdependence can be seen particularly between families living in and around Chicago, where several
sets of brothers jointly own restaurants. Most Presparë, however, including the majority living in Canada, have jobs that are independent of each
other. These families still need other households to be supportive of
their family celebrations, as well as to provide marriage partners for
their children. But these households do not have to live near each other,
and they need not be relatives; after all, one's children cannot marry *soj.*

Since the early 1980s, significant economic discrepancies have begun
to develop between overseas households, and the community seems to
have begun to return to the sort of economic stratification that characterized it in the days before Yugoslav socialism leveled such distinctions. As individual families become more well-to-do, they often prefer
to associate more with other households at their same economic level.
In the process they may gradually distance themselves from those who
are "beneath" them, even if those households are their kin. If such
changes are carried out too abruptly, the families that are cast off become

bitter and, feeling that their "honor" has been impugned, then cease to honor their obligations toward the offending party. This is a pattern that I saw repeated several times while I was in Toronto, with the result that the circle of families that was willing to offer their support to certain prominent households was becoming more select but also considerably smaller. In short, economic standing is challenging "honor" as the basis for relations between Prespa households.

The Younger Generation

In my first months in Toronto, one couple turned the tables on me during an interview and began asking me about *anglezë* (lit. "English people"), the term that Presparë use for English-speaking Euro-Americans. Do *anglezë* have dialects? Do they live in extended-family households? Do they gossip about each other and, as many Presparë put it, "mind each other's business"? Few adult Presparë have any first-hand knowledge of the home life of *anglezë*. Their only glimpses come from talking to fellow employees or, more commonly, watching situation comedies and soap operas on television. Nevertheless, various friends commented to me that they found some of the attitudes that they detected among *anglezë* to be appealing. *Anglezë*, they said, pay less attention to the affairs of others, they don't worry so much about how tidy their house is or how dressed up they are when visiting friends, and they have more time to spend with their immediate family. In the spirit of mainstream practices in North America, a few couples did go camping or take a trip to Niagara Falls or Canada's Wonderland (an amusement park north of Toronto) with their children from time to time. But none was willing to compromise either attention to social obligations or household orderliness and opulence to the point of risking their continued acceptance by other Prespa households.

If adult Presparë have been unwilling to adopt too many aspects of a new lifestyle, their children have not. Young people growing up in North America, even if they were born in Prespa, have been exposed to "English" ways not only through television but also through the friends they have made at school and in their neighborhoods. Many speak English with their siblings and attempt to speak it with their parents, who worry that children will soon not be able to communicate with their grandparents or their relatives still in Prespa. The greatest complaint of adults is a more general one: that young people don't "listen to," in the sense of respecting, their elders. During a large family get-together that I attended, for example, one of the men was holding forth on some topic when his young niece interjected, "You think you're perfect, don't you." Appalled at her behavior, he responded that she should listen to whatever her uncle says "because I'm older," and that she was not to speak to him that way.

> This young generation, they don't care about respecting no more, except if their parents are strict. You know, if you tell them to do it, they will have to do it. But if you just let them go, they will do anything they want—they wouldn't respect nobody. (Interview, in English, with a woman in Chicago, 1987)

In serious instances of disrespectful or shameful behavior, some parents have turned their children out of the house. Threats to that effect are also made by many families who might never actually do so. As children reach their teens, they are faced with a choice between behaving in a way that assures them a place in a cohesive and supportive community, or leading a life of freedom mixed with isolation outside the Prespa community. One teenager told me of a south Albanian girl who was engaged to a young Albanian in Australia. When she went for a physical exam, they found that she was pregnant. "Now she's out on the streets," my friend commented, "and she was going to marry into such a nice family. I don't want my family to disown me." She continued that she herself was one of only a few "good people" among young Prespa women. By "good people" she meant: they stay at home, do things and go places with their families, go to community events, don't wear makeup, and don't go out with boys. Her description can be contrasted with that offered by another community member of an *anglezkë* ("English woman"): "Take the car, go downtown [here she imitated a woman smoking], tell your husband, 'You take care of the kids.'"

Even those young people who most embrace the Prespa "system" and have tried hardest to live by it find that they have adopted North American views toward marriage and careers that vie with those of their parents' generation. One bride who graciously went through an elaborate, traditional wedding to a Prespar was astonished when he expected their earnings to go into a common till with those of his parents. She had assumed that the money would be put aside to save toward a home of their own. Living together with his parents, surrounded by his relatives, she found that she stood little chance of defending her position and changing the way her husband and his parents conceived of "family."

Most parents in North America hope to intercede in their children's exposure to North American attitudes before there is reason to disown them. Many forbid their children to play with young people who are not from the Prespa community. "I didn't know about 'friends,'" one young woman explained to me, speaking of the years when she was about ten or eleven years old. Another common parental strategy has been to have children enter the work force right out of high school, and to marry them off at a young age: for boys, between 18 and 24; for girls, perhaps as young as 16. These marriages are for the most part still "arranged," in the sense that negotiations between the two families are carried out primarily by the parents, although often the couple dates periodically before their wedding. As in the past, weddings and similar large occasions are one of the major contexts in which potential marriage partners are spotted, both by parents and their children. The young people may subsequently express their interests to their parents, who then begin the necessary negotiations. Generally, no parents will force a marriage partner on an unwilling child; but most will not tolerate what to them would be an unsuitable choice. If a young person is determined to marry against parental wishes, or simply cannot wait for a suitable match to be found, then he or she may choose to elope.

The future of the Prespa community rests in great part on the attitudes that will develop within this next generation of Prespare as they become heads of households. They will be responsible not only for the care of their parents, but also for the reformulated set of values that will emerge out of the confrontation of the "system" of their parents' generation with those aspects of North American life that they choose to adopt. Families thus see the choice of a marriage partner for their children as crucial. Most families attempt to find a partner from another Prespa household, but this is increasingly difficult. The community is small and families are becoming far too intermarried. Parents of sons also find that many young women growing up in North America have already absorbed too many "English" ways and are thus not considered suitable partners. Even when a family is able to find an appropriate and unrelated marriage candidate, the two young people may not like each other. For all these reasons, families with sons now conduct their search for a bride on a worldwide basis, contacting relatives and friends in Kosova and Macedonia, in Scandinavia, and in Australia in addition to other cities in North America. In many ways, the search for marriage partners is much more complicated now than in the past, when families saw each other frequently and when children knew each other from school. The prospect of a bride's marrying into a "household of strangers"—long a theme of southeast European wedding songs—is often more real today than it was a generation ago.

If a suitable Prespa bride cannot be found, families are most likely to request a daughter from another Muslim Albanian family: north Albanians from Kosova or Macedonia, or south Albanians from Albania. Here families emphasize the importance of their *besë*, or "faith," in both an ethnic and a religious sense. Most families regard the Albanian language as the key to Prespa identity. Without knowledge of Albanian, children will not even be able to communicate with their grandparents, let alone preserve many of the characteristic customs that symbolize community life. One father spoke to me adamantly several times about the necessity of finding Albanian husbands for his daughters. A non-Albanian spouse in the midst of the Prespa community, he insisted, would be like "a goat among sheep."[9]

A few Prespa men have nevertheless married out of the community. These have been men who came on *gurbet* to North America as young, single "bachelors." Of two whom I knew in Toronto, one had married an Italian woman and the two lived with her parents. As the years passed, he became more and more removed from the life of the community, in part because his life revolved around his wife's family, but also because he felt that others disapproved of him. For whatever reason, he was often excluded from the guest list of community functions, although that has now begun to change. Another man married a Canadian woman years ago. When I first met her, she was virtually indistinguishable from other Prespa women in appearance. She dressed as they did, had her hair coiffed in a like manner, and sported the same gold necklaces and earrings that Prespa women commonly wear. Although she did not actively speak Albanian, she inserted Albanian exclamations into her speech frequently and used the characteristic hand gestures of community members. I met her several times before I realized that she wasn't a Presparkë. Due at least in part to her willingness to embrace the *radhë* of Prespa life, she and her husband have remained active in the community and can in no substantial way be differentiated from other Prespa households. She has even begun to learn appropriate songs to sing at community events. The extent to which such a couple is seen as giving precedence to the Prespa community thus seems to be a major factor in its household's continued acceptance by others. In contrast, I know of no young Prespaarë growing up in North America under the watchful eye of parents who have married anyone other than a Muslim from Albania or the former Yugoslavia; and I am aware of only a handful of parents who would even consider such a possibility for children who are now approaching marriageable age.

Once married, most young couples are pressured to have children immediately. Parents fear that a young adult, attending college in North America, stands a far greater chance of falling under the influence of "English" friends than does a young person who has married within the community and is concerned with supporting a growing family. This is not to say that there are no young Presparë who have attended college here, but only to note that they are rare. One young man that I knew in Toronto was committed to attending university and then law school. He was embarrassed with the image of his community as one of dropouts and unskilled workers with little chance of improving their economic status in North American society. "If I drop out now," he remarked to me cynically, "I'll be a perfect Albanian." [10]

In contrast, among those families who have chosen to remain in the former Yugoslavia, higher education has been regarded as a young person's most assured route to economic advancement. A large number of children from village families, and from those families who have resettled in towns in Kosova or Macedonia, have attended university and have gone on to become physicians, dentists, teachers, professors, lawyers, and government officials. Until the late 1980s, when its Albanian-language programs were closed as part of a rescinding of Albanian rights in Kosova, most young Presparë attended the University of Prishtinë (Serb. Priština), which offered a full course of studies in the Albanian language. Smaller numbers attended the universities in Beograd and Skopje. Now that Macedonia has become an independent country, Albanians living there find themselves with very limited possibilities for advanced studies in their own language, and this is at present a source of much tension in Macedonian political life. [11]

For overseas Prespa families, sending their children to university in the former Yugoslavia was in past decades an appealing prospect, for two reasons: first, they would receive renewed exposure to Albanian language and society; and second, they could then seek better employment either in Yugoslavia or in North America. A few families therefore sent their children back to Kosova or Macedonia to university. Several others spoke to me in the past of plans to move the family back to Prespa so that their children could attend high school and marry there, and then decide whether to stay or to return to North America. The issue of whether to move back to Prespa is one that every family considered in years past. Until the breakup of Yugoslavia I met few families who had made the unequivocal decision to stay in North America. Most expressed a firm desire to return or had left the choice open to ongoing debate. Children were the first reason that a family would cite in wishing to return, but most also admitted that their children would probably not be happy in Prespa. As one woman explained, they don't know how to care for farm animals or do farmwork, and they're used to watching television when they come home from school, rather than doing farm chores.

Women with greater exposure to North American attitudes had also become used to their newly elevated status within their household, and some expressed to me a concern that a return to the village would mean a return to more oppressive conditions for them. One woman exclaimed to me repeatedly that she would never return to Prespa because the women there "work like slaves":

> As a "bride," she said, she was "too good." When any visitor, even a child, entered the house, she sprang to her feet, and stood up again when [the visitor] left. She worked as hard as she could, fetching two heavy containers of water from the fountain, even when she was pregnant. . . . "I don't know how I did it. I didn't know I was that strong. I don't know if I would do it again." (Field notes, Chicago, 1986)

Most frequently, families acknowledged that, despite deeply nostalgic feelings about village life, they had grown used to a higher standard of living in North America and would not be content with Macedonia's more meager standard. More recently, the severe inflation experienced by residents of Macedonia during the late 1980s, followed by the outbreak of war and the dissolution of Yugoslavia, have provided even stronger incentives for Prespa families to remain in North America. Despite their reservations about overseas life, very few families have returned to Macedonia or Kosova to live.

Because of the elaborate set of circumstances that informs their experience as immigrants, most Presparë retain deeply ambivalent feelings regarding their residence in North America. At one wedding in Canada in the mid-1980s that brought together relatives from Scandinavia, Australia, and elsewhere, the bride's grandfather expressed the frustration that many overseas Presparë feel when he exclaimed, *Neve s'jemi për këtu!* "We just don't belong here!" To which others replied, "Then where do we belong?" And another concluded, "Nowhere!" As another man put it, on another occasion, "When we're here we miss Prespa; when we're there we miss Canada. But we've learned to live as we live here."

Changing Weddings

During my stay in Toronto, I often found myself at small gatherings among Prespa families at which a recent wedding became an avid subject of discussion. In the intense conversations that ensued, speakers frequently mentioned qualities such as orderliness, predictability, and conformity to community norms: as manifested in household furnishings, in seating arrangements, in menus, in attention to forms of etiquette, and in song performances. If a celebration had exhibited such qualities, then individuals generally deemed it successful, praising the fact that it "had *radhë*," that it was *rregulluar* ("regulated") or even *kontrolluar* ("controlled"). If some aspect of the event had not projected such an image, then they perhaps complained that it "had no *radhë*" or that it "was tasteless" (*s'kishte lezet*), meaning that it failed to be aesthetically pleasing.

Today many of the practices connected with wedding celebrations are retained simply because they are traditional, because that is "the way things are done." But conformity to carefully defined community expectations carries moral implications as well. Just as a tidy, well-appointed home demonstrates the disciplined industriousness of its women and the "mindfulness" of all its inhabitants, so an orderly and predictable event suggests a community that is disciplined: one in which each individual knows his or her place within the moral order and behaves accordingly. Certainly the most reassuring image that Prespare have constructed through their *radhë*, in its most comprehensive sense, has been one of a society that provides a secure and well-defined slot for each of its members, so long as they agree to uphold its ideals through their behavior. It is not so much that Prespare have reproduced a cohesive *sistem* through their celebrations, as that they have been prompted to see it as a "system" through their participation in such events.

In recent years, Prespare living overseas have begun to alter the character of their family celebrations, and particularly their weddings. Some of these changes result from accommodations made to the exigencies of North American life, others are responses to shifting relationships within and between households, while others still are attempts by individuals to assert new aspects of identity that are emerging in response to such shifts. As a result of such changes, overseas Prespa weddings currently project a rather disorderly and unpredictable mix of Albanian and North American elements, one that betrays the deep-seated conflict currently being waged in the community between two contrasting social constructs. As these two constructs confront each other through the medium of symbolic practices, weddings have become a major site for the renegotiation of the Prespa "system."

Periods of Change

Although families have always made alterations and introduced innovations into their wedding celebrations, there have been certain periods in which major changes have taken place in conjunction with larger societal changes (table 6). One such period was in the 1960s and 1970s, when families first began to emigrate or to resettle in towns outside the district. Before that time, weddings were held sometime after St. Demetrius' Day (November 8), usually during midwinter. Presparë explain that, at this point in the year, the major season of agricultural labor was past, the harvest was in, cash crops such as tobacco and apples no longer needed attention, and a generous supply of food had been set aside for the winter. Families had time to rest from their work and food to feed their guests. Winter was also the time of year when the earth was plowed in readiness for being sown with seeds for the coming year's crops. Holding a wedding at that time was therefore consistent with the homology recognized between the cycles of human reproduction and agricultural fertility.[12]

The overall schedule for wedding activities was also somewhat different in that period. The bride was taken on a Thursday, a common practice among Muslim Albanians in the neighboring Korçë region as well. On the Thursday a week beforehand, both the henna and the *rroba* for the bride were brought to her. It is not clear from the accounts of those I have interviewed whether there was a separate custom of sending the *rroba* with adult *sinitorë* at weddings held before the 1960s, or whether the young boys who brought the henna also brought the bride's clothes.

Beginning in the late 1960s, families began to adjust the wedding schedule to changing living conditions. In order to make it convenient for relatives living abroad or elsewhere in Yugoslavia to return to Prespa for the celebration, most weddings were scheduled during the period extending from late May to mid-September. This placed them during the most intensive work period for families that still farm. Likewise, as more

TABLE 6 Periods Of Change In Prespa Wedding Celebrations

Prespa			North America
Winter (1930s–1950s)		Summer (1960s–)	Any Season (1970s–)
Day	Event	Day	Event
We		Sa	henna and *rroba* brought either day (if far away)
Th		Su	(if nearby)
	henna brought to bride		
	rroba brought		
Fr		Mo	
	henna put on bride		
Sa		Tu	
Su		We	
Mo		Th	
	bride is adorned		
	qeshqek crushed at groom's		(not done)
Tu		Fr	
We		Sa	
			sinitorë bring *rroba* to bride (if nearby) (or Sa)
Th		Su	bride's dowry taken—(brought by her family)
	groom bathed and shaved; given gifts		
	bride taken		
	dowry taken		
	- - - - - "bride's dance"		
	rituals incorporating bride into new home		(if return to groom's home)
	groom and bride closed in		celebration in banquet hall; "bride's dance"; couple leaves for honeymoon

of those individuals who remained in Prespa took government jobs in the nearby town of Resen (Alb. Resnjë) or at stores in the villages, the day of the taking of the bride was moved from Thursday to Sunday so that the core of the celebration could take place on a weekend. By the early 1980s, weddings were held on Sundays unless a family had problems scheduling a Sunday wedding, such as securing their favorite *daulle* for the final two days. There were also a few instances when a family had two sons that were married on Thursday and Sunday of the same week.

In the first years that immigrant Prespa families lived in North America, the great majority returned to Prespa for their sons' marriages, as some families still do (see chapter 2 for one example). When there were still many relatives in the village, holding a wedding in Prespa was the easiest way to assemble one's kin for such a major event. Most families had homes in the village that were more spacious than the ones in which they lived in North America. The groom's family in particular could accommodate a large number of guests in its courtyard during the day and in the evenings could distribute the men among various *konak*s at neighboring houses. Another factor in their decision to return was the absence in North America of Rom musicians who could provide the traditional *daulle* repertoire.

By the early 1970s, however, a Rom clarinetist from Prespa had formed a band in Toronto and thus provided one incentive for having a wedding at one's North American home. In the years to follow, a number of younger men in the Chicago area began to learn to play clarinet, accordion, guitar, bass, or drums, so that for the first time Albanians provided wedding music for themselves. Since then, several bands have formed and reformed in and around both Chicago and Toronto and have performed for Prespa weddings all over North America (plate 16). As more and more Prespa families have emigrated, and as they have been able to purchase larger homes abroad, they have felt less need to return to Prespa to hold a wedding. The large number of guests that gather on the groom's side can now be accommodated by transferring the final stage of the celebration to a banquet hall, generally one owned by Italians or Greeks, who are able to provide food that is not wholly unacceptable to Prespa tastes.

Alterations to the Ritual Sequence

When faced with planning a wedding in North America, most Prespa families try to include to whatever extent possible the major steps in the traditional ritual sequence, as detailed in previous chapters. As the arguments at Memet's wedding illustrate, it is important to older relatives in particular to have an "Albanian" wedding. For the portion of the wedding that takes place at their home, most of their decisions as to which ritual activities to include and how to schedule them revolve around logistical factors. If the bride and groom live in the same city or nearby, they may follow closely the schedule that is observed in Prespa.

If, however, the groom lives in one town while the bride lives in another, they may decide that the *sinitorë* should travel to the bride's on one weekend and that the bride should be taken on the next, usually on Sunday but occasionally on Saturday. An alternative strategy is for the full entourage on the bride's side to check into a hotel or motel near the groom's home so that a more traditional schedule may be observed.

Two of the major ritual activities of village weddings are now commonly omitted in North America, also for logistical reasons. The crushing of the *qeshqek,* which in Prespa takes place on Thursday afternoon, is not performed, both because it would require a large outdoor area, which many urban families do not have, and because it would be held on a weekday when few adults would be free to attend. The "closing in" of the groom and bride has also been eliminated in favor of the evening celebration in the banquet hall, from which the young couple now departs with little fanfare, often to go on a North American–style "honeymoon." At many weddings, the groom's family proceeds directly from the bride's home (or hotel) to the banquet hall without returning to their house. As a consequence, the many small rituals incorporating the bride into their household may not be observed. The "bride's dance" is now customarily danced at the hall rather than in the courtyard of the groom's home. At some weddings, the pressure to arrive at the banquet hall at a designated hour cuts short the observance of still other customs, as it did at the wedding of Memet and Feime, when the giving of gifts to the groom by his female relatives was interrupted.

The most drastically curtailed wedding I attended in Prespa was one in which the bride had eloped and was already living with the groom and his family. In such an instance, it is common for a wedding to be celebrated with the usual festivities on the groom's side, omitting those activities that would take place at the bride's home. A similar, one-sided wedding might be held in North America if the bride has recently come from Prespa and does not have relatives close by, or if she is not from the Prespa community, as was the case at the wedding described in chapter 6. If the groom is not from Prespa, or is not an ethnic Albanian, then the wedding is carried out according to his family's local traditions, except for gatherings held at the bride's home.

As the focus of the celebration has shifted from the home to the banquet hall, some families have opted to eliminate virtually all activities at their house. Sometimes this is a cost-saving measure, as it obviates the need to feed visiting guests and to pay the musicians, who would normally be hired on the groom's side for a full day of activities. Most families, however, still prefer to retain those activities that are logistically feasible: ones that can be carried out on evenings or weekends. In retaining these rituals, families may nevertheless revise their content somewhat or may choose not to observe some of the subsidiary customs, with the result that somewhat different meanings than the traditional ones may emerge.

Among the most prominent of the rituals still widely observed, for example, are those that mark the coming of age of the bride and groom. While many brides still have henna put on their hair, others now go to a hairdresser to have their hair dyed an appropriate shade or simply to get a special hairdo, eliminating the home ceremony altogether. The groom, for his part, now bathes himself rather than being bathed by female relatives, and he very often shaves himself moments before a mock shaving is performed by a relative. In both cases these ceremonies are changing away from actions that are carried out on the bride or groom by close members of their family, toward actions that they themselves initiate or perform. In the process, the two are presenting themselves as young adults who have increasing autonomy over their lives.

These rituals, together with the "adorning" of the bride on Thursday evening, probably also remain popular because the attainment of adult status continues to be a major aspiration for young Presparë, reinforced by its desirability within the Euro-American value system that many of them at least partially espouse. In contrast, it has become far less common for the father-in-law's hat or shirt or mother-in-law's headscarf to be burned at any North American wedding, and this may be indicative of changing views on the prospect of aging. Many women in their thirties and forties have been affected by media images extolling youthfulness to such an extent that they are unwilling to undergo the changes in dress and appearance that would set them off as elders. Moreover, as their generation gains increasing control over household decision-making, the thought of joining a marginalized older generation offers little attraction for them in return for the loss of their youth. During one interview that I conducted with a younger woman on the subject of wedding customs, she stopped in the middle of an explanation to exclaim, with a note of anxiety, "My daughter is going to marry in maybe seven years—how will I dress like that?!"

A second group of ritual activities that is still commonly observed are those that constitute reciprocity between the two families through gift-giving. These have, in fact, become far more elaborate than in earlier decades, as the economic standing of the families involved has become a more important measure of their status within the community. An increased emphasis on both the bride's dowry and the *rroba* given her by the groom's family is apparent both at weddings currently held in Prespa and at those in North America. Before families began to emigrate from Prespa, the *rroba* were very modest: perhaps two dresses, two pairs of stockings, and two pairs of shoes or slippers. In contrast, those for a wedding that I attended in Prespa in 1981 included three short dresses (made in Yugoslavia); four summer-weight suits (three from Turkey, one from the United States); two long evening dresses (made in Turkey); two pairs of dress shoes; two pairs of slippers; one handbag; one hat with veil; one large wooden box filled with cosmetics; a dresser set of comb, brush, and mirror; several pairs of underwear and hosiery; and four at-home gowns. Her wedding outfit consisted of a white wedding dress with a long train, trimmed entirely with pearls and made in the United States; a crown of white silk flowers with a white veil; white gloves; and white high-heeled slippers. The *rroba* at North American weddings are at least as lavish. One recent bride, for example, insisted that all clothes sent to her, in addition to her bridal gown and those of her attendants, be custom-made.

Likewise, a bride's dowry from the period before emigration typically consisted of two trunks filled with clothing, bedding, and decorative items such as crocheted doilies or embroidered towels; two mattresses; four to six cushions; and a selection of copper pots and pans for cooking. The bride was expected to have made the cloth items herself, as well as items of clothing to be given as gifts to each close relative of the groom: a headscarf or dress for women; undergarments or shirts for men. At recent weddings in both Prespa and North America, however, a bride has provided many of the furnishings for a home. Her parents are currently expected to give the couple a complete bedroom set, including furniture, bedding, and perhaps even the carpeting for their floor. Relatives of the bride provide bedroom accessories, as well as a complete set of kitchen and living room items: dishes, cutlery, glasses, cooking pans, small appliances, and the like; and generous gifts of clothing are sent by the bride to the groom and his immediate family. While the bride might embroider a couple of small pillows or tapestry pieces to be framed and mounted on the wall, virtually all items in present-day dowries are purchased. In these various ways, items that once demonstrated the bride's industriousness and skill or the groom's ability to provide for his new wife now display, above all, the economic status claimed by the two families. In the case of the bride's dowry, it is ironic that it may be years before the bride and groom are able, or are permitted, to move out of his parents' household and actually use many of the items that she and her family have provided.

The many changes being introduced into wedding celebrations are bringing about a significant decrease in the symbolic coherence of the traditional ritual sequence. Now that the *qeshqek* ritual has been eliminated and the groom is often shaved in the living room of his home rather than in the yard, the "public" nature of his coming of age is no longer affirmed through an outdoor setting. In the context of urban North America, a family's decision to hold any part of the wedding outdoors does not so much announce the groom's social responsibilities as a male as it points out to neighbors the family's distinctiveness, and possibly their marginality, as members of an "ethnic" community. Many families are unwilling to draw attention to themselves in such a way, even if they do have the outdoor space. The indoor/outdoor opposition, which once deeply informed Prespa ritual, has been further undermined by the substitution of the dance in the banquet hall for the "closing in" ceremony. At present, the one part of the wedding that is commonly celebrated outdoors is the procession to take the bride, a practice that is congruent with "English" wedding practices.

In a similar manner, the omission of the *qeshqek* ceremony, as well as of the serving of *bukëvale* to the bridal couple, has removed two of the major customs through which human and agricultural fertility have been linked metaphorically. If no customs incorporating the bride into the groom's home are performed, more such symbolic actions are eliminated. It is still common for the groom's family to send *kokolinkë* to the bride's family, to serve a *bakllava* after the groom's shaving, and to throw rice and candies over the bride when she is taken. Some families also have the bride bake *kulaçka* once she is married. But with several important grain-related rituals now removed from the sequence, the coherence of this symbolism has been severely eroded. With so little spatial and agricultural symbolism remaining, the ritual wedding sequence is losing its capacity to construct traditional gender relations as natural and self-evident.

Home Gatherings

If ritual activities at a wedding have served primarily to construct gendered relations within a patriarchal framework, then social gatherings have highlighted interfamilial relationships and consolidated the community's sense of moral order. For immigrant Pesparë, however, it is becoming harder to generate the utopian image of self and community that village weddings have often constructed, and the images that emerge at present-day weddings are not necessarily consistent with the realities of their current lives.

One of the ways that Presparë in North America mask their current situation at wedding celebrations is through the ethnic makeup of their guest list. In Prespa in the early 1980s, it was not uncommon for Albanians from other districts or for Macedonian or Turkish neighbors to be included in home gatherings at weddings. By welcoming such families into their homes, Presparë were acknowledging that they and their guests shared some common moral ground. In North America, however, it is unusual for anyone except an Albanian or Turk from Prespa, or perhaps from the neighboring Bitola district, to be present at home gatherings. An image is thus set forth of a social world peopled almost entirely by Presparë, as if the North American world outside, with all the challenges that it presents to the community's "system," does not exist. If non-Prespa or non-Albanian "strangers" (*njerëz të uaj*) are included in a wedding at all, they are invited to the portion that takes place at the banquet hall, where they contribute to an alternative image of a more assimilated Prespa society. My partial interpretation of the exclusion of my husband and myself from the home portion of some weddings is that our presence as "English" people was simply too inconsistent with the fragile vision of homeland that families wish to take away from home events.

Likewise, the strict observance of *radhë* that still characterizes most gatherings belies the realignments in power relations that are taking place in other contexts between genders and generations. At one wedding that I attended in Prespa, a young woman did in fact comment to me that she didn't like to kiss older women's hands: she felt it was "too traditional" and "not progressive." And, indeed, at a gathering in Toronto several years later, I watched congenial rounds of greetings stop abruptly when another young woman refused to kiss her father's hand. Such instances of rebellion are in my experience extremely rare, especially at a large event. Most younger adults readily kiss the hands of their parents and other elders at wedding gatherings, and defer to them in other ways, despite the fact that they are far less willing than in the past to heed the advice of the older generation in everyday matters.

Through their meticulous observance of *radhë*, today's adults are not so much "honoring" their elders as they are drawing attention to themselves as "mindful" and hence honorable individuals. They are also providing models of honorable behavior for the upcoming generation, in the hopes of countering the more egalitarian nature of intergenerational relations characteristic of "English" families. Above all else, Prespärë signal through their observance of *radhë* that they consider their community, as symbolized by its etiquette, to be viable and relevant to their daily lives. For those who observe it, their *radhë* is itself a form of resistance: to total assimilation to North American society and its values.[13]

On a superficial level, home gatherings project a particularly conservative view of Prespa society, one that fails to register fundamental changes in other domains of familial and community life. Nevertheless, some configurations emerge at such gatherings that overtly suggest the sorts of realignments that are currently taking place. Most striking in this regard is the relative importance placed on various kinds of kin and friends. In former decades, in Prespa, the early stages of a wedding were attended primarily by a family's *xhaxhallarë* (such a gathering is described in chapter 2). Later in the week, other close kin, generally maternal relatives and affines living in other villages, arrived to augment the number of celebrants. Finally, other relatives and friends with less close ties to the family came to participate in the climactic final days. Each family's patriline was thus set apart temporally as the core of the wedding's celebrants. An emphasis on the patriline was heightened on the groom's side on Saturday and Sunday evenings, when the men of visiting families were sent to *konak*s at the homes of his *xhaxhallarë*, whose houses physically defined that portion of the village named for his lineage. When the bride was taken, the effect was one of a young woman being wrested from one lineage by another, which then "danced" her triumphantly in the "bride's dance." Because the Prespa community is now so widely scattered, those who gather at the bride's and groom's homes at North American weddings may now be any type of relative—patrilineal or matrilineal, blood relative or affine—or even just acquaintances from the host's home village. The bride is most assuredly still "taken," to live in most cases with the groom and his parents. But the image of the two households that is suggested in the transaction is one of nuclear families surrounded by a network of other such families, all of whom are connected more by ties of expediency than of "blood."

The configuration of guests that attends a home gathering is not merely a reflection of current social networks, for a wedding may also provide the occasion for a household to signal a realignment in relationships. If a household of relatives or presumed friends chooses not to attend a wedding, this may be the host's first indication that a rift has occurred between the two families. The host, in turn, may suggest such a change either by not extending an explicit invitation to a family, or by treating a guest with less than the expected regard. At one Toronto wedding, for example, a cousin of the groom was deeply angered when he was not designated to be one of the *sinitorë*. This appeared to be the decisive moment of rupture between two households that had been growing distant over some time. The incident was not a mere falling out, but an expression of a reformulation of priorities on the part of the host family, one in which notions of "obligation" (*ua*) and "honor" (*nder*), as conceptualized within an egalitarian framework, were giving way to a strategy through which they pursued relationships that complemented their assessment of their own degree of wealth and prestige. In response, the cousin then had to consider whether or not he accepted the view of social order that the hosts were asserting through their actions.

As rifts such as this multiply throughout the community without finding resolution, it may be difficult for a family to assemble a large group of guests at any wedding gathering who will even try to get along for the course of the evening. Aside from heavy work schedules, this seems to be the major factor influencing yet another dramatic change in home events. Whereas families in the past could count on a large number of guests on most evenings, who then met separately in groups of men and women, today many gatherings are so small in size that all meet in a single room (as, for example, at the event described in chapter 4). The construction of completely separate male and female realms is thus no longer automatic at home events, and the public/private opposition informing the wedding as a whole is further undermined. Although integrated gatherings are becoming more common, men and women nevertheless sit most often in separate areas within the *odë* of the host's home, and the refreshments offered them continue to construct the nature of their *muabet*, and hence the nature of gendered relations, in contrasting ways. Here, as with age, the meaning of the observance of these aspects of *radhë* is perhaps being transmuted to a more general affirmation of the community's centrality in the lives of those present.

"English" Innovations

Just as a present-day marriage ultimately requires the consent of the young people involved, so the character of a present-day wedding depends on the willingness of the bride and groom to participate in its various stages. When I commented to Feime that I had been surprised by the number of "traditions" that were included in her wedding, she responded by exclaiming, "You only get married once!" She had wanted to observe all the *traditë,* she said, to make her mother happy. Like most contemporary brides, Feime retained the grueling stance that the bride is expected to maintain with particular pride. By being a "good bride," as she was widely said to be, she signaled her respect, not only for her parents and those of her husband, but also for the values of the community around which she expected her life to revolve for decades to come. Memet's attitude to their wedding had been similar. Feime's younger brother, however, was less enchanted by the proceedings. "It sure is a lot to go through just for one wedding," he commented, as we showed the family our video of the event.

In cases when the younger generation agrees to retain the traditional wedding format, whether for themselves or for the sake of older relatives, they may nevertheless agitate to introduce various features from "English" weddings into the event, particularly the portion that takes place at the banquet hall. As a result, participants in a wedding may find that their identity is constructed at different points in the celebration in highly contradictory ways. At the home portion, by holding to practices of long standing, they present themselves very much in terms of the "system" to which they were socialized a generation ago. In the banquet hall, they may find themselves framing their actions in terms of North American views of social order that they are not yet willing to accept in other domains of life.

The Connecticut wedding of Fatmir and Merita, of which the home portion was described in chapter 7, illustrates one extreme in the Americanization of present-day overseas weddings. Merita had come to the United States as a small child and grew up in a community with only a few Prespa families. Having attended college, she then began work as a nurse. She wanted her wedding to express her sense of being an American as well as an Albanian. Much of the celebration was personally planned by her, and she coached her new husband—who had arrived from Skopje only months before—through most of it, whispering directions to him under her breath rather than retaining the traditional unmoving bridal stance. When his relatives came to take her, she remained dignified and self-possessed, but she looked up and smiled rather than staring at the ground. She was to be her own person at her wedding, rather than a depersonalized image of femininity whose movements were directed by others.

Once she had been taken, all guests on both sides of the wedding drove in a procession to the banquet hall. One section had been partitioned off and folding chairs arranged to accommodate a "congregation." When all the guests were seated, Fatmir and Merita processed in, preceded by a flower girl, a ring-bearer, and three young couples dressed as bridesmaids and ushers, while the band hired for the occasion played "Here Comes the Bride." The local *oxha* then officiated over the standard American wedding ceremony, translated into Albanian.

When the ceremony had ended, the bride and groom took their seats at a special head table in the main hall, flanked by their young attendants. As everyone ate dinner, guests intermittently clinked their cutlery against their glasses, upon which Fatmir and Merita stood and kissed to loud applause from the guests. Pieces were then served of an extremely elaborate wedding cake: three separate, multi-layered cakes joined by plastic bridges, with a fountain of champagne glasses set beneath the elevated middle cake that was decorated with a small statuette of a bride and groom. Following dinner, the "bride's dance" was danced midway through a long sequence of line dances. Then, toward the end of the afternoon, Merita threw her bouquet, and Fatmir her garter, as one of the waiters, serving as emcee, announced the happenings over a loudspeaker to the roomful of guests.

Even at this wedding, however, not all the North Americanisms that could have been included were carried out. Just after dinner, the emcee announced that the bride and groom would start off the dancing with a couple dance. Immediately several older relatives protested that Albanians did not do such things. After some heated exchanges, he announced that the groom would dance instead with his mother. Later, once the bouquet and garter had been thrown, the emcee wanted the boy who caught the garter to put it on the leg of the girl who caught the bouquet. Again several male relatives swarmed around him, yelling their disapproval at what promised to them to be an indecent display. At this wedding, as at that of Memet and Feime, relatives expressed their concern that North American customs might overshadow the Albanianness of the event and challenge the values that a wedding is intended to project. At any wedding, and often through extended debate, each family decides for itself which innovations are appropriate and which violate its perception of *radhë*.

The introduction of North American customs is a way for young Preparë to assert their sense of being Canadian or "American," with all the implications held by those terms of being "progressive" and "modern" as well. Such customs can readily be adapted to the Prespa wedding format because they often share a great deal of parallel symbolism. The "English" bride's white dress and veil traditionally symbolized her virginity, as did the red *duvak* that Prespa brides formerly wore. Her bouquet, through allusions to plants, likewise symbolizes her fertility. "English" people, like Presparë, throw rice over the bride, and they serve a cake—a cooked grain product that is distributed to all—at the wedding meal.[14] Ironically, many of the practices that Presparë are borrowing convey the same messages regarding power relations, particularly gendered ones, as do the traditions that they are abandoning, for Euro-American wedding customs also constitute social relations within a patriarchal framework. To take just one example, when a Prespa bride dons a floor-length white wedding dress, she is constructed in the image of fragile Victorian femininity, in marked contrast to that of male-as-protector as provided by the groom in his broad-shouldered tuxedo. Even if she eschews the traditional stance of Prespa brides, she is still nearly immobilized by a long, cumbersome train. In many instances, borrowed "English" customs do not so much affirm changing gender relations as substitute one set of patriarchal symbols for another.

Among the new practices evident at Prespa weddings, however, are some that suggest a reformulation of traditional power relations. The beginnings of such a reformulation were, in fact, registered several decades ago in Prespa villages when two new customs were introduced: the inclusion of the groom in the party that fetched the bride, and the "bride's dance." For the first time the bride and groom were seen publicly as a couple as they stood in the doorway of the bride's home and then processed back to his house on foot. Then, rather than being hustled indoors, the bride was taken out into the courtyard where she and the groom were "danced" by his relatives. The "bride's dance" was the first custom to violate the strict indoor/outdoor division between male and female realms that had been observed at village weddings. But in its introduction can also be seen the beginning of the construction of the bride and groom as a distinct social entity.

At a North American wedding, the bride and groom are particularly prominent as a couple during the celebration at the hall. Usually they process into the hall together, as the "new couple" is introduced by a band member over the loudspeaker system. They then sit together at the center of the head table throughout the evening. At most weddings, they dance at least one slow couple dance together, alone on the floor, in addition to being the focal point of the "bride's dance." Late in the evening, as the party is winding down, they generally don street clothes and then depart for their honeymoon. In all these ways the image of bride-as-possession, which is still asserted strongly at the home portion of a wedding, is challenged by the image of an autonomous married couple that emerges at the hall.

The bride and groom as couple are echoed at many weddings by the young people who attend them as bridesmaids and ushers. In some cases these are recently married couples, in others young single people of eligible age. Often they process in as couples just ahead of the bride and groom and are then seated at the head table, together with the two sets of immediate relatives. At some weddings they also initiate the evening's dancing, with several line dances performed exclusively by them. Whereas the *konak*s that once occupied the evening's activities were dominated by male elders and married men in their thirties and forties, the festivities in the banquet hall give increasing prominence to younger Prespare. As the generation that will soon be among the community's leaders, setting the tone for future relations among households, it is crucial that they be incorporated into wedding celebrations on terms that they find acceptable.

Older household members are also increasingly likely to be grouped as couples at the banquet hall. Most often families are seated at tables in integrated groups, rather than at separate tables of men and women. At some weddings, relatives also lead the line in the "bride's dance" in couples rather than singly. Many older guests protested these sorts of innovations at weddings that I attended in the 1980s. As Memet's uncle said, such practices show "no taste." Nevertheless, these and other practices strongly suggest an emergent reconfiguration of Prespa society as composed of autonomous nuclear-family households rather than extended patrilineal groups.

Certainly the most striking innovation in overseas weddings is the inclusion of the bride's family in the festivities at the banquet hall. In Prespa, the bride was traditionally the only member of her side of the wedding who attended the celebration at the groom's house. But at North American weddings, as at "English" ones, the bride's entire wedding party proceeds on to the hall, where her family is only slightly less prominent in the celebration than is the groom's. Both families are generally seated at the head table, and each set of relatives takes its turn leading the new couple in the "bride's dance." Again a clash in constructs is evident. The image that still dominates home events is that of a bride making a sorrowful departure from her family home, accompanied by the groom's full retinue. At the hall, however, a contrasting image emerges of a young couple brought together by, but also set somewhat apart from, two complementary sets of relatives.[15]

As at village weddings, relations between the host families and the larger group of guests that attends the wedding continue to be confirmed through acts of reciprocity. Economic display is now foregrounded in these exchanges, as it is in the exchanges that take place between the two families themselves. A generation ago in Prespa, guests arrived at the groom's or bride's home with food items to be used for meals served during the wedding period. Families less close to the host might bring dry goods such as sugar or rice, while close relatives might bring a tray of baked sweets such as *bakllava,* as well as a head of livestock. One woman described to me how, when she was a girl, a family might process to a wedding leading a ram whose horns had been decorated with mirrors and beads. Upon arrival, the ram would be "danced" around the courtyard, somewhat as the bride is now danced. At present-day North American weddings, sweets are still brought to home events. Guests now appear at the banquet hall, however, with a generous monetary gift for the couple (in the mid-1980s, generally $100 per family) nestled in a greeting card enclosed in an envelope. Early in the evening's activities, they form a long reception line that passes slowly by the head table. As each family group steps forward to extend their best wishes, they drop the envelope into a large decorated basket placed just in front of the bride and groom.

Since the greatest number of guests see each other at the banquet hall, special attention is given to what each person will wear. Most families expect to purchase complete new outfits, at least for the mother and all daughters, for every wedding that they attend. For this reason alone, weddings command a sizable chunk of a household's yearly expenses. A family living in Prespa in the 1980s might have been closely involved in one or two weddings each summer and might have attended portions of three or four more. Today in North America, as guest lists have grown, families are often invited to eight or ten weddings a year. No family can afford to expend exorbitant amounts of money on every wedding, so the lavishness of the clothing that a family wears to any single celebration has become an important measure of their esteem for the host family. The groom's family returns the investment of its guests, and suggests its economic standing, in any number of ways: through the number of guests it invites to the hall, through the opulence of the hall it rents, through the meal it provides, through the band that is hired to play, and perhaps by providing favors such as napkins or matchbooks inscribed with the young couple's names.

The innovative features of Prespa celebrations that have come about as a result of borrowings from Euro-American culture should by no means be interpreted as reflecting current realities within the Prespa community, but rather as experiments pointing the way toward a possible future social order. By imposing elements of "English" weddings on their celebrations, younger Prespare prompt all who are present, regardless of gender or generation, to articulate through their actions views of themselves that they might not find acceptable in other contexts. As they move through the novel configurations these borrowed practices entail, wedding participants are given an opportunity to "try on" an identity formulated around Euro-American ideals, in contrast to the community notions of social order that they exemplify through their actions during the home portions of a celebration. In the juxtaposition between "Albanian" and "American" identities that is set up between events at home and in the hall, Prespare stake out for themselves the ideological poles between which they are currently reformulating their community's "system."

While I was in Toronto, a wedding took place that illustrates both the opulence of many present-day Prespa weddings and the vulnerability that such apparent prosperity may mask. Among the Toronto families are those of several brothers whose family was one of the richest and most influential in their village in the late Ottoman period. Although by the mid-1980s their economic level was only slightly above that of many other families in the community, the aura of their prominence in the past continued to hover over their households. During my stay, the only son of one of the brothers became engaged to a young Prespa woman, and the wedding plans became the talk of the community. The father of the groom bought a large new home in the suburbs, to be inhabited by himself, his wife, their daughter, and their son with his new bride. Both father and son acquired new cars. For the wedding a five-person team was hired to record the event on video and in still photographs, and musicians were flown in from Chicago. Hundreds of guests turned out for the celebration, held in a large hall. It was the wedding of the year. Families strained their budgets to buy especially dressy outfits for each member to wear to the wedding, and each gave a monetary gift as well. Although some felt that the affair was overly lavish, many of those same individuals were flattered to be included in such a spectacular occasion and would not have considered missing it. In rating the success and importance of the event in subsequent days, community members cited both the large number of guests and the large amount of money paid for the video team.

Six weeks after the wedding, the bride deserted her new husband and went home to her father's household. Rumors flew through the community, with little solid information to back them up. Each family supported its own child's actions and blamed the other, deploying their own version of the events in conversation whenever they could. Soon the incident had begun to cause deep rifts in the community, prompting anguish for households that had ties to both families. Other community events were disrupted whenever members of the two families or their relatives had to be accommodated. At the time I left Toronto six months later, the wedding, together with its aftermath, was still uppermost in many families' minds. The incident brought home to Prespa families the intersection of two of their major concerns: their ambivalence toward the materialism that has come to command such precedence in their lives, and the loss of community values among their children. The particular lavishness of the wedding simply served to heighten the irony that all families recognize at the core of their own lives: that the way of life they embraced in order to shield their children from poverty and disenfranchisement in Macedonia has ultimately prompted some of those children to repudiate the values that form the basis of their community.

In recent years, a number of painstakingly arranged Prespa marriages have failed. Although families remain reticent about the reasons, the one most commonly cited is the resistance of the bride to the demands of her husband's parents, and particularly their stipulation that she remain at home and immediately raise a family. Some of the young people involved have quickly remarried other Prespare; some have remained divorced. Other young Prespare have put off marrying to hang out with their single friends and are for all practical purposes lost to the community, although some have eventually returned to the flock. The frequency of such incidents suggests, both for community members and for an outsider such as myself, a community that is weathering a crisis: a crisis that is succinctly articulated at wedding celebrations in the clash of opposing visions of family and community that they set forth. No present-day Prespa wedding is thus the unabashedly joyous event that the festivities surrounding it are meant to suggest. As the two host families embark on the long sequence of ritual activities, they are concerned not only that the celebration itself will go smoothly, but also that the primary relationship that it constitutes will endure, and that there will continue to be a community of Presparë.

Changes in Singing

One day I was sitting with a young Prespa woman in the kitchen of her Chicago home while we transcribed the words of a wedding song, as it is sung by the groom's relatives when they take the bride:

Nusja tonë anedanë	Back and forth goes our young bride,
e vogël si protokallë.	little like an orange.
Beu i madh ashu ç'e do	The great *bey* [her father-in-law] likes her
për kafe e për liko,	for the coffee and sweets that she brings,
për të shtruar odat,	for the way she arranges the *odë*,
për të pritur zonjat,	for the way she greets the ladies,
zonjat e mejallës.	the ladies of the neighborhood.[16]

(wedding in Krani, 1980)

Suddenly she exclaimed excitedly, in English, "That's it! That's what it's all about!" And she launched into a diatribe about being a Prespa "bride." "That's what [your father-in-law] wants! You don't care about your husband, you care about what your father-in-law wants!" One thing that was changing in North America, she declared emphatically, is that she could now pay more attention to her husband. This woman has been one of the more rebellious of young Prespa adults, although she still participates actively in community events. But in her reaction to the song, she articulated an understanding that many Presparë must share, however implicitly: that their performances of songs at weddings and other occasions embody and affirm many aspects of the community's "system" that they have otherwise begun to question.

Within the context of North American weddings, which set forth an opposition between the "systems" of Prespa and North America, singing is one of the aspects of the celebration that continues to evoke most forcefully an image of village patriarchy. As one of the principal components of the home portion of a wedding, it is also one of the most effective means through which family members can highlight the "Albanian-ness" of the event. It might be tempting to assume that today's adults sing as they do simply because they are preserving a time-honored tradition in an unquestioning way. But each generation of adults also has its specific reasons for wishing to preserve the singing tradition of its youth in a largely unaltered form.

The oldest of these generations, those individuals who are now grandparents or even great-grandparents, is composed largely of people in their sixties and seventies. These are the true "elders" of the community, who have traditionally been granted precedence by the community's "system" and the singing that embodies it. At weddings that I have attended, such elders have related to polyphonic singing in two quite different ways. Some have relished the opportunity to serve as the ceremonial leader of singing gatherings, to participate actively in the singing at ritual moments, or to dominate the occasion with particularly poignant and emotional performances. Others have readily declined to perform prominently and have left the singing largely to younger adults. One younger man in fact pointed out to me how frequently he had been at gatherings where this had happened:

> The elders used to sing *me radhë*. Now if you tell the elders to sing, they say, "Why doesn't one of you young men 'take' it." Haven't you heard that sometimes? "Well, now, why don't we let the boys sing!" Our *sistem* has changed. (Interview in Toronto, 1986)

On the surface, two such different attitudes toward singing might seem contradictory, but I see them as being motivated by a single point of view. In the past the elders' dominance of the early stages of a gathering was a means of asserting their authority. Now many older men seem resigned to filling a ceremonial role within their family. For them it is most important that the traditional wedding repertoire is performed, but it does not so much matter to them who is singing. If younger adults dominate the occasion, they are nevertheless showing their respect to the community's traditions and thus, by extension, to its most senior members. For those elders who truly enjoy singing, they can still invoke their right to claim center stage. But for those who are not so inclined, they have earned the right to decline to perform if they wish.

The second generation of adults is composed of men and women in their middle years, couples whose children have recently married or are approaching marriageable age. The men of this parental generation are presently the most enthusiastic singers among North American Presparë, for a variety of reasons. The songs in their traditional repertoire extol qualities with which they still identify strongly, particularly those associated with male "honor." As they lift their voices in a heroic song, they portray themselves as staunch defenders of family and community: the "masters" of their household whose actions determine its fate. However much their wives might now contribute to family income, and however much they might at present collaborate with them in decision-making, in the world of song a man's precedence within household and society remains absolute. Men also know that a night of singing offers as its reward the possible attainment of a "peak experience," so long as they show their willingness to submit to the regimen of *radhë* in the evening's earliest stages. In the best of circumstances, communal singing allows them to suspend their everyday, existential concerns through their inducement of a transcendent state.

Men of this generation also have a particular interest in invoking traditional power relations between generations. While they may still have living parents, they are also the parents of children who will soon be agitating for greater autonomy within their households. As active participants in North American society, with years of practical experience in the working world, they are already assured of their own autonomy vis-à-vis their fathers. Their shows of deference toward elders at singing gatherings may therefore be motivated more by a desire to imbue a similar degree of respect in their own children.

For women of this generation, the traditional repertoire presents them with contradictions that men do not have to confront. Women tend to regard their singing as more of a functional activity than do men: another of their many social obligations. Rather than promise them a period of escape from everyday concerns, singing thrusts those concerns to the forefront of their consciousness, reminding them not only of the preciousness of family ties but also of the weight of familial responsibilities. As a result, some younger women have lost an interest in singing and perform in a lackluster manner at community events. Younger women are also constrained in their song performances by the pressure to defer to their mothers-in-law and other female elders, whose authority within their households has not been significantly eroded. If a young woman refuses to sing in a restrained and deferential manner, she risks dishonoring herself and thus her household before the women of the community, and she provides a poor model of feminine demeanor for her daughters or her own young *nuses*. Thus it is that the wives of men who are the most exuberant singers at gatherings often adopt the most subdued and "modest" demeanor as they sing. In most respects, the requirements of the women's song repertoire bring into sharp focus the dilemma that Prespa women share with many other women in North America: their enduring association with domestic responsibilities and their continuing subordinate status, despite their substantial contributions to the success of their families. It is little wonder, then, that a younger woman might balk, as my friend in Chicago did, at song texts that highlight some aspect of that dilemma in especially blatant terms.

At the smallest and most informal of wedding gatherings, however, men and women have in recent years experimented with ways of structuring their song performances that register the sorts of realignments that are taking place between genders and generations. The evening of singing that opens chapter 4 was one such event and illustrates two patterns that I began to notice at some weddings. On that occasion, men and women gathered together in the *odë* of the bride's home and sat on separate sides of the room. The singing, as would be customary, was initiated by the bride's father. But from that moment, men and women of different ages took turns leading the singing, in an order that ranked singers neither by gender nor by age. And at one point, a young woman leading a polyphonic women's wedding song was accompanied on the second vocal line by her husband rather than another woman (CD #20).

For as long as today's adults can remember, there have been a few women who have successfully performed men's songs or have sung in the men's more ornamented, elastic style, such as the younger female elder who sang so movingly at the gathering in chapter 2. There have also been women singers who have sung the supporting second line for a man when a suitable male partner has not been present. This type of pairing has been regarded as an appropriate one, for it is the male singer of the first line who is regarded as "singing" the song, while the woman merely "accompanies" him or "goes behind." So long as a woman has maintained a feminine demeanor and vocal timbre in her performances, her forays into the men's repertoire have been viewed as evidence of an unusual degree of intelligence and musical talent. At the same time, however, it has been embarrassing for a man to associate himself too much with the women's style or repertoire, which is considered much less challenging to perform. Even an accomplished male singer might be criticized if he sings in too "thin" a voice. And if one has never sung publicly in the forceful, *lartër* style, can one fully claim one's precedence as a male?

Now, however, there are some couples in the Prespa community who maintain a small repertoire of songs that they can sing together at more informal occasions. As the couple in Toronto illustrates, the singing configuration in such performances is a new one. In this format it is the woman who "sings" the song while the man "accompanies" her, and the songs that they sing are generally women's songs sung in a sparsely ornamented, *shtruar* style. In short, it is a manner of performance that requires more stylistic concessions on the part of the man than of the woman.

One of the younger men that I knew in Toronto had considered singing in this way with his wife but had eventually rejected the idea. Even the man who did perform at the Toronto gathering threatened afterward not to sing with his wife again. His reason was that it forced him to sing at too high a pitch level and thus to sacrifice the quality of his subsequent performance as the "singer" in a song of his own choosing. Clearly, such performances construct a view of masculinity, and of power relations between men and women, that many men may be unwilling to accept at present. Nevertheless, they may be seen as parallelling several of the innovative features of recent weddings, in that they suggest an image of husband and wife as an autonomous entity and partners in life, without offering a challenge to the man's preeminence in the public sphere.

Perhaps the most important reason that adult Presparë continue to sing as actively as they do is that the discourse that surrounds singing as an activity emphasizes values that they continue to espouse. That discourse recognizes explicitly a link between singing and the fostering of constructive relations between households, and it explicitly outlines the role of singing—especially at ritual moments—in the evocation and expression of deep emotional bonds between family members. In short, singing is for Presparë a way of both affirming and assuring their connections to others. In the face of frequent ruptures in both social networks and familial ties, Presparë feel all the more compelled to cherish and nurture the relationships that remain. Even if their circle of kin and friends is becoming smaller and their hold on their children less secure, it is a far safer strategy for them to revise their expectations of others and to support their reconstituted social worlds, rather than to forsake their ties to others for a life amid strangers.

These are factors that prompt Presparë to participate in wedding singing in any form, but they do not suggest why, for the most part, adult Presparë retain their traditional repertoires and styles of singing.

Here I believe the reason is that aspects such as singing style, vocal quality, and the themes of songs—those aspects that have traditionally differentiated men's and women's singing—have been linked to notions of gender in ways that have not been explicitly formulated through speech. Because of explicit connections made between singing and the moral code, singers recognize that they have a choice in those aspects of their performance, and they are well aware of what is at stake in deviating from the norm. The discourse surrounding singing stipulates, for example, that if a woman refuses to drone, she is making a statement about the "honor" of the "singer"; or that if she refuses to sing at all, she is not sufficiently acknowledging the happiness of the occasion. Most Prespärë, however, continue to regard the distinctions between men's and women's singing as *nga natyra*: as "natural" and self-evident. If no discourse exists that explains these aspects of performance—that points out their constructedness—then individuals do not consider that changing them is an option.

Of all these aspects, it is vocal production and personal demeanor that seem to be regarded most often as *nga natyra*. This is why even the finest of male singers is suspect if he sings too "thinly," and why a woman who sings in the emotional style of men's *lartër* songs nevertheless retains her customary "thin" voice and "modest" demeanor. If a woman were genuinely to sing a song "like a man"—that is, in a "thick" voice, waving clenched fists, and with eyes directed straight at the listener—she would not come across to others as immodest so much as abnormal. This also explains why it is potentially acceptable for a woman and man to perform the two solo lines of a song as a couple. The polyphonic structure of Prespa songs is one of those features for which an explicit discourse exists: one that links it not to gender, but to notions of "honor" and *muabet*. So long as the woman and man each retain an appropriate demeanor and sing with a gender-specific vocal quality, their performance will fulfill the requirements regarding singing that community discourses stipulate.

Changes in the Song Repertoire

The circumstances surrounding wedding singing are changing much more drastically than are performance styles. Because of alterations to the sequence of wedding rituals, there are far fewer moments in a celebration when ritual singing is performed. With the *qeshqek* ceremony omitted and often the henna ceremony as well, men may sing ritual songs only for the bathing and shaving of the groom, and women only for the packing or unpacking of the *rroba*, the bathing of the groom, and the taking of the bride.[17] Home gatherings continue to be held in the evenings, but they may begin later in the week of the wedding, and most are concluded well before midnight so that guests can get up for work the next morning. The bride's family may indeed host a luncheon for the *sinitorë*, which is now often the only lengthy men's gathering of the wedding. Rarely does the groom's family host a similarly lengthy *konak* of the sort described in chapter 6, and only on the night before the taking of the bride. Instead, the exultant men's singing that once marked the climax of a wedding has been transmuted into boisterous rounds of dancing at the banquet hall.

At the same time, other contexts for singing are also disappearing. Since the mid-1980s, a number of families have chosen to hold circumcision celebrations in a banquet hall rather than at their home, although not all families do this. Families might hold *gostis* for visiting relatives, but they host far fewer informal *muabets* in the absence of a specific occasion to celebrate. Amidst a general reduction in home-based celebrations, there is only one new context for singing: *muabets* that some families hold on New Year's Eve.

The more heterogeneous guest list of North American weddings has also affected communal singing, particularly at evening gatherings. Today's occasions often bring together families from many different Prespa villages. Adults from the lower villages grew up in large communities of Albanians, where they were imbued not only with a strong tradition of singing but also with a strong regard for the fostering of *muabet*. For many individuals from upper villages, however, Albanian singing is a fairly recent family tradition, as is the whole discourse surrounding singing that emphasizes the concept of *muabet*. Some upper villages had so few Albanian-speaking families that there was little opportunity for individuals to learn Albanian songs at all.

When wedding gatherings bring together guests from both upper and lower villages, as is increasingly the case, it is often hard for the hosts to maintain the customary singing *me radhë*, since many of those attending do not know how to, or do not wish to, sing. If the gathering is dominated by individuals from the upper villages, they may also not contribute so graciously to the nurturing of *muabet* and may even behave in ways that irritate other guests. In Toronto, tensions arose at a few weddings in the mid-1980s because the hosts were less committed to the practice of singing than were a number of their guests, even to the extent of discouraging guests from initiating a round of songs. Through such processes, the many rifts and points of ideological difference that have been festering between families may be brought into particular focus at singing occasions.

It is hardly surprising that, amidst such changes, fewer older, local songs are being sung. Because there are fewer contexts in which singing occurs, many songs that are less popular are being forgotten:

> Once, not at a wedding . . . it was a gathering. Somebody was over, or [it was] a *gosti*. . . . I couldn't remember any songs, so I asked one woman, "Could you please tell me how this song goes?" So I had to write it down. I sang it real nice, but—I get confused now. 'Cause I haven't sung for a long time now. (Interview in English with a younger woman in Chicago, 1987)

Today many singers get by with knowing just a few all-purpose songs that they can adjust to any point in a celebration.

The state of the Prespa repertoire can be assessed by comparing today's performances at weddings with recordings of about 200 Prespa songs that were made for the Institute of Folklore in Macedonia in the early 1970s. Of these, whole categories of songs are virtually never sung in North America, and perhaps in Prespa also. Men no longer sing polyphonic dance songs, and their formerly large repertoire of ritual wedding songs has shrunk to about five. *Gurbet* songs are sung rarely if at all. Of the songs recorded for the Institute, there are perhaps thirty women's wedding songs and over twenty men's historical songs that I have never heard performed live or on a community recording. Those numbers are ameliorated somewhat by the fact that I have heard quite a few songs that were not recorded by the Institute, but this only indicates that there may be others not recorded that are also not being sung.

At first I theorized that certain wedding songs might fall out of use if they seemed particularly old-fashioned, such as ones with a large number of obsolete Ottoman terms, but this does not appear to be the case. Songs that are still frequently sung often appeal to singers because of a particular turn of phrase or flow of lines, or an especially evocative image, and among these are songs that are unusually archaic in their language or subject matter. Other songs are sung again and again because their texts are short and easy to remember. For all these reasons, one of the marks of a good singer at present is the ability to grace those gathered for a wedding with a longer or more unusual song that has not been recently heard.

To some extent, the shrinking of the older, local repertoire has been countered by the introduction of new songs learned from the media. The use of such songs in traditional performance contexts is, in fact, one of the signs of vitality in current wedding singing. Men, for example, have learned new *këngë të lartëra* which, if anything, are more elaborate than the ones that have been sung in Prespa for several decades. Younger men in particular have also learned a number of love songs sung to simple, *shtruar* melodies. The men have replaced the dance song repertoire that once capped off a long night of singing with humorous songs sung in a similar rapid, metric style. Some of the women's new songs resemble those learnt by the men: rapid and unornamented, often with a long refrain after each verse. In a number of cases, the same songs are being learned by men and women, and these are often the ones that couples sing together.

Most songs popularized through the media are characterized by a less elaborate performance style, one that could be read as indicating a decline in the quality of performances in terms of traditional aesthetics. Fewer singers than in the past are able to distinguish themselves through the elaborateness of their ornamentation, and fewer still extemporize lines of songs or of *bejte*. There are also fewer singers who have either the repertoire or the self-confidence to comfortably sing the second solo line, let alone to execute it in a virtuosic style. By traditional standards, many performances seem pro forma, bereft of the features that would indicate spontaneity and therefore depth of feeling.

But it is possible that such trends have been prompted not so much by lesser musical competency than by a shifting sense of gendered identity on the part of younger singers. Younger adults seem gradually to be moving toward an aesthetic in which lively, rhythmic performances by women are as acceptable as subdued, *shtruar* ones, and in which men may perform lyric love songs with as much confidence as the more bombastic heroic ones. Overall, performances by younger singers, whether men or women, exhibit a tendency toward greater melodic simplicity and metric strictness, as well as an overlap in repertoires between men and women and a convergence in their performance styles. If such tendencies were to continue, it is possible that a reconstituted Prespa singing tradition would emerge that approached a "unisex" repertoire and performance style, in which male/female couples were featured as soloists in addition to all-male or all-female pairs. Were this to happen, then Presparë would no longer be constructing through their singing the image of two innately and profoundly different genders, inhabiting polarized domains of activity and concern, that they have conveyed for so long through their older repertoire.

At present, however, these innovations should be seen as suggesting future possibilities rather than expressing newly consolidated social realities. Just as younger Presparë have drawn on "English" wedding customs, so somewhat older adults have seized on styles of singing propagated through the Albanian media that suggest alternative visions of social order. As with wedding celebrations as a whole, the older song styles and repertoires and the newer media songs dramatically articulate two contrasting expressive poles, and it is somewhere between these poles that a reconsolidated practice of Prespa singing might eventually take shape. Such a development will not, however, depend on the present generation of adults, but rather on those who are now approaching or attaining adulthood. For them, singing has played a far more peripheral role in their socialization to the community.

The Future of Prespa Singing

> Yes, my mother taught us: the words [of songs], where to sit, to work, to make things, to sing. "So that when you marry you will bring honor upon me and not shame me . . . so as to honor others." (Interview with a woman elder in Chicago, 1986)

Prespa children growing up in North America are no longer learning to sing in the ways that their parents did. There are no longer *muabet*s to attend each winter evening with a roomful of people singing *me radhë*, and children are no longer asked to perform the sorts of daily farm chores, such as herding livestock or stringing tobacco, for which singing once provided an ideal accompaniment. The process of learning to sing by listening and then polishing by group practicing and mutual coaching is no longer a possibility. During my stay in Toronto I began to realize that a number of younger children were interested in learning to sing. Many of their parents were waiting for them to try to learn a song before they interceded, however, and so their children did not learn.

There were some exceptions. One mother responded to her eight-year-old daughter's interest by choosing a simple dance song and working with her until she had memorized the words, with all the appropriate *e-os*, *mojs*, and *ajdos* specified. She then painstakingly led her daughter through the melody of the first solo line while she accompanied on the second. The father in another family taught his three young sons the words to several songs *si vjershë* ("as poems"), and then gradually taught each of them one of the two solo lines. For him, singing was part of a broader program of imbuing a strong sense of Albanian identity in his sons. The interest that these parents showed in teaching their children to sing has since paid off. One of those sons is now prominent among younger men who play the *daulle* repertoire at weddings in Toronto, and the young girl—now a young woman—recently sang that same dance song at her brother's wedding. In these families, and some others, children have been given an introduction to Prespa singing that they can draw on in the future if they choose to do so.

Many Prespa parents, however, do not regard polyphonic singing as one of the crucial aspects of their cultural heritage that must be passed on to their children. When I spoke with parents about such things, language was the one aspect of behavior that they emphasized to me. For daughters, it was also important that they learn to roll by hand the filo dough used to make *bakllava* and vegetable pies. A number of parents have chosen instead to teach their children monophonic north Albanian songs, which do not require so much of their attention as instructors. In one instance, a younger couple even complained that their teenage son "drove them crazy" by singing Prespa songs to himself whenever they were in the car. "How will I be able to sing 'in public' if I don't practice?" he countered them.

Once children enter their teens, it becomes harder for them to reconcile their Albanian heritage with the mainstream North American sense of identity that they are anxious to espouse. During these years, parents begin to intercede in their children's social activities, often forcing them to choose between family-centered "Albanian" values and "English" ones centered around an active youth culture. At this point, some young people rebel by moving away from home or hastily eloping. But even for those who choose to remain firmly within the community, they may find that its singing tradition represents a set of values and way of life from which they hope to gradually distance themselves.

Today, many Presparë in their teens and twenties do not know how to sing the local repertoire, or know at most only one or two songs. Those who wish to participate in some sort of expressive activity that is appropriate for community occasions have turned to ones that offer greater room for the accommodation of aspects of North American identity. Several younger men, for example, have taken up the instrumental repertoire of the *daulle* and have become active in the bands that play for weddings and other occasions. Aside from the fact that instrumental music does not require the proficient knowledge of Albanian that is needed for singing, playing in a band has some of the feel for them of playing rock-and-roll, which a few of them do as well. As with most rock bands, the Prespa bands are exclusively the domain of younger men and thus allow them to carve out a musical role at social occasions that is different from that played by their elders. In some instances, a band has indirectly served as a route to singing for younger men, who have been prompted to learn specific Prespa songs to round out their repertoire of dance music. At the banquet hall at a wedding, they perform these songs onstage and to amplification, perhaps joined by a few older men from among the guests. In such a setting, singing is transformed from a participatory activity to a performative genre, and the status that it brings to a performer may provide incentive for other young men to learn to sing as well.

It is far rarer, however, for young women to participate in such bands. Several years ago, the wife of one younger band member in Chicago, a young woman from Kosova, was encouraged by her husband to begin singing songs with his band. At first she sang only north Albanian songs but later began to include southern songs (CD #24), as well as a few Turkish numbers. In Kosova, young women have had careers as professional "folk" singers for some time, and that precedent may have eased the way for this woman's career as a singer. But she explained to me that she endured a few years of gossip from community members before they were willing to accede that singing in public into a microphone, as a soloist, was an acceptable pursuit for a younger woman. Now a second woman in the Chicago area, also married to an instrumentalist but from a Prespa family, sings primarily a southern Albanian repertoire with her husband's band.

The expressive activity that is challenging singing the most at social occasions is line dancing. Whereas few children are being taught to sing, virtually all have either been taught to dance or have learned on their own. The pride that parents once took in seeing a child lead a song at an evening gathering in the bride's or groom's home is now channeled into the moment at the banquet hall when their son or daughter proudly leads the dance line. At a home event, only those guests gathered in the host's *odë* or side room are able to hear a child's song performance or to offer support on the drone. But in the dance hall, all wedding guests in both the bride's and the groom's party can watch a child's dancing, and relatives and friends can dance at the front of the line, just behind the child, to underscore their support of his or her performance.

Whereas few younger women have shown an interest in singing, most are exuberant participants in line dances. Through the dances they request, they can project images of themselves that vie with the demure, self-effacing pose of traditional women's singing. Two of the favorite dances of younger women during my stay in Toronto were *shota* and *çoçek*. The first is the Prespa version of the most popular dance from Kosova, danced there most often by a woman and a man. Prespare usually dance it in a line from which the first two dancers—often two women—break off and dance facing each other. The second is a slower line dance in Ottoman style, danced to a sultry Turkish clarinet improvisation. In both dances, younger women may wave their arms and move their shoulders flirtatiously, or twirl the kerchief that the line's leader holds in a sinuous "Oriental" manner. In so doing, they may suggest a more sensual type of femininity than would ever be permissible in a song performance.

Prespa singing as practiced by preceding generations depended on a division of musical labor, in which each participant in a social occasion contributed actively as a singer. It is highly unlikely that singing of this sort will continue among overseas families, even if a certain number of younger Prespare become interested in the traditional repertoire as performed in home contexts. But as members of the younger generation become more involved in familial concerns and the lives of their growing children, the community's singing may yet present itself to them as a means of instilling a sense of heritage, of community solidarity, and of aesthetic challenge and satisfaction.

Emergent Subjectivities

The preceding two chapters outline the central role of ritual and musical practices in constructing the "system" that Prespa families lived within as they began to emigrate to North America somewhat over two decades ago. Currently in North America, Prespa families are confronting an alternative "system" composed of myriad, often contradictory discourses and practices. Some of the practices that they are choosing to incorporate into community events, such as elements of the standard Euro-American wedding ritual and the repertoire of pop songs that is often associated with it, are structured in accord with older, patriarchal assumptions about social relations. More often, they encounter practices that articulate and embody aspects of an unfolding North American modernity, typified by a leveling of gender and generational hierarchies, a loosening of kinship ties beyond the household unit, and a decline in the capacity of religion to outline moral behavior.

To a great extent these changes have been propelled within North

America by its central participation in the expansion of a world market economy: the same phenomenon that initially compelled Prespa families to leave their villages and to emigrate. Within this system, younger generations are empowered through the market niches that they represent, economic ties often replace those founded on kinship or mutual "honor," and economic pragmatism often overrides community-based religious or moral codes. In response, members of the Prespa community find themselves experiencing the same contradictory mixture of confusion, malaise, and exhilaration as other North American families, including my own, whose negotiations with received notions of family, community, and society have produced the "system" that Presparë have confronted as they have arrived from overseas.

Daily life for Presparë represents a continual encounter with and accommodation to this new set of life circumstances, as members of different genders, generations, and households negotiate the new terms within which their lives will be led. It is this ongoing process of accommodation that dominates the discussions that family members have among themselves, or with other families at social events, as individuals frame their senses of self and of community, and their place in a new economic order, in discourses that they are gradually adopting from the larger North American society. But much of this process is also being carried out nonverbally, as individuals and families experiment within the realm of cultural forms by altering such practices as ritual sequences, music and dance repertoires, food, dress, and household decor. Through such processes, Presparë are taking on new forms of subjectivity implicitly, as "habitus," often without conscious recognition of the assumptions that those practices were developed to embody.

Through such intricate negotiations, Prespa families seem to me to be arriving at a new sense of social order within which there is considerable consensus, at least among adult generations. It is one that involves being "modern" without fully being "North American" and that fosters an ethos in which family life within the Prespa community is central, while involvement with the larger North American society is tolerated as a necessary nuisance. Within such a schema, women may come to feel that they occupy the more favored position, shielded from the most threatening aspects of contemporary family relations among anglezë. While older adults are now willing to relax somewhat the strict hierarchies that were formerly maintained regarding both age and gender, younger adults are also willing to maintain those hierarchies to some degree for the sake of household and community cohesion. In this respect, Prespa families have achieved remarkable success up to this point: young people are marrying largely within the community and are agreeing to uphold its slowly changing "system" to a great degree. And they continue to participate in cultural forms that play a central role in the ongoing formulation of this altered "system," whether by exploring new song repertoires and styles of singing or by dancing avidly to the new electric bands.

In Yugoslavia in the early 1980s, a number of young Presparë involved in amateur folklore groups in Skopje and Prishtinë adopted their polyphonic song repertoire as a primary emblem of community identity: a feature of their folklore that proclaimed their Albanian heritage while distinguishing them from the majority north Albanian population. To do so, they selected as their performance vehicles song texts and styles of singing that were representative of their community but which also affirmed their emerging sense of themselves as worldly, well-educated Yugoslavs. If the Prespa song repertoire continues in any form in North America, it will be because the younger generation continues to restructure it and, in a sense, to reinvent it as a performative activity. Perhaps they will take their cue from the sorts of developments initiated by adults somewhat their seniors and will perform as couples or emphasize the energetic, melodically straightforward style of many media songs. Perhaps they will sing to the accompaniment of an instrumental ensemble or combine singing with dancing, as is common for folkloric performances by immigrant communities from elsewhere in southeast Europe.[18] Perhaps they will choose instead to emphasize current hits from the north Albanian repertoire, clearly the most potent symbol of Albanian ethnicity among families from the former Yugoslavia. As they do so, they will simultaneously be taking on new forms of subjectivity: as men and women, as adults, as Albanians, as North Americans. If any of these strategies should be adopted, then the plea that I heard one young wedding instrumentalist utter will not go unheeded. "It's our tradition!" he called out to his fellow band members when they balked at a full day of playing. "Let it live!"

allo (Tk. *hala*, Arab. *khāla*)   A female paternal relative of one's father's generation; an "aunt" or "father's female first cousin"

anglezë   Lit., "English people"; a term used by Prespare in North America to
refer to Euro-Americans

bakllava (Arab. *bāqlawā*)   A pastry made from layers of filo pastry filled with
chopped nuts and soaked in honey or sugar water

bej (Tk. *bey*)   An Ottoman honorific title, used in the past by Prespa women to
address men of the community; also used in the Ottoman period to
refer to a local feudal lord

bejlerë (from pl. of Tk. *bey*)   The former feudal lords of Prespa and their
descendants

Bektashi (Tk. Bektaşi)   A Sufi order with connections to Shiʿa Islam, of which
the descendants of the Prespa overlords are members

besë   Lit. "credo," in the sense of religious belief; in its broadest sense, the
shared discourses and practices that define the Prespa community

bejte (Tk. *beyit* or *beyt*, from Arab. *bayt*, a line of verse or a rhymed couplet)   A
type of short, extemporized couplet, generally with a teasing theme,
that may be added by singers to the end of a song; pairs of singers
might also exchange such couplets in a sort of contest

beqar (Tk. *bekâr*, from Pers. *bīkār*, "idle, unemployed")   An unmarried man, a
bachelor

boçe (Tk. *bohça*)   A square of white fabric used to wrap gifts that are exchanged
by central figures in a wedding

dai (Tk. *dayı*)   A male maternal relative of one's father's generation, an "uncle"
or "mother's male first cousin"

daicë   The wife of one's *dai*

daillarë (pl. of *dai*)   All the men of one's mother's lineage

dasmë   Wedding; may refer to the entire celebration or, more narrowly, to the
day that the bride is taken

daulle (from Tk. *davul,* "drum")   Rom musicians who sing and play instrumental music for Albanian weddings in Prespa; or their Albanian counterparts in North America

fuqi   Male strength/potency/virility

Geg   (1) term for the dialects spoken in northern Albania and contiguous areas; (2) an Albanian from a Geg-speaking area

gosti   An evening gathering hosted by a Prespa household to honor visiting relatives

gurbet (Tk.)   The practice of venturing abroad in search of work

kaba (Tk.)   A type of solo, nonmetric instrumental improvisation, played most often on the clarinet; see also *me të qarë*

këngë   A song

këngë me të rënkuar   "Songs with droning"; songs in the local polyphonic style of Prespa

këngë të lartër (pl. *këngë të lartëra*)   A specific type of men's nonmetric song with a large range, sung in a loud, high-pitched style with much ornamentation (see *lartër*)

këngë të shtruar (pl. *këngë të shtruara*)   A specific type of men's metric song with a small range, sung more softly and with minimal ornamentation (see *shtruar*)

kokolinkë   A mixture of roasted chickpeas and candies that is distributed to wedding guests by the groom's family; it is then sent to the bride's home, where it is distributed among guests on her side of the wedding; also known as *pemë* ("fruit")

Kolonjarë   Lit. "people from Kolonjë," a region in southern Albania; term for the descendants of the former feudal lords of Prespa, whose families believe that their ancestors moved to Prespa from Kolonjë

konak (from Tk. "residence," "mansion")   An all-night gathering hosted by a relative of the groom for male guests of his wedding party; in Prespa, *konak*s have customarily been held both the night before and the night after the taking of the bride

krushq   The men of the groom's lineage who form the core of the group that takes the bride on the day of the wedding

kryetar (from *kryes,* "head")   The ceremonial host of a men's gathering, usually the oldest male member of the host household or another senior relative; if this man is an elder, he may be referred to as the *kryeplak,* lit. "head elder"

lartër (lit. "high" /"loud")   (1) term used by women for a relatively loud and
high-pitched, rapid, and sparsely ornamented style of singing;
(2) term used by men for a loud, high-pitched, nonmetric, and highly
ornamented style of singing

lulkë (lit. "little flower")   A face decoration made of sequins and /or glitter that
is worn by the bride

llokum(e) (Tk. *lokum*)   A type of gelatinous, nut-filled candy rolled in powdered sugar, "Turkish delight"

me gjith zëmbër (lit. "with all one's heart")   Phrase used to describe a seemingly
heartfelt song performance, characterized by features such as dense
ornamentation, changes in vocal register, relaxed realization of the
meter, and verbal or melodic elaboration of the basic song

me dy kolla (lit. "in two circles")   The practice of singing in two alternating
groups

me radhë (lit. "with order")   To carry out an activity in an ordered way (see
radhë)

me të qarë (lit. "with crying")   (1) a men's vocal technique involving any type of
shift in vocal register, including yodeling and lapses into falsetto; (2) a
type of nonmetric, solo instrumental improvisation (see *kaba*); both
usages are meant to imply an allusion to women's funeral lamenting
and thus refer to styles of performance intended to evoke a sense of
longing and melancholy

melodi   The underlying tonal structure of a song

mevlyd (Tk. *mevlûd;* from Arab. *mawlid,* "birth")   (1) the Mevlûd is an Ottoman
poem describing the birth of Muhammad, written by Süleyman Çe-
lebi; (2) a *mevlyd* is a ceremony hosted by a family in their home at
which the Mevlûd is recited

mënçëm, i (masc.; fem. *e mënçme;* lit. "mindful")   Properly socialized to the
Prespa community's moral code (see *mënd*)

mënd (lit. "mind")   A state of behaving in a way conforming to the Prespa
community's moral code; cf. Arab. *'aql,* Tk. *akıl,* S. Slav. *um* or *pamet*

meze (Tk.; from Arab. *maza*)   The array of appetizers that may be served at a
Prespa social occasion

muabet (Tk. *muhabbet,* from Arab. *maḥabbah,* "affection")   (1) an atmosphere of
openness and intimacy that members of the Prespa community seek
to evoke at their social gatherings; (2) an informal, family-hosted gathering not held in connection with a particular celebration, at which

the attainment of *muabet* is a major goal for those attending; (3) any kind of good-natured interchange, such as friendly conversation, singing, dancing, or playing an instrument, that might induce *muabet* among those at a social gathering

nder "Honor"; the regard or esteem in which a person or household is held by community members; cf. similar terms among other Mediterranean communities, such as Arab. *sharaf*, Tk. *şeref* and *namus*, Gk. *timi* and *filotimo*, S. Slav. *čast* or *čest*

njeri (1) a person; (2) a person whose behavior conforms to the moral ideals of the Prespa community

nuse (1) a bride; (2) any young woman in the years between her marriage and that of her first child; (3) term of address for any such young woman by her husband's relatives

odë (Tk. *oda*)   The formal reception room in a Prespa home where guests, particularly men, gather to socialize

oxha (Tk. *hoca*, from Pers. *hage*)   A Muslim religious teacher

plak (masc.; fem. *plakë*)   "Elder," an adult of whom at least the oldest child is married

Prespar (masc.; fem. Presparkë, pl. Presparë)   A person from Prespa

qejf (Tk. *keyif*, from Arab. *kayf*)   A state of heightened emotion or elation (cf. Mac. *kef*, Gk. *kefi*); a person in this state is said to be *qejfli*

qeshqek (Tk. *keşkek*, from Pers. *kešk*)   (1) a boiled dish made with crushed wheat berries and meat, served at the groom's home on the final night of a Prespa village wedding; (2) the ceremony held at the groom's home three days before the taking of the bride, at which the wheat berries are crushed by men of the groom's family

radhë (lit. "order")   (1) the order in space and/or time in which some activity is executed; (2) more generally, the full range of codified practices that characterize Prespa social life

raki (Tk. *rakı*; from Arab. *araq*)   A type of homemade liquor distilled from fruit; in North America, may refer to any type of hard liquor such as whiskey

Ramazan (Arab. *Ramaḍān*)   The ninth month of the Muslim lunar calendar, during which a fast is observed each day from sunrise to sunset

rroba   The gifts of clothing and related items (shoes, accessories, toiletry items) given to the bride by the groom and taken to her by the *sinitorë*

shtruar   (1) a calm, reserved manner of behaving; (2) a style of singing characterized by a moderate pace, a relatively soft vocal quality, moderate to extensive ornamentation, and a relaxed sense of meter; men's *shtruar* singing is often slower and less metric than women's

sinitorë   A group composed of an odd number of adult male relatives of the groom who take the *rroba* to the bride, generally a day or a week before she is taken

soj (Tk. *soy*)   One's kin, whether paternal or maternal

tel (Tk.)   Long strands of silver wire that are worn by the bride on either side of her face

Tosk   (1) term for the dialects spoken in southern Albania and contiguous areas; (2) an Albanian from a Tosk-speaking area; (3) (adj.) a descriptive term for a style of polyphony sung in all Tosk-speaking areas but south central Albania (Labëria)

turp   (1) shame or dishonor; (2) embarrassment or self-consciousness; (3) for women, modesty or propriety; cf. similar terms among other Mediterranean communities such as Arab. *'ayb, ḥishmah,* or *iḥtisham;* Tk. *ayıp;* Gk. *dropi;* S. Slav. *sram*

valle e nuses   The "bride's dance"; a line dance performed after the bride is taken, in which members of the groom's wedding party take turns leading the bride; cf. Mac. *nevestinsko oro*

xhaxha (probably from Slav. *djadja*)   A male paternal relative of one's father's generation, an "uncle" or "father's male first cousin"

xhaxhallarë (pl. of *xhaxha*)   All the men of one's father's lineage

xhaxhicë   The wife of one's *xhaxha*

zoti i shtëpisë   Lit. the "master of the house"; the male head of a multi-generational household, generally the oldest male

NOTES

Chapter One: Approaching Prespa Singing

1. Macedonia declared its independence from Yugoslavia in November 1991.

2. Most Albanian scholars assert that Albanians are the descendants of the ancient Illyrians, but other theories have been advanced as well (see for example Georgiev 1972).

3. Throughout this study, place-names have been given as they are spelled and pronounced in Macedonian, only because this is how they appear on virtually all maps of the region. Names of settlements having an Albanian population, together with their name as rendered in Albanian, are as follows: Resen (Resnjë), Sopotsko (Sopockë), Kozjak (Kozjak), Gorna Bela Crkva (Bollacërkë e Sipërme), Dolna Bela Crkva (Bollacërkë e Poshtme), Grnčari (Gërnçar), Asamati (Asamat), Krani (Kranjë), Arvati (Arvat), and Nakolec (Nakolec).

4. This is the terminology used in Kŭnčov 1891 and Trajčev 1923. Kŭnčov 1990 includes Grnčari within lower Prespa.

5. This impression on my part was confirmed in interviews with Rom musicians who perform regularly for weddings in all the Prespa villages.

6. Other early writings on north Albanians include Lane 1923, Coon 1950, and Hasluck 1954. Although there are no formal ethnographies of south Albanians, two books deserve mention. Zaimi 1937 is an account by the daughter of a prominent Muslim urban family of her childhood in southwest Albania. And the Federal Writers' Project of Massachusetts prepared a handbook on the Albanian community of Boston (1939) that provides much valuable information about family and community life, as well as about Albanian political history.

7. See, for example, Peristiany 1965; Erlich 1966; Hammel 1967; Simić 1969; Schneider 1971; Michaelson and Goldschmidt 1971; Denich 1974; W. Lockwood 1975; Meeker 1976; Bourdieu 1977, 1979; Herzfeld 1980, 1985; Eickelman 1981; Sciama 1981; Abu-Lughod 1985, 1986; Dubisch 1986; Gilmore 1982, 1987. Major works that have appeared since that time include Cowan 1990, Delaney 1991, and Abu-Lughod 1993.

8. Marshall 1982 is a notable exception, although I do not agree with his conclusions.

9. One of the best ethnographic essays to explore this state of affairs is Schieffelin 1985.

10. To cite only one instance, Buchanan 1991 and Rice 1994 both analyze changes in the performance of various types of Bulgarian village music following

the introduction of a socialist government in 1944, and the controversies that such policies unleashed.

11. See, for example, Wallis and Malm 1984, Turino 1993.

12. My characterization of Foucault's position relies primarily on his later works, in particular the *History of sexuality*, vol. 1 (1980). For a discussion of shifts in his use of the term "discourse," see Dreyfus and Rabinow 1983. Abu-Lughod and Lutz 1990 provide a lucid exposition of how Foucault's notion of discourse contrasts with more standard linguistic and anthropological usages of the term. A particularly probing discussion of Foucault's writings as they might be accommodated to a hermeneutic perspective may be found in Tomlinson 1993.

13. For an excellent application of the notion of "multiple discourses" to the analysis of one community's social practices, see Tapper and Tapper 1986.

14. For folklore see particularly Bauman and Sherzer 1974 and Bauman 1977; reviews of this literature include Limón and Young 1986 and Bauman and Briggs 1990. Anthropological analyses of performance events include Geertz 1973c, Kapferer 1979, Karp 1980, Kligman 1984 and 1988, Brenneis 1985, Caraveli 1985, Schieffelin 1985, Sugarman 1988, and Stewart 1989. Bourdieu's emphasis on practice resonates with a body of anthropological literature that has examined the effects on participants of formalized behavior and the structure of ritual itself; see Geertz 1973b, Bloch 1974, Moore and Myerhoff 1977, Cohen 1979, Irvine 1979, Rappaport 1979 and 1980, Jennings 1982, and Kapferer 1986. Nketia's article on the importance of the performance context to musical meaning (1962) presages many of my own concerns in the present study.

15. See, for example, many but certainly not all of the articles in the major ethnomusicological anthologies to date: Koskoff 1987, Keeling 1989, and Herndon and Ziegler 1990. Koskoff 1991 and Sarkissian 1992 provide overviews and assessments of much of this scholarship.

16. Rubin, in fact, points out the limitations of the notion of a "sex/gender system" and includes considerations of kinship and the division of labor in her analysis. See also Collier and Yanagisako 1987 on the interrelationship between gender and kinship.

17. Koskoff's recent critique (1993) of much anthropological work on gender may be read in part as a criticism of the propensity of researchers to focus on a community's explicit "gender ideology" to the exclusion of other considerations.

18. For recent studies that touch on these issues see Robertson 1989 and 1991, Oldenburg 1990, and Rowson 1991. Brett et al. 1993 and Koestenbaum 1993 explore musical activities of "homosexuals" in the West as composers, performers, and audience members.

19. In anthropology, see for example Abu-Lughod 1986 and 1990 on Egyptian Bedouin poetry, Boddy 1989 on *zār* in the Sudan, Cowan 1990 on Greek Macedonian dance, and Novack 1990 on American "contact improvisation." The practices analyzed by Cowan in her exemplary study provide striking parallels, as well as a few notable contrasts, to those presented here. Gender issues have recently become a major focus of interdisciplinary work in musicology as well;

representative examples include McClary's anthology of articles (1991) and her handbook on *Carmen* (1992), and the volumes *Musicology and difference* (Solie 1993) and *Cecilia reclaimed* (Cook and Tsou 1994). Solie's introduction to *Musicology and difference* is helpful in tracing the turn in feminist musicology toward critical approaches.

Scholars from the tradition of British cultural studies have long considered such questions with regard to popular music; see particularly Frith and Mc-Robbie 1978 and the response by Taylor and Laing (1979); as well as recent work by Bradby (1993). A range of approaches to questions of social reproduction and resistance in popular music can be seen in the literature on Madonna (such as the articles assembled in Schwichtenberg 1991). Denski and Sholle 1992 and Walser 1993:108–36 provide welcome explorations of constructions of masculinity, specifically in heavy metal; while Rose 1994:146–85 provides an excellent discussion of "sexual politics" in rap.

20. For critiques of ethnography, see for example Said 1987 and Clifford 1988. Ong (1988), Trinh (1989), Mohanty (1991), and others have specifically addressed the question of representation with regard to accounts of non-Western women.

21. Turino (1993:279) proposes that ethnographers conduct a "neighbors test": "Would I feel comfortable describing myself and my own neighbors in the same terms I use for discussing Peruvians or the people in other societies?" See also Rosaldo 1989:46–54. At its best, the type of approach that I envision should be capable of offering an equally satisfying interpretation of one's own life.

Chapter Two: Singing as a Social Activity

1. The word *bey*, which occurs frequently in women's songs, is an Ottoman honorific title applied to males.

2. To illustrate this point, one man recounted to me that, in the days before massive emigration, families in his village would perform farm chores during the day, and then the men would gather at dusk at the threshing floor to discuss work-related issues, such as which fields would be irrigated the next day or who would guard the livestock against wild animals during that night. Any such concerns were then deliberately excluded as topics of conversation during evening gatherings, when preference was given to singing or other more sociable activities.

3. This is a continuation of the song sung by the outgoing blond woman at the gathering held before Asan's wedding (ex. 2.4).

4. This is in contrast to most Christian communities in the Balkans, where a deceased person may be lamented for three years or more. For writings on funeral lamenting see particularly Kligman 1984 and 1988 for Romania; Alexiou 1974, Auerbach 1987, Caraveli 1980 and 1986, Danforth 1982, and Seremetakis 1990 and 1991 for Greece; Kacarova 1969 and D. Kaufman 1981 for Bulgaria; Sachs 1979 for Macedonia; Vukanović 1965, Gojçaj 1973, Ahmeti 1983, and Fetiu 1983 for north Albanians in the former Yugoslavia; Mehmeti 1978 for northern

Albania; Stockmann 1966, Mitrushi 1974, and Shituni 1982 for southern Albania; and Racy 1986 for Lebanon.

5. The "Lab" style, characterized by a largely homophonic, three- or four-part texture, is found in portions of the districts of Vlorë, Fier, Tepelenë, Përmet, Gjirokastër, and Sarandë (see Kruta 1980; Shituni 1989). Examples of both Tosk and Lab styles may be heard on Lortat-Jacob 1988; there is also an excellent example of Çam men's singing on Cellier 1995. For descriptions of specific south Albanian singing styles, see Kruta 1968 on the Myzeqe region and 1973 on the district of Skrapar; Stockmann, Fiedler, and Stockmann 1965 on Çamëri; Shituni 1989 on Labëri; and Stockmann and Stockmann 1964 for an overview of both Tosk and Lab styles. Sokoli 1965, Lloyd 1968, Stockmann and Stockmann 1980, and Sugarman (in press) provide general discussions of music from all parts of Albania; and Lloyd 1966 provides an exemplary selection of recordings of both northern and southern Albanian music.

Neither of the polyphonic textures characteristic of south Albanian singing is unique to Albanians. The Lab style is shared with Greeks in the northwestern district of Epirus (see Samiou and Fakinos 1984), while the Tosk style is common among Aromân communities from the Kolonjë region of Albania, the so-called Fărşeroţii (see Lortat-Jacob and Bouët 1983), and among Slavs from the Kastoria district of northern Greece (see N. Kaufman 1959). Macedonians in the lower villages of the Prespa district also formerly sang in this style. Pentatonic, drone-based polyphonic singing is thus a practice common to all the rural, pre-Ottoman linguistic groups living within and adjacent to southern Albania. As is true for many world areas, musical styles may be specific more to geographic regions than to individual ethnic groups.

6. This usage in many ways parallels that of the South Slavic word *glas* (see Vasiljević 1964).

7. The verb *këndoj* evidently derives from the Latin *cantare* ("to sing"; see Huld 1984:80). In its range of meanings, however, it more closely resembles both Persian *khandan* and Ottoman *okumak* ("to read, recite, sing"; Martin Schwartz and Walter Feldman, personal communication). It is possible that the Albanian word gradually took on the more extensive meaning of its Ottoman counterpart as Albanians participated more in Ottoman urban society. If this is so, then it may have displaced older terms for the first solo line among Muslim south Albanians in both Prespa and the Korçë region.

8. For example, *vodi* and *prati* ("leads" and "accompanies") among Croats (Dubinskas 1983:239) and Serbs (R. Petrović 1972:334), *prednjak* and *zadnjak* ("person going before" and "person going behind") among Serbs (ibid. 335), and *vodi* and *sledi* ("leads" and "follows") among Bulgarians (N. Kaufman 1968: 16–17). A striking counterpart from outside the Balkans is the polyphonic yodeling or *jüüzli* from the Muotatal region of Switzerland, in which the three vocal lines enter in succession as they do in Prespa singing. Singers refer to the first melodic line as *vorjuuzä* ("to yodel in front" or "lead the yodel"). The second line is referred to as *abnää* ("to take something from someone"; cf. Alb. *merr*), as *sekundierä* ("to second"), or, if crossing to go above the first line, as *überjuuzä* ("to yodel above"; see Zemp 1990).

9. The word *iso* is clearly related to the Byzantine word *ison,* which refers to the drone in Greek Orthodox liturgical singing.

10. I conducted research among families from this area in Skopje between 1979 and 1982; see also N. Kaufman 1959. My comments are by no means intended to imply either that Prespare are Slavs or that Kosturčani are Albanians, but rather to suggest that a convergence of terminology has come about in the Balkans between different linguistic groups.

11. Cf. the South Slavic term *prati* for the second line of polyphony; see note 8.

Chapter Three: Singing as a Gendered Activity

1. A *boçe* (Tk. *bohça*) is a square of white cloth, often decorated with lace and/or embroidery, that is wrapped around the various gifts that are exchanged between relatives during the course of a wedding.

2. A *temena* (Tk. *temenna;* from Arab. *tamannī*) is an elaborate gesture of the arms and hands performed by north Albanian brides in Kosova and elsewhere, deriving from Muslim forms of greeting. Reineck 1991:94–96 discusses the *temena* specifically; her study as a whole details issues of the status of women in north Albanian households in the district of Opojë in Kosova.

3. The word *bir,* which most commonly means "son," is often used by Prespare for children of either sex.

4. *Llokume* (Tk. *lokum*), known in English as "Turkish delight," is a type of gelatinous, nut-filled candy that has been rolled in powdered sugar.

5. A. Petrović 1990 provides a valuable discussion of the loud, resonant singing of Bosnian Slavic women and its relationship to notions of gender.

6. One woman commented to me that such ornamented singing "sounds like an instrument," and that it *ka muzikë,* ("has music," the word *muzikë* being generally reserved for instrumental music played by professionals). Certainly women ornament their songs in a manner similar to that of the Rom clarinet players in Prespa and perhaps were influenced by the instrumental tradition. When compared with women's singing in other southern districts, even in the Bitola district just to the east, the singing of Prespa women is unusually florid.

7. Such ornaments are sometimes referred to as "glottal stops," although the glottis is not fully closed in their execution. M. Caton (1974) provides an excellent discussion of this technique as it is used in Iranian singing. In her description, as a singer vocalizes in chest register, he or she lifts the back of the tongue slightly, at the same time sending a small puff of air past the vocal cords. The shift in tongue position causes a reconfiguration and tightening of the vocal cords, so that they momentarily vibrate in head register, producing a pitch somewhat higher than that of the melody line. Once the tongue is dropped, the vocalization continues in chest register. The effect is similar to that produced by bagpipe players, who often articulate between two notes by momentarily fingering a higher pitch; or by string players who perform rapid "hammering" on the neck of their instrument.

8. Although she writes about Javanese singing, Poedjosoedarmo (1988) offers an excellent discussion of the mechanics of a type of vocal production that is, from my experience as a singer, characteristic of much Balkan singing as well. It should be noted that one highly regarded Prespa male singer, the "singer" in CD #13, sings in an unusually nasal manner.

9. *Bukëvale* is a dish made of squares of bread that are soaked in melted butter and then baked in the oven.

10. For the original poem see Frashëri 1978:145. Haxhihasani (1971) has written about the close relationship between Frashëri's poetry and southern Albanian village songs.

11. Men have occasionally alluded to the word *mekam* when speaking of a man who sings in this highly ornamented way. *Mekami e bën këngën* ("He does the song in the manner of *mekam*") was one man's remark, and another commented, *Ay këndon me mekam* ("He sings with *mekam*"). This is no doubt a reference to Ottoman classical music, which is based on a system of melodic modes called *makam*s (see Signell 1977). Such comments are reminiscent of the woman's remark discussed in note 6. Together they suggest that the highly melismatic ornamentation of Prespa singers has been modeled on Ottoman urban music as introduced into southern Albania by Rom instrumentalists.

12. At a talk given in Prishtinë in 1981, Beniamin Kruta played an example of a southern women's *gurbet* song in which the second soloist began her line with a note in falsetto and then sang a long sequence of turns around one note. He later explained to me that these techniques were intended to depict weeping, because of the sad nature of the text. Although Prespa women do not speak of their singing in this way, the glottal ornaments that they insert in their songs, particularly at cadential points, may be seen as a practice parallel to that of the men's more dramatic register changes. For information on Tosk laments and their relation to men's polyphonic singing, see Sugarman (in press).

13. In speech both genders may exclaim *o-bo-bo!* whereas women are more likely to use *o-i!* Although these sounds are more exclusive to south Albanians, words such as *aman* and *lele* pepper the speech of most ethnic groups in Turkey and the Balkans.

14. I have found it interesting that heroic characters in Albanian historical films often speak in particularly rich baritone voices. A good example is the character of Bajo Topulli in the film *Liri a Vdekje* ("Liberty or Death"), which chronicles the exploits of a guerrilla unit that fought against Ottoman rule at the turn of the century.

15. Sokoli (1965:128–29) has written that singers in southern districts in Albania often distinguish between men's songs sung in a style *pleqërishte* ("of the older men") and those sung in a style *djemurishte* ("of the younger men"). The first are sung *"shtruar"* while the second are performed in a more "lively" and *"naltë"* (a variant of the word *lartër*) manner. These clearly correspond to the associations that Presparë hold for men's *shtruar* and *lartër* songs, although Prespa songs are never spoken of as exclusively the domain of a particular generation of singers.

16. Lloyd 1966 features performances of men's singing from both the My-zeqe (B2 and B6) and Korçë (B8) regions. See also Kruta 1968 on men's singing from Myzeqe.

17. The word *bejte* derives from the Arabic *bayt,* meaning a line of poetry or, more specifically, a rhymed couplet. For related traditions of recited or sung extemporized couplets see Dubinskas 1984 for Croatia, Y. Lockwood 1983 for Bosnia, Herzfeld 1981 and Caraveli 1985 for Greece, Kligman 1984 and 1988 for Romania, Herndon and McLeod 1980 for Malta, Haydar 1989 for Lebanon, Abu-Lughod 1985 and 1986 for Egypt. Compared to most of these traditions, Prespa *bejte,* at least as currently performed, are less often extemporized.

Chapter Four: The "Order" of Weddings

1. In this and subsequent seating diagrams, I have indicated myself as JS and my former husband as EF.

2. The use of wedding imagery to speak of death is common in southeast European heroic songs of the late Ottoman period. Most often the hero "marries" the land that he has fought to free (i.e., is buried in its soil).

3. Rheubottom 1976 provides an excellent analysis of four types of saint's day celebrations (*slavas*) in one region of Macedonia. See also Rice 1980b for an account of a "church *slava*," in Rheubottom's terminology, in the Skopje district.

4. Dojaka 1978 provides a thorough account of wedding customs in various parts of Albania. Durham 1928:197–202 describes a wedding in the town of Shkodër, Memija 1962 details wedding customs in the district of Malësia e Gja-kovës in northern Albania, Çaushi 1974 describes weddings in the town of El-basan, and Reineck 1986 and 1991 discuss weddings in the Opojë district of Ko-sova. Other descriptions of Balkan weddings may be found in Dunin 1971, on Macedonian Roma; Vasileva 1969, comparing Slavic and Turkish weddings in eastern Bulgaria; Koleva 1961 on the contemporary Bulgarian wedding; Genčev, Vasileva, and Stojkova 1985:171–92 on wedding customs throughout Bulgaria; Rice 1994:152–62 on weddings in eastern Bulgaria; Cowan 1990:89–133 on weddings in the Thessaloniki region of Greece; and Delaney 1991:99–146 on marriage and weddings in a Turkish village. A number of articles on weddings in Balkan countries appear in the journal *Makedonski Folklor,* 5 (9–10) (1972).

5. She may also be said to *niset si nuse,* "adorn herself as a bride"; hence the subtitle of the first section of this chapter.

6. For descriptions of such events in widely divergent areas and historical periods, see Caraveli 1985 for contemporary Greece, Andrews 1985 for Ottoman Turkey, Birge 1937 for Bektashi Sufi services, Sawa 1989 for medieval gather-ings in the 'Abbasid court in Baghdad, Varzi 1988 for pre-Revolution Iran, and Qureshi 1986 and 1987 for Sufi gatherings in Pakistan. Racy 1991 discusses the notion of *ṭarab* with respect to modern Arab musical performances. In Sugarman 1988 I provide an analysis of the longest of Prespa men's singing events, whether held in conjunction with weddings or with other celebrations such as circumci-sions and betrothals.

7. See, for example, Sawa 1989, Andrews 1985, and Birge 1937.

8. The roles of the *kryetar* and *sak* at Prespa men's events may also be compared to those of the *Baba* (leader of the dervish order) and the *saki* (cup-bearer) in Bektashi worship services (Birge 1937:198–99). For general information on Bektashism among Albanians, see also Norris 1993 and Trix 1993.

9. Leibman 1974 and Vuylsteke 1981 both include performances by Prespa *daulle*. The Leibman disc features one *kaba*, four dance melodies, and a polyphonic song, *Dardhë rrumbullake*. The Vuylsteke includes one song (*O bilbil*) and one dance played by an unusual combination of two clarinets, violin, trombone, accordion, *dzhumbush* (banjo-like plucked lute), *def* (large frame drum), and *tarabuka* (goblet drum).

10. Macedonians speak of the "three coffees" served at a social occasion, all designated with Turkish names. The first, *bujrum kafe* (Tk. *buyurun*; "Welcome! Make yourself at home!" coffee), is served when guests first arrive; the second, *muabet kafe* (Tk. *muhabbet*; "friendly conversation" coffee), is brought out once a pleasant interchange is underway. The last, *sikter kafe* (Tk. *siktir*; "Get lost!" lit. "Go get fucked!" coffee), signals that the event is over and that guests should leave. Notably, these designations are not presently used in Turkey. At Prespa wedding gatherings, coffee is served only at the end, but it bears the same message that *sikter kafe* does among Macedonians.

Chapter Five: The Prespa "System"

1. American linguist Eric Hamp suggests that the word "Shqipëria" may instead "be derived from a term meaning 'pronounce clearly, intelligibly'" (Hamp 1974:422 = 1985:682).

2. Within "Western" thought, Battersby traces what she terms the "flowerpot" theory of procreation to the writings of Aristotle (1989:29ff.; see also Ahmed 1992:29). Delaney 1991 provides a comprehensive analysis of the agricultural metaphors of "seed and soil" as they pertain to rural Turkish notions of gender, procreation, and Islamic monotheism and notes (p. 30) the Qur'ānic directive, "Women are given to you as fields to be sown, so go to them and sow [your seed] as you wish" (Sura 2:223). The idea of a patrilineal group that is related through "blood" (*gjak*) is an integral component of the blood feuds that were traditionally carried out between rival north Albanian clans or *fisë* (see Durham 1909, Gjeçov 1933, Hasluck 1954, Reineck 1991). For a similar idea of relationship through "blood" among Egyptian Bedouins, see Abu-Lughod 1986: 41ff.

3. Kolonjë is the district from which several leaders of the Albanian national renaissance of the nineteenth century hailed, most notably Abdyl, Naim, and Sami Frashëri, who were from a Bektashi family. It should be noted that such stories of origin are common in most Albanian communities. Albanian scholars take them seriously and have used them to trace population movements within Albanian-speaking areas (see particularly Zojzi 1962).

4. Cf. Bourdieu's description of Kabyle homes in Algeria, where the "master beam" of the house is linked symbolically to the husband (Bourdieu 1979:

133–53). In Lebanon, a son is referred to as the "pillar of the house" (Ali Jihad Racy, personal communication); this phrase (*shtylla e shtëpisë*) is also found in Albania.

5. Hasluck (1954:25) relates that north Albanian customary law alludes specifically to a woman's role as bearer of children when it states that "'a wife is a sack for carrying' things."

6. For a pertinent analysis of the concept of "privacy" in the Mediterranean area, see Sciama 1981.

7. Hasluck (1954:30) points out similar usages in north Albanian households.

8. Some accommodations are possible within this system. If a couple is unable to bear children, they may adopt a child either formally or informally, by raising the child of a close relative. Divorced individuals also remain within the community, although in a somewhat marginal capacity. Having been married and having perhaps had children, they have already attained adult status even if no longer married. In my years working with the Prespa community, however, I have never met a couple who intentionally had no children, nor have I met any individual who remained unmarried well into adulthood or who identified himself or herself as "homosexual." This is not to say that no individuals have ever chosen these options. By making such a choice, however, they would simultaneously be opting for a life outside the community, and so an outsider such as myself would not be likely to meet them at a community function, or perhaps even to hear about them. As Borneman (1996:229) argues, the privileged position of marriage within most societies produces "a domain of practical abjection" peopled by those individuals who do not live according to the norms that it constructs.

The situation among Presparë contrasts with that documented for north Albania and adjacent areas, where in the past a woman could swear perpetual virginity, either to avoid an arranged marriage or because her parents had no sons that survived childhood (Durham 1928:194–95; Grémaux 1994). Particularly in the latter instance such a woman, known as a *virgjineshë* or *vajzë e betuar* ("sworn virgin"), might dress in male clothing, perform male chores, become head of household, and even perform the male song repertoire (Grémaux 1994: 255). It remains unclear what the sexual orientation of such individuals has been, nor do these practices translate into a present-day tolerance for constructions of gender or sexuality that would challenge either the binary gender system or the assumption of heterosexuality that characterizes rural Albanian communities. At present, for example, it is illegal in Albania to declare oneself to be homosexual.

9. Black, the color of mourning among Balkan Christians, is generally eschewed by Prespa elders, including widows, since it implies an unwillingness to accept God's will that an individual should die. Nevertheless, some Prespa women have worn black to mourn the death of a close relative.

10. Even more rarely, a boy and girl might become "blood brother" and "blood sister." Kavaev 1972 discusses another type of fictive kinship observed between Christians and Muslims in the Struga district of Macedonia.

11. Cf. Arab. *'aql*, Tk. *akıl*, S. Slav. *um* or *pamet*. Ali Jihad Racy (personal communication) has suggested that Presparë may have come to use the word *mënd* as a translation of the Arabic.

12. In contrast, Andrews (1985:115) notes that, according to Ottoman law and social convention, a male was considered to have "matured from a life of pure emotion to a stage at which he [could] be considered capable of reason" by age seven.

13. Speaking of her husband's having gone to college, one woman explained to me that he was *me shkollë* ("with school"), whereas a lot of the men in the community were merely *me lopa* ("with the cows"); in other words, while he had been away at school, they had remained in the village on their farms. The implication was that he would have far better information to give me regarding singing than men with less education. Her remark sheds some light on my unusual position as a woman researching the community's singing. Because I am also *me shkollë*, I have always been perceived as being capable of carrying out a scholarly project. Furthermore, as many other women fieldworkers have noted, I have been treated in many circumstances as an "honorary male," in the sense that I am often given the same consideration as a male guest and, at times, allowed to observe men's gatherings. Even when my presence might override community conventions, it does not threaten the terms of the Prespa "system" as would an outside man's presence at a women's gathering. As more Prespa women gain a higher education, it is conceivable that one of them might be able to carry out similar research in the future, so long as she comported herself in a proper and respectful manner.

14. *Zoti* is the most frequently used word for God, whereas *Alla* (Arab. *Allāh*) is reserved for fixed Islamic expressions such as *inshalla* ("if God wills it"). Writing of a rural Turkish community, Delaney (1987:44) relates gender issues and the concept of "honor" both to beliefs about procreation and to monotheism:

> In this cosmological system the material, unregenerate, and eventually perishable aspects of life and women associated with it are devalued in relation to and encompassed by the creativity and spiritual essence of men and God. It is not a relation of opposition and duality, for that would imply separate but potentially equal status; instead, it is a relation of hierarchy, dominance, and encompassment. As the world is dependent on and encompassed by God, so too are women dependent on and encompassed by men. In this world men are God's representatives.

See also Delaney 1991.

15. A Serbian wedding song, sung by women to guests seated at the banquet table, explicitly links the "power" of the sons of a household both to their labor and to the drinking of homemade brandy that so frequently accompanies men's singing:

Kad pevamo zašto ne pijemo?	When we sing, why don't we drink?
Ovo pivo nije pokradeno,	This drink is not stolen,

već je ovo snagom zarađeno,	it took power to make it,
desnom rukom i motikom tupom,	with the right arm and a dull hoe,
s volovima i sa sinovima.	with oxen and with our sons.
Nije gazda koj ima volove,	The rich man is not the man who has oxen,
no je gazda koj ima sinove.	but the rich man is he who has sons.

(R. Petrović 1981, band B11; translator's name not given)

16. Comparable terms in other Mediterranean areas would include Arab. *sharaf,* Tk. *şeref* and *namus,* Gk. *timi* and *filotimo,* S. Slav. *čast* or *čest.* Abu-Lughod 1986 also analyses Egyptian Bedouin social relations in terms of a "discourse of honor."

17. Again, comparable terms would include Arab. *'ayb, ḥishmah,* or *iḥ-tisham;* Tk. *ayıp;* Gk. *dropi;* S. Slav. *sram.*

18. One of the ironies that I have confronted in drawing on contemporary social theory is that my interpretations are often very much in sympathy with those of scholars in Albania and the former Yugoslavia who, during the socialist period, asserted a Marxist stance in their writings. Scholars in these countries have not hesitated to label rural social relations as "patriarchal" and are very aware of the close relationship between village practices such as wedding observances and aspects of the local social order (see, for example, Dojaka 1978). In his collection of songs from the Korçë region of Albania, Panajoti (1982:718) groups a version of this song with several others that, he feels, exemplify "social themes from the past", meaning, before socialist reforms were introduced.

19. Abu-Lughod has interpreted the Bedouin concept of *ḥasham* in much the same way:

> The modesty code minimizes the threat sexuality poses to the social system by tying virtue or moral standing to its denial. To overcome the moral devaluation entailed by less self-mastery and control over one's own body and by closer association with that which threatens the social system, people must distance themselves from sexuality and their reproductive functions. . . . the more women are able to deny their sexuality, the more honorable they are. (1986:152)

Other scholars of the Mediterranean, however, go further in suggesting that the female body is regarded as innately tempting to men and therefore "shameful." Speaking of Egyptian women entertainers, Nieuwkerk writes:

> . . . female performers are bad because their bodies are *'awra,* shameful. The female body is shameful because it is by definition eroticizing and enticing, whereas the male body has several dimensions and is not by nature seductive. . . . the body of male performers is a "productive body" whereas that of female performers is by definition a "sexual body." (1995: 154)

Ahmed (1992) provides a comprehensive history of such attitudes in the Islamic world, emphasizing a legacy of discourses and practices regarding sexuality and the body that is shared by both Westerners and Middle Easterners. While present-day Prespa women have not spoken to me in such ways about themselves, they nevertheless maintain practices that are informed by such historical discourses.

20. A north Albanian bride was traditionally expected to show even greater deference to her husband and his kin, such as for example standing in the presence of any of his blood relatives. See the song *Bien tri daire* as sung in chapter 3.

21. It strikes me that the Prespa community's expectations of "human nature," when it is not restrained by deliberate effort or customary etiquette, can be summarized as follows: two women when placed in the same setting will relate in a docile manner (no one ever suggested to me, for example, that they might quarrel); a woman and a man together will copulate; and two men will fight. It is a formula that might apply equally well to livestock: to *ajvanë* (beasts of burden) precisely.

22. Cf. Egyptian Bedouins, who feel that a man progresses from a more passionate to a more "wise" and "reasonable" nature around age forty (Abu-Lughod 1986:91).

23. It would seem that, in their political isolation from other southerners, Presparë have looked to north Albanian communities in Kosova and western Macedonia as their major point of reference for what constitutes "Albanianness." Whereas I would interpret the differences between northerners and southerners in terms of different types of social formations that have developed in line with different means of livelihood ("pastoralists" vs. "agriculturalists"), most Presparë speak as if their society only recently evolved away from a common Albanian form now typified by northerners, and only because of their exposure to Western ways. Schneider 1971, Denich 1974, Meeker 1976, and Herzfeld 1980 all include more detailed discussions of these two types of societies within Mediterranean regions.

24. Speaking of burial customs in the north Albanian district of Kelmend, the ethnographer Fadil Mehmeti relates that, according to community members, a man is buried somewhat deeper than a meter, whereas a woman is buried deeper still, *për mëkatet që ka bërë në këtë botë* ("for the sins she has committed in this world"). Mehmeti ascribes this practice to "the influence of religion and patriarchy" (1978:350).

25. In the fall of 1994, however, I did attend seven days of a wedding celebration, hosted by a family who were among my first Prespa friends.

Chapter Six: Singing and the Discourse of Honor

1. This is one of several humorous strophic songs in which the same verse formula is applied in turn to the three generations of females, named in descending order of age: "elders," then "brides," then "girls." The physical appearance of each group is then stereotyped in specific ways.

2. What was actually sung here was a mixture of two standard *bejte*. The second soloist could not quite hear the first, and so completed a different line of

text from what the first soloist had begun. The *bejte* initiated by the first soloist is usually sung:

Ajde mor ISMAIL, aman o-i,
më t'u mbledhshim më shtëpi!

3. The groom's father drove a vintage Mercedes at the time.

4. Such reciprocity lies at the basis of the notion of friendship. When I questioned Presparë as to which families were among their "friends," they invariably cited reciprocal social visits as the main criterion. One older woman, for example, explained why her household and another were not "friends" in the following way:

S'kemi ryrë, s'kemi dalë [We haven't entered or exited each other's homes].
We know each other to say "Hello." But we haven't gone to their house
for supper, and they haven't come to ours. (Interview in Toronto, 1986)

Similarly, Abu-Lughod (1986:66) notes that Egyptian Bedouin use the phrase "we go to them and they come to us" to convey the existence of social bonds.

5. One man suggested to me that the practice of having multiple *konak*s at village weddings came about as a means of segregating male guests who harbored ill feelings toward each other. This may have been one factor in the development of that practice, but spatial constraints would seem to have been a more fundamental motivation.

6. Note that here "honor" is taken to be a male prerogative, perhaps with reference primarily to north Albanians. Slavic Montenegrans, whose notion of "honor" is extremely close to that of northerners, in fact denote the concept of "honor" by the term *obraz*, meaning "face" or "cheek," as if to emphasize that "honor" involves conveying a social persona. Their parlance is reminiscent of Goffman's use of the word "face" to refer to "the positive social value a person effectively claims for himself . . ." (1967:5). Bourdieu quotes from a Kabyle tale that suggests yet another dimension of the association of "face" with "honor": "Custom requires men to look others in the face, not look at their feet. It's a man's face, his honour, that counts" (1979:119).

7. This pattern is true of social visits in general. If a woman goes calling by herself, she is sincerely welcomed by her hosts, but much more informally than if her husband visits alone or if the two go as a couple.

8. Such an attitude recalls Bloch's celebrated but simplistic statement regarding ritual singing, that "You cannot argue with a song" (1974:71).

9. Stewart 1989 has advanced similar arguments regarding singing among Vlach Rom men in Hungary. See also Myers 1979:354 on singing among Pintupi in Australia and Feld 1989 on Kaluli vocal genres in New Guinea.

10. It is important to note that the two families whose children are to be married must be economically capable of hosting the various gatherings that are connected with the wedding celebration, at least at a minimal level. When I interviewed villagers in the Korçë region of Albania in 1994, several men explained that *konak*s had not been held there for some time because families did not have enough money to pay for the refreshments that would be a required

part of the event. Singing occasions are thus to some extent contingent on the economic well-being of the community as a whole.

Chapter Seven: Singing as the Practice of Patriarchy

1. In contrast, one young woman explained to me that she considered the consummation of the marriage to be the point at which she was married, and I would suspect that this would be the more common answer.

2. In southern Albania, the scarf that is burned at a wedding is said to be *shami e beqarit:* the "scarf of bachelorhood," and thus a symbol of the groom's leaving behind his single years. I have not, however, heard this designation used by Prespare, and any scarf that is burned is inevitably associated with the groom's mother.

3. Durham encountered this same sort of explanation many times in her travels among north Albanians. Here she recounts one such instance while visiting the town of Pejë or Peć in Kosova:

> The thing that bothered everybody was my straw hat; they had never seen one before; "Why do you wear wheat on your head?" Every one broke a little bit off the brim to make sure it really was "wheat."
>
> "Do you wear it in the house?" "Do you sleep in it?" "Do you wear it to show you are married?" "To show you are not married?" "Are all the women in your vilayet (province) obliged to wear wheat on their heads?" "Is there a law about it?" "Or do you wear it *per chef* (for pleasure)?"
>
> "I wear it because of the sun," said I desperately. "Why because of the sun?" "It is hot," said I. "No, it isn't," said they. They did not wear wheat because of the sun. Would I tell them the real reason? . . . I fell back on the answer that has so often tried me in others: "I wear it because I do. It is *nash obichaj* ([Serb.] our custom)."
>
> This satisfied them wholly, for there is a proverb which says: "It is better that a village should fall than a custom." (Durham 1909:258–59)

See also Turino 1989:1 for similar responses among Aymara families in Peru.

4. The most complete study of the relationship between marriage and death as expressed in Balkan ritual is Kligman 1988. In some parts of eastern Europe, the bride or one of her relatives has traditionally sung a lament upon her departure from her family home. Zemtsovsky (1980:390) writes for parts of Russia that "at the crucial moment of the ritual the bride changes the melody, falls to the ground and laments *na myortviy golos* ('in the voice of the dead'), that is, in the melody of the funeral lament."

5. In the Korçë district of Albania, the common explanation for this is that every action in the wedding is associated with an odd number because the addition of the bride then "makes it even" (*nusja e bën çift*).

6. Speaking of rural Turkish weddings, Delaney recounts that the bride's henna is considered

> the sacred soil of *Cennet* (Heaven, Paradise), which is envisioned as a garden, and it exudes the smell of Heaven as opposed to earthly soil. The

woman (human soil) is anointed with sacred soil, and the flame [a candle placed in the moistened henna], a symbol of male (but divine) procreative power, transforms her into a bride of Heaven. (1991:137–38)

I have never heard such an explanation from Prespa women, although the henna ceremony is no doubt a practice that was introduced to them in the Ottoman period. For actual amulets against the evil eye, such as the bracelets and charms that are placed on infants, Presparë favor the color blue, as do Turks and many Arabs.

7. See Rice 1994:18 for a similar description of all-male mumming at a Bulgarian wedding. Vakarelski (1952:198–99) describes erotic dances performed by men at weddings in the Pazardžik district of Bulgaria, accompanied by songs about "planting peppers." One such song, *Dilmano dilbero,* has become a standard performance vehicle for all types of Bulgarian folk ensembles.

8. In Korçë villages, a mixture literally of dried fruits (*pemë*) may be sent instead.

9. In the one instance where I was able to stay with the groom's family for several days before the taking of the bride, I was present for yet another *traditë* involving grains and legumes. At midnight on Wednesday, chickpeas (*qiqra*) were ground and then made into a yeast mixture to be used for baking the wedding bread. The grinding was initiated by the groom's younger brother, but soon his sister and female cousin, each wearing a red scarf, took over. While the sister prepared the bride's yeast mixture, the cousin prepared that of the groom. Jars with the two mixtures were left overnight to rise and were inspected the next morning to see whose had risen more. The yeast mixtures were then used as the basis for a dough that was first kneaded by an unmarried cousin with a living father and mother, sister and brother. The other young women joined in the kneading, and eventually the dough was shaped into loaves and baked in several large metal trays. Enough bread was made to serve the wedding guests at the many meals offered them by the hosts during the wedding period. Throughout these activities, the women who were present sang songs in honor of the groom.

10. At least three of the songs that Prespa women sing to the bride allude to this in their opening lines: *Vetëtin në fund të odës* ("There is something shining at the end of the room"; see chapter 4; CD #21); *Sh'të vetëtin vëndi ku rri* ("The place where you sit is shining"; see chapter 8); and *Moj e vogla në lëmë/sh'të ndritin tynë ato llërë* (O small one on the threshing floor/how your forearms are glistening; CD #9).

11. In fact, Prespárë use the word *bereqet* most often to mean "wheat." For a similar homology in Andean rituals, see Turino 1993:105.

12. Some families instead break the loaves into small pieces and distribute them to members of the groom's party at the time of the bride's arrival at his home. The fertility and abundance symbolized by the bread are thereby extended to the full lineage group. In this regard, the bread loaves and their distribution may be compared to the North American custom of the wedding cake, a piece of which is served to each wedding guest.

In past decades, the groom's mother also inspected the bedclothes on the morning after the taking of the bride, to look for traces of blood that would confirm the bride's virginity. The bedding was not then publicly displayed, however, as has been the case in some other regions of the Mediterranean.

13. Speaking of rural Turkey, Delaney 1991:95 also discusses the implicit connection drawn between procreation and women's bread-baking. I should note here that my Prespa women friends regarded my learning how to make cooked grain products, particularly a type of vegetable pie made with filo dough known as *lakror*, as the most important sign of my symbolic entry as a woman into their community.

14. A young woman is so commonly referred to as a "partridge" or a "turtledove" that this usage forms part of the definition of these words in the principal dictionary of the literary language published in Albania (Kostallari 1980). When Prespa women translated their songs for me, they often rendered these words simply as "young woman" or "bride," without mentioning that they also refer to birds.

15. In parts of southern Albania, a young man is often depicted in songs as a "falcon" (*petrit*) rather than a nightingale, as if to highlight his "preying" on the bride.

16. The absence of women's names in the men's historical songs is reminiscent of Graham-Brown's remarks about a Lebanese family's memories of past generations:

According to a member of the present generation of the family, the women of that era are "like shadow figures" in the family memory. Even her great-aunt, born in 1898 and regarded as a repository of family history, always talks about what the men in the family did, and says little about the women. It seems that because they stayed at home and reared children they were perceived as having no history. In the eyes of women as well as men, family history was seen as rooted in the achievements of men. (Graham-Brown 1988:97)

17. I explore the relationship between south Albanian men's historical songs and notions of gender and nation in Sugarman 1994.

18. See, for example, Lloyd 1968:215–16 for Albania in general. Lloyd points out that north Albanian men in particular have often felt that love songs were not becoming for men to sing:

Some mountaineers still feel it is shameful to sing love songs ("They aren't made for heroes", is a remark overheard by Sokoli), and if they sing them at all it is *nënkrahçe* (literally, "under the arm"), namely in a barely audible voice. (1968:213)

19. Becker coins the phrases "speaking the past" and "speaking the present" to refer to any linguistic activity, but specifically within the context of an analysis of the Javanese puppet theater or *wayang*. I have here extended his phrases to the activity of singing.

20. Most of these expressive techniques have been noted by linguistic anthropologists as cross-cultural indicators of heightened emotion: broken syntax

and the use of intensifiers (Irvine 1982); glottal ornamentation, use of falsetto, and a falling intonational contour in general (Urban 1988). Urban relates the features that he cites specifically to the affect of grief. This is not the case among Prespare or other singers of Tosk polyphony, however, who seem to have drawn upon local lament styles as a source of emotional expressivity for both singing and instrumental music.

21. The rendition of this song on CD #5, which was performed solely for a recording session and not in a wedding setting, is slower than would be usual.

22. Until very recently, no south Albanian woman from Macedonia had ever performed at an event as a professional singer, nor had Prespa women participated in stage performances of their folklore, as had several of the men. See chapter 8, however, for some recent exceptions. For similar Egyptian attitudes toward women entertainers, see Nieuwkerk 1995.

23. Likewise, the word *shtruar* may be used to describe the demure dance style of young women. In one popular song from the town of Vlorë in southwestern Albania, young women are once again represented as "partridges":

Dilni, shihni ju thëllëxat-o	Come out to see the partridges
që na marrin vallen shtruar-o.	leading the dance line *shtruar*.

Shtruar dancing involves taking small steps close to the ground and keeping one's torso relatively still.

24. A similar association of women with "ritual" singing and of men with "social" singing is found among Christian south Slavs, among whom the distinction is much more pronounced. Throughout Macedonia and Bulgaria, women have traditionally sung as accompaniment to the majority of their daily work activities, as well as for calendrical and life-cycle rituals and for community dancing. Men's singing has been restricted for the most part to raucous singing "around the table" (*na trapeza*) at family and community celebrations, when those taking part have been generously fueled by food and drink. As Rice (1980a:48) points out for Bulgarian men, "in these cases they are more commonly called drunks (*pianitsi*) than singers (*pevtsi*)." At wedding celebrations in particular, Slavic women have performed all the ritual singing, whether for the groom or the bride, whereas men have dominated the social singing that takes place around the banquet table. (See Rice 1994 for a more extensive account of men's and women's music-making in Bulgaria.)

This same division is observed by Muslim north Albanians in Kosova and Macedonia, although it is the young unmarried girls of the family who perform ritual wedding songs, rather than married women. In these communities, women past the age of puberty are not generally permitted to sing, even in the courtyard of their home. But an additional factor might be the importance to north Albanians of "blood" (*gjak*), in the sense of patrilineal relations, which would leave the task of ritual observance to females of the household's own lineage.

25. For the most part, I found that it was only among Kolonjarë families that the details of most historical songs were known.

26. Nelson (1982:43) reports that she heard Egyptian listeners respond to

recitations of the Qur'ān with the phrase, "Oh nightingale of the Nile!" (*Ya bulbul in-Nil!*).

27. Durham (1909:177) relates how a priest in the north Albanian highlands once summarized a "true Albanian day" by reciting to her a short verse:

| Duhan, rakia, | Tobacco, brandy, |
| Pushke, dashtnia. | guns, love. |

His formula is equally apt for Prespa men's gatherings.

28. Dubinskas (1983:254) describes a similar instance of singing as "dispute management" in Slavonia, Croatia. His account of Slavonian men's gatherings offers interesting comparative material, in that the structure of occasions allows men to assert their status within the community through their domination of the singing event.

29. In his analysis of beer-drinking parties among the Iteso of East Africa, Karp has noted a similar need for participants to control their demeanor carefully in order for the event to unfold successfully. His term "engrossment" can be compared to the *qejf* sought by Prespa men:

> Engrossment is a critical feature of the beer party, but it is not a preconscious experience; nor is it inevitable. Instead much of their action is directed towards achieving it and celebrating that achievement. The beer party is "a managed accomplishment." (Karp 1980:113, quoting Harold Garfinkel, *Studies in ethnomethodology,* 1967)

Prespa men are generally far less unruly in their shows of *qejf* than are the men of neighboring ethnic groups. In the final hours of a Macedonian wedding that I attended, the groom's brother was to be seen kneeling in the courtyard of his family's home, opening bottles of beer one by one and pouring them over his head in a display of complete elation (Mac. *kef*). Such behavior would be beyond all bounds of propriety for a Prespar.

30. The behavioral syndrome that surrounds Prespa men's *lartër* songs, including such elements as a full-voiced delivery, dramatic demeanor, heroic values, heavy drinking, and pistol-shooting, together with all its connotations of male strength and virility, is one that is not by any means unique to Albanian men. Américo Paredes has captured very much this same ethos in his description of songs about Latino "warrior-heroes" and the way that they are performed:

> Men should sing with their heads thrown back, with their mouths wide open and their eyes shut. Fill your lungs, so they can hear you at the pasture's furthest end. And when you sing, sing songs like *El Corrido de Gregorio Cortez.* There's a good song that will make the hackles rise. You can almost see him there—Gregorio Cortez, with his pistol in his hand. (*With his pistol in his hand,* 1958, p. 34, as quoted in Rosaldo 1989:154–55)

Chapter Eight: Emerging Subjectivities

1. Had there been more room, more women would have danced in the line and also joined in on the drone.

2. This song is usually sung with additional verses such as:

Ma ke buzën si kuti . . .	You have a mouth [as full as] a box . . .
Ma ke ballën si çini . . .	You have a forehead [as round as] a plate . . .
Ma ke synë si ylli . . .	Your eye is [as sparkling as] a star . . .

3. Young women at a north Albanian urban wedding are "like ducks" because they dress in shiny white polyester *shallvarë*, or Turkish trousers, and a white homespun silk blouse, over which they wear a vest of gold braid. They are also "ducks" because they carry themselves proudly and with dignity.

4. Unlike many neighboring communities, Presparë do not seem to have a polyphonic song that is sung consistently when the bride departs from her home. Instead, they often sing this monophonic song, which is a direct rendering into Albanian of a song that is popular among Macedonians, "Creša se od koren korneše."

5. This song is usually repeated with the names of other close relatives inserted in place of "father." The phrase *Rri me shëndet!* ("Remain in health!") is the customary way of saying "Goodbye."

6. A bride kisses a small boy so that she will bear sons, but kisses a child who is ill or disabled so that he or she might recover.

7. The rather cryptic first verse of this song seems to describe a type of large headscarf made of cotton gauze, printed with a steamship design around its edges. A similar one, with sailing ships at its borders, is illustrated in Ioannou-Yiannara 1984:356. Such a scarf might have been brought by a husband as a present to his wife, to highlight his status as one who had worked abroad.

8. One younger woman in fact pointed out to me that, together with her outside job and her household duties, she has also taken on tasks such as going to the market that would have been men's work in Prespa. She was quite familiar with the feminist term "second shift" for a woman's household duties.

9. Some families arrange a marriage between their child and that of a Turkish-speaking Muslim family from Prespa. Such families commonly speak Albanian as well, and their *sistem* is virtually indistinguishable from that of Presparë.

10. On the other hand, one of the prominent musicians for weddings in the Chicago area was completing a Master of Music degree in choral conducting when I met him, and he asked me to edit his term paper on composer Elliott Carter in return for an interview. His need to support a wife and three small children, however, as well as the volatility of the academic job market, have precluded his studying the field that holds most interest for him: ethnomusicology. Because of such constraints, it will be a long time before any member of the community, at least among overseas families, is able to "represent" it in a scholarly way.

11. At present some Albanians in Macedonia are attempting to open an Albanian-language university in the city of Tetovo (Alb. Tetovë).

12. See also Delaney 1991:115 for rural Turkey. Rice (1994:128–32) discusses this same homology with regard to the Bulgarian cycle of calendrical rituals. In the past, Bulgarian men initiated the ritual year by singing *koleda* songs at the time of the winter solstice, an activity that coincided with their winter plowing and that occurred approximately nine months before harvest. For the remainder of the year, women performed both agricultural tasks and the ritual songs connected with them.

13. Reineck (1986) offers a similar analysis of north Albanian weddings in Opojë, Kosova.

14. Sometimes Presparë observe "English" wedding customs in ways that bring them into even closer conformity to their Prespa counterparts, usually because they have learned about them mostly from each other rather than non-Albanians. At one wedding, for example, in actions reminiscent of the breaking apart of the bread loaves that are traditionally placed under the bride's arms, the cake was distributed to guests in bite-sized pieces rather than in the more customary large slices.

15. A number of North American wedding innovations have also been incorporated into weddings held in Prespa villages. These now generally culminate with a large dinner dance, attended by guests from both sides of the wedding, that is held in the tourist hotel located by the lake near the village of Krani (Kranjë). Music at the hotel, as well as that played for outdoor dancing at the groom's, is provided by the same Rom *daulle* families, who now augment the standard ensemble with saxophone, electric guitar and bass, electric keyboard, and drum set.

16. This song may also be sung by the bride's relatives before she is taken, in which case it begins with the word *çupa* ("young girl"). By changing the first word from *çupa* to *nusja,* singers on the groom's side can signal the bride's transformation from "girl" to "bride" at the moment she is taken.

17. If the shaving of the groom is held indoors, then women might sing for that ritual rather than the men. The result is that the association of ritual singing with women is even more strongly enforced than at a village wedding. At some weddings, as at Memet and Feime's, the men's singing at some moments may be preempted by the playing of the *daulle,* something that does not happen in Prespa.

18. Presparë did in fact form a dance group in Toronto in the early 1990s, composed mostly of young people in their late teens, that performed at a few community events. As of this writing, however, it is no longer active.

Abu-Lughod, Lila. 1985. "Honor and the sentiments of loss in a Bedouin society." *American Ethnologist* 12:245–61.

———. 1986. *Veiled sentiments: Honor and poetry in a Bedouin society.* Berkeley and Los Angeles: University of California Press.

———. 1990. "The romance of resistance: Tracing transformations of power through Bedouin women." *American Ethnologist* 17:41–55.

———. 1993. *Writing women's worlds.* Berkeley and Los Angeles: University of California Press.

Abu-Lughod, Lila, and Catherine Lutz. 1990. "Introduction: Emotion, discourse, and the politics of everyday life." In *Language and the politics of emotion,* ed. Catherine A. Lutz and Lila Abu-Lughod, 1–23. Cambridge: Cambridge University Press.

Ahmed, Leila. 1992. *Women and gender in Islam: Historical roots of a modern debate.* New Haven: Yale University Press.

Ahmeti, Ali M. 1983. "Gjëmëtarët shqiptarë nga Gucia dhe Plava" [Albanian male lamenters from Gucia and Plava]. *Gjurmime Albanologjike: Folklor dhe Etnologji* 13:219–26.

Alexiou, Margaret. 1974. *The ritual lament in Greek tradition.* Cambridge: Cambridge University Press.

Andrews, Walter. 1985. *Poetry's voice, society's song: Ottoman lyric poetry.* Seattle: University of Washington Press.

Auerbach, Susan. 1987. "From singing to lamenting: Women's musical role in a Greek village." In *Women and music in cross-cultural perspective,* ed. Ellen Koskoff, 25–43. Urbana: University of Illinois Press.

Bateson, Gregory. 1972. "A theory of play and fantasy." In *Steps to an ecology of mind,* 177–93. San Francisco: Chandler.

Battersby, Christine. 1989. *Gender and genius: Towards a feminist aesthetics.* London: The Women's Press.

Bauman, Richard. 1977. *Verbal art as performance.* Prospect Heights, Ill.: Waveland Press.

Bauman, Richard, and Charles L. Briggs. 1990. "Poetics and performance as critical perspectives on language and social life." *Annual Review of Anthropology* 19:59–88.

Bauman, Richard, and Joel Sherzer, eds. 1974. *Explorations in the ethnography of speaking.* Cambridge: Cambridge University Press.

Becker, A[lton] L. 1979. "Text-building, epistemology, and aesthetics in Javanese shadow theatre." In *The imagination of reality: Essays in Southeast Asian coherence systems,* ed. A. L. Becker and Aram A. Yengoyan. Norwood, N.J.: Ablex.

Becker, Judith, and Alton Becker. 1981. "A musical icon: Power and meaning in

Javanese gamelan music." In *The sign in music and literature*, ed. Wendy Steiner, 203–15. Austin: University of Texas Press.

Birge, John Kingsley. 1937. *The Bektashi order of dervishes*. London: Luzac.

Blacking, John. 1973. *How musical is man?* Seattle: University of Washington Press.

Bloch, Maurice. 1974. "Symbols, song, dance and features of articulation: Is religion an extreme form of traditional authority?" *Archives Européenes de Sociologie* 15:55–81.

Boddy, Janice. 1989. *Wombs and alien spirits: Women, men, and the zār cult in northern Sudan*. Madison: University of Wisconsin Press.

Borneman, John. 1996. "Until death do us part: Marriage/death in anthropological discourse." *American Ethnologist* 23:215–38.

Bourdieu, Pierre. 1977. *Outline of a theory of practice*. Translated by Richard Nice. Cambridge: Cambridge University Press.

———. 1979. *Algeria 1960*. Translated by Richard Nice. Cambridge: Cambridge University Press.

Bradby, Barbara. 1993. "Sampling sexuality: Gender, technology and the body in dance music." *Popular Music* 12:155–76.

Brenneis, Donald. 1985. "Passion and performance in Fiji vernacular song." *Ethnomusicology* 29:397–408.

Brett, Philip, Gary Thomas, and Elizabeth Wood, eds. 1993. *Queering the pitch: The new gay and lesbian musicology*. New York: Routledge.

Buchanan, Donna. 1991. "The Bulgarian folk orchestra: Cultural performance, symbol, and the construction of national identity in socialist Bulgaria." Ph.D. dissertation, University of Texas at Austin.

Caraveli[-Chaves], Anna. 1980. "The Greek women's lament as communicative event." *Journal of American Folklore* 93:129–57.

———. 1985. "The symbolic village: Community born in performance." *Journal of American Folklore* 98:259–86.

———. 1986. "The bitter wounding: The lament as social protest in rural Greece." In *Gender and power in rural Greece*, ed. Jill Dubisch, 169–94. Princeton, N.J.: Princeton University Press.

Caton, Margaret. 1974. "The vocal ornament *takīyah* in Persian music." *Selected Reports in Ethnomusicology* 2 (1):43–53.

Caton, Steven C. 1986. "*Salām tahīyah*: Greetings from the highlands of Yemen." *American Ethnologist* 13:290–308.

Çaushi, Abedin. 1974. "Martesa në qytetin e Elbasanit" [The marriage in the town of Elbasan]. *Etnografia Shqiptare* 5:231–56.

Cellier, Marcel, comp. 1995. *L'Albanie mystérieuse*. Disques Pierre Verany PV 750010.

Clifford, James. 1988. *The predicament of culture*. Cambridge: Harvard University Press.

Cohen, Abner. 1979. "Political symbolism." *Annual Review of Anthropology* 8:87–113.

Collier, Jane Fishburne, and Sylvia Junko Yanagisako, eds. 1987. *Gender and kinship: Essays toward a unified analysis*. Stanford: Stanford University Press.

Cook, Susan C., and Judy S. Tsou, eds. 1994. *Cecilia reclaimed: Feminist perspectives on gender and music*. Urbana: University of Illinois Press.

Coon, Carleton S. 1950. *The mountains of giants: A racial and cultural study of the North Albanian mountain Ghegs.* Cambridge: Peabody Museum of American Archaeology and Ethnology.

Cowan, Jane K. 1990. *Dance and the body politic in northern Greece.* Princeton: Princeton University Press.

Csikszentmihalyi, Mihalyi. 1975. *Beyond boredom and anxiety.* San Francisco: Jossey-Bass.

———. *Flow: The psychology of optimal experience.* New York: Harper and Row.

Danforth, Loring M. 1982. *The death rituals of rural Greece.* Princeton, N.J.: Princeton University Press.

Delaney, Carol. 1987. "Seeds of honor, fields of shame." In *Honor and shame and the unity of the Mediterranean,* ed. David D. Gilmore, 35–48. Washington, D.C.: American Anthropological Association.

———. 1991. *The seed and the soil: Gender and cosmology in Turkish village society.* Berkeley and Los Angeles: University of California Press.

Denich, Bette S. 1974. "Sex and power in the Balkans." In *Woman, culture, and society,* ed. Michelle Z. Rosaldo and Louise Lamphere, 243–62. Stanford: Stanford University Press.

Denski, Stan, and David Sholle. 1992. "Metal men and glamour boys: Gender performance in heavy metal." In *Men, masculinity, and the media,* ed. Steve Craig. Newbury Park, Calif.: Sage Publications.

Dheri, Eftim, Mexhit Daiu, and Qemal Haxhihasani, eds. 1964. *Këngë popullore* [Folk songs]. Tiranë: Instituti i Folklorit.

Dheri, Eftim, Mexhit Daiu, and Arsen Mustaqi, eds. 1966. *250 këngë popullore dasme* [250 folk wedding songs]. Tiranë: Instituti i Folklorit.

Dojaka, Abaz. 1978. "Ceremoniali i dasmës shqiptare" [The Albanian wedding ceremony]. *Etnografia Shqiptare* 9:115–50. French translation: "Le cérémonial nuptial en Albanie." *Ethnographie Albanaise* 9 (1979):117–54.

Dreyfus, Hubert L., and Paul Rabinow. 1983. *Michel Foucault: Beyond structuralism and hermeneutics.* 2d edition. Chicago: University of Chicago Press.

Dubinskas, Frank Anthony. 1983. "Performing Slavonian folklore: The politics of reminiscence and recreating the past." Ph.D. dissertation, Stanford University.

Dubisch, Jill, ed. 1986. *Gender and power in rural Greece.* Princeton: Princeton University Press.

du Boulay, Juliet. 1986. "Women—Images of their nature and destiny in rural Greece." In *Gender and power in rural Greece,* ed. Jill Dubisch, 139–68. Princeton: Princeton University Press.

Dunin, Elsie. 1971. "Gypsy wedding: Dance and customs." *Makedonski Folklor* 4 (7–8):317–25.

Durham, Mary Edith. 1904. *The burden of the Balkans.* London: Nelson.

———. 1909. *High Albania.* London: Edward Arnold. Reprinted by Arno Press, 1971; and by Beacon Press, 1987.

———. 1928. *Some tribal origins, laws, and customs of the Balkans.* London: George Allen & Unwin.

Eickelman, Dale F. 1981. *The Middle East: An anthropological approach.* Englewood Cliffs, N.J.: Prentice-Hall.

Erlich, Vera St. 1966. *Family in transition: A study of 300 Yugoslav villages*. Princeton: Princeton University Press.

Federal Writers' Project of Massachusetts. 1939. *The Albanian struggle in the Old World and the New*. Boston: The Writer.

Feld, Steven. 1982. *Sound and sentiment: Birds, weeping, poetics, and song in Kaluli expression*. Philadelphia: University of Pennsylvania Press.

———. 1984. "Sound structure as social structure." *Ethnomusicology* 28: 383–409.

———. 1989. "Aesthetics as iconicity of style, or 'Lift-up-over sounding': Getting into the Kaluli groove." *Yearbook for Traditional Music* 20:74–113.

Fetiu, Sadri. 1983. "Pesë vajtime nga Malësia e Madhe" [Five laments from Malësia e Madhe]. *Gjurmime Albanologjike: Folklor dhe Etnologji* 13:229–43.

Foucault, Michel. 1972. *The archaeology of knowledge*. New York: Pantheon Books.

———. 1980. *The history of sexuality. Volume 1: An introduction*. Translated by Robert Hurley. New York: Vintage.

Frashëri, Naim. 1978. "Bagëti e Bujqësija" [Livestock and farming]. In *Vepra* [Complete works], vol. 1, ed. Nazmi Rrahmani. Prishtinë: Rilindja.

Friedrich, Paul. 1977. "Sanity and the myth of honor: The problem of Achilles." *Ethos* 5:281–305.

Frith, Simon, and Angela McRobbie. 1978. "Rock and sexuality." *Screen Education* 29:3–19. Reprinted in *On record: Rock, pop, and the written word*, ed. Simon Frith and Andrew Goodwin, 371–89. New York: Pantheon.

Geertz, Clifford. 1973a. *The interpretation of cultures*. New York: Basic Books.

———. 1973b. "Religion as a cultural system." In Geertz 1973a, 87–125.

———. 1973c. "Deep play: Notes on the Balinese cockfight." In Geertz 1973a, 412–53.

Genčev, Stojan, Margarita Vasileva, and Stefana Stojkova, eds. 1985. *Etnografija na Bŭlgarija. Tom III: Duhovna Kultura* [The ethnography of Bulgaria. Volume 3: Spiritual culture]. Sofia: Bŭlgarskata Akademija na Naukite.

George, Kenneth M. 1993. "Music-making, ritual, and gender in a Southeast Asian hill society." *Ethnomusicology* 37:1–27.

Georgiev, Vladimir I. 1972. "The earliest ethnological situation of the Balkan Peninsula as evidenced by linguistic and onomastic data." In *Aspects of the Balkans: Continuity and change*, ed. Henrik Birnbaum and Speros Vryonis Jr., 50–65. The Hague: Mouton.

Gilmore, David D. 1982. "Anthropology of the Mediterranean area." *Annual Review of Anthropology* 11:175–202.

———, ed. 1987. *Honor and shame and the unity of the Mediterranean*. Washington, D.C.: American Anthropological Association, Special Publication 22.

Gjeçov, Shtjefën Konst. 1933. *Kanuni i Lekë Dukagjinit*. Shkodër: Franceskane. Reprinted 1989 with English translation by Leonard Fox. New York: Gjonlekaj Publishing Co.

Goffman, Erving. 1967. *Interaction ritual: Essays on face-to-face behavior*. Garden City, N.Y.: Anchor Books.

———. 1974. *Frame analysis: An essay on the organization of experience*. Cambridge: Harvard University Press.

Gojçaj, Mirash. 1975. "Vdekja dhe vajtimet ndër shqiptarët e Malësisë të rrethit të Titogradit" [Death and lamenting among Montenegran Albanians from the Titograd district]. *Gjurmime Albanologjike: Folklor dhe Etnologji* 3 (1973): 85–114.

Graham-Brown, Sarah. 1988. *Images of women: The portrayal of women in photography of the Middle East 1860–1950.* London: Quartet Books.

Grémaux, René. 1994. "Woman becomes man in the Balkans." In *Third sex, third gender: Beyond sexual dimorphism in culture and history,* ed. Gilbert Herdt, 241–81. New York: Zone Books.

Hammel, E. A. 1967. "The Jewish mother in Serbia, or Les structures alimentaires de la parenté." In *Essays in Balkan ethnology,* ed. William G. Lockwood, 55–62. Berkeley: Kroeber Anthropological Society, Special Publications 1.

Hamp, Eric P. 1974. "Albanian language." In *Encyclopaedia Britannica (Macropaedia),* 15th edition, volume 1, pp. 422–23 (= 15th edition revised [1985], volume 22, pp. 682–83).

Hasluck, Margaret. 1954. *The unwritten law in Albania.* Cambridge: Cambridge University Press.

Haxhihasani, Qemal. 1971. "Naimi dhe folklori" [Naim and folklore]. *Studime Filologjike* 8/2:41–49.

Haydar, Adnan. 1989. "The development of Lebanese *zajal:* Genre, meter, and verbal duel." *Oral Tradition* 4:189–212.

Herndon, Marcia, and Norma McLeod. 1980. "The interrelationship of style and occasion in the Maltese *spirtu pront.*" In *The ethnography of musical performance,* ed. Norma McLeod and Marcia Herndon. Norwood, Pa.: Norwood Editions.

Herndon, Marcia, and Suzanne Ziegler, eds. 1990. *Music, gender, and culture.* Wilhelmshaven, Germany: Florian Noetzel Verlag.

Herzfeld, Michael. 1980. "Honour and shame: Problems in the comparative analysis of moral systems." *Man* (n.s.) 15:339–51.

———. 1981. "An indigenous theory of meaning and its elicitation in performative context." *Semiotica* 34:113–41.

———. 1985. *The poetics of manhood: Contest and identity in a Cretan mountain village.* Princeton: Princeton University Press.

Hill, Jonathan. 1979. "Kamayurá flute music: A study of music as meta-communication." *Ethnomusicology* 23:417–32.

Huld, Martin E. 1984. *Basic Albanian etymologies.* Columbus, Ohio: Slavica.

Ioannou-Yiannara, Tatiana, comp. 1984. *The Greek folk costume. Volume 2: Costumes with the kavadi.* Translated by Philip Ramp. Athens: Melissa Publishing House.

Irvine, Judith T. 1979. "Formality and informality in communicative events." *American Anthropologist* 81:773–90.

———. 1982. "Language and affect: Some cross-cultural issues." In *Contemporary perceptions of language: Interdisciplinary dimensions,* ed. Heidi Byrnes, 31–47 (Georgetown University Round Table on Languages and Linguistics, 1982). Washington, D.C.: Georgetown University Press.

Jennings, Theodore W. 1982. "On ritual knowledge." *Journal of Religion* 62: 111–27.

Kacarova, Rajna. 1969. "Oplakvane na pokojnici" [Lamenting the dead]. *Izvestija na Instituta za Muzika* 13:177–200. English translation: "Bulgarian funeral laments." *International Folklore Review* 2:112–30.

Kaeppler, Adrienne L. 1978. "Melody, drone and decoration: Underlying structures and surface manifestation in Tongan art and society." In *Arts in society*, ed. Michael Greenhalgh and Vincent Megaw, 261–74. London: Duckworth.

Kapferer, Bruce. 1979. "Entertaining demons: Comedy, interaction and meaning in a Sinhalese healing ritual." *Social Analysis* 1:108–52.

———. 1986. "Performance and the structuring of meaning and experience." In *The anthropology of experience*, ed. Victor W. Turner and Edward M. Bruner, 188–203. Urbana: University of Illinois Press.

Karp, Ivan. 1980. "Beer drinking and social experience in African society." In *Explorations in African systems of thought*, ed. Ivan Karp and C. S. Bird, 83–119. Bloomington: Indiana University Press.

Kaufman, Dimitrina. 1981. "Oplakvanija na pokojnici v Bŭlgarija" [Laments for the dead in Bulgaria]. In *Obredi i obreden folklor* [Rituals and ritual folklore]. Sofia: Bŭlgarskata Akademija na Naukite.

Kaufman, Nikolaj. 1959. "Triglasnite narodni pesni ot Kostursko" [Three-voiced folk songs from the Kastoria region]. *Izvestija na Instituta za Muzika* (Sofia) 6:65–150.

———. 1968. *Bŭlgarskata mnogoglasna narodna pesen* [The Bulgarian polyphonic folk song]. Sofia: Nauka i Izkustvo.

Kavaev, Filip. 1972. "Kosmenjeto (striganoto kumstvo) kaj makedoncite hristijani i kaj makedoncite muhamedanci i kaj makedoncite hristijani i albancite muhamedanci vo Struga i Struško" [Fictive kinship between Macedonian Christians and Muslims and between Macedonian Christians and Albanian Muslims in Struga and the Struga district]. *Makedonski Folklor* 5 (9–10):111–17.

Keeling, Richard, ed. 1989. *Women in North American Indian music: Six essays.* Bloomington, Ind.: Society for Ethnomusicology, Special Series 6.

Kiçi, Gasper. 1978. *Albanian–English dictionary.* Washington, D.C.: Author.

Kligman, Gail. 1984. "The rites of women: Oral poetry, ideology, and the socialization of peasant women in contemporary Romania." *Journal of American Folklore* 97:167–88.

———. 1988. *The wedding of the dead: Ritual, poetics, and popular culture in Transylvania.* Berkeley and Los Angeles: University of California Press.

Koestenbaum, Wayne. 1993. *The queen's throat: Opera, homosexuality, and the mystery of desire.* New York: Poseidon.

Koleva, Tatiana. 1961. "Sŭvremennata narodna svatba v razložkija kraj" [The contemporary folk wedding in the Razlog district]. *Izvestija na Etnografskija Institut i Muzej* 4:277–83.

Koskoff, Ellen, ed. 1987. *Women and music in cross-cultural perspective.* Westport, Conn.: Greenwood.

———. 1991. "Gender, power, and music." In *The musical woman: An international perspective, Vol. III, 1986–1990*, ed. Judith Lang Zaimont et al., 769–88. New York: Greenwood.

———. 1993. "Miriam sings her song: The self and other in anthropological discourse." In *Musicology and difference: Gender and sexuality in music scholarship*, ed. Ruth A. Solie, 149–63. Berkeley and Los Angeles: University of California Press.

Kostallari, Androkli, chief editor. 1980. *Fjalori i gjuhës së sotme shqipe* [Dictionary of the contemporary Albanian language]. Tiranë: Akademia e Shkencave e RPS të Shqipërisë.

Kruta, Beniamin. 1968. "Vështrim rreth këngës popullore polifonike të burrave në krahinën e Myzeqesë" [An examination of men's polyphonic folk songs from the Myzeqe region]. *Studime Filologjike* 22 (3):161–206.

———. 1973. "Polifonia e Skraparit dhe disa çështje tipologjike të saj" [The polyphony of the Skrapar region and several of its typological characteristics]. *Studime Filologjike* 27 (2):209–36, 27 (4):131–51.

———. 1980. "Vështrim i përgjithshëm i polifonisë shqiptare dhe disa çështje të gjenezës së saj" [A general examination of Albanian polyphony and some considerations as to its origins]. *Kultura Popullore* 1:45–63.

Kŭnčov, Vasil. 1891. "Bitolsko, Prespa i Ohridsko" [The Bitola, Prespa, and Ohrid districts]. *Sbornik za Narodni Umotvorenija i Narodopis* 4/1. Reprinted in *Izbrani proizvedenija* 1, 374–499. Sofia: Nauka i Izkustvo, 1970.

———. 1900. *Makedonija: Etnografija i statistika* [Macedonia: Ethnography and statistics]. Sofia: Izdanie na Knižovnoto Društvo. Reprinted in *Izbrani proizvedenija* 2, 285–600. Sofia: Nauka i Izkustvo, 1970.

Lane, Rose Wilder. 1923. *The peaks of Shala*. New York: Harper.

Leibman, Robert Henry, comp. 1974. *Traditional Tosk (South Albanian) songs and dances from the Lake Prespa area*. Selo LP-2.

Limón, J. E., and M. Jane Young. 1986. "Frontiers, settlements, and development in folklore studies, 1972–85." *Annual Review of Anthropology* 15:437–60.

Lloyd, A. L. 1966, comp. *Folk music of Albania*. Topic 12T154 (reissued as TSCD 904).

———. 1968. "Albanian folk song." *Folk Music Journal* 1:205–22.

Lockwood, William G. 1975. *European Moslems: Economy and ethnicity in western Bosnia*. New York: Academic Press.

Lockwood, Yvonne R. 1983. *Text and context: Folksong in a Bosnian Muslim village*. Columbus, Ohio: Slavica.

Lortat-Jacob, Bernard, comp. 1988. *Albania: Vocal and instrumental polyphony*. Chant du Monde LDX 274897.

Lortat-Jacob, Bernard, and Jacques Bouët, comps. 1983. *Rumania: Vocal polyphony of the Arumanians*. Chant du Monde LDX 74803.

Marcus, George E., and Michael M. J. Fischer. 1986. *Anthropology as cultural critique*. Chicago: University of Chicago Press.

Marshall, Christopher. 1982. "Towards a comparative aesthetics of music." In *Cross-cultural perspectives on music*, ed. Robert Falck and Timothy Rice, 162–73. Toronto: University of Toronto Press.

McClary, Susan. 1991. *Feminine endings: Music, gender and sexuality*. Minneapolis: University of Minnesota Press.

———. 1992. *Georges Bizet:* Carmen (Cambridge Opera Handbooks). Cambridge: Cambridge University Press.

Meeker, Michael E. 1976. "Meaning and society in the Near East: Examples from the Black Sea Turks and the Levantine Arabs." *International Journal of Middle East Studies* 7:243–70.

Mehmeti, Fadil. 1978. "Zakone, rite e besime vdekjeje në Kelmend" [Customs, rituals, and beliefs about death in Kelmend]. *Etnografia Shqiptare* 9: 333–56.

Memija, Myftar. 1962. "Dasma e Malësisë së Gjakovës" [The wedding in the district of Malësia e Gjakovës]. *Etnografia Shqiptare* 1:276–306.

Michaelson, Evalyn J., and Walter Goldschmidt. 1971. "Female roles and male dominance among peasants." *Southwestern Journal of Anthropology* 27: 330–53.

Mitrushi, Llambrini. 1974. "Zakone e rite të ceremonialit të vdekjes në Myzeqe" [Traditions and ceremonial rituals for the dead in Myzeqe]. *Etnografia Shqiptare* 5:257–81.

Mohanty, Chandra Talpade. 1991. "Under Western eyes: Feminist scholarship and colonial discourses." In *Third world women and the politics of feminism*, ed. Chandra Talpade Mohanty, Ann Russo, and Lourdes Torres, 51–80. Bloomington: Indiana University Press.

Moore, Henrietta L. 1988. *Feminism and anthropology.* Minneapolis: University of Minnesota Press.

Moore, Sally F., and Barbara G. Myerhoff, eds. 1977. *Secular ritual.* Amsterdam and Assen: Van Gorcum.

Myers, Fred R. 1979. "Emotions and the self: A theory of personhood and political order among Pintupi Aborigines." *Ethos* 7:343–70.

Nelson, Kristina. 1982. "Reciter and listener: Some factors shaping the *mujawwad* style of Qur'anic recitation." *Ethnomusicology* 26:41–47.

Newmark, Leonard, Philip Hubbard, and Peter Prifti. 1982. *Standard Albanian: A reference grammar for students.* Stanford: Stanford University Press.

Nieuwkerk, Karin van. 1995. *"A trade like any other": Female singers and dancers in Egypt.* Austin: University of Texas Press.

Nketia, J. H. Kwabena. 1962. "The problem of meaning in African music." *Ethnomusicology* 6:1–7.

Norris, H. T. 1993. *Islam in the Balkans: Religion and society between Europe and the Arab world.* Columbia: University of South Carolina Press.

Novack, Cynthia J. 1990. *Sharing the dance: Contact improvisation and American culture.* Madison: University of Wisconsin Press.

Nurbakhsh, Javad. 1987. *Sufi symbolism: The Nurbakhsh encyclopedia of Sufi terminology (Farhang-e Nurbakhsh),* vol. 2. London: Khaniqahi-Nimatullahi Publications.

Oldenburg, Veena Talwar. 1990. "Lifestyle as resistance: The case of the courtesans of Lucknow, India." *Feminist Studies* 16:259–87.

Ong, Aihwa. 1988. "Colonialism and modernity: Feminist re-presentations of women in non-Western societies." *Inscriptions* 3/4:79–93.

Ortner, Sherry B. 1978. "The virgin and the state." *Feminist Studies* 4:19–35.

———. 1990. "Gender hegemonies." *Cultural Critique* 14:35–80.

Ortner, Sherry B., and Harriet Whitehead, eds. 1981. *Sexual meanings: The cultural construction of gender and sexuality.* Cambridge: Cambridge University Press.

Panajoti, Jorgo, ed. 1982. *Këngë popullore të rrethit të Korçës* [Folk songs from the Korçë region]. Tiranë: Instituti i Kulturës Popullore.

Peristiany, J. G., ed. 1965. *Honour and shame: The values of Mediterranean society.* London: Weidenfeld and Nicolson.

Perry, Duncan M. 1988. *The politics of terror: The Macedonian Liberation Movements 1893–1903.* Durham, N.C.: Duke University Press.

Petrović, Ankica. 1990. "Women in the music creation process in the Dinaric cultural zone of Yugoslavia." In *Music, gender, and culture,* ed. Marcia Herndon and Suzanne Ziegler, 71–84. Wilhelmshaven, Germany: Florian Noetzel Verlag.

Petrović, Radmila. 1972. "Dvoglas u muzičkoj tradiciji Srbije" [Two-voiced singing in the musical tradition of Serbia]. *Rad XVII Kongresa Saveza Udruženja Folklorista Jugoslavije — Poreč 1970,* 333–37. Zagreb: Savez Udruženja Folklorista Jugoslavije.

———. 1981. Notes to *Srpska narodna muzika* [Serbian folk music]. Radio Televicija Beograd RTB 2510057.

Poedjosoedarmo, Gloria R. 1988. "A phonetic description of voice quality in Javanese traditional female soloists." *Asian Music* 19:93–126.

Qureshi, Regula Burckhardt. 1986. *Sufi music of India and Pakistan: Sound, context and meaning in Qawwali.* Cambridge: Cambridge University Press.

———. 1987. "Musical sound and contextual input: A performance model for musical analysis." *Ethnomusicology* 31:56–86.

Racy, Ali Jihad. 1986. "Lebanese laments: Grief, music, and cultural values." *World of Music* 28 (2):27–37.

———. 1991. "Creativity and ambience: An ecstatic feedback model from Arab music." *World of Music* 33 (3):7–28.

Rappaport, Roy A. 1979. "The obvious aspects of ritual." In *Ecology, meaning, and religion,* 173–221. Richmond, Calif.: North Atlantic Books.

———. 1980. "Concluding comments on ritual and reflexivity." *Semiotica* 30:181–93.

Reineck, Janet. 1986. "The place of the dance event in social organization and social change among Albanians in Kosovo, Yugoslavia." *UCLA Journal of Dance Ethnology* 10:27–38.

———. 1991. "The past as refuge: Gender, migration and ideology among the Kosova Albanians." Ph.D. dissertation, University of California, Berkeley.

Rheubottom, D. B. 1976. "The saint's feast and Skopska Crna Goran social structure." *Man* (n.s.) 2:18–34.

Rice, Timothy. 1980a. "Aspects of Bulgarian musical thought." *Yearbook of the International Folk Music Council* 12:43–66.

———. 1980b. "A Macedonian *sobor*: Anatomy of a celebration." *Journal of American Folklore* 93:113–28.

———. 1994. *May it fill your soul: Experiencing Bulgarian music.* Chicago: University of Chicago Press.

Ricoeur, Paul. 1971. "The model of the text: Meaningful action considered as a text." *Social Research* 38:529–62.

Robertson, Carol E. 1979. "'Pulling the ancestors': Performance practice and praxis in Mapuche ordering." *Ethnomusicology* 23:395–416.

———. 1989. "The *māhū* of Hawai'i." *Feminist Studies* 15:313–26.

———. 1991. "The ethnomusicologist as midwife." In *Music in the dialogue of cultures: Traditional music and cultural policy*, ed. Max Peter Baumann, 347–64. Wilhelmshaven, Germany: Florian Noetzel Verlag.

Rosaldo, Renato. 1989. *Culture and truth: The remaking of social analysis*. Boston: Beacon.

Rose, Tricia. 1994. *Black noise: Rap music and black culture in contemporary America*. Hanover, N.H.: University Press of New England.

Roseman, Marina. 1984. "The social structuring of sound: The Temiar of peninsular Malaysia." *Ethnomusicology* 28:411–45.

———. 1991. *Healing sounds from the Malaysian rainforest: Temiar music and medicine*. Berkeley and Los Angeles: University of California Press.

Rouget, Gilbert. 1985. *Music and trance: A theory of the relations between music and possession*. Chicago: University of Chicago Press.

Rowson, Everett K. 1991. "The effeminates of early Medina." *Journal of the American Oriental Society* 111:671–93.

Rubin, Gayle. 1975. "The traffic in women: Notes on the 'political economy' of sex." In *Toward an anthropology of women*, ed. Rayna R. Reiter, pp. 157–210. New York: Monthly Review Press.

Sachs, Nahoma. 1979. "The facts of death: An anthropologist views musical symbolism." *World of Music* 21:36–49.

Said, Edward. 1987. "Representing the colonized: Anthropology's interlocutors." *Critical Inquiry* 15:205–25.

Samiou, Domna, and Aris Fakinos, comps. 1984. *Grèce: Chants polyphoniques et musique d'Epire*. Ocora 558631.

Sarkissian, Margaret. 1992. "Gender and music." In *Ethnomusicology: An introduction*, ed. Helen Myers, 337–48. New York: Norton.

Sawa, George Dimitri. 1989. *Music performance practice in the early 'Abbasid era, 132–320 A.H./750–932 A.D.* Toronto: Pontifical Institute of Mediaeval Studies.

Schieffelin, Edward L. 1985. "Performance and the cultural construction of reality." *American Ethnologist* 12:707–24.

Schneider, Jane. 1971. "Of vigilance and virgins: Honor, shame and access to resources in Mediterranean societies." *Ethnology* 10:1–24.

Schwichtenberg, Cathy, ed. 1993. *The Madonna connection: Representational politics, subcultural identities, and cultural theory*. Boulder: Westview.

Sciama, Lidia. 1981. "The problem of privacy in Mediterranean anthropology." In *Women and space: Ground rules and social maps*, ed. Shirley Ardener, 89–111. London: Croom Helm.

Seeger, Anthony. 1980. "Sing for your sister: The structure and performance of Suyá *Akia*." In *The ethnography of musical performance*, ed. Norma McLeod and Marcia Herndon, 7–42. Norwood, Pa.: Norwood Editions.

———. 1987. *Why Suyá sing: A musical anthropology of an Amazonian people*. Cambridge: Cambridge University Press.

Seremetakis, C. Nadia. 1990. "The ethics of antiphony: The social construction of pain, gender, and power in the southern Peloponnese." *Ethos* 18:481–511.

————. 1991. *The last word: Women, death, and divination in Inner Mani.* Chicago: University of Chicago Press.

Shituni, Spiro. 1982. "Vezhgime etnomuzikore rreth vajtimit lab" [Ethnomusicological observations on the Lab lament]. *Kultura Popullore* 1982, No. 2: 139–51.

————. 1989. *Polifonia Labe* [Lab polyphony]. Tiranë: Instituti i Kulturës Popullore.

Signell, Karl L. 1977. *Makam: Modal practice in Turkish art music.* Seattle: Asian Music Publications.

Simić, Andrei. 1969. "Management of the male image in Yugoslavia." *Anthropological Quarterly* 42:89–101.

Skendi, Stavro. 1967. *The Albanian national awakening, 1878–1912.* Princeton: Princeton University Press.

Sokoli, Ramadan. 1965. *Folklori muzikor shqiptar (Morfologjia)* [Albanian musical folklore (Morphology)]. Tiranë: Instituti i Folklorit.

Solie, Ruth A., ed. 1993. *Musicology and difference: Gender and sexuality in music scholarship.* Berkeley and Los Angeles: University of California Press.

Stacey, Judith. 1988. "Can there be a feminist ethnography?" *Women's Studies International Forum* 11/12. Reprinted in *Women's words: The feminist practice of oral history,* ed. Sherna Berger Gluck and Daphne Patai, 111–19. New York: Routledge, 1991.

Stewart, Michael. 1989. "'True speech': Song and the moral order of a Hungarian Vlach Gypsy community." *Man* (n.s.) 24:79–102.

Stockmann, Doris. 1966. "Totenklagen der südalbanischen Çamen." *Rad XI Kongresa Folklorista Jugoslavije,* 433–41. N.p.: Kongres Folklorista Jugoslavije.

Stockmann, Doris, and Erich Stockmann. 1964. "Die vocale Bordun-Mehrstimmigkeit in Südalbanien." *Ethnomusicologie III: Les Colloques de Wégimont V 1960,* 85–135. Paris: Les Belles Lettres.

————. 1980. "Albania." *New Grove Dictionary of Music and Musicians,* ed. Stanley Sadie, vol. 1, 197–202. London: Macmillan.

Stockmann, Doris, Wilfried Fiedler, and Erich Stockmann. 1965. *Albanische Volksmusik I: Gesänge der Çamen.* Berlin: Akademie-Verlag.

Stone, Ruth M., and Verlon L. Stone. 1981. "Event, feedback, and analysis: Research media in the study of music events." *Ethnomusicology* 25:215–25.

Sugarman, Jane. 1988. "Making *muabet:* The social basis of singing among Prespa Albanian men." *Selected Reports in Ethnomusicology* 7:1–42.

————. 1989. "The nightingale and the partridge: Singing and gender among Prespa Albanians." *Ethnomusicology* 33:191–215.

————. 1993. "Engendering song: Singing and the social order at Prespa Albanian weddings." Ph.D. dissertation, University of California, Los Angeles.

————. 1994. "Singing for the fatherland: Folklore, poetry, and nation in Albanian men's narrative songs." Unpublished manuscript.

————. In press. "Albanian music." *Garland Encyclopedia of World Music.* New York: Garland.

Süleyman Çelebi. 1943. *The Mevlidi Sherif.* Translated by F. Lyman MacCallum. London: John Murray.

Tapper, Richard, and Nancy Tapper. 1986. "'Eat this, it'll do you a power of good': Food and commensality among Durrani Pashtuns." *American Ethnologist* 13:62–79.

Taylor, Jenny, and Dave Laing. 1979. "Disco-pleasure-discourse: On 'Rock and sexuality'." *Screen Education* 31:43–48.

Tomlinson, Gary. 1993. "Approaching others (Thoughts before writing)." Chapter 1 of *Music in Renaissance magic: Toward a historiography of others*, 1–43. Chicago: University of Chicago Press.

Traerup, Birthe. 1974. "Albanian singers in Kosovo: Notes on the song repertoire of a Mohammedan country wedding in Jugoslavia." In *Studia instrumentorum musicae popularis* III, ed. Gustaf Hillestrom, 244–51. Stockholm: Musikhistoriska Museet.

Trajčev, Georgi. 1923. *Prespa*. Sofia: P. Gluškov.

Trinh, T. Minh-ha. 1989. *Woman, native, other: Writing postcoloniality and feminism.* Bloomington: Indiana University Press.

Trix, Frances. 1993. *Spiritual discourse: Learning with an Islamic master.* Philadelphia: University of Pennsylvania Press.

Turino, Thomas. 1989. "The coherence of social style and musical creation among the Aymara in southern Peru." *Ethnomusicology* 33:1–30.

———. 1993. *Moving away from silence: Music of the Peruvian Altiplano and the experience of urban migration.* Chicago: University of Chicago Press.

Turner, Victor W. 1969. *The ritual process.* Chicago: Aldine Publishing Company.

Urban, Greg. 1988. "Ritual wailing in Amerindian Brazil." *American Anthropologist* 90:385–400.

Vakarelski, Khristo. 1952. "Muzikata v života na rodnoto mi selo: Bitovi materiali ot s. Momina klisura, Pazardžiško" [Music in the life of my native village: Cultural materials from the village of Momina Klisura in the Pazardžik district]. *Izvestija na Instituta za Muzika* 1:43–91.

Varzi, Morteza. 1988. "Performer–audience relationships in the *bazm*." In *Cultural parameters of Iranian musical expression*, ed. Margaret Caton and Neil Siegel, 1–9. Los Angeles: Institute of Persian Performing Arts.

Vasileva, Margarita. 1969. "Shodstva i otliki v bŭlgarskata i turskata svatba v grupa sela na razgradski okrŭg" [Similarities and differences between Bulgarian and Turkish weddings in the Razgrad district]. *Izvestija na Etnografskija Institut i Muzej* (Sofia) 12:161–88.

Vasiljević, Miodrag A. 1964. "Funkcije i vrste glasova u srpskom narodnom pevanju oblasnjenje reci" [Functions and types of melody types in the explanatory terminology of Serbian folk singing]. *Rad VII Kongresa Folklorista Jugoslavije—Ohrid 1960*, 375–79. Ohrid: Savez Folklorista Jugoslavije.

Vernant, Jean-Pierre. 1989. "At man's table: Hesiod's foundation myth of sacrifice." In *The cuisine of sacrifice among the Greeks*, by Marcel Detienne, Jean-Pierre Vernant, et al., 21–86. Translated by Paula Wissing. Chicago: University of Chicago Press.

Vukanović, T. P. 1965. "Plačeno naricanje kod Šiptara i Makedonaca" [Professional lamenting among Albanians and Macedonians]. *Gjurmime Albanologjike* 2:169–212.

Vuylsteke, Herman C., comp. 1981. *Yougoslavie 2. (Macédoine: Polyphonies tosques.) Sous les peupliers de Bilisht.* Ocora 558572.

Walser, Robert. 1993. *Running with the devil: Power, gender, and madness in heavy metal music.* Hanover, N.H.: University Press of New England.

Wallis, Richard, and Krister Malm. 1984. *Big sounds from small peoples: The music industry in small countries.* New York: Pendragon.

Waterman, Christopher Alan. 1990. *Jùjú: A social history and ethnography of an African popular music.* Chicago: University of Chicago Press.

Wikan, Unni. 1984. "Shame and honour: A contestable pair." *Man* (n.s.) 19: 635–52.

Williams, Raymond. 1977. *Marxism and literature.* Oxford: Oxford University Press.

Zaimi, Nexhmie. 1937. *Daughter of the eagle.* New York: Ives Washburn.

Zemp, Hugo. 1990. Notes to " 'Jüüzli' Yodel of the Muotatal." Chant du Monde LDX 274 716.

Zemtsovsky, Izaly. 1980. "Union of Socialist Soviet Republics, IX, 2: Russian SFSR, Russian folk music." *New Grove Dictionary of Music and Musicians,* ed. Stanley Sadie, vol. 19, 388–98. London: Macmillan.

Zojzi, Rrok. 1962. "Ndamje krahinore e popullit shqiptar" [Regional divisions of the Albanian people]. *Etnografia Shqiptare* 1:16–62. French translation: "L'ancienne division régionale ethnographique du peuple albanais." *Ethnographie Albanaise,* édition spéciale (1976):7–19.

DISCOGRAPHY OF
SOUTH ALBANIAN MUSIC

Bariu, Laver. 1995. *Songs from the City of Roses*. GlobeStyle CDORBD 091.

Cellier, Marcel, comp. 1995. *L'Albanie mystérieuse*. Disques Pierre Verany PV 750010.

Ensemble "Ibe Palikuqa" (Skopje). n.d. *Ti moj dardha rrumbullake*. Jugoton CAY 1705.

Harding, M., L. McDowall, J. Wozencroft, and Spiro Shituni, comp. 1990. *There where the avalanche stops: Music from the Gjirokastra Folk Festival, Albania, 1988*. Vol. 1. Touch T33.11.

Islami, Ramiz K. 1992. *Grupi Sazet e Ohrit*. Ramiz K. Islami RKI 225.

Kruta, Beniamin, comp. 1982. *Albania I. Canti i danze tradizionali: Polifonia vocale e musica strumentale*. I Suoni / Fonitcetra Cetra / SU 5009.

Leibman, Robert Henry, comp. 1974. *Traditional Tosk (South Albanian) songs and dances from the Lake Prespa area*. Selo LP-2 (available from Festival Records, 2773 W. Pico Blvd., Los Angeles, CA 90006).

Lela, Remzi. 1992. *Famille Lela de Përmet: Polyphonies vocales et instrumentales d'Albanie*. Label Bleu LBLC 2503 / Harmonia Mundi HM 83.

Lloyd, A. L., comp 1966. *Folk music of Albania*. Topic TSCD 904 (formerly LP 12 T 154).

Lortat-Jacob, Bernard, and Beniamin Kruta, comp. 1988. *Albania: Vocal and instrumental polyphony*. Chant du Monde LDX 274 897.

Strictly Albanian. n.d. Strictly Albanian 1001–1003.

Vuylsteke, Herman C., and Kaim Murtishi, comp. 1981. *Yougoslavie 2 (Macédoine: Polyphonies tosques): Sous les peupliers de Bilisht*. Ocora 558 572.

etiquette and, 8; female, 172; gendered, 169, 182, 252, 339; and nationalism, 257; North American, 325, 341; and singing, 23–24; social, 168–82

immigration, of Prespa families, 12, 26, 58, 168, 178, 299, 301, 312, 345

Institute of Folklore, Macedonia, 338

Islam, 11, 29, 133, 168; marriage contract of, 120, 146, 244; sexuality and, 363n.19; tenets of, 167, 281. *See also* Muslims

Kaeppler, Adrienne, 24–25

Karp, Ivan, 370n.29

kinship: affinal, 179, 322; agnatic, 174–75, 179–80, 186, 190; ceremonial, 227; fictive, 361n.10; and gender, 354n.16; groups, 134, 169, 193–94; household, 167, 202; and identity, 182; and lineage, 237; obligations of, 243; patrilineal, 187, 302; and reciprocity, 214; ties of, 2, 21, 39, 171, 343

Kligman, Gail, 354n.14, 366n.4

Kolonjarë, 11, 13–14, 70–71, 77, 100, 111, 166–68, 181–82, 369n.25

Kolonjë (district), 76, 356n.5, 360n.3

konak (gathering), 205–12, 216, 219, 273, 277, 322, 327, 337, 365n.5, 365n.10. *See also* gatherings

Korçë (district), 11, 71, 75–76, 111, 131, 314, 356n.7, 359n.16, 365n.10, 366n.5, 367n.8

Koskoff, Ellen, 354nn. 15, 17

Kosova, 5, 60, 168–69, 205, 309–12, 342, 357n.2, 364n.23, 366n.3, 369n.24

Krani (village), 9–13, 15, 76, 79, 111, 174, 195, 236, 266, 372n.15

Kruta, Beniamin, 62, 356n.5, 358 n.12

lamenting: funeral, 355n.4, 366n.4; styles of, 369n.20; Tosk, 358n.12; women's, 61, 106, 110, 153, 281

language: Albanian, 9, 36, 62, 69, 165, 182, 217, 305, 310–11, 371n.11; Arabic, 362n.11; and cultural heritage, 341; English, 305; Macedonian, 166; Serbian, 14; Turkish, 9, 11, 14, 51, 180, 182

lartër singing style, 95, 98–101, 103–5, 110–11, 113, 115, 125, 131, 153, 157, 161, 163, 165, 206, 262, 269, 271, 273, 276, 278, 358n.15, 334, 336, 339, 370n.30

life-cycle, ceremonies of, 2, 17, 19, 58–59, 135, 220, 261, 303, 369n.24

lineage, 169, 171–72, 181–82, 187, 199, 203, 223, 237, 243, 263, 322

Ljubojno (village), 11

Lloyd, A. L., 356n.5, 368n.18

localism, Prespa, 166–67

Macedonia, 4–5, 13, 311–12

Macedonians, 4, 7, 9, 135–37, 182, 321

Marshall, Christopher, 353n.8

Mehmeti, Fadil, 364n.24

melismas, 132, 156, 265, 269, 276. *See also* ornamentation

me radhë. See radhë

mevlyd, 17, 58

mindfulness, 182–89, 193, 215, 218, 224–25, 263, 265, 271, 313, 322

modesty: Bedouin, 363n.19; bride's, 242–43, 270; female 188–91, 196, 224. *See also* demeanor

Moore, Henrietta, 201

morality, 22, 25, 59, 182–97, 213, 225, 321, 336, 343

muabet: atmosphere of, 161, 276; attainment of, 152, 165, 274; and honor, 336; in households, 197; informal, 154, 337; level of, 132; loss of, 163, 304–5; making of, 59, 136–37, 153, 215, 277, 303; nature of, 118, 134, 146, 148, 156, 202, 209–11, 213–14, 216, 220, 222, 254, 278–80, 323, 340; and obligation, 283; through singing, 58, 62, 92, 219; and women, 79, 268, 271

mumming, 211–12, 245, 367n.7

music: commercial release of, 38; and
gender, 30–32, instrumental, 73,
153; Ottoman, 358n.11; national,
77–78; north Albanian, 205, 286–
87; popular, 355n.19; Tosk, 74
musicology: interdisciplinary work
in, 354n.19; feminist, 355n.19. *See
also* ethnomusicology
Muslims, 4, 5, 9–14, 17, 135, 150, 165,
167–68, 180, 182–85, 194, 310–14,
353n.6, 356n.7, 369n.24, 371n.9
Myzeqe, 104, 111, 359n.16

Nakolec (village), 9–13, 195
Nelson, Kristina, 369n.26
Nieuwkerk, Karin von, 363n.19,
369n.22
Nketia, J. H. Kwabena, 354n.14
North America: Christians in, 185;
economic status in, 311; mainstream practices in, 307; gender in,
285, 308; Prespa children in, 74–
75, 192, 310, 312, 330, 335, 340;
Prespa families in, 12, 18–19, 174,
305, 313; Prespa women in, 302

order: by age, 122–23, 125, 141, 149,
151, 157, 212, of departures, 154; by
gender, 121, 149, 212, of seating,
122–24, 133, 149, 165; of singing,
20, 49, 82, 86, 153, 157–59, 222; social, 2–3; undermining of, 153; of
weddings, 137–54. *See also radhë*
ornamentation, 7, 21, 82, 96, 101, 113,
132, 157, 159, 161, 231, 276, 334,
339, 357nn. 6, 7; emotionality of,
270; extensive, 266; glottal, 106,
265, 269, 358n.12, 369n.20; little,
111, 127; melismatic, 66, 113,
358n.11; melodic, 71, 97–98, 105,
110, 116, 263; types of, 100, 117
Ortner, Sherry, 31, 172, 198
Ottoman Empire: fall of, 13; former
territories of, 29, 136, 139; period
of, 4, 9, 11, 58, 104, 150, 181, 298,
329, 358n.14, 362n.12, 367n.6; urban culture of, 167, 257, 356n.7

Panajoti, Jorgo, 363n.18
patriarchy: in extended families, 170;
naturalization of, 244–51; practice
of, 227–85; Prespa system as a, 35,
198, 320, 326; and sexuality, 189;
and singing, 282; rural, 299; village
331
patrilineal descent, 31, 169, 197, 236,
263, 322, 327, 360n.2, 369n.24
patrilineality, 170, 171, 174, 177–78,
185, 187
pentatonic scales, 66
performance: and agency, 33; anthropology of, 32; men's, 76, 116; musical, 24, 27, 29–30; polyphonic, 221;
praise of, 47; public, 163; as self-
conscious, 138; song, 16, 22, 43,
369n.22; styles of, 92, 95–96, 113;
women's, 116, 266
Përmet (district), 76
personhood, Prespa, 182–88
Petrovič, Ankica, 357n.5
Poedjosoedarmo, Gloria, 358n.8
polyphony: in song structures, 3, 7,
12, 62, 67–70, 71, 73–74, 76, 78, 80,
138, 141, 153, 219, 221–22, 282,
332, 334, 336, 338, 341, 356nn. 5, 8,
357n.11, 358n.12, 360n.9, 371n.4;
Tosk style, 70, 75, 77. *See also* singing; songs
Prishtinë, 311, 345
procreation, beliefs about, 169, 175–
76, 247, 360n.2, 362n.14, 368n.13

qejf (elation), 61, 148, 151–52, 161,
206, 258, 268, 272, 276, 370n.29;
and alcohol use, 278–79; and flow,
280
Qur'ān, recitation of, 58–59, 69, 133,
150, 183, 249, 369n.26

Racy, Ali Jihad, 359n.6, 361n.4,
362n.11
radhë (order): in approaching bride,
293; in approaching groom, 293–
94; of community, 139, 225, 323;
and formal behavior, 138, 149; of